Environmental Policy and Technological Innovation

NEW HORIZONS IN THE ECONOMICS OF INNOVATION

Series Editor: Christopher Freeman, *Emeritus Professor of Science Policy, SPRU – Science and Technology Policy Research, University of Sussex, UK*

Technical innovation is vital to the competitive performance of firms and of nations and for the sustained growth of the world economy. The economics of innovation is an area that has expanded dramatically in recent years and this major series, edited by one of the most distinguished scholars in the field, contributes to the debate and advances in research in this most important area.

The main emphasis is on the development and application of new ideas. The series provides a forum for original research in technology, innovation systems and management, industrial organization, technological collaboration, knowledge and innovation, research and development, evolutionary theory and industrial strategy. International in its approach, the series includes some of the best theoretical and empirical work from both well-established researchers and the new generation of scholars.

Titles in the series include:

Environmental Policy and Technological Innovation

Why do firms adopt or reject new technologies?

Carlos Montalvo Corral

Senior Adviser in Science and Technology Policy
TNO, Netherlands Organisation for Applied Scientific Research,
Delft, The Netherlands

NEW HORIZONS IN THE ECONOMICS OF INNOVATION

Edward Elgar
Cheltenham, UK • Northampton, MA, USA

Published by
Edward Elgar Publishing Limited
Glensanda House
Montpellier Parade
Cheltenham
Glos GL50 1UA
UK

Edward Elgar Publishing, Inc.
136 West Street
Suite 202
Northampton
Massachusetts 01060
USA

A catalogue record for this book
is available from the British Library

ISBN 1 84064 957 7

Printed and bound in Great Britain by MPG Books Ltd, Bodmin, Cornwall

Contents

Figures

Tables

Abbreviations

:	Page citation
α	Chronbach alpha, an index of scale reliability
Σac_b	Scale to assess acceptance of environmental risks
Σal_b	Scale to assess perceived strategic alliances capability
Σcp_b	Scale to assess perceived community pressure
Σer_b	Scale to assess economic risk perception
Σevr_b	Scale to assess environmental risk perception
Σmp_b	Scale to assess perceived market pressure
Σnwk_b	Scale to assess perceived networks of collaboration capability
Σol_b	Scale to assess perceived organisational learning capability
Σrp_b	Scale to assess perceived regulatory pressure
$\Sigma tcpp_b$	Scale to assess perceived technological capability
σ^2	Standard variance
A	Attitude towards the behaviour
AC	Acceptance of environmental risk
ac_b	bth belief of acceptance of environmental risk
AL	Strategic alliances capabilities
al_b	bth belief of perceived strategic alliances capability
μ	Average item-scale correlation
BECC	Border Environmental Cooperation Commission
CEC	Commission for Environmental Cooperation
CEO	Chief executive officer
C_n	Factor nth or component nth
COLEF	El Colegio de la Frontera Norte
CONACYT	Concejo Nacional de Ciencia y Tecnología
CP	Community pressures
cp_b	bth belief of perceived community pressure

cs	Scale of the favourable or unfavourable condition of the observer of risk
CT	Clean technologies
ctr	Scale of the perceived controllability of environmental risks
dts	Scale of discount of benefits and costs in time and socio-geographic space
EMS	Environmental management system
EPA	United States Environmental Protection Agency
ER	Economic risk
er_b	bth belief of perceived economic risk
EV	Expectancy value model
EVR	Environmental risk perception
evr_b	bth belief of perceived environmental of risk
GNP	Gross Net Product
H_n	nth Hypothesis
INEGI	Instituto Nacional de Estadística, Geografía e Informática
ISO	International Standardisation Organisation
LCA	Life cycle analysis
LGEEPA	Ley General de Equilibrio Ecológico y Protección Ambiental
MEP	Mexican Environmental Project
MP	Market pressures
mp_b	bth belief of perceived market pressure
NADBank	North American Development Bank
NAFTA	North American Free Trade Agreement
NWK	Networks of collaboration
nwk_b	bth belief of perceived networks of collaboration capability
OC	Organisational capabilities
OL	Learning capabilities
ol_b	bth belief of perceived organisational learning capability
PBC	Perceived behavioural control
PIAF	Plan Integral Ambiental Fronterizo
PSP	Perceived social pressure
r	Index of bivariate correlation (Pearson)
R&D	Research and development
R^2	Index of determination

RP	Regulatory pressures
rp_b	bth belief of perceived regulatory pressure
SECOFI	Secretaría de Comercio y Fomento Industrial
SEDESOL	Secretaría de Desarrollo Social
SEDUE	Secretaría de Desarrollo Urbano y Ecología
SEMARNAP	Secretaría del Medio Ambiente Recursos Naturales y Pesca
SETAC	Society of Environmental Toxicology and Chemistry
SEU	Subjective expected utility
$\propto$	Proportionality between two scores
SMEs	Small and medium size manufacturing firms
S_n	nth policy scenario
SN	Subjective norm
sr	Scale of perceptions of the firm operations as 'safe' or 'risky'
TCPP	Technological capabilities
$tcpp_b$	bth belief of perceived technological capability
TPB	Theory of planned behaviour
TR	Technological regime
VAT	Value added tax
vol	Scale of voluntariness of exposure to risk
W	Willingness to develop clean technologies
We	Empirically calculated willingness to develop clean technologies
WTS	Waste water treatment system

Preface

'So, once you have identified some problems, what would you do if you had the power to protect the environment from pollution?' This was the last question that my examiners posed in the public defence of my MSc dissertation. The thesis explored the environmental misbehaviour of transnational firms manufacturing locally and exporting globally. At that moment, although I was aware of the relevance of the question, I took the question rather badly and was genuinely annoyed. I felt like in a beauty contest …and the last question is! What would you do if… To save my neck I had to say that the question posed was out of the scope of the research project and it was too broad! A few days later I started a job as a manager of a small R&D firm on environmental technologies for industrial applications. There I had the opportunity to see in praxis the state-of-the-art of environmental technologies and the interaction of regulatory authorities and our main customer, the firm. Soon after I confirmed that the question above was in fact broad but realised that the problem 'What to do?' is in fact of central relevance for policy making. This experience led me to distinguish two major constraints that the design and enforcement of policies directed to protect the environment face. These are set out below in a stylised manner.

The first relates to the development of science and its technological applications in the last two hundred years. It has to be acknowledged at the highest political level that there is a serious anomaly in the evolution of our current industrial technological stock that is related to the ecosystem resiliency capacity. That is, at the moment we are facing an infinite regress concerning current technological fixes, as these do not solve industry's environmental problems but only extend and increase their range. After more than 250 years of industrial development the implications of the first and second laws of matter and energy have not been fully understood at a social level. Nothing is created, nothing in destroyed, but transformed (Lavoisier 1743–94), and all process is entropic (Carnot, 1796–1832). Thus, in principle, concepts like clean production and industrial ecology have a chance of becoming operative once these two laws have been integrated in the scientific and technological paradigms that are embedded in industrial production.

The second constraint refers to the current industrial organisation and the social system that it helps to reproduce under a dominant ideology mirrored in a concept, the market. The ruling behavioural principle is that of agents maximising their individual (or group) interests. Although this principle is a vulgarisation of Bernard Mandeville's (1714) poem *The fable of the bees*, initially used in economics by Adam Smith (see *The wealth of nations*) to describe an industrious collective, currently this principle is supposed to optimise the human societal welfare. Experience has shown that the operation of this principle leads to the persistence of behaviours that are rational in the short term but irrational in the long term, and rational at individual level but irrational on the social level. Specifically, concerning the behaviour of the firm, environmental problems are situations in which the short-run individual (or group) interests guiding firms' behaviour are inconsistent with the long-run global best interest of the firm and the society.

It is against these challenges that more than 30 years of direct regulation in the form of command-and-control, taxes, subsidies and covenants have had very little success in promoting innovation towards clean production. Current trends of liberalisation of international trade, privatisation of national assets and economic concentration are likely to reduce the already limited independence and power of regulatory agencies to enforce environmental protection against the individual or group interests. In this sense in this situation the old rule of natural law – the more power the more right – applies.

Thus, radical technological and organisational innovations at the firm and regulatory levels are required. Radical innovation implies high risk for long-term capital investments. But, few firms are willing to expose themselves to failure, especially when the needed behavioural change implies redesigns of entire portfolios of products and processes. In this context, if governments lack political independence to set and enforce behavioural standards the question that this book addresses is: Is it possible to influence the innovative behaviour of the firm other than by direct regulation? If it is possible, under which conditions? After almost ten years I can give a response to the question made at the end of my master's exam. What would you do if you had the power to protect the environment from pollution. Concerning the question, this book offers a response to those that are in a position to test a different paradigm of policy analysis based on principles of conflict resolution with power asymmetry.

The book is primarily written for environmental and technology policy analysts, practitioners and lobbyists. But due to the increasing relevance of environmental challenges, to the diverse academic areas of enquiry that the book draws from, and to the quasi-ontological subject that it addresses, it is also of interest to academics, researchers and students in areas of risk perception, innovation studies, institutional change, social and cognitive psychology and economists interested in exploring new horizons concerning the theory of the firm. In addition, as the book operates as a model to understanding and predicting the propensity of the firm to invest in new technologies, it can be used as an industrial marketing research tool for companies commercialising environmental technologies.

I gratefully acknowledge the funding from the Mexican National Council for Science and Technology (CONACYT) for the research project that produced this book; the logistics support during the fieldwork provided by El Colegio de la Frontera Norte; and the scholarship from the Center for

xiv   *Environmental Policy and Technological Innovation*

US–Mexican Studies of the University of California San Diego that enabled me to write the first draft chapters in a relaxed environment. I want to express my gratitude to Anamaría Escofet G. (CICESE), Frans Berkhout (SPRU), Jim Skea (PSI), Robin Mansell (LSE), Nick von Tunzelman (SPRU) and Mark van Vugt (University of Southampton) and Cynthia Little (SPRU) for their contribution to the coherence of this book at different stages, from the very early stages of the research project to the elaboration and structure of the manuscript. I owe much appreciation to the firms' managers because without their patient participation this research would not have been possible. Specials thanks go to Mario Peregrina and Federico Salas because their contacts in industry opened many doors despite to the fact that research on firms' environmental behaviour in the US–Mexican border region is highly controversial. I am grateful to my friends especially to Tim Girven, Arturo Torres and Alex Vera Cruz for their support throughout this endeavour. Finally, I want to thank Uta Wehn de Montalvo who came to be an invaluable interlocutor in critical stages of the writing process.

Carlos Montalvo Corral
Delft

1. Resistance to change

INTRODUCTION

The firm is, by definition, a profit maximising organisation (Varian, 1978, p. 1). One classical way to increase its profits is by reducing costs. As environmental protection increases the firm's structure of fixed operation costs, it is widely accepted that in the absence of regulatory enforcement a firm will tend to externalise these costs, at the expense of broader societal interest. In this regard, environmental policies are conceived ideally, as a means to render such opposing interests compatible. The challenge here is to design ways to achieve socially desirable goals while allowing people to pursue their individual self-interests or companies the maximisation of profits. Is it possible, however, to reconcile individual self-interest with the societal interest regarding environmental protection? If so, under what conditions? Since self-interest is the dominant paradigm of market economies, these questions have become a central issue for environmental policy design. This book addresses these questions by searching for the preconditions that determine a firm's willingness to develop clean technologies. It also seeks to determine under what conditions it may be possible to reconcile the interests of a given firm with the social interests in the context of the In-Bond industry in the northern border region of Mexico.

The main argument of this work is that existing environmental policies are flawed in principle since they do not address the origin of problems but only their symptoms. At the core of most environmental problems lies a conflict between individual interest in the short term, with long-term individual and social interests. It can be argued, therefore, that designing policies which increase the possibilities of reconciling both interests requires a clear understanding of the determinants upon the involvement of environmental protection of any given firm. Following Fisher's framework, this work can be located at the first stage of a constructive conflict resolution (Fisher, 1994). This stage focuses on the sources of the conflict by searching and distinguishing the values, beliefs, fears and goals of the parties in conflict. It is the final goal of this work to produce a behavioural simulation instrument that includes an inventory of the possible combinations of belief systems upon which firms may be optimally willing to innovate in clean technologies (CT).

In the following sections, first, a justification for and the relevance of the present work in terms of environmental policy and technical change is discussed. Second, within the framework of the theory of social traps the rationale underlying the contradiction between economic development and environmental protection is explored. Third, some of the reasons why actual environmental policies are still largely sub-optimal are discussed. Fourth, a new approach that may lead to a better policy design is proposed. Fifth, a structural behavioural theory used as the method to operate this new approach is presented. Finally, the structure and content of the book is outlined.

RESISTANCE TO CHANGE

Achieving environmental conservation is a desirable goal for both industrialised and newly industrialising countries. This requires the promotion of a process of change involving conflicting political, organisational, technological and cultural dimensions (Binswanger *et al.*, 1990; Brawn, 1995; Everett *et al.*, 1993; Hukkinen, 1995; Ojeda, 1995; Yuñes-Naude, 1994; PCSD, 1999). Not surprisingly, adherence to the goals proposed by the World Commission on Environment and Development (WCED, 1987) and the Comisión de Desarrollo y Medio Ambiente de America Latina y el Caribe (CDMA, 1990) by governments, firms and institutions has been, in practice, quite limited. Even when actors recognise the need for change in the patterns of production for the sake of environmental protection, there is still a huge gap between intent and the real operation of the concept of clean technology.[1]

The clean production concept represents an example of those contributions of science and philosophy that are problematic to implement at a societal level. If implemented at all, this occurs only after the ideas overcome a long chain of resistance to change from individuals and institutions. The implementation of new ideas at a societal level implies a causal sequence of the diffusion, resistance, acceptance, adoption and finally implementation of new ideas by the differentially affected group interests (Daly, 1995; Ziman, 1984).

These conditions constitute a 'social trap' (see p. 4) in which social actors promoting the implementation of new paradigms find themselves confronting the strong resistance to change of economic actors (Costanza, 1987; Binswanger *et al.*, 1990). Thus, to design environmental policies that have any chance of being effective, a set of variables must explicitly be taken into account. These range from social factors (i.e., values, institutions and political power) (Beck, 1995; Boehmer-Christiansen, 1995; Gabaldón, 1994; Lander, 1994) to the technological opportunities underlying the current techno-economic regime and the available technological capabilities (Dosi, 1982; Dosi *et al.*, 1988; Kemp, 1994). This pattern is repeated in both industrialised and non-industrialised countries, but is worse in the latter, in part because of their condition of economic dependency and the scant resources applied to environmental protection (García-Guadilla and Blauert, 1994; Bojórquez and Ongay, 1992; Casson, 1990; Leff, 1986). It is of interest, therefore, to determine those factors which hinder the success of the environmental policies intended to promote clean technologies.

A closer analysis of those resistances toward the adoption of clean technologies found in industry gives some insight into these factors. Following the Neo-Schumpeterian theory of economic change, it can be said that the creation of a sustainable industry is an endogenous process dependent on government environmental policy, the capabilities and incentives of firms to achieve cleaner operations and the goals and characteristics of potential users of capital goods, intermediate and consumer products. This process will, of necessity, be gradual, rather slow, and disruptive at the start, because of the strong dominance of the pre-existing technological trajectories (Nelson and Winter, 1982; Kemp and Soete, 1992; Kemp, 1994). Even though this theory helps the understanding of macro dynamic processes of innovation, it remains very general and does not help to operate environmental policy analysis at the micro level.

Over the last decade, studies analysing the determinants of the 'greening' of industry have provided numerous important insights about the determinants of a firm's innovative behaviour in cleaner technologies. Although there is some degree of overlap, the studies can be categorised into three types of recurrent determinants according to the degree of importance given to the factors mentioned. The first group considers factors that can be seen as arising from social norms. Among these factors are public and shareholder pressures, regulations enforcement, market demand, community concerns, customer demands, liability, public image and social responsibility (e.g., Ashford, 1993; Bhatnagar and Cohen, 1997; Cramer and Schot, 1993; den Hond and Groenewegen, 1993; Dillon and Baram, 1993; Geffen and Rothenberg, 1997; Henriquez, and Sadorsky, 1996; Kemp, 1996a; Maxwell *et al.*, 1997; Orsatto, 1997; Rondinelli and Vastag, 1996; Steger, 1993; and Williams *et al.*, 1993).

The second group emphasises cognitive and attitudinal factors such as perceptions, personality, efficacy, leadership, environmental awareness and the ethics of mangers and CEOs. This group also considers factors such as the economic efficiency and opportunity, and the risk and uncertainty of the innovative process (e.g., Andrews, 1998; Cramer and Schot, 1993; EPA, 1998; Everett *et al.*, 1993; IOD, 1995; Hart and Ahuja, 1996; Kemp, 1993; King, 1997; Konar and Cohen, 1997; Morrison, 1997; Petts *et al.*, 1998; Steger, 1996; Prakash, 1997)). The third group concerns technological factors hampering the 'greening' of industry. Recurrent factors include the lack of technological opportunities and the necessity of generating a new knowledge base prior to attaining a sustainable industrial development; the industrial and trade relationships across the supply chain; the relation between end-users and suppliers; the firms' technological and organisational endowments; technological trajectories, and so on. (e.g., Ashford, 1993; den Hond, 1996;

Kemp, 1994; Kemp and Soete, 1992; Florida, 1996; Hall, 1999; Rodgers, 1998; Roome, 1994; Schot *et al.*, 1994).

Although the above works provide much qualitative information about the factors influencing the development and adoption of clean technologies, it was not possible to assess the importance of individual factors nor to explore the relationships among determinants in a quantitative manner. Progress has been restricted by a lack of sufficient theoretical and methodological rigour to enable hypotheses testing (Kemp, 1994; Fuchs and Mazmanian, 1998). As Fisher and Schot (1993), Gladwin (1993) and Fuchs and Mazmanian (1998) remark, most of the prevailing research on 'greening' of industry is merely descriptive. The primary difficulty is to apply adequate theories to analyse the phenomena which could help to organise and build upon the existing findings in order to produce generalisations, shape and guide empirical enquiry and produce useful corporate and public policy recommendations.

SOCIAL TRAPS

From the discussion developed in the previous section it can be inferred that the implementation of environmental policy schemes that effectively promote the process of change towards sustainable industrial development requires an adequate grasp of the human dynamics that drive economic development. Since Pigou (1924) proposed the economic notion of 'externalities', many authors have remarked on the fact that firms tend not to bear the total cost of production mitigating them via externalities to the environment because of the underlying rationale of individual self-interest (e.g., Baumol, 1972; Baumol and Oates, 1975, 1993; Coase, 1960; Harret, 1968; OECD, 1991b, 1993, 1995; Templet, 1995). Written from an economic perspective most of these works neglect the complex dynamic that underlies human decision processes.

From a different perspective, Costanza (1987), based on the socio-psychological work of Platt (1973) and Cross and Guyer (1980), applies the concept of *social traps* to explain the persistence of behaviours that are: 1) rational in the short term but irrational in the long term, and 2) rational at individual level but irrational on the social level.[2] Specifically, Costanza relates the environmental problems with 'situations in which the short-run, local reinforcements guiding individual behaviour are inconsistent with the long-run, global best interest of the individual and the society' (Costanza, 1987, p. 408).[3]

Costanza's argument proved incorrect in its policy conclusions in assuming, on the one hand, that there are technological 'fixes' available to current environmental problems,[4] and on the other hand, supposing that regulatory mechanisms such as subsidies and taxes could modify the behaviour of firms. As discussed in the next section, the economic instruments for environmental policy have been proven not to work efficiently.

Nevertheless the importance of Costanza's contribution stems primarily from his questioning of the basic principle of market economies, 'the invisible hand', as the main restriction upon the achievement of environmental protection; and secondly from the idea that local reinforcements lead people towards paths that in the long-run have negative potential. Some examples of social traps are given in Table 1.1.

Table 1.1   Social traps

Type of trap	Examples
Time delay	Discounting, smoking, drug addiction
Ignorance	Slot machines, gambler's fallacy
Slider reinforce	Pesticide overuse
Externality	Pollution, prisoner's dilemma
Collective	Tragedy of the commons
Hybrid	Any combination of the above

Source: Costanza (1987).

The above work and those mentioned previously opened a new perspective for the analysis of *market failures* in relation to the environment. The originality of these works is related to the implicit proposition that social psychology may help to account for the rationale underlying any given individual or group interest(s). However, efforts to systematically account for the nature of the conflict between the individual and societal interest have been limited. Although some interesting studies have been carried out to apply the theory of social traps in combination with game and conflict theories, these studies show limitations that impede both their further application and the generalisation of results. These limitations include: the small size of samples (no more than 40 people); the measurement of 'outcome behaviour' without a clear explanation of the reasons underlying specific choices; weak predictive power, the measurement of simple behaviours; and the fact that studies were carried out within limited contexts such as university laboratories (e.g., Messick and McClelland, 1983; Kondo, 1990; Fleishman, 1988; Brann and Foddy, 1988; Parks and Vu, 1994; Ward, 1993; Braver and Wilson II, 1986).

Even though all these studies contribute to our understanding of the dynamic underlying the persistence of environmental problems, they do not define effective ways to unlock the current environmental social trap. Rather the above works constitute developments in the theory of environmental economics and environmental policy leading to the, now apparently obvious, idea that self-interest (i.e., the interest of the firm) must be regulated.[5]

THE FAILURE OF THE SELF-INTEREST FOCUS POLICY PARADIGM

For more than 30 years the conventional process of environmental policy design has been a process of trial and error (Tietenberg, 1992; Levèque, 1996; Clayton *et al.*, 1999). Most of it has been based on theories of distribution and power, under the assumption that *self-interest* (i.e., profit seeking) explains *per se* firms' behaviour towards compliance with regulations and/or the development of clean technologies. However, these theories provide few insights about the conditions under which incentive-based instruments designed to promote environmental protection could be chosen and implemented (Baumol and Oates, 1993; Hahn, 1989).

Because of this basic assumption regarding self-interest, actual environmental policies generally function sub-optimally, as they seek to regulate the firm's self-interest in a direct way. Some additional causes of this sub-optimality are:

- the influence of industrial lobbying upon the setting of environmental standards;
- the strong resistance to compliance produced by command-and-control policies;
- the fixed cost of the regulations implicit in command and control policies which necessarily require enforcement and monitoring of the degree of compliance;
- the design of tax legislation for the purposes of revenue yield as opposed to purposes of inducing behavioural change;
- the fact that conceptually, economic instruments are not environmentally but monetarily optimal;
- virtually all incentive-based systems focus on individual pollutants;
- the overly 'moderate' tone of voluntary agreements resulting from regulators having to compromise stringent policy objectives in order to secure industry co-operation (Pearce and Turner, 1991; Tietenberg, 1992, 1994; Hahn, 1989; Kemp, 1993, 1996a, 1996b; Baumol and Oates, 1993; den Hond, 1996, Clayton *et al.*, 1999; EPA, 1998; PCSD, 1999).

Furthermore, these studies show that ill-designed environmental policies can and do remain in force overlong even though it may be obvious that they do not induce the desired outcomes (Tietenberg, 1994; EPA, 1998). Experience shows that this has resulted in firmly entrenched antagonistic positions. On one side, regulators with the power to penalise or prosecute violators; on the other, the industrial lobby which not only resists compliance with those environmental regulations in force, but also fails to develop clean technologies (ELI, 1998; CSIS, 1997; PCSD, 1999). This dynamic leads to a vicious circle in which: 1) policy makers, without knowing the conditions under which incentive-based instruments might succeed, encounter strong lobbying on the industrial side, lobbying that normally reshapes the original policy (reducing the original objectives) (Levèque, 1996); and 2) in the long term both regulators and firms prove resistant to change, the regulators because they obtain benefits from their position as prosecutors and firms because they see the environmental problem as a threat rather than a source of new ideas to improve economic efficiency (see Figure 1.1).

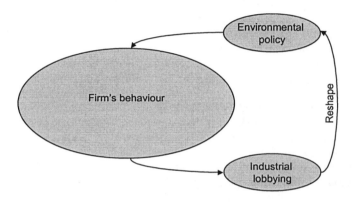

Figure 1.1 Vicious cycle of resistance to engage in clean production

Figure 1.1 illustrates a dynamic in which regulators' penalising and firms' lobbying reach a point where they become part of a social network composed of actors engaged in resource exchanges. Because of this, regulatory agencies oscillate between autonomy and capture lacking any real institutional power to promote a process of change as required by the concept of *clean production* (Echeverry-Gent, 1992; Hukkinen, 1995; Panayotou, 1993). It can be argued that conventional policy making is convenient for both regulators and firms, because it minimises political risks for regulators and investment risk for firms. However, it always postpones the resolution of the conflict and the long-term solution of environmental problems to the future (e.g., Hukkinen, 1995). There remains the question, then, of how to change behaviours which at individual level are perfectly rational, but which at the social level become irrational.

A NEW ENVIRONMENTAL POLICY APPROACH: INDUCING BEHAVIOURAL CHANGE

Due to the limitations of the actual policy paradigm, a new approach may be proposed. From the discussion above, it can be said that the self-interest focused policy approach emphasises learning-by-doing and conflict as the central means for the abatement of environmental problems (Lee, 1993). Regarding this *modus operandi* it can be argued that:

1. Although learning-by-doing has played a very important role in most areas of human activity in the process of solving problems it is generally desirable to have a more systematic approach. Modelling the phenomena in question, for example, helps to foresee a majority of possible future malfunctions or mistakes (Hippel and Tyre, 1995). The production of a model of a systematic account of the factors causing resistance to behavioural change, therefore, followed by the operation of that model to give a simulation of the resistance or willingness to innovate in clean technologies, would help in constructing better designed environmental policies and allow more accurate and efficient allocation of the policy effort.
2. The dynamic generated by the cycle of penalisation and lobbying leads to the creation of networks of resource exchanges that 'lock in' those social actors intending to promote innovation not only within firms but also within regulatory agencies.
3. Although self-interest is a natural source of conflict, it has become obvious in the contemporary period that the solution to environmental problems involves collaboration between both economic and social actors.

In order to be able to search for schemes of collaboration, it may be necessary to deepen our perspective regarding the *self-interest* of the firms. Here it is proposed to do that by changing the focus of environmental policies towards the sources of resistance to behavioural change. Analysis of the elements constituting the resistance allows a better understanding of the failure of innovative behaviour in clean technologies within firms. This new emphasis enables us, conceptually, to operate the conflict between the firm's interest and the social interests and potentially break the vicious circle of conflict. It could open up the possibility of locating negotiable areas between groups of interests by promoting schemes of collaboration based on a willingness to change. These negotiable areas would be related to the specific preconditions that may enable policy makers to induce that behavioural change.

An accurate identification and weighting of the factors that account for the resistance or willingness to change would allow policies to be formulated that prioritise the encouragement of behavioural change on a collaborative basis over and above (penal) regulation (Figure 1.2). Such a perspective concurs with the relatively recent recognition that collaboration is the only way to find long-term radical solutions to environmental problems related to industrial activities (e.g., Arthur D. Little, 1996; Clayton *et al.*, 1999; CSIS, 1997; PCSD, 1999).

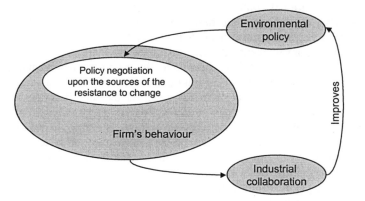

Figure 1.2   Virtuous cycle of willingness to engage in clean production

A BEHAVIOURAL MODEL FOR ENVIRONMENTAL AND TECHNOLOGY POLICY ANALYSIS

In this section a model to operate the concept of *resistance-to-change* is proposed. It is based on Ajzen's theory of planned behaviour (TPB), a theory designed to understand and predict human social behaviour (Ajzen, 1991). As discussed above, the theories underlying environmental policy design gain few insights into the 'rationality' of the precondition of decision making. All these theories are based on the same simple assumption, i.e., that 'thought moves things'. In reality the process of cognition transformed into action is not a direct path. Although this latter point seems obvious, the theoretical and practical development in many policy fields based on approaches as different as stimulus-object-response behaviourism,[6] social learning theory, consistency theories, expectancy theories, and expectancy-value theories of motivation and decision making have neglected to take it into account (Kuhl and Beckman, 1985; Kuhl, 1985).

By taking into account the issue of the *control* over actions, recent theoretical developments in social psychology have led to the construction of models with a high explanatory and predictive power for human social behaviour. This leads to the possibility of the rigorous testing of hypotheses with regard not only to the understanding of the sources of variance but also predicting the predisposition of people towards specific behaviours. The theory of planned behaviour specifies three major sources of cognition-behaviour inconsistency.

The first source is a change in the initial intention before the behaviour is carried out; the second, people's lack of confidence that the attainment of a behavioural objective is under their (volitional) control; the last is the question of whether a behavioural expectation formed on the basis of such an attainment of volitional control actually leads to the achievement of a given objective. This is contingent on the relation between people's confidence in their ability to exercise control over their own action and the extent to which they actually do control events (Ajzen, 1988, 1991).

This work aims at applying the above theory to environmental policy analysis in order to go beyond an enumeration of the obvious factors that hamper development of cleaner technologies, via the identification of those predispositional factors that are the sources of resistance to change. Following this identification phase, the possibility of predicting the predisposition of a firm to behave in favour of, or against the development of, clean technologies, may arise. In addition, applying of such a theory to research adds to previous studies by contributing to the opening of the previous monolithic input-output (black box) perspective of the rational decision-making process.

Indeed, the approach adopted for policy analysis, by including variables such as beliefs, expectancies, values, intentions and control between cognition and action, takes into account that the relationship between cognition and action is not a straightforward process (Ajzen, 1985, 1988, 1991; Fishbein and Ajzen, 1980; Beck and Ajzen, 1993; Fishbein and Ajzen, 1975; Kuhl and Beckman, 1985; Kuhl, 1985). This provides the opportunity to look at individuals (or firms, groups and organisations) as social actors seeking changes but encountering any number of resistances that hamper the achievement of an ideal goal. Thus, as will be discussed in Chapter 3 and demonstrated in Chapter 4, the approach adopted makes it possible to relate and merge several theoretical bodies into a synthesis directed towards the understanding and prediction of the behaviour of organisations in specific contexts and, more specifically, towards the analysis and prediction of the willingness of firms to engage in innovative activities towards clean production. The process of building and testing the theoretical model for devising strategies for a better allocation of the environmental policy effort is outlined below.

THE CASE STUDY

This research takes as its case study the determinants of innovative behaviour in clean technologies in the In-Bond industry ('Maquila') in the northern region of Mexico. In-Bond refers to the state of taxable goods stored under a bond in charge of the government. The term 'In-Bond' refers to the fact that the inputs required for production are temporarily imported to the host country. The inputs are processed, finished and exported back to the country of origin. As the firm's product is not sold in the country where the goods are finished the firm does not make profits on its operations in the host country. In turn, because of the latter this industry is considered a 'centre of costs, and companies therefore do not pay revenue taxes in the host country, just valued added tax (VAT) on labour (Gonzalez-Arechiga and Ramirez, 1990, Taylor 2000).

In contrast, local or national industry sells in the national market or exports with national certificates of origin; as a consequence they are taxed as their revenues are tied to the national territory. In this sense the In-Bond industry is an *ad hoc* sample of highly mobile firms seeking optimal deregulated regions; and maximum flexibility on labour, fiscal regimes, and environmental regulations (Gereffi and Wyman, 1992; Icasa, 1993; Sklair, 2000a). These are the common features that many corporations seek when they operate at a global level. Elsewhere it has been argued that the In-Bond industry represents an example of how multinationals through foreign direct investment, promote and manage an accelerated economic integration towards a global economic system. The In-Bond industry is a Mexico–US variant of an almost universal pattern of economic development (Sklair, 2000b, 2000c; Koido, 2000, Mortimore, 2000). Although the analysis and conclusions are limited to the a specific region and industry, it is assumed that by focusing on firms that seek these conditions, the results of this study could be useful in other countries or regions with similar contexts (e.g., export platforms, tax-free zones, international subcontracting of manufactures, etc.).

STRUCTURE OF THE BOOK

In Chapter 2 it is argued against the generally held belief that a firm's *strategic* environmental behaviour, in particular innovative behaviour in clean technologies, is mainly dependent on the macro and micro *structural* features of the prevailing techno-economic regime, rather than only on 'positive' environmental attitudes and values on part of the corporate boards. Those macro *structural* features are discussed within the context of regional industrial activities and their relation to environmental management on the northern border of Mexico. The purpose in doing so is to contextualize the description of the findings of the empirical work and to offer a link to and basis for the regional policy analysis undertaken in Chapter 7. The micro *structural* determinants of the innovative behaviour of firms are addressed in Chapter 4.

In Chapter 3, a theoretical basis for the development of an instrument of policy analysis that may allow a new environmental policy approach (i.e., inducing change rather than regulating behaviour) is discussed. This approach is built upon Ajzen's theory of planned behaviour. This theory is introduced and briefly discussed in comparison with other theories of decision making. After this comparative approach it is argued that the TPB can be applied to understand the innovative behaviour of firms regarding the development of clean technologies. Finally, a system of hypotheses regarding the relationship of dependence of the willingness to innovate in clean technologies upon nine behavioural correlates is proposed.

Chapter 4 builds on the framework presented in Chapter 3. This chapter seeks to go beyond the enumeration of factors already presented in the literature of the past ten years. This is undertaken by exploring further those factors upon which the firms' managers build their perceptions of possible outcomes, social pressures and capabilities which in turn may influence their willingness to promote the development of clean technologies in their firms. First, drawing on theories of environmental risk perception, economic risk perception, competitiveness and technology strategy, product life cycle analysis, organisational learning, strategic alliances and networks of collaboration, the chapter explains how the theoretical pool of the determinants of attitudes, social pressure and behavioural control was drawn up. Second, the scales used to measure and assess each domain are presented. Finally, a series of definitions that link willingness to undertake innovative behaviour to a specific system of beliefs is presented. This allows a system of hypotheses of the relationships of dependence between behavioural correlates and the planned environmental behaviour of the average firm in the sample to be stated.

Chapter 5 describes and justifies the research strategy to test the proposed behavioural model for policy analysis; the connection of the theoretical approach with the research design and unit of analysis; a basis for the selection of the case study, and the criterion for data analysis. It also includes a description of how the research was conducted; how data was collected, and the criteria for the sample selection.

Chapter 6, based on descriptive statistics, presents the first insights of the behavioural trend expected in the sample under study. That is, the weakness or strength of the resistance to change towards the development of clean technologies (CT). The description is based on the 'scores' achieved for perceived environmental and economic risk; the perceived pressures from the community, regulations and the market and the perceived organisational and technological capabilities to develop CT. Subsequently, a scenario of the firms' environmental planned behaviour based on the current and long-term managers' rational expectations is used to respond to two of the main questions of this work.

Chapter 7 seeks to go beyond the descriptive and explanatory stages of preceding chapters to advance into a scenario simulation of changes in the different behavioural correlates proposed to influence the firm's intention or willingness to develop CT and, as a consequence, its behaviour. With the combination of the scenarios obtained from this simulation, policy suggestions for the encouragement of innovation towards cleaner technologies for the In-Bond industry are outlined.

Chapter 8 presents the conclusions of this work as to the main findings regarding the determinants of willingness to innovate, the policy implications of these findings in the context of the Mexican northern border region, the generalisations of the instruments developed, the work's contributions to the realm of environmental policy and innovation literature are discussed.

The Appendix deals with the consistency of the results presented in Chapter 6. That is, it tests the consistency of the theoretical model developed in Chapters 3 and 4. The test of the theoretical model is undertaken in two steps. First, an assessment of the *reliability* of the contents of the questionnaire used as an instrument to measure the determinants of the behaviour under study is carried out. Then, second, an assessment of the *validity* of the theoretical construct underlying the structure and contents of the questionnaire is performed. These analyses enabled the test of the system of hypothesis proposed in Chapter 4 and the simulation of scenarios in Chapter 7.

NOTES

1. Clean technologies are defined as 'production processes and products which minimise energy, resource consumption and hazards over the product life cycle. This life cycle includes design, extraction, transport, processing, use and disposal of a product or material' (OECD, 1995).
2. Platt's definition of *social trap: The* term refers to situations where men, organisations or whole societies orient themselves in a direction or a set of relationships that later prove to be unpleasant or lethal and from which they see no easy way back out of. *Counter trap*: This term refers to situations in which the consideration of individual advantage prevents an action that might nevertheless be of great benefit to the group or society as a whole (Platt, 1973). Cross and Guyer's definition: A social trap is a situation characterised by multiple but conflicting rewards (reinforcements) (Cross and Guyer, 1980).
3. These local reinforcements refer to social recognition; values; institutions; monetary incentives; pleasure; in summary the realisation and enhancement of self (see Binswanger *et al.*, 1990).
4. This argument will be discussed at length in Chapter 2.
5. Currently, although new industrial technologies are scaled and diffused to commercial and industrial activities mainly through the participation of the private sector, many scientific discoveries and technological innovations are achieved through research projects carried out with public funds. Thus, the investment in clean technology development could be seen as a public choice problem. In this regard, the 'public good' properties that clean technologies might have or imply are beyond the scope of this work. Further discussion of social traps related with the environment and public goods can be followed in Cross and Guyer (1980), Costanza (1987), Messick and McClelland (1983), Rapoport (1988a, 1988b), Ward (1993), Brann and Foddy (1988), Harret (1968), Cropper and Oates (1992), Pearce and Turner (1991).
6. The works of Platt (1973), Cross and Guyer (1980) and Costanza (1987) fall into this category.

2. Background: strategy follows structure

The notion of sustainable development, seemingly simple, intuitively rational and morally correct, has become global in recent years as part of the discourse of both academics and policy-makers. The US-Mexican Border Region is no exception; after the signing of the North American Free Trade Agreement (NAFTA) in 1992 two commissions were created to deal with the challenge of sustainability. However, the possibility of making such a concept practicably operable beyond the rhetoric appears increasingly remote. This is due, according numerous authors, to the need for a radical shift in both the societal attitudes and the values held by corporate decision makers (e.g., Andrews, 1998; Petts *et al.*, 1998; Beck, 1995; Boehmer-Christiansen, 1995; Gabaldón, 1994; Lander, 1994).

In opposition to this general belief, in this chapter it is argued that the strategic environmental behaviour of firms, particularly innovative behaviour to prevent the generation of pollution, is mainly dependent on the structural features of the actual 'techno-economic regime'. In other words, firms' strategies and behavioural change are strongly dependent on both the external (macro) and the internal (micro) dynamics of technical change, rather than solely on positive environmental attitudes and values. This constitutes a restatement of the notion that the movement from cognition to action does not necessarily follow a direct path.

This chapter looks at the macro-structural determinants of the innovative behaviour of firms towards clean technology development. First there is a brief overview of the In-Bond industry. Second, the dynamics of technological change are then briefly outlined. Third, it is discussed what is being wrongly understood by environmental protection in industrial activities. Fourth, it is suggested what type of changes may be necessary in industrial activities in order to achieve environmental sustainability. Fifth an overview of environmental management activities and the regulatory framework within which the In-Bond industry operates is given. Lastly, some conclusions are presented.

THE IN-BOND INDUSTRY

The In-Bond Industry along the US–Mexican border has been widely studied elsewhere, so this section presents only a brief overview of its development and main features (e.g., Godinez and Mercado, 1996; Gonzalez-Arechiga and Ramirez, 1990; Perez, 1990; Icasa, 1993; Taylor, 2000; De la O, 2000). This region is one of most dynamic platforms for export in the world, with an average rate of industrial growth of over 15% per annum during the last decade (Godinez and Mercado, 1996). Most of this growth stems from the reallocation of factories from the USA and Japan along the entire US–Mexico border. The In-bond industry moved to Northern Mexico in 1965 as part of the Program of Border Industrialisation (Taylor, 2000). Firms continued to relocate their operations on the grounds of (1) cheap, highly qualified and virtually non-unionised labour, (2) tax exemption for inputs and revenues, (3) land subsidies, (4) low costs of services and infrastructure, (5) the proximity to the firm's headquarters and markets in the USA and (6) economies of agglomeration (González-Aréchiga and Barajas, 1988; Taylor, 2000; Kiodo, 2000).

Lax enforcement of environmental regulations has probably also played a part in this process of industrialisation. At its outset, this program involved only 65 factories, generating 3000 jobs along the border. In 1984 there were 672 factories (Carrillo, 1986) and by 1998 3,833, generating 1,003,918 jobs (INEGI, 1998). This industry is segmented into the following ten sectors: auto parts; textiles; chemical products; electrical and electronic consumer and intermediate goods; food processing; timber and furniture; leather products; plastics; services; tools and metal mechanics (Gonzales-Arechiga and Barajas, 1989).

The number of sectors and the rate of growth clearly convey the dynamism and heterogeneity present in this industry. Heterogeneity also exists in terms of productivity and sophistication of the production processes of different firms. These span from (1) very simple and old-fashioned assembly lines to long and complex manufacturing processes; (2) rigid, standardised and intensive forms of labour employment to flexible labour and flexible automation; (3) small local factories to regional centres of production (Godines and Mercado, 1995); and (4) firms that operate with no environmental considerations to firms that have environmental management groups.[1]

Although direct investment funded relocation is another form that has occurred frequently, in recent years this industry operates primarily within a 'shelter' scheme. This type of scheme reduces firms' economic and political risks to the minimum, thus, it has been used as an intermediate strategy covering the time during which the firm knows little about the culture, regulations, labour and ·politics of the host country. In such cases the firm receives certain services from a Mexican contractor. Such services may include the obtaining of necessary licenses and documentation, labour recruitment, the construction of facilities, and installation of production lines, plant management and the securing of import and export permits.

After a lengthy trial period and once they have learned the culture and adapted their management techniques to the regional context, many firms decide to transform their operation to direct investment. In this case, the firms construct their own facilities, expand production and manage almost all aspects of their operations independently. Nevertheless, common to both the shelter scheme and the direct investment form of plant operation is a predominance of Mexican employees. Generally, only a few members of senior management are from the 'country of origin – i.e., the USA, Japan, etc. While they generally supervise their entire operation, most firms contract Mexicans to act as plant managers.

Although this industrial development represents a partial solution to the problem of unemployment in this region, its operations – similar to the programmes in a number of southern Asian countries (Gassert, 1985, p. 46) – generate only low added value, minimal integration of national inputs (less than 2%), zero technology transfer (Icaza, 1993; Carrillo, 1986), and tend to cause regional wages contraction. In addition, because the rapid urbanisation and population expansion induced by re-location of this industry, state and local government are frequently unable to provide basic public services and many problems arise regarding labour and environmental health (Ganster and Sanchez, 1998). Some of these problems are related to the improper disposal of hazardous and solid wastes, discharges of industrial wastewater, heavy metals and organic-chlorinated compounds in municipal sewage, pollution of underground drinking water, and so on (cf., Kopinak and García 2000; Mercado, 2000; Ganster and Sanchez, 1998; EPA, 1996; Alvares and Castillo, 1986; Baker, 1989, 1990; Carrillo, 1986; Franco; 1991; Montalvo, 1992; Mendez, 1995; Perry *et al.*, 1990; Sanchez, 1990a, 1990b, 1991).

Though a regulatory framework for the operation of this industry exists, in many cases local and state authorities have to choose between environmental quality and employment. This dilemma is a consequence of the above structure under which this industry operates. Most of the firms involved enjoy the services of industrial holdings that provide shelter plans, facilities, management, transport and import–export services, and labour (González-Aréchiga and Ramírez; 1990; Godinez and Mercado, 1996). They have a high rate of openings and closures, as many firms are set up for specific short-term production projects. On top of this, the local authorities must compete, not only with other countries but also with other Mexican states, to attract investment. This situation – the prevalence of an easily cancellable shelter scheme and the intra-regional locational opportunities – grants an even greater degree of negotiating power to already highly mobile (multinational) firms.

It is precisely at the time of any policy negotiation that stakeholders should have attained a better understanding of what it is that is being negotiated, of what is and what is not possible to do, particularly with regard to environmental protection and sustainability, in order to devise viable environmental policies to promote these goals. An analysis of whether the firms that constitute the In-Bond industry have any capacity to contribute to regional sustainability, can be best achieved from the perspective of the dynamics of technical change and industrial evolution. Such analysis aims to locate where this industry stands on the road to sustainability by establishing a background against which contrast: (a) the scope of the efforts of those regional environmental authorities and institutions to meet the challenge of environmental sustainability discussed below (p.27); and (b) the description (Chapter 6) and analysis (Chapter 7) of current capabilities of the firm to make the transition to a new 'technological regime' that is more environmentally benign. The term 'technological regime' is defined below.

PARADIGMS, TRAJECTORIES AND CYCLES OF TECHNICAL CHANGE

Although it is not clear whether science and technology alone can solve industrial pollution problems (Kemp, 1994; Freeman, 1996), governmental and private sector policy agendas have started to consider them as more politically viable and a source of potential solutions (e.g., EPA, 1996; PCSD, 1999; CSIS, 1997; AIST, 1993; MPW, Canada, 1999). This agenda departs from the premise that neither population nor consumption can be reduced. It assumes therefore, that an easier and more viable solution to environmental problems is the development of clean technologies (Iarrera and Vickery, 1997). As technology is believed to be the central tool for responding to the challenge of sustainability, it is necessary to discuss how technology evolves and intertwines with the logic of industrial organisation. This evolution can be viewed from at least two perspectives. The first is a macro perspective looking at the paradigms that determine the direction of technological progress, and the second a micro perspective considering the cycles and stages along which industry evolves.

Paradigms and Trajectories of Technical Change

At the macro level, the School of Evolutionary Economics has shown that technological change has its own inner logic (Nelson and Winter, 1977, p. 56). Following Dosi (1988), at the core of any technological development is a *technological paradigm*. This is:

> "a pattern for the solution of selected techno-economic problems based on highly selected principles derived from the natural sciences. Therefore, it defines contextually the needs that are meant to be fulfilled, the scientific principles used for the task, the material technology to be used. A technological paradigm is both a set of exemplars – basic artefacts which are to be developed and improved and a set of heuristics – Where do we go from here? On what sort of knowledge should we draw?" (Dosi, 1988, p. 225).

Once a technological paradigm is fixed, it determines and conditions the evolution of technologies in specific and selected directions termed *technological trajectories* (Dosi, 1988).[2] The dominance of a particular technological trajectory is determined by all kinds of evolutionary improvements that have a self-reinforcing effect. Kemp and Soete (1992) include among these factors the costs and performance of product and production process design and their integration in a socio-economic context in terms of accumulated knowledge and skills; production capabilities; infrastructure; regulations and social norms; and peoples' lifestyles. Some examples of technological paradigms that have followed definite trajectories of optimisation to their possible limits include: (1) maximisation of automation; (2) maximisation of speed in computer processing capacity; and (3) introduction of microelectronics into industrial, capital and consumer products, etc.

The concatenation of diverse technological paradigms and trajectories form a *technological regime*. A technological regime represents a 'set of design parameters which embody the economic principles that generate the physical configuration of products and processes and materials from which they are constructed' (Georghiou *et al.*, 1986, p. 32). The notion of regime needs be understood here as having a dual aspect: as the ruling system and as a prevailing system. On the one hand it constitutes the frontier of achievable capabilities, defined in their relevant economic dimensions, limited by physical, biological and other constraints, and giving a broadly defined way of doing things (Hayami and Ruttan, 1971, cited in Nelson and Winter, 1982, p. 258). The technological regime represents a framework shared by the totality of engineers, technologists and economic actors as a basis for the search of improvements in production processes and products (Kemp, 1994) and of economic opportunities. On the other hand, as the regime evolves along its 'natural trajectories'[3] it becomes in itself the *modus operandi* of the broader 'techno-economic system'. In this sense a technological regime rules and defines – that is, organises – the boundaries of technological progress, demarcating those directions of progress based on '...what is feasible or at least worth attempting' (Nelson and Winter, 1982, p. 258).

It is within this notion of what is 'worth attempting' (in terms of technological feasibility and economic opportunity), that the concept of technological paradigms, trajectories and regimes mixes with the *value chain system*. According to Porter, a value chain is that system whereby value is created and added at each stage of the transformation of raw materials into goods and services, flowing incrementally from the primary to the tertiary sector (Porter, 1985, p. 36). As the technologies required to maintain marketplace competitiveness become more complex and expensive to research, develop and perform, intra- and inter-firm trade also becomes more complex.

Such trade constitutes a way in which the costs and risks involved in production and innovation can be offset to some degree, and increases firms' flexibility to cope with drastic changes in the demand for their products (Tirole, 1988; Schoemberger, 1990). Hence, industrial organisation develops into an interdependent chain of value creation making the possibility of environmental sustainability a phenomenon that involves not only the firm or sector undertaking technological innovation towards the development of clean technologies, but the whole industrial supply–demand chain.

Cycles of Industrial Evolution

At a micro level, the degree of evolution and maturity of a given industry at a given moment is intrinsically linked to the evolution of those technologies required for the manufacture of a competitive product through its specific production processes. According to Abernathy and Utterback (1975), the form taken by the industrial innovation of manufactured goods can be described as cyclic departing from a frantic product and process concepts generation to maturity and decline and final replacement by a new wave of product and process concepts. The three main phases that make up these cycles have been further refined by Utterback (1994) (see Figure 2.1 below).

The first 'fluid' phase is characterised by the development of the concepts of both the product and the production process. In this phase, the rate of product innovation is rapid with frequent and major changes in the products' features. Diverse and often customised designs of the same product frequently exist. The primary source of innovation is generally located within the firm that pioneers the product. Here, however, the research and development (R&D) effort is to some degree diffuse. This is due to the very nature of new product development in which the operational specifications it seeks to impart to the new product (and which define its novelty) require technical solution *for the first time*. Plant facilities are generally small with flexible but inefficient production processes due to the use of general-purpose equipment and highly skilled labour. Major changes in production lines can be easily accommodated at a relatively low cost. The end of this phase is marked by the emergence of a product design that wins customer loyalty in the marketplace. The pioneering firm normally reaps the benefits arising from the novelty of its product as a result of the timing of its entry into an existing market or the creation of a new market with no competitors. As a consequence, competitors and new entrants in the same industrial sector must adhere to the dominant design if they are to gain a significant market share.

	Fluid phase	Transitional phase	Specific phase
Innovation	Frequent major product changes	Major process changes required by rising demand (and desire of scale economies)	Incremental for product, cumulative improvements in productivity and quality
Source of innovation	Industry pioneers; product users	Manufacturers; users	Often suppliers
Products	Diverse designs, often customised	At least one product design, stable enough to have significant production volume	Mostly undifferentiated, standard products
Production process	Flexible and inefficient, major changes easily accommodated	Becoming more rigid, with changes occurring in major steps	Efficient, capital intensive, and rigid; cost of change high
R&D	Focus unspecified because of high degree of technical uncertainty	Focus in specific product features once dominant design emerges	Focus on incremental product technology; emphasis of process technology
Equipment	General purpose, requiring skilled labour	Some sub-processes automated, creating islands of automation	Special purpose, mostly automatic, with labour focused on tending and monitoring equipment
Plant	Small scale, located near the user or source of innovation	General purpose with specialised sections	Large scale, highly specific to particular products
Cost of process change	Low	Moderate	High
Competitors	Few, but growing in numbers with widely fluctuating market shares	Many, but declining in numbers after emergence of dominant design	Few; classic oligopoly with stable market shares
Basis of competition	Functional product performance	Product variation; fitness for use	Price
Organisational control	Informal and entrepreneurial	Through project and task groups	Structure, rules, and goals
Vulnerability of industry leaders	To imitators, and patent challenges; to successful product breakthroughs	To more efficient and higher quality producers	To technological innovations that present superior product substitutes

Rate of major innovations — *Process* — *Product*

Figure 2.1 Innovation cycles of industrial products and processes
Figure based on: Utterback (1994)

20

The second 'transition' phase is distinguished by diminishing product innovation and its replacement by frequent changes in the production process. In this phase at least one product design has achieved the stability to obtain a significant market share and sufficient production volume to meet further rises in demand. At this stage, the major sources of innovation are the manufacturers themselves and suggestions from the product's users. Further R&D efforts focus upon specific product features. Plant facilities are generally of medium size with the automation of some parts of the production process creating 'islands' of automation; and major changes in production can be accommodated at moderate cost. At the end of this phase, the numerous firms struggling for a market share will rapidly give way to competitive pressures.

The third 'specific' phase is defined by a levelling off of the rate of innovation and the slowing of technical change in both the product and the production processes. Products become standardised and process improvements focus almost exclusively upon productivity and quality. The sources of innovation at this stage are mainly the suppliers of components, machinery and equipment. Research and development efforts focus on incremental changes in the technologies in both the product and the production process, the emphasis being on the latter. Plant facilities are large, efficient, capital-intensive and rigid, with purpose-built machinery and equipment that is mostly automated. Labour activity is primarily focused on tending and monitoring this equipment. The cost of major changes to the product or the production process – that is, to their concepts and design – is, therefore, very high. Normally the number of competitors is low; a classic oligopoly with a stable market share.

In sum, the evolution of an industry and its associated technologies departs from a technological paradigm in which it struggles to survive in an environment of competitive selection driven by market laws. It proceeds through the 'fluid' and 'transitional' phases and becomes a dominant and rigid design in the 'specific' phase of product and process maturity. Once a product is in the 'specific' phase, the technological paradigms underlying the dominant designs provide the direction in which the technological trajectories for products, production processes and industries evolve. Such paradigms and trajectories have a powerful exclusionary effect. Blind to other needs and possibilities, the creativity and efforts of engineers and entire organisations are concentrated in rather precise directions (Dosi, 1982). As a consequence, technological 'progress' follows certain trajectories due to any number of marginal evolutionary improvements, e.g., the cost and performance of the design; its integration into a socio-economic context in terms of accumulated knowledge and skills, production capabilities, infrastructure, regulations and social norms, etc. (Nelson and Winter, 1977, pp. 56–9; Kemp, 1994).

An absurd example of how reinforcing factors transform prevailing paradigms and trajectories into regimes is that of 'pollution control' as embodied in end-of-pipe technologies and transformed into a regime of environmental regulations. For more than 30 years the mandatory use of end-of-pipe technologies has created and boosted an industrial sector that provides environmental management technologies that purport to be a solution. As will be illustrated in the next section, this 'solution' not only postpones but also increases the pollution problem. This is one illustration, as noted in Chapter 1, of how ill-defined policies can last for many years.

POLLUTION PREVENTION: A NEW TECHNOLOGICAL REGIME

Since the nineteenth century, it has been widely accepted that any industrial activity generates pollution. Environmental economists have put emphasis mainly on determining optimal levels of pollution (e.g., Coase, 1960; Hahn, 1989; Pearce and Turner, 1991; Opschoor and Vos, 1991) while the environmental debate, policy and practice have focused on limiting the release of noxious substances into water, air and soil (Skea, 1995; CSIS, 1997). This has created a tacit correspondence between pollution control and environmental protection. It has only recently been recognised that controlling pollution (in the long term) does not avoid environmental degradation. The main reason is that once pollution has been generated, its control fails in the long term, substances eventually escaping to mix and travel from one physical medium to another (see Figure 2.2).

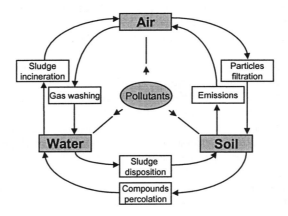

Figure 2.2   Cross mediums pollution cycle
Based on: Ferrer (1986)

If pollutants, for example, are released into water and subsequently *controlled* through settlement, filtration and/or flotation, these treatments produce not just clean water but also sludge as a 'side' product. This is then either 'treated' by incineration – thereby being transformed into gases that pollute the air – or confined, either in landfills or more specialised facilities from which there is always percolation through the soil and eventual return to ground water. If the pollutants are released directly into the air for subsequent control through filtration, adsorption or gas washing, a side-product is still produced, i.e., the captured pollutants, which in turn need to be treated via incineration or confinement, thus repeating the cycle described in the case of wastewater treatment. In other words, by whichever route, pollutants are always mixing with, or have the potential to return to, the environment (Ferrer, 1986; Skea, 1995).

Furthermore, the industry that produces and promotes these end-of-pipe technologies is just another interdependent link in the supply chain system. As a consequence, this industrial sector is caught within the framework of current technological trajectories. It poses, therefore, the same problems of pollution creation even as it produces technical 'fixes' aimed at pollution abatement. Industrial wastewater treatment systems (WTS) are a good example of such interdependence, since they are at the centre of virtually all integrated pollution control systems for air or soil. Typically WTS are composed of a tank (metallic or plastic in structure), an electro-mechanical system to pump water in and out and to administer and mix chemical reagents, and a control system for water flows, doses of chemicals, pH levels, and the quality of treated water at the system's outflow. The manufacture of the tank is linked to the steel, plastic and coating industries; the electro-mechanic system is linked to the metal-mechanic and electrical industry; and the control of the purification of water is linked to the electronics industry. As any possibility for innovation and technical change in WTS is dependent upon these supplier industries, end-of-pipe technologies cannot provide a solution to the problem they are intended to solve. Rather, they simply extend the chain of problems.

In some countries, this fact has been finally accepted at government policy level with the recent enactment of several initiatives calling for the application of a precautionary principle regarding pollution (e.g., van den Berg *et al.*, 1995; SETAC, 1993; PCSD, 1999; AIST, 1993; MPW, Canada, 1999). Currently for the first time, the environmental debate, some policy, and – to a minimal degree – practice, are putting emphasis on the necessity of shifting from technologies that control pollution at the end of a production process to technologies that seek to *prevent the generation of potential pollutants* from the inception of product design and production process (Krut, 1998; Gouldson and Murphy, 1998).

Thus, environmental protection is now conceived of as the prevention of pollutant generation. The term that embodies such pollution prevention practices is *clean technology*. Following Dosi's (1982) definition of technological paradigm, clean technologies can be seen as a new set of technological paradigms involving new goals, new scientific principles, and new material technologies for the production of all kinds of consumer goods and services. Some of the features of the current technological regime and those that are likely to feature in a new one that seeks to facilitate the transition to sustainability are presented in the following section.

A NEW TECHNOLOGICAL REGIME FOR SUSTAINABLE INDUSTRIAL DEVELOPMENT

The previous sections have helped to organise and anticipate the technological and social challenges that environmental protection poses. From the above discussion it can be inferred that in order to protect the environment it is necessary to advocate a new technological regime. To make such a shift, an initial – but in itself insufficient condition – is to change the basic principles of the current technological regime. This requires a reduction of the present institutional rigidities through the promotion of a set of core capabilities comprising collective long-term values embraced by corporate boards,[4] new knowledge and skills, and new technological and managerial systems at the firm level (Leonard-Barton, 1995). This new set of competencies represents a new knowledge base.

Following the definition of Georghiou *et al.* (1986) and the above discussion, the current technological regime (TR) can be defined as being bound by a set of features and economic principles that are embodied in the design and development of all products or production processes. Its *modus operandi* is such that it puts emphasis on product life cycle management. Its main features and economic principles are outlined below:

The current regime: product life cycle management

- By the very nature of their design, product concepts and production processes involve the use of natural resources in a dynamic of short-term exploitation.
- Products are conceptualised and marketed as disposable consumable goods.
- The supply chain of any production system progresses across different industrial sectors. It encompasses the extraction of raw materials, their material transformation into inputs for the manufacture of intermediate and final goods, consumption, and finally the disposal of these products.
- The supply chain is an 'open loop' with regard to natural resources management because all the work accumulated during materials extraction and their transformation into manufactured consumable goods is disposed into the environment at the end of the product life.

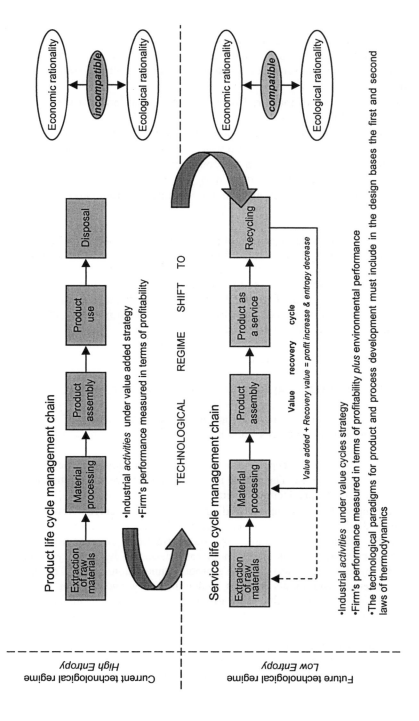

Figure 2.3   Technological regime shift: a new corporate strategy, changing from value added to value cycles

25

- Each link in the supply chain is governed by a value-added strategy. That is, along the supply chain raw materials – and subsequently components – pass through a sequence of transformations each of which adds monetary value.
- The performance of industrial firms is measured in terms of their short-term profitability.
- The management of residuals is performed at the end-of-the-pipe to control pollutants discharged into water or emitted to the atmosphere. Therefore, industrial activities and consumption are associated with a regime of high-energy consumption.
- As a consequence, economic and environmental rationalities appear incompatible.

The product life cycle management paradigm has been dominant since the Industrial Revolution. Several authors have argued that in order to achieve a clean technology system, a shift towards a new technological regime that places emphasis on services is required (e.g., Rodgers, 1998; Linnanen *et al.*, 1995; Van Weenen, 1995). Figure 2.3 summarises the features of the current technological regime and those most likely to constitute a new regime which emphasises the management of products as services.

The new regime: service life cycle management

Some of the features that may form the new regime are that:

- By the very nature of product conceptualisation, the design of products and production processes entails natural resources in a long-term management dynamic.
- Products will be conceptualised by the services they provide, hence, marketed as services. The device providing the service is designed to be recycled into the production system.
- The supply chain encompasses all the stages of the current regime but closes the loop of resource management. The product is recycled in the supply chain at the stage of transformation of resources and manufacturing. Designs enable both easy disassembly for recyclability and easy reinsertion into the firm's product innovation cycles. The reuse of materials and inputs enables 'value recovery cycles' that can be integrated into the value addition strategy of the business, hence increasing the overall profitability of the firm. This implies that firms need to have an innovative capability so as to develop evolutionary architectures for their product concepts.
- With regard to natural resources the supply chain will be a loop. All the work accumulated during materials extraction and their transformation

into manufactured consumable goods is reintroduced into the production and innovation cycles at the end of the product life.

- The industrial activities at each link of the supply chain are governed by strategies for innovation and cycles of value recovery. This represents an advance in corporate strategies from value addition to value cycles.
- The performance of industrial firms is measured in terms of profitability, which incorporates their environmental performance.
- Ideally, the management of residuals is eliminated since the conceptual development of the product and the manufacturing process incorporates the natural laws of matter and energy into the very designs.[5] Thus pollution is prevented rather than controlled.
- As a consequence, economic and environmental rationalities are compatible.

The necessary scientific and technological base for the implementation of the service life cycle management paradigm does not yet exist (PCSD, 1999; NSF, 2000). Furthermore, according to Kemp (1994), the following conditions have to be present for a change of technological regime to occur: (1) new scientific insights that open new technological and economic opportunities must be in place; (2) pressing needs – environmental or otherwise – that are impossible to satisfy within the available technological paradigms; (3) exhausted technological trajectories the pursuance of which leads to increasing marginal costs; (4) the establishment of new firms or industries with a different knowledge base which permits them to diversify into new markets; and (5) the presence of an entrepreneurial propensity to undertake innovative activities with a high risk factor.

It is not clear, however, to what extent the change in the understanding of environmental protection – that is, its acceptance as the prevention of the generation of pollution and its interaction with technological regimes – is recognised at the *regional* policy-making level. The environmental policies and regulatory framework discussed in the following section suggest strongly that these notions are not reflected in the steps being taken towards implementation of the notion of environmental sustainability in the US–Mexican border region.

ENVIRONMENTAL MANAGEMENT IN THE USA–MEXICO BORDER REGION

The foregoing sections have provided an insight into the In-Bond industry, its relationship with the degradation of the border environment and the dynamics of technical change within which it operates. This section seeks to explain why considerable failures in enforcement persist despite the existence of environmental laws and regulations at local, state, and federal levels. It also attempts to highlight the absence of policies directed at promoting sustainability in the region, and hence the failure to address the problem of a shift in the technological strategy of firms necessary to move towards sustainability.

The first modern Mexican Environmental Law (Ley General de Equilibrio Ecológico) was passed in 1971 (DOFM, 1971), and subsequently revised in 1982, 1983 and 1988 (Ley General de Equilibrio Ecológico y Proteccion Ambiental (LGEEPA)). While the most recent version is the most stringent and comprehensive, significant loopholes remain, particularly with regard to the limited number of specific standards for a wide range of economic activities. In an attempt to remedy these shortcomings four additional regulations have been ratified since 1988. These concern air, air quality in Mexico City, environmental impact assessment and hazardous wastes. Being subject to political pressure and confronted by the immediacy of the need to take care of the environment, the Federal Government announced in 1990 an undertaking to promote *clean economic growth*.[6] A total of 64 technical norms and ecological criteria have been enacted to give weight to the four areas of regulation.

Before 1991, protection of the environment was the responsibility of the federal authority (the national government). Under the Mexican Environmental Project (MEP, Proyecto Ambiental Mexicano) and with assistance from the World Bank, the federal government initiated pilot programmes in several states to decentralise environmental management (SEDESOL, 1990).[7] In accordance with the MEP and the LGEEPA, it is now the responsibility of local and state authorities to regulate emissions and wastewater discharges into local authority drainage systems, excluding hazardous wastes and discharges into federal waters (Mexican Ecological Law, 1989: article 4).[8] In conjunction with the Ministry of Industry and Trade (Secretaría de Comercio y Fomento Industrial (SECOFI)), federal environmental agencies are responsible for controlling the import and export of hazardous substances and wastes. Notably, here, hazardous wastes created by the In-Bond industry must be returned to the country of origin (DOFM, 1983).

US–Mexican Environmental Cooperation Agreements

Concern with the environment in the border region reached the political agenda in 1983. In that year, the Mexican and US governments signed the 'La Paz Agreement',[9] which effectively created a framework for binational co-operation to address issues of common concern in the border region. The main goal and commitment of this agreement was to implement the necessary steps to prevent and control pollution in the border region.[10] The agreement set up six binational working groups: Air, Contingency Planning, Cooperative Enforcement, Pollution Prevention and Water. The first regulation of cross-border transportation of hazardous wastes emanated from the works of these groups in 1986 (Franco, 1991).

In 1991, the Mexican Ministry of Social Development (Secretaría de Desarrollo Social: SEDESOL) and the US Environmental Protection Agency (EPA) developed the *'1992–94 Integrated Environmental Plan for the US–Mexican Border Area'* (Plan Integral Ambiental Fronterizo: PIAF) (SEDUE–EPA, 1992). This new programme defined a further four specific goals: (1) to enforce existing law and regulations; (2) to reduce pollution through new resources and initiatives; (3) to increase co-operation in the areas of planning, training and environmental education, and (4) to widen knowledge of environmental issues in the border (SEDUE–EPA, 1992, p. 8). The authorities regarded PIAF as the beginning of a growing co-operative effort that aimed to achieve their goals during the next decade (SEDUE–EPA, 1992, p.101).

Arising from the strong criticisms directed at NAFTA regarding its potential impacts on the environment, the governments of the three countries signed the Parallel Agreements for Environmental Cooperation in 1993. As a consequence of this agreement, the Commission for Environmental Cooperation (CEC) was created. The CEC has five main tasks: (1) to promote sustainable development in North America; (2) to preserve, protect, and improve the environment; (3) to support the environmental objectives of NAFTA; (4) to avoid distortions in trade, and (5) to promote the effective enforcement of environmental law (DOFM, 1993).

Also arising from NAFTA was the joint creation by Mexico and the United States of the Border Environmental Cooperation Commission (BECC) and the North American Development Bank (NADBank), both institutions without any direct relation to the CEC. It is intended that these two institutions should address the most urgent environmental problems by providing technical assistance and funding to border communities. The priority is the creation of an infrastructure for drinking water provision, municipal wastewater treatment and solid waste management (sanitary landfills) facilities on both sides of the border. About US $8 billion are expected to be available for investment along the US–Mexican border to develop this environmental infrastructure during the next 10 years.[11]

The Commission is currently not addressing problems directly related to industry, focusing instead on the public infrastructure. In conjunction with the environmental authorities of both countries, the Commission has developed a new border plan, 'Border XXI', which covers the period 1996–2001 (EPA, 1996b). It is intended that these institutions (i.e., BECC and CEC) play the main role in addressing the priority environmental problems of the region and their establishment could be construed as suggesting that the solution to the environmental problems associated with the economic development of the region is on its way.

Recent Border Environmental Management: An Analysis

The rapid growth of the In-Bond industry has brought a heavy – arguably excessive – flow of goods (importation and exportation) and people (immigration, emigration and floating populations), as well as the unplanned growth of large urban centres. For most analysts, these are the primary explanation for the environmental problems in the region. Environmental problems of this nature are, however, only symptoms of the process of rapid industrialisation: policy solutions clearly need to be directed towards the origins and not at their symptoms. In this regard, here is presented an analysis of (1) the performance of regulatory authorities on the Mexican side of the border; (2) the control of hazardous wastes by the 1992–94 PIAF; (3) the Compendium of Binational and Domestic US–Mexico Activities;[12] (4) the CEC 1999–2001 action plan and 1998 report of activities; and (5) the activities of BECC and NADBank. The analysis intends to reveal that the actual proposed solutions for the environmental problems present many pitfalls.

1. *Enforcement of pollution control policies*: Local, state and federal authorities on the Mexican side of the border are still incapable of managing many of the delicate problems that afflict the region. Strong group interests hamper the success of environmental policy enforcement. Most of the appointments of senior officers and middle manager positions in the environmental agencies are determined more by political interests than by skills in science or engineering. This results in a severe lack of organisational, institutional and technological capabilities and thus hinders environmental protection, as detailed in Table 2.1 (see next page).
2. *Control of hazardous wastes by PIAF*: Amongst the main objectives of PIAF was that to assess the volume of hazardous and solid wastes generated in the area (and, in particular, the amount generated by the In-Bond industry) and how they are disposed of, and to increase the capabilities of monitoring and enforcing regulations (SEDESOL, 1990, p. 48–50). A comparison of these goals with the outcomes-to-date as summarised in the PIAF Compendium of Activities shows that the goals are yet to be achieved (EPA, 1995). The authorities do not have the necessary capacity, as presented in Table 2.1, to control and supervise the behaviour of the industry on a regular basis because they do not know how much hazardous waste is being generated and what it is composed of, and therefore its possible effects on the environment.
3. *Compendium of Binational and Domestic US–Mexico Activities*: Analysis of the 144 projects along the border detailed in the PIAF Compendium of Activities (EPA, 1995) evidences the following: (a) most research and other activities are related to the gathering of data on pollutants in the environment, risk assessments, best available end-of-pipe technologies,

best available recycling and waste minimisation practices, and with remedial rather than preventive activities; (b) the projects related to technical assistance could be seen as the promotion of new markets for end-of-pipe and solid waste management technologies, and (c) an overall lack of clear co-ordination of problem-solving efforts from the regulatory agencies (both EPA and SEMARNAP) and industry.

Table 2.1 Environmental management capabilities

Lack of institutional capabilities

- A basic problem lies in the general nature of most border state environmental laws which do not clearly specify all the responsibilities of the states and municipalities, resulting in some cases in overlapping functions or inaction at both levels
- Municipalities and states now have the responsibility of enforcing regulations to protect the environment, but most regulations are weak and underdeveloped
- Political change and lack of continuity in policies tend to reduce the likelihood of successful reforms
- There is no decision-making power or responsibility for environmental issues
- Lack of inter-sector co-ordination at a local, state and federal levels (water, urban planning, solid waste, etc.)
- Only big municipalities have environmental units
- Because of rent *seeking* behaviour by officials, violators find easy and in their interest to pay a fraction of the stipulated fine as a bribe and to the enforcement official who, being grossly underpaid, is often willing to accept or propose it.

Lack of technological capabilities
- Insufficient and weak infrastructures
- Excessive work demands on staff
- Inexperience, and lack of technical knowledge
- Lack of laboratories and monitoring equipment
- The environmental management activities are extremely limited in most cases. Municipalities that have only recently incorporated environmental protection into their administrative agenda, those that count with environmental units normally do not count with their own budget.

Sources: EPA (1996), and Panayotou (1993).

4. *The CEC*: The report of the Commission for Environmental Cooperation suggests a laudable effort on several fronts. The addressing of the numerous urgent environmental problems leaves little space for the promotion of schemes that may encourage the development of clean technologies. The current action plan for pollution prevention focuses the

effort on two projects. The first, considered a pilot project, focuses on the identification of by-product waste from one industry and the location of potential users in other industries. The second aims to consolidate a fund for pollution prevention directed to promoting the adoption of pollution prevention methods by small and medium sized manufacturing firms (SMEs) in Mexico. One of the major problems that limits the potential of the CEC is its organisational size and budget considering its role of clean technology promotion in three countries and across *all* industrial activities. The total operational budget for all its projects in 1998 amounted to less than three million US dollars (CEC, 1999).

An idea of the type of economic resources and the time required for such technological endeavour can be obtained by a comparison with the resources invested in the R&D effort on the technological development of five products within the current technological regime. From Table 2.2 it can be inferred that promotion of the development of a new knowledge base – the fundamental prerequisite for the development of a new set of technologies for the transformation of a whole technological system – cannot be achieved by a single organisation of the resource and capacity base as that managed by the CEC.

Table 2.2   Attributes of five products and their associated development effort

	Stanley Tools Jobmaster screwdriver	Rollerblade	HP DJ 500 Printer	Chrysler Concord Automobile	Boeing 777 aeroplane
Develop time	1 year	2 year	1.5 year	3.5 year	4.5 year
Team size	3 people	10 people	100 people	1400 people	10,000 people
Develop cost	US$15^{E}4	US $75^{E}4	US $5^{E}7	US $1^{E}9	US $3^{E}9
Production investment	US$15^{E}4	US $1^{E}6	US $25^{E}6	US $6^{E}8	US $3^{E}9

Source: Ulrich and Eppinger (1995, p. 6).

Furthermore, its strategy of building a capacity for pollution prevention through the creation of a pollution prevention fund is ill-defined. On one side, there is the intention to obtain funds from a set of organisations such as industrial associations and business councils with no real economic power. On the other – although in some of its documents pollution prevention is defined 'as the avoidance of the generation of pollutants' (CEC, 1996a, p. 45) – the working definition found in its action plans refers to the 'minimisation of wastes and its associated impacts' (CEC, 1999, p. 90). As a consequence, the possible outcomes of this conflict of definitional and operational frameworks could be expected to be rather limited in relation to the dimension of the challenges.

5. *BECC and NADBank*: The activities of the BECC and NADBank officially started in October 1994 in response to the pressing need for an environmental infrastructure. The political and economic interests related to the creation of these institutions and the development of selection criteria for the certification of submitted projects are enormous. The potential pitfalls for these institutions are numerous: (a) the absence of an overall strategy for what it is sought to achieve;[13] (b) domination of their programme by political rather than engineering/scientific considerations; (c) the outweighing of human and environmental health concerns by commercial interests; (d) an inability to correlate costs and risk; (e) a lack of mechanisms to ensure the quality of contract work; (f) the lack of interest in the local communities along the border in the projects certified and funded by these institutions; and (g) conflicts of interest between BECC and NADBank and their contractors (Casagrande and Morgan, 1995).

One of the main asymmetries of this border environmental programme is that there is a direct transfer of capital from Mexico to the US. This is occurring because the criteria set up by the commission to select projects and contractors excludes many Mexican contractors from the capital intensive bidding process. Associated with this is the fact that most Mexican contractors that remain in the market are associated with US contractors who provide the necessary environmental technologies. Furthermore, the list of government agencies and activities described in the US–Mexico Border XXI Program mainly presents policies to control the current environmental problems.

The programme intends to correct the deficit in the wastewater treatment infrastructure, improve the management of solid and hazardous waste, cover the deficits in the drinking water supply, avoid impacts on the environment and biodiversity and increase the urbanisation of the region (*La Jornada*, 19 December 1996). The pollution prevention programme does not present clear links with institutions that may be able to promote technological change in industry such as the US Office of Technology Administration, the US National Science Foundation, or Mexican Science and Technology National Council, the Mexican Chamber of the Manufacturing Industry (CANACINTRA), etc. (EPA, 1996b).

From the above discussion it can be argued that, although an environmental law, very specific regulations, and some institutions that promote pollution prevention exist in the region, these are largely just 'paper tigers'. Most environmental protection efforts are directed towards pollution control leaving schemes for pollution prevention through technological change outside the policy realm. As a result, a solution to environmental problems, not to mention sustainability, is increasingly remote.

CONCLUSION

The foregoing sections describe aspects of the regional development dynamic based primarily on industrial growth, the dynamics of technical change and the environmental management of the US–Mexican border region. They can be seen as the macro structural determinants of the innovative behaviour of the firms under study. From these sections the following conclusions can be drawn: First, the environmental problems must be understood in a global context. The globalisation of market economies is based in the use of, and search for *flexible* labour, technologies and financing. This so-called flexibility empowers multinationals by increasing their level of mobility, thus reducing the negotiating power of host regions and local authorities. As the region urgently need sources of investment and employment there is a tendency to accept any kind of firms including those using technologies that harm the environment and the health of the labour force.

Second, the implementation of – or even the search for – possible technological solutions is directly related to the conflict among different economic actors. The fact that there is no definite effort to link the activities of government and the new institutions to the development of prevention schemes overwhelmingly hinders the development of CT. Not only does the lack of institutional, technological and organisational capabilities strongly constrain both the success of actual programmes, and above all, the possibility for the regulatory agencies and commissions to develop R&D programmes that address the development of CT.

In short, the tools that exist in the region for the promotion of a sustainable industrial development are: (1) government agencies which, subject to national and international economic and political interests have minimal organisational, institutional and technological capabilities to enforce environmental protection policies, and (2) technological capabilities shaped by overarching technological trajectories along which the products of a dominant design (i.e., pollution control and monitoring technologies) can still benefit from new markets (USA White House, 1998; CEC, 1996b). One can question, then, whether or not the issue of sustainability is in practice being faced or denied.

In order to address environmental problems effectively, it is crucial to promote collaboration among the different interests groups. Although the actual institutions seem committed to tackling environmental problems, the fact that the sources of the conflict between actors are not addressed will always constrain the range of solutions proposed. This leads to a vicious circle of resistance to change (see Figure 1.1) in which a lack of understanding of the conditions under which the resistance and willingness of industry towards environmental protection is shaped, does not allow the real promotion of the technical change necessary.

A better understanding of the dynamic of technical change at the micro level may help to find a way out of this 'vicious circle'. The following questions emerge: *What* are the factors that determine the development of clean technologies on manufacturing firms? *How* can these determinants be organised? *How* can they be rated and ranked? *How* can the degree of conflict between the interest of the firm and the protection of the environment be measured? How can change in the firm's behaviour be promoted towards the development of clean technologies? In summary, how can the effectiveness of environmental policies be improved in order to reconcile opposing interests? To answer these research questions in the following chapters a behavioural model is developed to explore this problem at the 'micro level'. This model intends to provide a tool for analysis of the sources of the firms' resistance or willingness to innovate in clean technologies, as perceived by their managers.

NOTES

1. Unfortunately, very few firms have environmental management departments.
2. These are termed natural trajectories by Nelson and Winter (1982, p. 268).
3. This notion refers to the latent scale improvements in product and process (Nelson and Winter, 1977).
4. The broad societal interest as opposed to the actual short-term interest of the firm.
5. The first law is that matter can neither be created nor destroyed but only transformed. The second refers to the fact that every anthrophogenic work produces a degradation of energy and matter. These laws have many implications in particular for product and process development and in general for the whole economic system. For an ample discussion see, Georgescu-Roegen (1971).
6. 'The Federal Government has the responsibility for promoting *clean economic growth* throughout the training and motivation of the human resources that the development requires and the promotion of favorable industrial technologies that do not harm the environment' (SECOFI, 1990).
7. This programme was elaborated by the Secretaria de Desarrollo Social (SEDESOL).
8. Mexican Ecological Law (*Ley general de equilibrio ecológico y la protección al medio ambiente*).
9. This agreement is also called by some authors 'The Friendship Agreement' (*'El tratado de la Amistad'*, e.g., Franco, 1991).
10. This region extends 100 kilometres on both sides of the US–Mexican border.
11. This technical assistance will be provided by the private companies that win the contract through international public bidding. The funding provided is being channelled through the local authorities. The payment of the investment to NADBank is expected to be assumed by the communities that will benefit.
12. The activities mentioned in this compendium represent a summary report of the progress of efforts to date of the '1983 La Paz working groups' and PIAF 92-94.
13. This critique refers to those disclosed 'official' goals of these institutions.

3. Structure: A behavioural model for environmental and technology policy analysis

In the last 30 years environmental regulations have generated strong conflicting positions between firms and regulators (PCSD, 1999; CSIS, 1997). This chapter introduces the theoretical basis for the development of an instrument for environmental policy analysis that may enable a better understanding of the sources of such conflict on the part of the firm. The instrument is based on a behavioural model, the theory of planned behaviour (TPB), a theory designed to understand and predict human social behaviour. This theory has shown that people's behaviour in most situations can be explained and predicted in terms of intentions, attitudes, subjective norms and behavioural control.

The TPB in this work is used as a definitional system and method to explore, organise, and test the determinants of firms' innovative behaviour in clean technologies. After comparing the TPB with other decision-making theories discussed in this chapter it is argued that it can be applied to understand the firm's innovative behaviour with regard to clean technologies (CT). It is proposed that a firm's willingness (and ultimately behaviour) to develop clean technologies can be explained in terms of its managers' attitude towards clean technologies, perceived social pressures and their perceived control over the innovation process.

In turn it is proposed that: (1) attitude towards the development of CT is dependent on beliefs that arise from the domains of economic and environmental risk perception; (2) the perceived social pressure to develop CT is dependent on beliefs that arise from the domains of market and regulatory community pressures; and (3) perceived control to develop CT is dependent on beliefs that arise from the domains of technological and organisational capabilities. This chapter is divided into three parts. First, the theory of planned behaviour is briefly presented. Second, the TPB is compared with other models of decision making. Based on this comparison it is argued that the TPB can be applied to the understanding and prediction of firm behaviour. Third, the TPB model is adopted to develop a tool for policy analysis in order to devise strategies to optimise the policy effort when intending to foster cleaner environmental behaviour in the firm. Finally, two hypotheses of causality between willingness to innovate and its determinants are proposed.

FROM INTENTIONS TO ACTIONS

The Theory of Planned Behaviour (TPB) is concerned with the prediction and understanding of human social behaviour. The theory is found to be well supported by empirical evidence, the model performs with an explanatory reliability up to 91% of the variance on behaviour (Ajzen, 1991; Jonas and Doll, 1996; Ajzen and Krebs, 1994). The TPB has offered a framework to understand and predict behaviours in topics such as: problem drinking (Fishbein *et al.*, 1980b; Conner *et al.*, 1999), family planning (Fishbein *et al.*, 1980c), consumer behaviour (Fishbein and Ajzen, 1980), voting (Fishbein *et al.*, 1980b), AIDS prevention (Terry, 1993), employment programmes (Van Ryn and Vinokur, 1992; Sperber *et al.*, 1980), drugs abuse (Armitage *et al.*, 1999) adoption of technologies (Lynne *et al.*, 1995), adoption and use of information technologies (Taylor and Todd, 1995; Harrison *et al.*, 1997; Wehn de Montalvo, 2001), and organisational change (Metzelaar, 1997).

Recently the TPB also has been used to explain environmental proactive behaviours (e.g., Harland *et al.*, 1999; Bamberg, 1999; Griffin *et al.*, 1999), water conservation (Lam, 1999), paper recycling (Boldero, 1995; Cheung *et al.*, 1999), public transport use (Bamberg and Schmidt, 1997), waste management (Taylor and Todd, 1997). The TPB will be briefly presented putting emphasis only its most relevant aspects. A complete exposition of the theory can be found in Ajzen (1985, 1988, 1991, 1994, 1996a, 1996b).

According to Ajzen (1985, 1996b) and Gollwitzer and Bargh (1996) there appears to be a general agreement among social psychologists that most human behaviour is goal-directed. This implies that social behaviour can be accurately portrayed as moving along paths of more or less well formulated plans. Therefore, the TPB postulates that a person's *intention* to perform (or not to perform) a behaviour is the immediate determinant of that action (Ajzen, 1985). Discounting contingencies, people are expected to behave according to their intentions. Underlying this statement is the main assumption of the theory, that is that generally speaking human beings are *usually rational*[1] and make systematic use of the information available to them before acting (Ajzen and Fishbein, 1980). This assumption is more likely to be correct when considering the planned behaviour of the firm.

Determinants of Intentions

The TPB specifies three major sources of cognition-behaviour inconsistency. The first source is a change in the initial intention before it is carried out. The second source is people's lack of confidence that the attainment of their behavioural goal is under their volitional control. Finally, whether a behavioural expectation formed on the basis of such an attainment of volitional control leads to actual goal attainment is contingent on the relation between people's confidence in their ability to exercise control over their own action and the extent to which they actually do control events (Ajzen, 1985). These sources of cognition-behaviour inconsistency have been classified and defined as:

- *Attitude toward the behaviour* (A): 'is the degree to which a person (organisation) has a favourable or unfavourable evaluation or appraisal of the behaviour in question'.

- *Subjective norm* (SN): 'is a social factor, is the perceived social pressure to perform or not to perform the behaviour'.

- *Perceived behavioural control* (PBC): 'is the perceived ease or difficulty of performing the behaviour and it is assumed to reflect past experience as well as anticipated impediments and obstacles' (Ajzen 1991, p. 188).

Determinant of Attitudes, Subjective Norm and Perceived Behavioural Control

At its most basic level of explanation, the TPB postulates that behaviour is a function of *salient beliefs* or information relevant to the behaviour. The nature of these beliefs can be explained by looking at how they are shaped. Generally speaking we form beliefs about an object (or people, activity, institution, etc.) by associating it with various characteristics, qualities and attributes. Depending on this connotative meaning, automatically and simultaneously we acquire an attitude towards that object (Ajzen, 1991, p. 191).[2] In a similar fashion, we associate our skills, resources, time, etc., with the control over our own and/or others' behaviour.

According to Ajzen and Fishbein (1980), although people may hold many beliefs about any given object or behaviour, they can attend to only a relatively small number – perhaps five or nine – at a any given moment; these are called salient beliefs. This idea is in agreement with a broad body of literature dealing with complex decisions. Its main proposition and finding is that the more complex the decision problem, the more people will use simplifying decision heuristics (Payne *et al.*, 1992, p. 98). Following the Ajzen model, three kinds of salient beliefs can be distinguished:

- *behavioural beliefs*: which are assumed to influence attitudes toward the behaviour;

- *normative beliefs*: which constitute the underlying determinants of subjective norms, and

- *control beliefs*: which provide the basis for perceptions of behavioural control.

Defining a Behaviour

The TPB states that the first step towards understanding a behaviour, is to define clearly the behaviour under study. In order to achieve a clear definition of a behaviour the TPB proposes four criteria. The first is related to the problem of distinguishing between *behaviours* and events that may be the *outcomes* of those behaviours. To do this the TPB divides behaviour into single actions and behavioural categories. Single actions are specific behaviours performed by an individual (e.g., eating, reading, writing, running, etc.), while behavioural categories are composed of a set of single actions (e.g., dieting, raising funds, stealing, recreational activity, developing clean technologies, etc.). Outcomes are the result of single or behavioural categories (e.g. slimming, success in exams, recycling garbage, protecting the environment, etc.). The second criteria is the *target* (i.e., object, subject, institution, etc.) towards which the behaviour is directed. The third is the *time* when the action should or would take place or occur. The fourth is the situational *context* in which the behaviour occurs or is supposed to occur. A clear definition of each of these four *behavioural criteria* is essential for the accurate measurement of any behaviour under study (Ajzen, 1991).[3]

Predicting Behaviour from Intention

As stated above, from a theoretical point of view, *intention* determines behaviours, but this should not be taken to mean that a measure of intention will always be an accurate predictor of behaviour. A reliable prediction is contingent on two factors that influence the relationship between intention and behaviour. The first is the *degree of correspondence* between the measure of intention and the behavioural criterion, i.e., there must be a high correspondence between action, target, context, and time – elements of the behavioural criteria – and intention with the behaviour under study. Intentions and behaviours correspond only to the extent that their elements are identical.

At this point it is important to clarify that when eliciting these beliefs the researcher must be aware that the set of salient beliefs will be very different depending upon the definition of the behaviour involved. Changing any one of the four elements (action, target, context and time) that define the behaviour can call out completely different sets of salient beliefs.

But this must not be confused with the lack of predictive potential of the TPB. This potential depends on *general or specific measurements* of the behavioural predisposition in question. The level of specificity or generality is contingent on the behavioural criterion selected. If we are interested in predicting and understanding a single action (or a behavioural category), directed at a certain target, in a specific context, and a given time, then the measurement of attitude, subjective norms and perceived behavioural control have to correspond to the criteria selected in all of these elements (Ajzen and Fishbein, 1980, p. 247).

The second factor is the *stability* of intentions over time. Intentions can change over time, the longer the time interval, the greater the likelihood that events will occur or new information will produce changes in intentions. Long-term predictions are usually not concerned with the behaviour of any given individual but rather with projecting or forecasting behavioural trends in relatively large segments of the population (Ajzen, 1988, pp. 92–111). The distinction between predicting behaviour at the level of the individual, and at the aggregate level, is important because aggregate intentions are apt to be much more stable over time than individual intentions (Ajzen, 1988, pp. 45–61). According to Ajzen, there is considerable evidence that even when individual predictions are relatively poor, predictions of behaviour from intention at the aggregate level are often remarkably accurate (Ajzen, 1991, 1996b).

Understanding, predicting and influencing behaviour: The TPB model

To solve applied problems and make policy decisions (or recommendations) it is often necessary to predict people's behaviour. In this regard Ajzen and Fishbein (1980) argue that although prediction is possible with little or no understanding of the factors that cause behaviour, for producing change some degree of understanding is necessary. In many instances, as is the case in this study, our goal goes beyond prediction in that we attempt to produce policy recommendations that influence or change firms' behaviour (Ajzen and Fishbein, 1980). Within the TPB framework, a specific behaviour is considered explained once its determinants have been traced to the underlying beliefs. In order to reach a deeper understanding and predictive reliability, and understanding of any behaviour, it is necessary to examine the attitudes, subjective norms and perceived behavioural control as determinants of intention. To analyse any behaviour the model to operationalise the TPB is presented as follows.[4]

Behavioural beliefs and attitudes toward behaviours

Attitudes are indexes of the degree to which people like or dislike (approve or disapprove of, agree or disagree with, etc.) any aspect of the individual's world. Each behavioural belief links behaviour to an outcome or an attribute that is valued positively or negatively. In this way, we tend to prefer behaviours we believe have desirable consequences. An index of attitude can be obtained, as shown in equation (3.1), by multiplying the subjective evaluation (e) of each belief attribute and the strength (b) of each salient belief, with the resulting products summed over the n salient beliefs.

$$A \propto \sum_{i=1}^{n} b_i e_i \qquad (3.1)$$

Where:

    A is the individual's attitude towards performing behaviour;
    b_i is the belief (subjective probability) that performing behaviour will lead to outcome i;
    e_i is the evaluation of the outcome i, and
    Σ is the sum of the n salient behavioural beliefs.

Normative beliefs and subjective norms

The subjective norm is an index of the importance that the person gives to his or her important individual referents or groups and whether they are perceived to approve or disapprove of the behaviour in question. This can be seen also as the social pressure that the actor perceives. This index can be calculated by multiplying the strength of each normative belief (n) with the person's motivation (or necessity) to comply (m) with the referent in question. The subjective norm is directly proportional to the sum of the resulting products across the n salient beliefs, as shown in equation (3.2).

$$SN \propto \sum_{j=1}^{n} b_j m_j \qquad (3.2)$$

Where:

    SN is the subjective norm;
    b_j is the organisation's motivation to comply with referent j, and
    m_j is the normative belief concerning referent j;
    n is the number of salient normative beliefs.

Control beliefs and perceived behavioural control

The beliefs that ultimately determine intention and action are those that have a relation to the presence or absence of requisite resources and opportunities. These beliefs may be based on past experience, second–hand information or any other factors that increase or reduce the perceived difficulty to perform the behaviour in question. An index of the perceived behavioural control can be estimated by multiplying the control belief strength (c) with the perceived power (p) of the specific factor that facilitates or inhibits the performance of the action. The resulting product is summed across the n salient beliefs as shown in equation (3.3).

$$PBC \propto \sum_{i=1}^{n} c_i \, p_i \qquad (3.3)$$

Where:

PBC	is the perceived behavioural control,
c_i	is the control beliefs strength,
p_i	is the perceived power of the particular control factor to facilitate or inhibit performance,
Σ	is the sum of the n salient control beliefs to produce the perception of behavioural control.

Finally, in order to integrate the above equations, equation 3.4 suggests that the variance in intention or willingness is proportional to the contribution of each of the factors in the model. The mathematical form of the relation among attitudes, subjective norms and perceived behavioural control must be determined empirically. In its simpler form we could hope to find a linear relationship between intention and its determinants as shown in equation 3.4:

$$B \sim I \propto (w_0 + w_1 A + w_2 SN + w_3 PBC) \qquad (3.4)$$

Where:

B	is the behaviour of interest,
I	is the individual's intention,
A	is the individual's attitude toward performing the behaviour,
SN	is the individual's subjective norm concerning performance of the behaviour,
PBC	is the individual's perceived behavioural control,
w_n	are weighting parameters empirically determined, and
$\sim$	suggests that intention is expected to predict behaviour only if the intention has not changed prior to performance of the behaviour.

Linking Beliefs to Behaviour: Implications for Inducing Behavioural Change

The TPB specifies that behaviour is ultimately determined by beliefs. Salient beliefs, in turn, influence attitudes, subjective norms and perceived behavioural control. The latter variables determine intention and intention determines behaviour. Therefore, the TPB essentially consists of a *system of hypotheses linking beliefs to behaviour*, with each hypothesis requiring empirical verification. Once the behaviour is explained, the question of influencing behaviour remains open. The TPB argues that beliefs reflect people's past experiences and that behavioural change is ultimately the result of changes in their beliefs (Fishbein and Ajzen, 1980).

This assumes that, to influence people's behaviour: (a) it is necessary to expose people to new information, and (b) such new information is expected to produce changes in their beliefs. The change in behaviour will be contingent upon: (1) the weight that those selected salient beliefs holds; (2) its empirical correlation with their respective indexes (A, SN, and PBC), and (3) the empirical relations that A, SN and PBC hold with the intention (Ajzen 1980 p. 81; Ajzen, 1988).

In sum, the TPB recognises that global attitudes towards a broad target cannot be expected to predict specific behaviour with respect to that target. Fishbein and Ajzen (1975) formulated a *principle of compatibility* to clarify the conditions under which strong attitude–behaviour correlation can be expected. The principle of compatibility states that measures of attitude and behaviour are compatible, and thus should correlate with one other especially to the extent that they address the same behaviour, and directed at the same target, in the same context and at the same time. It can be seen that the principle of aggregation is a special case of the principle of compatibility. Compatibility can be established either by aggregating behaviours to elevate the generality of the behavioural measure to that of a general attitude (aggregation), or by measuring attitudes with respect to the specific behaviour of interest (Ajzen, 1994).

The TPB applies the principle of compatibility to the prediction of specific behavioural tendencies. This is achieved by encompassing different levels of explanation for people's behaviour. At the most global level, a person's behaviour is assumed to be determined by his or her intention. At the next level, intentions are determined by attitudes towards the behaviour, subjective norms and perceived behavioural control. The last level, attitudes, subjective norms and perceived behavioural control, is explained in terms of beliefs about the consequences of performing (or not performing) the behaviour, about the normative expectations of relevant referents and about the perceived control over the behaviour or action. In the final analysis, a person's behaviour is explained by reference to his or her beliefs. Since people's beliefs represent the information they hold (be it correct or incorrect) about the world, it follows that people's behaviour is ultimately determined by this information.

Therefore, to understand behaviour completely it is necessary to identify the beliefs related to the performance of each behavioural alternative. In solving policy problems, when the interest is in promoting the protection of the environment (this is an outcome, not a behaviour), the behaviour of interest (complying with regulations or undertaking innovative behaviours) may require questions to be formulated in terms of a single intention to the correspondent behaviour, as will be presented below.

DECISION-MAKING THEORY AND THE TPB: A COMPARISON

Various models have been used to predict or understand strategic decisions in organisations. Following the taxonomy of Schoemaker (1993b), the work in decision making since the influential works of Edwards (1954), and Simon (1945) can be divided into four categories. The first refers to the *single rational actor*, that acts from a clear set of objectives and pursues a rational strategy with unlimited information processing capacity and perfect foresight to meet these objectives. Organisations are seen as monolithic entities who can be understood only in terms of individual rationality. The second are *organisational models,* in which multiple players pursue the same objectives. They practise a differentiated but integrated division of labour on their various activities with shared values and rationality.

The third category comprises *political models* in which individual or departmental goals supersede the overarching organisational ones. However, there is a fine balance between individual and organisational goals. This model uses partisan behaviour in understanding organisational decision-making. The fourth and last category, the *contextual view models,* hold that organisational environments are so complex, and human desires so varied, that each decision context becomes its own reality, with limited consistency across situations and goals. Therefore, the particularities of the context are the driving force for the decision, rather than the super-ordinate goals or comprehensive planning.

The TPB falls into the first class according to Schoemaker's (1993b) categorisation, as it focuses on *single rational actors*. However, it differs from the traditional linear process normative model of decision making based on the subjective expected utility (Edwards, 1954; Simon, 1977), i.e., it is supposed to follow a path of decision-making process as follows: (1) becoming aware of the problem; (2) defining possible courses of action; (3) collecting information about the alternatives; (4) identifying likely (events/circumstances) related to the decision; (5) estimating possible outcomes from alternative actions and the prevailing circumstances; and (6) choosing a preferred course of action. Out of the process of decision making, but in a cycle of decision–implementation–evaluation–decision would follow: (7) implementation; (8) feedback, and evaluation; and (9) upon feedbacks are expected modifications over behaviour in a cyclical fashion (Ajzen, 1996a). Instead, the TPB is a structural descriptive model that aims to gain understanding of the predispositional factors by looking at the structural relationships of the possible determinants of behaviour.[5]

The Basic Paradigms of Social Decision Making

Ajzen (1996a) points out that the different perspectives of decision-making depart from two basic paradigms. On the one hand, the *judgement and decision-making paradigm*, normative in nature, portrays the decision maker as an intuitive statistician who carefully considers the alternatives and makes full use of all available information in accordance with the normative, statistical principles of probability and logic. That is, *the decision maker acts in perfect rationality*.[6] The basic and most influential explanatory model used in the analysis of decisions under uncertainty is the optimisation of subjective expected utility (SEU) (Edwards, 1954). The model assumes that any decision will favour the outcome with the highest probability of maximising the subjective expected utility arising from the chosen course of action.

Ajzen (1996a), in agreement with Fransman (1994), Stevenson *et al.*, (1990), Schoemaker (1993b), Payne *et al.*, (1992), and Frank *et al.*, (1988), argues that much of the research on decision making in the last 20 years has been designed to show that real life decision makers are far removed from the ideal decision maker portrayed in the early propositions of Bernard (1938) and Edwards, (1954). Such a mismatch, it is argued, results from the cognitive limitations of the decision maker (bounded rationality) and bias towards the subjective probability estimates that deviate from normative values (Simon, 1945, 1977; Lindblom, 1959; Fransman, 1994). In general, it is accepted, but not explained, that decisions often seem to follow paths that are incompatible with the principle of the maximisation of utility.

On the other hand, *the theories of social action* from social psychology explore decision-making in a descriptive rather than a normative fashion (Kuhl, 1985). Generally, any given decision is associated with a target behaviour. Then the decision is assimilated with the intention or commitment to engage in a behaviour. Intentions, in turn, are associated with a predisposition to behave: such predispositions are used to explain intention and, ultimately, behaviour. The model that underlies this approach is based on the expectancy value model (EV). As in the SEU model, in the EV model the evaluation of each outcome contributes to the predisposition to behave in direct proportion to the decision maker's subjective probability that the behaviour will lead to the outcome in question.

Differences Between SEU and EV

Although the basic structure of the SEU and EV models is essentially the same, there are important differences between them. First, the EV does not assumes consistency with the optimisation principle, instead it relies upon internal consistency of beliefs with the aggregate variables (attitude, subjective norm and behavioural control), and these aggregate variables with intention, and intention with behaviour. Whether true or false, biased or unbiased, the beliefs represent the subjectively-held information on which decisions are based. A second important difference is concerned with how the subjective probability is calculated. In the SEU, if there are two different courses of action, the subjective probability of two outcomes must sum to one. Meanwhile, in the EV the probabilities of two events are taken as separate events (Ajzen, 1996a).

A third major difference implicit in the EV model – not recognised by any of the authors reviewed – is the concept of *relative rationality*. This concept arises from two sources. On one side, the basic process of reasoning is an operation of comparison between two or more courses of action or concepts. On the other side, any process of optimisation has an objective function, rule, or SEU to be optimised. Then the rationality of any decision is contingent on: (1) the objective function to be optimised, and (2) the relative match or mismatch of an actor's objective function and that of the nth observer.

Thus, the rationality of a decision or action depends on convergence of the objective function of the nth observer. The latter means that there are no irrational decisions but only a mismatch of perceptions between the decision maker and that of the nth observer. The concept of relative rationality has relevance to the understanding of the conflict between the individual interest in the short-term with the social interest in the long-term regarding the protection of the environment. There is a mismatch between the individual and the social *objective functions* to be optimised.

Understanding Organisations and Organisational Behaviour: The Same Lens?

The application and modification of the TPB to the study of the *organisation's behaviour* allows Schoemaker's idea of a meta-theory that integrates and reconciles elements of the four models mentioned above to be followed (Schoemaker, 1993b). The study of the organisation's behaviour can be achieved by applying the rule of specificity or generality of the behavioural criterion. The definition of an appropriate behavioural criterion could take into account the behaviour of the organisation through the perception of its managers. This would allow managers to be seen as the primary decision makers in organisations (Shapira, 1994; Frank *et al.*, 1988; Hickson *et al.*, 1986).

However, far from being absolute optimisers, highly reflective, strategic or tactical and top-down planners, their decisions could be seen as far from optimal, but having full rationality. It is more likely that managers should be seen as action oriented, with lives that are controlled mostly by the never-ending stream of demands placed on them from all sides. Changing the level of analysis to *organisational behaviour*, that is to the analysis of tactical or operational decisions, would imply only the selection of the appropriate target behaviour, behavioural criterion and redefinition of the behavioural domains (e.g., Metselaar, 1997).

In the following chapters, a simile is made between the 'perception' of the entity 'the firm' with the perceptions of the managers. In principle, these are two different units of analysis. In the sections above it has been said that decision-making within the firm is socially constructed (Hickson *et al.*, 1986). In this construction process the firms' managers are considered to be the best positioned to express the preferences of their firm. They are assumed to be the trustees of the strategic vision of the firm. This strategic position enables them to be the hub of information, communication, control and decision making. Because of this, managers are the best informed about the internal and external contexts in which their organisation operates (this aspect is further discussed in Chapter 5, p. 114). The assessment of managers' perceptions in this work is considered as a proxy to infer the planned behaviour of the firm. That is, this research is not interested in the behaviour of managers but only in the behaviour of the firm as seen through the perceptions of the managers.

INDUCING BEHAVIOURAL CHANGE: THE ENVIRONMENTAL POLICY PERSPECTIVE

The TPB puts emphasis on the possibility of influencing or changing behaviour when designing policy programmes for social intervention. The application of the TPB framework to the environmental policy context aims to systematise and gain a deeper *understanding* of the sources of the *resistance* or *willingness to* develop clean technologies. Following the theories of conflict resolution, *understanding* is conceived as the first step in the negotiation towards the design of better environmental policies based on agreements upon solid terms of reference (Fisher, 1994; Deutsch, 1994). The justification of the framework is based on the need for validation that the sources of resistance to change assumed in the academic literature correspond with reality, and that they condition or hamper the process of clean technology development.

This work aims to apply a behavioural model in order to go beyond an enumeration of the factors that hamper the development of clean technologies, through the identification of the predispostional factors (the resistance-to-change) that underlie such behaviour. Following this first phase, the possibility of predicting the predisposition of multiple firms to behave positively or negatively towards the adoption of cleaner technologies may arise. In addition, the application of such a framework adds to the existing studies by its contribution to the opening of the previous monolithic input-output 'black box' perspective of a rational decision process.

The TPB, by including variables such as beliefs, expectancies, values, intentions and control between cognition and action, takes into account that the relationship between cognition and action is not straightforward (Ajzen, 1985, 1988, 1991; Ajzen and Fishbein 1969, 1980; Beck and Ajzen, 1991; Fishbein and Ajzen, 1975; Kuhl and Beckman, 1985; Kuhl, 1985). The theory provides the opportunity to look at individuals (firms, groups and organisations) as dynamic social actors searching for change but encountering many resistances that hamper the achievement of an ideal goal. Thus, the TPB makes it possible to relate different areas of scientific enquiry to gain deeper understanding and enable the prediction of behaviour of organisations in *specific contexts.*[7]

Understanding and Predicting the Firm's Innovative Behaviour

In this section the previous framework is applied to understanding and predicting the firm's innovative behaviour regarding the development of clean technologies. A very important element in the operation of the TPB is the application of the principle of compatibility of the behavioural criterion when defining the behaviour to be studied. The behavioural criterion is made up of an *action*, performed in a *target*, in a specific *context* and *time*. This criterion must be the same for the behaviour of interest and the items assessing intention (willingness) to perform the behaviour. Following the definition given above, (pp. 38–9), *clean technology development* is considered here as a behavioural category as it is composed by a set of single actions.[8] The necessary actions considered as capabilities to carry out the behaviour are discussed in Chapter 4 (pp. 86–103). The *action* to carry out is 'development' and its *target* is 'clean technologies', the *context* refers to the 'Mexican Northern Border Region' and the *time* encompasses four points in time (i.e., at the present moment, within the next two years, within the next five, and in the long term).

Once the behaviour has been defined the next step is to define the intention and the variables attitude, subjective norm and behavioural control in agreement with the behaviour seeking to optimise the principle of correspondence between intention and behaviour established by Fishbein and Ajzen (1980). Therefore, the Ajzen model will be adapted in the following way: intention will be translated as *willingness to develop clean technologies*; attitude will be applied as *attitude towards developing CT*; the subjective norm will be equated with the *perceived social pressure to develop CT* and the perceived behavioural control with the *perceived control over the development of CT* that the firm can exert. In general, the notion behind the willingness of the firm to develop clean technologies is willingness to change current practices, to innovate (see Figure 3.1).

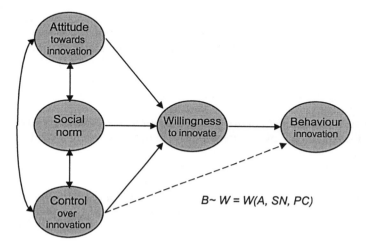

Figure 3.1   Understanding why firms adopt or reject new technologies
Figure based on: Ajzen (1991)

Definitions of Attitude, Perceived Social Pressure, Perceived Control and their Behavioural Domains

As stated in the introduction to this book, the idea of measuring the willingness to develop clean technologies and its determinants is to define the degree of conflict between the necessity of the firm to produce profits for its shareholders and the general wellbeing of the environment.[9] In the firm context strategic planning is based on the goals to be achieved. These goals can be seen as intentions to perform behaviours, that is, the firm's planned behaviour. Thus, it is assumed that an explicit greater willingness to develop clean technologies is in agreement with socially desirable goals, and therefore, indicates lower conflict with the social interest. The *definitions* of the three determinants of behaviour applied to environmental policy in the context of the firm are as follows:

The firm's *attitude* (A) toward the development of clean technologies is defined as the degree to which the *firm's managers* expect good or bad outcomes from the performance of such behaviour. The attitude towards the behaviour results from the accumulated connotative load associated with the behavioural salient beliefs or relevant information towards the implication of the adoption of cleaner technologies. An example of an attitudinal salient belief is: *clean technologies can be unreliable.* Such a belief is likely to imply a negative connotation leading to a negative outcome. This belief could contribute to the formation of a negative attitude toward the development of clean technologies.

The firm's *perceived social pressure* (PSP) refers to the importance that the firm's manager gives to different important referents to develop or not to develop cleaner technologies. It results from the accumulated connotative load of normative beliefs that managers may hold. For example: if the managers perceive *that no other firm in the same industrial sector is redesigning its products or process,* then that firm will be less inclined to develop cleaner technologies.

The firm's *perceived control over the development of clean technologies* (PBC) focuses on the management beliefs about how much control they can exert over the innovation process to develop clean technologies. The perceived control arises from the accumulated connotative load of beliefs with regard to the perceived ease or difficulty of developing cleaner products and production process. For example: *a long-term solution implies a rethinking of the product and the associated production process.* Depending on the perceived control over the technological change, the willingness to innovate will be strong or weak.[10]

Behavioural Domains Definition

Once the behaviour, intention (or willingness), attitude, the social pressure and the perceived control are defined consistent with the behavioural criterion (i.e., action, target, context and time), then it is necessary to go in search of the beliefs that may determine willingness. It is at this point that the TPB works as a meta-theory to integrate several bodies of theory that may help to provide a deeper understanding of the behaviour under study. The first step in generating the beliefs is the definition and mapping of the *behavioural domains* that underlie attitudes, the perceived social pressure, and perceived behavioural control. The behavioural domains are defined as 'the specific areas of experience and knowledge from which the salient beliefs arise' (Ajzen, 1988, Ch. 1).

With the definition of the notion of *behavioural domain* it is possible to analyse the diverse insights from the literature of the determinants of the greening of industry mentioned in Chapter 1. These insights are reviewed in detail and classified in Table 3.1 according to the definitions of attitude, the social pressure and perceived behavioural control over innovation.

Table 3.1   Classification of the determinants of the innovative behaviour in clean technologies in the greening of industry literature

Authors	Attitude	Social pressure	Behavioural control
Andrews (1998)	Managers' perceptions and attitudes		
Clayton et al. (1999b)	Anticipation of regulation changes, financial pressures for cost reductions, investment cycles	Regulation, stricter standards	Technological opportunity
Ashford (1993)		Regulation and enforcement	Firm endowments and capabilities
Baas et al. (1999)	Responsible care, cost reductions, waste minimisation, environmental improvement	Market pressures, ISO9002	
Bhatnagar and Cohen (1997)	Benefits offsetting the costs of compliance; anticipation of future significance of environmental issues		
Cramer and Schot (1993)	Economic opportunities		
den Hond (1996)		Regulatory pressure	Technological capabilities
den Hond and Groenewegen (1993)	Improved value of the product	Market position and regulatory pressure	
Dillon and Baram (1993)		Regulatory requirements, liability, market forces, customer demand, public pressures	

51

Table 3.1 Continued

Authors	Attitude	Social pressure	Behavioural control
Duffy *et al.*(1999a)	Environmental concerns, cost reductions from reduced material use, environmental ethos of the firm	Regulations, community pressure	Technological opportunity, production expansion, collaboration inter- and intra-firms
Duffy *et al.* (1999b)	Cost reduction of water treatment, firm investment cycles	Regulation, public concerns	
Everett *et al.* (1993)	CEOs' attitudes, personality		CEOs' self-efficacy
Florida (1996)	Productivity improvement, quality, cost reduction		Relationships across production chain and between end-users and suppliers
Geffen and Rothenberg (1997)		Regulation and public pressure	
Hall (1999)			Inter- and intra-trade, supply chain power relations
Hart and Ahuja (1996)	Economic opportunity based on increased efficiency and waste reduction		
Hartman and Stafford (1997)		Public and market pressures	
Kemp (1993, 1994)	Appropriability of innovation benefits, risk and uncertainty	Regulation, market demand, consumer expectancies	Technological paradigms and regimes, technological opportunities

Table 3.1 Continued

Authors	Attitude	Social pressure	Behavioural control
Kemp (1996a)		Regulation	
Kerndrup et al. (1999a)	Cost-saving investment that provided solution to long standing environmental problem	Regulatory pressure	Collaboration with suppliers, research institutes, and environmental authorities, lack of technological opportunities
Kerndrup et al. (1999b)	Business strategy, potential cost saving, environmental concerns	Regulation, Government grants for cleaner production	Technological opportunity: awareness of cleaner technology, radical change in process technology, collaboration with suppliers
King (1997)	Economic efficiency, local strategic objective		
Klemmensen et al. (1999)		Legal pressure (federal law)	
Konar and Cohen (1997)	Potential economic gain		
Maxwell et al. (1997)	Rising cost of waste disposal	Threat of regulation	
Morrison (1997)	Economic benefit, environmental awareness	Employee morale	

Table 3.1 Continued

Authors	Attitude	Social pressure	Behavioural control
Orsatto (1997)		Regulation, competition/collaboration, consumer pressure	Organisational culture
Prakash (1997)	Performance evaluation of managers		Principal–agent problem, leadership
Rodgers (1998)			Supply chain management
Rondinelli and Vastag (1996)		Public concern and emphasis on industry responsibility	
Roome (1994)			Technological capabilities, organisational change, learning
Steger (1993)	Cost reductions	Market pressures, public image, social responsibility, regulation, and CEO values	
Thompson *et al.* (1999)	Market opportunity, commercially motivated by economic opportunity	Regulations and market pressure	
Williams *et al.* (1993)	Cost reductions	Legislation and enforcement, commercial, investors, and community pressures	

The behavioural domains that might influence attitudes, social norms and perceived control over innovation are depicted in Figure 3.2 and discussed below. From the analysis of those determinants of environmental responsive behaviour classified in Table 3.1 under attitude, it can be said that the rationale underlying these determinants refers to the expected outcomes derived from the development of cleaner technological options. For example: cost reductions, cycle investment timing, economic opportunities, anticipation of regulatory changes, improvement of value product, improvements in environmental performance, good outcomes from environmental protection, etc., all these connote the potential outcomes from the development of clean technologies. All the determinants classified under attitude fall within the definition of attitude given above (p. 41). Therefore, attitude is assumed to be formed upon the possible outcomes expected to arise from the development of clean technologies. Good outcomes are assumed to form a positive attitude and, therefore, a predisposition to develop clean technologies.

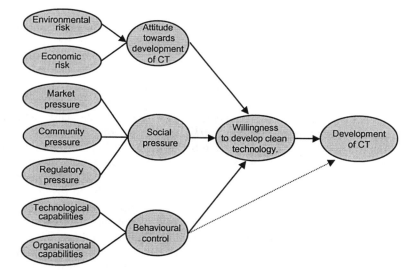

Figure 3.2   Understanding and predicting the firm's willingness to develop clean technologies

The main concept behind this evaluation of possible outcomes is risk. The perception of risk is assumed to stem from two domains. The first relates to the perception of the possible environmental impact of the firm's operations, coupled with the perceived relevance of environmental improvement derived from the development of a clean technological portfolio. The second domain concerns the possible economic consequences for the firm (Shapira, 1994, p.

3; Matten, 1995). This implies an evaluation of possible outcomes arising from the investment in innovative activities under risk or uncertainty, either in process or product changes, being incremental or radical. Therefore, the salient beliefs, and ultimately the formation of the attitude towards the development of clean technologies to protect the environment, will stem from the domains of the perception of environmental and economic risk. The perceptions that may determine the environmental and economic components of managers' attitude towards the development of clean technologies will be explored in Chapter 4, pp. 60–75.

Similarly, as with attitude, the analysis of the determinants classified under the social pressure fit the definition provided before, p. 41 (see column 3 in Table 3.1). The main sources of social pressure mentioned in the literature are regulation, industrial standards (ISO), market position, market forces, customers' expectations and demands, and public concerns. The perception of a high or low social pressure is assumed to depend on the subjective importance given by the managers to their social referents. For example, a firm could be giving high importance to consumer demands or their competitors' technological position or moves. It also could be that the community in which it operates is believed to be very concerned about the hazards that the firm generates, but such concern might not be considered important by the firm.

The perceived *social pressure* concerns how the 'firm perceives' the social context within which it operates.[11] The sources of social pressure mentioned above can be summarised as: (1) the *regulatory regime*, this refers to the perceived stringency of environmental regulations and standards and the degree of enforcement; (2) the *market pressures* that may arise from consumers or from the reaction of other firms regarding the adoption or development of cleaner technologies. Firms may be forced to become pioneers or followers in product or process innovation and, (3) the perceived (real or not) lobbying capacity of *the community* in which the firm operates. Therefore, the normative salient beliefs are assumed to arise from the perception of these domains, that is, the contextual pressure that the firm may perceive. These domains will be further explored in Chapter 4 (pp. 75–86).

Finally, the determinants classified under the *perceived control* over the development of clean technologies conform to the definition provided before (p. 42). The most frequent determinants found were the current technological capabilities of the firm, the availability of technological opportunities, collaboration with research institutions, collaboration and influence with suppliers, perceived internal control of the firm, and learning capability. All these factors have in common the underlying notion of control upon the capabilities to innovate. Upon consideration of these factors it is proposed that the perceived control to innovate arises from two domains of the internal sphere of firm. One is the perceived organisational capabilities that the firm holds to guide a radical technological change. The other area refers to the perceived technological capabilities within the firm and the technological opportunities that the market has to offer. The specific capabilities to innovate towards a clean technology portfolio will be discussed in Chapter 4, pp. 86–103.

In sum, the behavioural domains from which the beliefs that determine the firm's willingness to innovate in clean technology arise are: the perceived economic and environmental risk; the perceived social pressure attributed to the regulators, market, and the community; and the perceived technological and organisational capabilities to innovate in a cleaner product and production process. As mentioned above, the structure of the decision-making model depicted in Figure 3.1, is presented in Figure 3.2 with the corresponding domains for each variable. The basic premise of the application of the model presented above is that willingness to innovate forms a positive behavioural intention (+I), whereas resistance forms a negative behavioural intention (–I). The possibility of aggregating the degrees of predisposition towards the development of clean technologies at the sector level may allow an accurate image of the sources of resistance or willingness of the different firms under study to be built, thereby allowing a better understanding of the different rationales at stake.

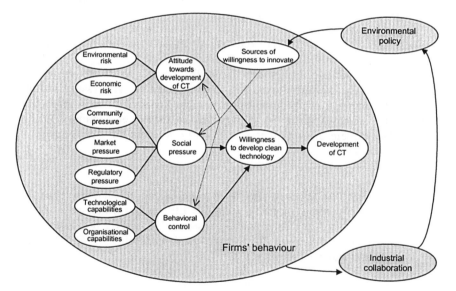

Figure 3.3 Virtuous cycle of willingness towards the development of clean technologies

If we apply this behavioural model to our previous model of the policy making paradigm discussed in Chapter 1, p. 9, and we search for sources of *resistance or willingness to innovate* (i.e., the salient beliefs), policy design can be improved and the collaboration of the firm in policy making may arise (compare Figures 1.1, and 1.2, with Figure 3.3 above). The latter is believed because, in principle, it is easier to negotiate or shape the specific underlying micro-motives of behaviour than behaviour itself (Cronbach, 1994; Schelling, 1971).

Summary

The discussion in this chapter can be summarised by proposing two hypotheses to test the theoretical framework presented here. The first concerns the first level of explanation of the willingness to develop clean technologies, that is, its dependence on attitudes, social pressure and perceived behavioural control.

H_1:   The firms' willingness (W) to develop clean technologies can be explained in terms of the managers' attitude towards the development of clean technologies (A), the perceived social pressure to develop clean technologies (PSP) and the control over the innovation process (PC) as perceived by their managers.

$$H_1: W = W(A, PSP, PC) \qquad (3.5)$$

The second hypothesis brings into focus the coherence of the theoretical framework. If the managers' attitudes, the perceived social pressure and the perceived control over the innovation process arise from their respective behavioural domains, then the perceptions in these behavioural domains should also explain the willingness to innovate towards the development of clean technologies.
Thus:

H_2:   The firms' willingness (W) to develop clean technologies can be explained in terms of the perceptions of: environmental risk (EVR), economic risk (ER), community pressure (CP), market pressure (MP), regulatory pressure (RP), technological capabilities ($TCPP$), and organisational capabilities (OC).[12]

$$H_2: W = W(EVR, ER, CP, MP, RP, TCPP, OC) \qquad (3.6)$$

As it is shown in the Appendix, p. 211, the function proposed in H_1 is similar in its form to the function proposed by the TPB. The form and level of analysis proposed in H_2 has not been proposed in any previous work that used the TPB. The notion behind both hypotheses is to test whether, within the environmental policy realm, it is possible to link the perceptions at the domain level to willingness and ultimately to behaviour. In Chapter 4, several bodies of literature will be discussed in order to explore, from a theoretical perspective, the beliefs that managers may hold when deciding whether or not to develop clean technologies. In addition, a system of hypotheses – including H_1 and H_2 – will be proposed in order to contrast, and to go beyond, the general wisdom regarding the determinants of the 'greening of industry' and to integrate several bodies of theory into a single and testable theoretical body.

NOTES

1. This concept will be discussed in the comparison of TPB with other theories of decision making.
2. The connotative meaning of a concept includes all of its suggestive or implicit significance. That is, the concept or object has significance only by association to the subject's reality. Thus, the connotation of a specific concept can be expected to vary from person to person according to their experience and expectations (see Carlsmith *et al.* 1976).
3. The behavioural criterion for this study is defined in Chapter 3, pages 39–40.
4. A complete presentation of the TPB model can be seen in Ajzen (1988 and 1991).
5. For a comparison between process and structural models of decision making, see Abelson and Levi (1985).
6. The definition of *rationality* will be discussed below.
7. Once a catalogue of the preconditions has been built up and the weight of belief clusters determined, the possibility of guiding institutional change within organisations may arise.
8. The notion of adopting or rejecting new technologies here is considered implicit on the willingness of the firm to develop or to innovate on the features of their products and processes.
9. From here onwards 'willingness to innovate' will refer to willingness to innovate in clean product and production process.
10. In order to measure the control (i.e., the perceived capability) to perform a particular activity the respondent was asked to rate the activity in a differential semantic scale whose extremes were easy–difficult. The higher the capabilities, the higher the score on the perceived ease to perform the activity.
11. At this point, it is necessary to bear in mind that we are dealing with general managers' perceptions of manufacturing firms. The managers are assumed to be in the appropriate position to know best the firm's planned behaviour, its context and its capabilities to perform any given behaviour.
12. The domain of organisational capabilities will be better defined and complemented in Chapter 4. Hypothesis H_2 will contain three variables more.

4. Content: A theoretical exploration of the behavioural domains in the search for salient beliefs

This chapter builds upon the framework presented in Chapter 3. It describes how the 'pool' of theoretical beliefs that may determine the attitude of a firm's managers towards clean technology development, perception of social pressure and control over the innovation process was drawn up. In order to narrow down the literature review in each of the behavioural domains and to avoid, as much as possible, arbitrariness in the selection of beliefs, the search for the relevant literature was strictly guided by the definitions of attitude, perceived social pressure and perceived control over the innovation process provided in Chapter 3.

The chapter is divided into four sections. The first three discuss and explore the behavioural domains proposed in Chapter 3 in order to gain a further understanding of the determinants of clean technology development. The final section presents a set of hypotheses that intend to link the belief system to 'willingness-to-innovate'. For purposes of clarity, the definitions of attitude, social pressure and perceived behavioural control are re-stated at the beginning their respective sections.

The discussion of each of the domains is developed as follows. Initially, the literature relevant to each domain is considered. Then, the approach and criteria for the selection of the beliefs chosen for inclusion in the questionnaire is presented. Next, a list of those attributes selected for the domain (i.e., beliefs or perceptions), and which will be assessed in Chapters 6 and 7, is presented. Finally, hypotheses of dependence and proportionality between 'behavioural domain scales'[1] and the 'direct measures'[2] of the overall perception in each behavioural domain are proposed.

ATTITUDES TOWARD THE DEVELOPMENT OF CLEAN TECHNOLOGIES

In Chapter 3, attitude was defined as the degree to which a firm's manager expects positive or negative outcomes from the development of clean technologies. This favourable or unfavourable *evaluation* of the behaviour in question arises from two domains. First the perceived risk generated by the firm's operations in the community and the environment. Second, the economic risk in terms of perceived possible capital losses/gains arising from innovative activities in cleaner products and production process. In the following sections these domains are explored from a theoretical perspective.

ENVIRONMENTAL RISK PERCEPTION

In Chapter 3 a set of hypotheses linking environmental risk perception and attitudes to willingness to innovate were proposed. This section explores this first domain that may influence the innovative behaviour in firms regarding clean technologies in greater depth (see Figure 4.1). The goal is to gain a better understanding of CEOs' and managers' concerns about the hazards that the operations of their firms may generate for host communities and the wider environment. The questions to be answered are: Under what conditions are the activities of the firm considered environmentally safe or risky? What do managers take into account in accepting or avoiding the creation of environmental risks?

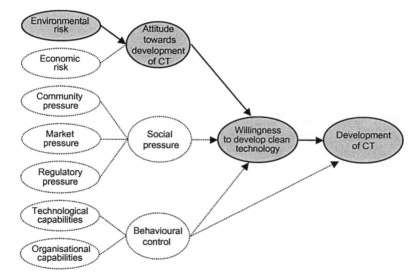

*Figure 4.1 Understanding and predicting the firm's willingness to innovate
Behavioural domain: Environmental risk perception*

The premise of this section is that managers who perceive a high level of environmental risk will be more likely to promote the development of clean technologies in their firms. This section presents a set of beliefs which, it is suggested, determines the perception and acceptance of environmental risks by a firm's managers. The scales proposed seek to facilitate the assessment of the managers' evaluation of the possible hazards imposed upon the community and the environment as a result of their manufacturing operations.

Risk Perception Approaches

The concept of *risk perception* has evolved from being considered a one-dimensional measurement of a multidimensional concept that involves people's beliefs, attitudes, judgements and feelings, as well as the wider social or cultural values and dispositions adopted towards hazards and their benefits (Royal Society, 1992). Its historical development can be traced through three main approaches:

The first focuses primarily on the quantification of risk acceptance through *revealed* preferences. This originated with the work of Star (1969) in which social benefits were correlated with the number of accidental deaths arising from the application of technological developments.[3] The main proposition of this approach is that objective and subjective risk can be maintained as separate, i.e., risk acceptance can be objectively assessed and measured from revealed preferences by using historical – in this case – data on fatalities in the public use of technology. A second aspect of this approach is that risk can be assessed objectively through statistical methods which calculate the probability of loss (Vlek and Stallen, 1980). Authors advocating this approach are here termed *objectivists* (e.g., Thompson, 1999; Murphy, 1986; Perrera, 1986; Onishi *et al.*, 1985; Kirkwood, 1985; Mantel, 1985; Kirschman, 1984; Smith, 1984; Wisniewskt, 1983).

The second approach, using *expressed* preferences, focused on the attributes of risk in order to infer its acceptability. As this trend evolved from cognitive psychology, it has come to be known as the *psychometric* approach. Insofar as it highlights the inadequacy of one-dimensional indexes to assess acceptance of risks (e.g., loss of life expectancy, annual probability of death) it constitutes a response to the objectivists. Pioneered by Fischhoff *et al.*, (1978) the main propositions of this approach are that: (1) perceived risk is determined by a variety of quantitative and qualitative attributes, (2) risk perception is quantifiable and predictable and (3) risk means different things to different people in different situations (Slovic *et al.*, 1984). The works on risk of Kunreuther and Slovic (1996); McDaniels *et al.* (1995); Covello (1983); Fischhoff *et al.* (1993); Fischer *et al.* (1991); Hartenian *et al.* (1993); Canter *et al.* (1993); Jungerman and Fermers (1995); Sockolowska and Tyska (1995); Wandersman and Hallman (1993) and Slovic (1987) all fall within this approach.

The third approach focuses primarily on values, personality and social differences to understand and predict acceptance of risk. This *socio-cultural* approach can be seen as a complement to the second approach.[4] It begins with the work of Douglas and Wildavsky (1982). Their central argument is that attitudes towards risk and hazards are not homogeneous but they vary systematically according to cultural biases. Seeking to explain and predict acceptance of risks, they propose four groups or types of cultural bias exhibited by people: (1) *hierarchists* are willing to accept high levels of risk so long as decisions are made by experts or in other socially approved ways; (2) *egalitarians* accentuate the risks of technology and economic growth so as to defend their own way of life and attribute blame to those who hold to other cosmologies; (3) *fatalists* do not knowingly take risk but accept what is in store for them, and (4) *individualists* see risk and opportunity as going hand-in-hand. This classification of social actors implies that social, cultural and political processes are involved in the formation of individual attitudes towards risk and their acceptance of the latter. That is, risk perception and its acceptance are socially constructed (e.g., Dake, 1992; Vaughan, 1993; Kuyper and Vlek, 1984; Douglas and Wildavsky, 1982).

Chosen Approach

The three approaches mentioned above focus on how and why individuals perceive technologies or activities as risky or safe and, as a consequence of such a perception, accept or reject that risk. For the purposes of this work, the psychometric approach will be used to assess risk perception and acceptance by managers. The justification for the selection of this approach is based on the following premises:

1. The *objectivist* approach works with revealed preferences through the analysis of historical data. In contrast to this, the instrument used here, stemming from the theory of planned behaviour, is a self-reporting questionnaire. The objectivist approach is therefore incompatible with this study. In addition, with regard to objective characterisations of risk perception, it has been proved that subjective biases affect both experts and lay people (Watson, 1981; Fischhoff *et al.*,1984; and Vlek and Stallen, 1980).

2. The *socio-cultural* approach attempts to theorise cultural biases and social relations. Even though it is generally accepted that risk perception is socially constructed, there is little research that has managed to integrate this theory with empirical studies. The results show limited explanatory power of the perceived risk (5 to 9% of explained variance, see Sjöberg, 1996). Furthermore, changing cultural biases and associated social relations could be seen as part of a process of social change that would have to start with the acknowledgement of the environmental hazards involved in the current forms of production and consumption.

3. The *psychometric* approach focuses on individuals and functions by assessing expressed preferences via self-report questionnaires. This focus and method are coherent with the TPB method as it enables the

identification of specific beliefs subject to policy intervention. In addition, according to the report on *Risk Analysis, Perception and Management* (Royal Society, 1992) this approach is considered to be a mature normal science. The construction of a scale to assess managers' risk perception will be based on the works of Slovic *et al.*, (1984) and McDaniels (1995) and the scale to assess the determinant of hazard generation acceptance, on the work of Vlek and Stallen (1980).

Risk Perception

According to Slovic *et al.* (1984) any activity or technology will be considered as *safe* if the possible hazards associated with it are: (1) meant to be controllable; (2) not dreaded; (3) not catastrophic; (4) the benefits and social costs are equally distributed; (5) of low risk for future generations; (6) voluntarily exposed; (7) do not affect the observer; (8) observable; (9) known to those exposed; (10) of delayed effect; (11) old and familiar; and (12) known to science. The perception of risk will vary moving from *safe* to *risky*, depending upon how each of these attributes is perceived in relation to its theoretical opposite (e.g., non-voluntary, non-observable, non-controllable, etc.).

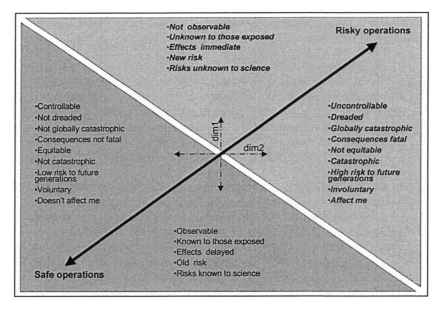

Figure 4.2   Risk perception attributes and dimensions
Diagram modified: Slovic *et al. (1984)*

From Figure 4.2, it can be inferred that those managers who perceive a given environmental hazards as familiar (i.e., old risks), controllable, non-personally affecting, as without apparent effects, etc., will consider the activities of their firm as safe. Therefore, the development of clean technologies will be considered irrelevant, and not necessary. Table 4.1 presents those 'items' employed in the questionnaire to assess risk perception. The left side of the table shows those beliefs that would generate a low perception of risk, and as a consequence the notion of a given manufacturing operation being environmentally safe.

Table 4.1 Scale to assess environmental risk perception

Question. The environmental hazards generated by the operations of our company for this region* are likely to be:			
**	**Risk perception attributes**		
evr$_1$	Controllable	1 ...7	Uncontrollable
evr$_2$	Don't have global impact	...	Have global impact
evr$_3$	Consequences not fatal	...	Fatal consequences
evr$_4$	Evenly distributed	...	Unevenly distributed
evr$_5$	Not catastrophic	...	Catastrophic
evr$_6$	Low risk to future generations	...	High risk to future generations
evr$_7$	Voluntary for those exposed	...	Involuntary for those exposed
evr$_8$	Doesn't affect me	...	Affects me
evr$_9$	Observable	...	Not observable
evr$_{10}$	Known to those exposed	...	Unknown to those exposed
evr$_{11}$	Delayed effects	...	Immediate effects
evr$_{12}$	Old risk	...	New risk
evr$_{13}$	Risk known to science	1 ...7	Risk unknown to science

* The region was defined to the respondent as the area that included a Mexican host city and a neighbouring city on the US side of the border.
** In this table the first column shows a nomenclature that indicates that the full wording of the concept in the form of a question can be found in the questionnaire appendix under such code. The same coding will be used in the following sections.

Sources: Slovic (1984) and McDaniels *et al.* (1995).

Acceptance of Environmental Risk

Risk perception is inherently multidimensional with particular risks or
hazards meaning different things to different people and varying according to
context (Douglas and Wildavsky, 1982).[5]   Exploring the concept of the
acceptance of environmental hazard generation thus becomes of central
importance to understanding the conflict between social and individual
interests. Apparently, the nature of the interest a person has in a particular set
of activities significantly influences his or her way of conceptualising and
judging those activities in terms of relevant decisional attributes (Kuyper and
Vlek, 1984). As managers are the trustees of the firm's interests, they are
assumed to directly benefit from the success of the firm's operations.
Therefore, assessing managers' perceptions presents an opportunity not only
to obtain an index of why they accept the generation of hazards, but also a
proxy-index of a firm's acceptance of environmental hazards.

Following Vlek and Stallen (1980), the degree of opposition to, or
acceptance of, the generation of risks by a firm's managers will depend
primarily on four variable aspects: (1) the discount of benefits and costs in
time and space; (2) the condition of the manager; (3) controllability of effects;
and (4) voluntariness to exposure, and secondarily upon social factors, and
confidence in experts and regulators. Applying Vlek and Stallen to this work
four factors were considered to measure the managers' acceptance of hazards.

The first factor concerns the *space and time discount* of costs and benefits
resulting from the use of the current technology. If the benefits are intended
to accrue in the shortest term possible (ac_{11}),[6] and over the shortest social
distance (i.e., for the manager himself or his family) (ac_{14}, ac_{15}), and the
undesired consequences occur in the long term (ac_{12}), and at greater social
distance (i.e., to unknown people) (ac_{13}), the acceptance of the creation of
hazards will be greater. The second factor involves the *condition of the
observer* of the hazard (the managers). This refers to a decision maker's
accumulated 'risk load' due to personal experience $(ac_{16}, ac_{17}, ac_{18})$ and its
permanent or temporary condition in terms of the personal benefits that would
incline to favour risk acceptance (ac_{19}). The higher the risk load and the less
favourable the permanent condition, then the less inclined a manager would
be to accept the hazards generated by his company.

The third factor encompasses the perception of the *controllability of risks
and hazards,* a perception constituted by the relation between the possibility
of accidents and safety measures (ac_6), human error and equipment failures
(ac_7), rescue operations (ac_8), the reversibility of effects upon the
environment (ac_9), and their controllability (ac_{10}). The higher the perceived
possibility of accidents, the lower the acceptance of hazards. The last factor,
the voluntariness[7] *of exposure*, varies depending upon the range of product
and process technology options available on the market and their associated
cleanliness (ac_1, ac_2), the exertion of the manager's influence to promote or
oppose a radical change in the current technologies in usage (ac_3), the relative

importance given to the benefits derived from the use of certain technologies contrasted with the environmental impact of those technologies (ac_4), and the degree of freedom to opt for or against the creation of hazards (ac_5).

It follows that the fewer the options, and the lower the influence, benefits and degree of freedom of choice, the less the acceptance of environmental hazards. As a consequence, exposure to – or creation of – risks could be seen as unavoidable. Those factors of the acceptance of hazards are summarised in Table 4.2. The list of attributes enables us to understand why the perception of risk and the acceptance of environmental hazards is inherently multidimensional and subjective (as suggested above).

Table 4.2   Scale to assess environmental risk acceptance[8]

	Voluntariness of exposure		**Discount in time and space**
ac1	Technological options 1	ac11	Importance of short-term profits
ac2	Technological options 2	ac12	Discount of the pollution effects in time
ac3	Influence and power within the firm	ac13	Manager's home location
ac4	Economic benefits vs. environmental impacts	ac14	Knowledge of benefits appropriation
ac5	Influence and power in the supply chain	ac19	Overall social benefits vs. environmental Impacts
	Controllability of hazards		**Condition of the observer**
ac6	Safety procedures and skills	ac15	Personal benefits vs. environmental impacts
ac7	Likelihood of environmental accidents	ac16	Knowledge of environmental effects
ac8	Controllability by rescue operations	ac17	Manager's personal experience in environmental accidents
ac9	Reversibility of effects	ac18	Manager's perceived likelihood to be personally affected by pollution
ac10	Controllability of pollution effects		

Item sample:

ac10 The effects of released pollutants on the environment and human health are controllable.

agree	1	2	3	4	5	6	7	disagree
	extremely	quite	slightly	uncertain	slightly	quite	extremely	

In order to assess managers' acceptance of the generation of hazards, the factors proposed by Vlek and Stallen (1980) are employed. The format presented in Table 4.2 will be adopted to present the sets of scales for all the behavioural domains in the following sections. The items presented in Tables 4.1 and 4.2 are pitched at a level of generality that enables us to employ the same scale to capture the connotative load that environmental risk perception may generate in different contexts. They can be used, therefore, for different firms in different industrial sectors.[9]

The set of attributes presented in Tables 4.1 and 4.2 are an inventory of the set of beliefs that firms' managers may hold when appraising the possible environmental consequences of their firms' operations. Within the framework provided by the theory of planned behaviour (TPB), estimates of specific perceptions could be constructed by using conjoint additive measurement.[10] From the above discussion, and following on from the definitions of attitude provided in Chapter 3 for the estimation of attitude indexes, it can be stated that a manager's overall environmental risk perception (*EVR*) is proportional to the accumulated connotative load with regard to a given set of perceived environmental hazards and its possible range of outcomes. In order to test the link between managers' environmental risk beliefs and the overall attitude towards the development of clean technologies the following hypothesis is proposed:

H₃: The managers' environmental risk attitude (*EVR*)[11] is a function of the accumulated connotative load of beliefs arising from environmental risk perception (Σevr_b) and environmental risk acceptance (Σac_b).

$$H_3: \quad EVR = EVR \left(\sum_{b=1}^{13} evr_b + \sum_{b=1}^{19} ac_b \right)$$

Where:

EVR	is the item that assesses environmental risk perception,
evr_b	is the *b*th belief about risk perception attributes,
ac_b	is the *b*th belief about environmental hazards and possible outcomes in terms of personal damages/benefits.

ECONOMIC RISK PERCEPTION

This section explores and defines economic risk perception in greater depth and detail in order to better understand how good or bad attitudes towards innovation might arise (see Figure 4.3). Technological innovation has been characterised as an endeavour that involves non-exploited technical and economic opportunities, and a high degree of uncertainty (e.g., Kline and Rosenberg, 1986, Nelson and Winter, 1982; Kemp, 1993). In the literature on technological change 'uncertainty' is considered to be the central dimension that 'organises' innovative activities (e.g., Dosi, 1988; Kline and Rosenberg,

1986). Surprisingly, despite such importance, there is an absence of studies that clearly define and specify the sources of uncertainty in innovation projects. There are a number of authors that relate uncertainty or risk to innovation but do not explore their components in greater depth. As a result, they do not provide frameworks or generic procedures that permit the operation, assessment or management of these concepts in a decision-making sphere (e.g., Nelson and Winter, 1982; Dosi, 1988; Tidd *et al.*, 1997; Petts *et al.*, 1998; Andrews, 1998; den Hond, 1996; Kline and Rosenberg, 1986; Utterback, 1994; Schot *et al.*, 1994; Chattery, 1995; Freeman and Perez, 1988; Roome, 1994).

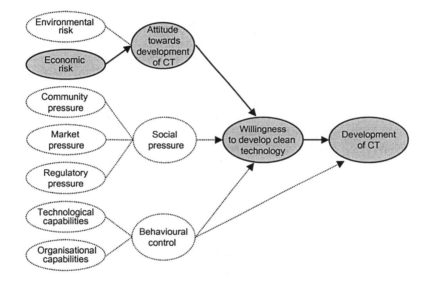

Figure 4.3   *Understanding and predicting the firm's willingness Behavioural domain: Economic risk perception*

Dosi, for example, has pointed out that uncertainty in innovative activities arises 'from the existence of techno-economic problems whose solution procedures are unknown and from the impossibility of precisely tracing consequences to actions' (Dosi, 1988, p. 222). This definition is in agreement with the differentiation between risk and uncertainty found in the literature of decision making under risk. There, uncertainty refers to situations or events in which each action leads to a set of consequences, the outcomes of which are unknown; risk however refers to situations in which each action leads to a few known outcomes, each of which has a specific probability of occurrence (e.g., Shapira, 1994; Lipshitz and Strauss, 1997).

The above definition provides some insight into what uncertainty is but does not include enough elements to permit an assessment of economic risk perception. In order to define and operate the concept of 'economic risk' within the context of innovative activities, there follows a review of the literature of decision making under risk. Two questions oriented this review to enable the assessment of managers' perceptions of economic risk regarding the development of clean technologies: 'What constitutes uncertainty?' and 'How do managers conceptualise economic risk and uncertainty?'

Decision Making Under Risk and Uncertainty

The literature of decision making under risk can be divided into three broad streams: risk assessment, risk management and risk behaviour in organisational settings. Here, risk is conceptualised as encompassing both gains and losses. Risk assessment literature deals mainly with the estimation of risk. Within this literature, risk refers to situations in which each action leads to a few known outcomes, each of which has a given probability of occurrence (e.g., van Groenendaal and Kleijnen, 1997; Lopes, 1994; Taha, 1989). In general, the reasoning used to calculate this is that uncertainty leads to hazards, and hazards have a probability of occurrence. Then the magnitude of the hazard multiplied the probability of occurrence is said to provide an estimate of the risk (Shapira, 1994). The assessment of this risk can be undertaken by using any of several techniques such as break-even analysis, sensitivity analysis, scenario analysis, decision trees and Monte-Carlo (Baker *et al.*, 1998; Hull, 1980; Brealey and Myers, 1991).

Risk management literature focuses on the systematic reduction of uncertainty through the application of operational research and planning methods (e.g., Wisniewskt, 1983; Smith, 1999; Colmer *et al.*, 1999; Turner and Hunsucker, 1999; Mulvey *et al.*, 1997). These methods seek to harness and manage uncertainty in any given development project by generating knowledge at each and every major project stage. According to Chapman and Ward (1997) uncertainty can be managed by responding to the following questions: (1) Resources: who are the parties to be involved in the project? (2) Motivations: what do the parties involved want to achieve? (3) Designs: what are the parties interested in? (4) Process: in what way is it to be achieved and what types of activities are necessary? (5) Wherewithal: what are the resources required?, and (6) Timetable: when does it need to be done by? The application of this framework to the management of innovative projects is immediate as it enables us to manage the process of innovation to operate and minimise uncertainty.

Risk behaviour literature focuses mainly on the determinants of 'risky' decision-making within organisations (Sitkin and Weingart, 1995). One of its primary goals is to enable the prediction of future risky behaviour for the selection and positioning of personnel (Weber and Milliman, 1997). Some of the recurrent predictors in the literature are individual traits, organisational settings and problem framing (Sitkin and Pablo, 1992). The individual traits focus, for example, proposes that risk-taking behaviour is moderated by personal preferences (Weber and Milliman, 1997), personal propensity to seek or reject risks (MacCrimmon and Wehrung, 1986) and risk perception (Vlek and Stallen, 1980; Weber and Milliman, 1997). The organisational setting approach points out that risk-taking behaviour depends also on group composition (Janis, 1972), an organisation's cultural values (Douglas and Wildavsky, 1982), and organisational control systems (March and Shapira, 1987). The problem framing approach suggests that depending on how a situation is framed, be it in terms of the perception of positive or negative outcomes (Kahneman and Tversky, 1979; Schoemaker, 1993b), past outcome history (Thaler and Johnson, 1990), or personal experience in overcoming obstacles (March and Shapira, 1992), people will be more or less prone to risk-taking behaviour. The general idea of all these studies is to find systematic relationships between personality traits, different situational factors, risk propensity, risk perception, etc., with risk-taking behaviour.

Chosen Approach

The ultimate goal of the assessment, management and risk behaviour approaches is to control uncertainty in order to reduce the negative consequences of risk-laden activities, whether by the estimation of risk, by managing uncertainty or by aiming to provide tools for the selection of appropriate decision makers. Some elements of these approaches can be gathered to assess the perception of economic risk in firms' activities as perceived by their managers.

The assessment approach was considered to be not applicable here because it focuses on the quantification of risk in terms of the product of magnitude of hazards and their probability distribution. According to Shapira (1994) managers are rather insensitive to estimated outcome probabilities; instead they put emphasis on detailed descriptions or particular events, such as worst outcomes scenarios.[12] In addition, the perception of risk cannot be reduced to a single subjective correlate of a particular mathematical aspect of risk, such as the product of the probabilities and consequences of an event (Vlek and Stallen, 1980; March and Shapira, 1992).

The management approach is not applicable in its full extent due to the type of strategic decision that the development of clean technologies represents. Analytical techniques such as operations research and planning can only be used with programmed decisions that are mainly factual. More complex, strategic, non-programmed decisions require value judgements, employ intuition and are not based on sequential linear analytic ways of thinking (Simon, 1977; Frank *et al.*, 1988). In addition, decision-makers tend to consider strategic decisions as unique and neither repetitive or frequent situations (Lovallo and Kahneman, 1993).

This approach does, however, provide a good breakdown of the generic sources of uncertainty in innovative projects (i.e., resources, motivations, designs, process, wherewithal, and timetable) (Chapman and Ward, 1997). Applying these questions to the stage of project planning provides the set of activities and resources needed to develop clean technologies that will be discussed below, for example: activities such as: performing deliberate organisational learning activities (which will be discussed below, p. 90); strategic alliances and collaboration (p. 99); and product life cycle analysis practices (p. 86), all of which imply economic opportunities and threats in terms of costs, time, and resources control. All this provided the theoretical elements through which to screen the beliefs to be included in the questionnaire.

The literature on risk-taking behaviour in organisational settings was valuable in two ways. First, in comparative terms, it permitted identification of the theory of planned behaviour as a robust model (the TPB allows integration of several common aspects of risk behaviour whereas many of the studies focus on single behavioural correlates). Second, although some authors in the literature on risk perception conceptualise risk as 'a chance of injury or loss' (e.g., Weber and Milliman, 1997; Lopes, 1994; Royal Society, 1992), there is general agreement that risk involves both the possibility of gains as well as the threat of losses (e.g., Highhouse and Yüce, 1996; March and Shapira, 1982; Douglas, 1990). In this work the latter understanding of risk is employed to operate the definition of economic risk in this section. The possible gains or losses arising from innovative activities in clean technologies are classified into four areas: economic and growth opportunities, appropriability,[13] technological risk and financial risks. A summary of the attributes proposed to explain the perception of economic risk derived from the performance of innovative activities towards the development of clean technologies is presented in Table 4.3 and disaggregated below.

In the literature on innovation, *economic opportunity* is regarded as the primary factor driving technological innovation (e.g., Abernathy and Utterback, 1977; Dosi, 1988; Utterback, 1994). Similarly, innovating in clean products has been argued as constituting a business opportunity by a number of authors (e.g., Baas *et al.*, 1999; Cramer and Schot, 1993; Duffy *et al.*, 1999b; Florida, 1996; King, 1997). Two of the advantages mentioned are gaining new market niches (*er1*) due to new environmental expectations of consumers (*er12*) (Kemp, 1994), and the opening in general of another source of growth for a firm (*er15*). Clean technologies are also said to reduce regulatory risk since environmental regulations tend to become more stringent over time (*er2*). An additional set of beliefs regarding economic opportunities arises from the notion of the timing of market entry (Ali, 1994). It is generally asserted that those firms that pioneer a product in 'time' (with regard to social and cultural demand (*er10*)) reap the benefits of the novelty of the product and its distribution effects (*er9*, *er11*).

A second important driver of firms' innovation activities is the *appropriability* of benefits (Nelson and Winter, 1982; den Hond, 1996). Some mechanisms employed to procure appropriability or the benefits of R&D effort are patenting, licensing, and the transfer of technology. Several studies detail evidence of firms that have pioneered products but failed to reap the benefits expected from their investments on R&D (*er8*) (Teece, 1986). Related to this is the frequent necessity of outsourcing knowledge through alliances (*er16*) or subcontracting as part of R&D activities (*er13*). Due to the nature of alliances one of the main concerns of managers is the loss of control over knowledge and technology (Porter, 1993).

Table 4.3 Scale to assess economic risk perception

	Economic opportunity		**Technological risk**
er1	Market niche opportunity loss	er3	R&D requirements
er2	Regulatory risk	er4	R&D costs
er9	Distribution and novelty effects	er5	Economic resources availability
er10	Entry timing	er6	Project life time
er11	Pioneer vs. follower	er7	Uncertainty of achievement and discovery
er12	Customer expectancies (willingness to pay)	er21	Compound risk
er14	Growth opportunities		**Financial risk**
er15	Market uncertainty	er17	Management uncertainty
	Appropriability	er18	Resources uncertainty
er8	Appropriability opportunities	er19	Capital risk
er13	Subcontracting risk (LCA)	er20	Competitiveness uncertainty
er16	Alliance risk (loss of technological control)		
Item sample:			

er10. We believe that launching a clean product venture would be 'ahead of its time'

disagree	1	2	3	4	5	6	7	agree
	extremely	quite	slightly	uncertain	slightly	quite	extremely	

Technological risk refers to the uncertainty of discovery regarding the feasibility of the concept of clean technology as perceived by managers (*er7*) (Porter, 1995a; Chapman and Ward, 1997). The perceived feasibility of clean technologies is given in terms of the amount of R&D required (*er3*), the R&D cost (*er4*), the time required (*er6*), the availability and opportunity of economic resources (*er5*) and the compound uncertainty that the launch of a new product concept implies (*er21*). In summary, it is the combined uncertainty that a new venture entails. Co-operation in the creation of a new knowledge base for the development of clean technologies implies the co-ordination of different operational areas of several organisations (i.e., strategy, market, product, technology, process, management team, etc.).

When explorations into new technologies are coupled with the development of new products for new markets, it is akin to solving a triple simultaneous equation with three unknowns (Porter, 1993, p. 281).

Financial risk refers mainly to what is perceived by managers as downside risk as it connotes mainly with possible losses of profits or capital (Shapira, 1994; Royal Society, 1992). The perception of financial risk is proposed to arise from the timing of resources availability (*er18*), the possibility of losing sums of capital investments on R&D (*er19*) and reduction on competitiveness due to the increase in fixed costs (*er20*).

The risk attributes discussed above and presented in Table 4.3 constitute the set of threats and opportunities that it is proposed, contribute to the perceptions of managers regarding the economic risk that the firms may face if they venture into the development of clean technologies. Derived from the above, it is proposed that a manager's perceived economic risk is proportional to the connotative accumulated load regarding the good or bad consequences arising from the development of clean technologies. In order to link the perceived possible outcomes associated will the innovation on product and production process to the managerial economic attitude towards the development of clean technologies the following hypothesis is proposed:

H₄: The manager's economic risk attitude towards clean technologies (*ER*) is a function of the connotative accumulated load of beliefs regarding the positive or negative economic consequences for the firm that may arise from developing clean technologies (Σer_b).

$$H_4: ER = ER \left(\sum_{b=1}^{21} er_b \right)$$

Where:

ER   is the direct measure of perceived economic risk,
er_b is the *b*th belief of the perceived possible outcomes and economic consequences arising from the development of clean technologies.

Summary

The potential sources of *attitudinal* predisposition in a firm's managers towards the development of clean technologies were proposed above. This predisposition was assumed to arise from the perceived possible outcomes for the firm and for the environment. Hypotheses H_3 and H_4 concern the relationship of dependence of the overall risk perception on the beliefs or information that the managers hold. The premise of these hypotheses is that, if such a relationship is empirically confirmed and also the hypotheses H_1 and H_2 proposed in Chapter 3 are accepted, then, a chain of causality from beliefs to willingness would be established. Therefore, it could be expected that, if it is possible to devise policies to modify the identified attitudinal (behavioural) beliefs, it may be possible to influence the willingness of managers to promote the development of clean technologies in their firms.

PERCEIVED SOCIAL PRESSURE

The second important determinant of the willingness to develop clean technologies proposed in Chapter 3 is the influence of the social context in which the firm operates. It refers to what a firm's manager perceives to be the dominant social norm in the firm's operating context. That is, this refers to how the managers perceive their referents in their context to be thinking about what their firms' behaviour should be; specifically, whether the firm is expected to develop radical solutions to protect the environment. It is assumed that those firms with high perceived social pressure will be more willing to develop clean technologies. However, such a perception may or may not reflect what the important referents really expect from or think about the behaviour of their firm.

In the literature on environmental policy, the importance of the social norms in shaping the behaviour of the firm regarding environmental protection has long been recognised. Some of the sources of social influence recurrent in the literature of environmental policy are the actions of competitors, customers' expectations, legal requirements, employees' suggestions, shareholder expectations, public perceptions, industry norms, and NGOs' demands. (e.g., Andrews, 1998; Henriquez and Sadorsky, 1996; Petts *et al.*, 1998; Welford, 1995; Linnanen *et al.*, 1995; Fuchs and Mazmanian, 1998; Levèque, 1996; Clayton *et al.*,1999). In this section, the possible sources of social pressure are classified into three groups: the market, the communities directly related to the firm and the regulatory regime. Each of these groups is discussed before hypotheses of dependence between the respective beliefs and the perceived social pressure are proposed.

PERCEIVED MARKET PRESSURE

The market operates under well-institutionalised rules that have matured as a result of a social development process. Instances of these rules are, for example, production relationships (i.e., prices, wages, working hours, etc.), trade rules (i.e., tariffs, taxes, patents, etc.), and the type of products that are in fashion for consumption and the way they are produced. All these are social constructions. In general, in these instances it can be said that the market operation is guided by, and within the limits of, the dominant social norms. The assessment of the perceived social pressure arising from the market intends to gauge the extent to which any form of social norm regarding clean technology development is present in the markets where the firm operates.

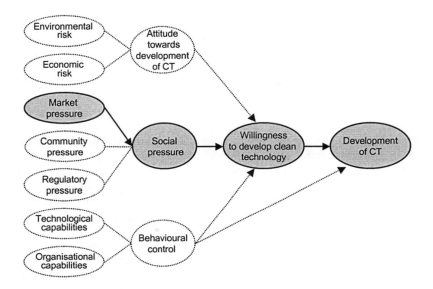

Figure 4.4   Understanding and predicting the firm's willingness to innovate
Behavioural domain: Perceived market pressure

The question here is, who are the important market referents that may be dictating a social norm that would modify the firms' technology strategy to include radical environmental parameters for the design of products and production processes? According to the literature of the 'greening' of industry, the market pressures for the firm to develop clean technologies stem mainly from their competitors and from their customers' expectations regarding specific environmental qualities of their products (e.g., Kemp, 1993; Steger, 1993; Hartman and Stafford, 1997; Dillon and Baram, 1993; Fuchs, and Mazmanian, 1998).[14] Although this literature does not specify any form in which any social norm might be present in the market, it has led this study to a review of the literature that relates the competitiveness of the firm with its technology strategy.

There is a vast body of research emphasising the importance of technology as a determinant of the competitiveness of the firm (e.g., Clark and Guy, 1998; Fagerberg, 1996; Tidd *et al.*, 1997; Teece and Pisano, 1994; Hamel and Prahalad, 1994; Golder and Tellis, 1993; Gustavsson *et al.*, 1999). Unfortunately, there are relatively few empirical studies that assess the firms' competitive context as a moderator of technology strategy through the perceptions of managers (Zahra, 1996; Ali, 1994).

The competitive context of the firm has been described to be characterised along three key dimensions: dynamism, hostility and heterogeneity (cf., Miller, 1987; Boyd *et al.*, 1993; and Zahra, 1996). Dynamism refers to the unpredictability of consumer preferences, competitors' behaviour, and the rate of technical change and growth opportunities in a specific industry (Miller, 1987). Hostility in a competitive environment refers to intense competition accompanied with unfavourable business climate due to market saturation or recessionary conditions (Boyd *et al.*, 1993). Heterogeneity indicates the diversity and complexity of market segmentation in which the firm operates (Zahra, 1996).

Miller (1987) and Zahra (1996) reported strong association between the perception of the firms' managers on these three key dimensions of the firm's competitive context and the pioneering or followership in the development of new technologies. According to Zahra, pioneering is more likely to occur among firms facing competitive environments that are highly dynamic, moderately hostile, and moderately heterogeneous. Followership is more likely to occur among firms operating on moderately dynamic, highly hostile, and homogeneous markets (Zahra, 1996). Thus, if the competitive context of the firm – as defined above – can motivate the pioneering or followership of new technologies, then the competitive context can be expected to be the referent that dictates social norms that determine, at least partially, what technologies gain currency in the marketplace. In this case, the motivation to develop clean technologies could be expected to arise if these technologies are demanded, and, therefore, seen as a competitive advantage by the firm. The form that such a social norm might take as perceived by managers is explained below.

Based on the foregoing discussion the possible sources of perceived social pressure that might arise from the market are classified into three groups: the competitive context, the customer demands and the perception of the need to be a pioneer on a follower. In the first group, concerning the competitive context, the following aspects were considered. The imitation of leaders, either by adopting their managerial systems or copying their technologies, is a common practice in industry (Tirole, 1988). When a firm is pioneering a product or process, its competitors are observing it for signals of success in order to imitate the behaviour and also to reap some of the expected benefits. The reasoning is to follow the competition closely to be able to catch-up, if needed. This aspect is to be captured by assessing whether the managers perceive that their competitors are developing clean technologies (*mp2*), and whether this activity will motivate them to follow their competitors (*mp3*).

In addition, the rate of change in the industry's technological conditions could lead the firm to see the development of clean technologies as an option to pre-empt rival entries (*mp10*). The extent to which technological innovation in the industrial sector that is relevant for the respondent is perceived as progressing towards clean technologies was also considered (*mp1*).

The assessment of the hostility of competition intended to assess whether the presence of an unfavourable business climate with intense competition and limited market opportunities might lead the firm to consider clean products as a good marketing strategy (*mp11*). The assessment of the heterogeneity of markets intended to capture whether clean products are a good option to introduce in the market to face the challenge of maintaining a broad line of products to match the diversity of customer needs (*mp12*).

The second group of market pressures considers how the firm perceives the current and possible future customer demands with regard to the development of clean products (*mp7*, *mp8*) and the motivation of the firm to comply with the preferences of their customers (*mp9*). The third group, pioneer-follower, was regarded as resulting from the firm's perception of its competitive context, its past history and its experience as a pioneer or follower of new products and production technologies (*mp5*, *mp6*, and *mp7*). Table 4.4 presents a summary of the attributes proposed to capture the perceived market pressure that might motivate the firm to carry out innovative activities towards the development of clean technologies.

Table 4.4 Scale to assess market pressure

	Competitive context		**Pioneer-follower**
mp1	Pace of technical change	mp4	Pioneer in product technology
mp2	Competitors' behaviour	mp5	Pioneer in process technology
mp3	Competition drive	mp6	Follower in innovations
mp11	Market competition		**Consumers**
mp10	Sector dynamism	mp7	Consumer expectations
mp12	Market heterogeneity	mp8	Future consumer pressure
		mp9	Motivation to comply with consumers

Item sample:

Mp Our customers will demand us to develop clean products and clean production process.							
unlikely 1	2	3	4	5	6	7	likely
extremely	quite	slightly	uncertain	slightly	quite	extremely	

From the above discussion it can be said that the perceived market pressure to develop clean technologies depends on the level of attention that firms give to their customers' expectations, to the behaviour of their competitors, and to the industry's competitive context in general. The various aspects presented in Table 4.4 constitute the set of market signals that might induce the development of clean technologies. From the above discussion, it can be expected that the firm's perceived market pressure is proportional to the accumulated connotative load regarding weak or strong perceived market signals for the opportunity and timing of the development of clean technologies. Based on the above discussion, the following hypothesis is proposed:

H₅: The firm's perceived market pressure (*MP*) is a function of the accumulated connotative load of beliefs held by their managers regarding the weak or strong signals coming from the market place to develop clean technologies (Σmp_b).

$$H_5: MP = MP \left(\sum_{b=1}^{12} mp_b \right)$$

Where:

MP is the item that assesses the perceived market pressure

mp_b is the *b*th belief about possible market pressures arising from customers, and the competitive context the motivate the firm to develop clean technologies.

PERCEIVED COMMUNITY PRESSURE

The demand for social responsibility through firms' environmental behaviour by the local and regional communities in which the firms operate is known to be what often sparks environmental issues and government intervention towards the solution of problems generated by the firm (Lee and McKenzie, 1994; Levèque, 1996). This only occurs when the local community becomes proactive and attempts to protect its physical and social landscape.

Such action is dependent first on the community's perception and awareness of the trade-off between the environmental effects and social benefits arising from the firm's operations in the locality, coupled with confidence in environmental regulators (Vlek and Stallen, 1980). Second, and even more important, the pressure the community is able to exert is dependent on the existence of neighbourhood associations, the social composition of the residents, and the political incentives available to the community (Mesch,

1996). Unfortunately, in general, the role played by local communities and NGOs is merely that of raising awareness and advocating government intervention. After this step, the community is excluded from the regulatory process, leaving the responsibility to look for solutions to regulators and, ultimately, to the firm (Levèque, 1996).

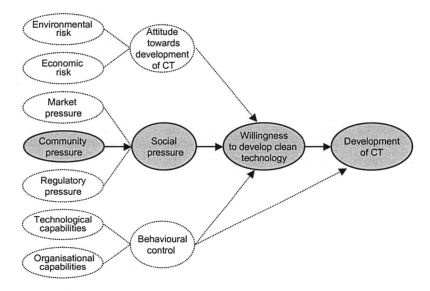

Figure 4.5   Understanding and predicting the firm's willingness to innovate
Behavioural domain: Perceived community pressure

The above aspects are assumed to be among those that managers would assess connotatively when considering the degree of social pressure that their company could be facing. The sources of community influence on the environmental social responsibility of a firm are proposed to be composed of outsiders that are important for the success of the company (*cp3*, *cp4*), environmental experts from universities and research institutes (*cp5*) and environmental consultants (*cp6*, *cp7*), how managers perceive the environmental expectations (*cp8*, *cp9*), and the self-organising and lobbying capability of the local community (*cp10*, *cp11*) (Mesch, 1996), how managers value the suggestions of their staff regarding the environment (*cp13*, *cp14*) (Andrews, 1998), and to what extent their local NGOs demand the development of clean technologies (*cp15*). As the manager is part of, and normally lives in, the locality in which the firm operates, the manager's moral norm is also taken into account (*cp1*) as well as the possible pressures that he will experience from his personal important referents (i.e., relatives, friends, wife, etc.) (Graedel, 1993; Lee and McKenzie, 1994). Table 4.5 (next page) presents the grouping of the set of beliefs proposed to assess the firm's perceived community pressure as perceived by their managers.

Table 4.5   Scale to assess community pressure

	Manager's personal important referents		Perceived community pressure
cp1	Manager's moral norm	cp9	Compliance with community demands
cp2	Manager's social norm	cp10	Community lobbying current capacity
	Firm's important external referents	cp11	Community lobbying future capacity
cp3	Outsiders social norm	cp15	NGOs' pressure
cp4	Outsider pressure capability		**Firm's important internal referents**
cp5	Environmental experts norm agreement	cp12	Important staff
cp6	Perceived pressure from experts	cp13	Staff capability pressure
cp7	Motivation to comply with experts	cp14	Motivation to comply with staff pressures

Item sample:

cp. The local community will push us to develop clean products and clean production process.

unlikely	1	2	3	4	5	6	7	likely
	extremely	quite	slightly	uncertain	slightly	quite	extremely	

The beliefs discussed and presented in Table 4.5 constitute the set of beliefs that may contribute to the perception of managers with regard to demands from the community, and may induce the development of clean technologies. It is proposed that a manager's perceived community pressure is proportional to the accumulated connotative belief load regarding weak or strong perceived community demands to develop clean technologies. In order to test the link of the proposed normative beliefs with the overall perceived community pressure towards the development of clean technologies the following hypothesis is proposed:

H$_6$:   The manager's perceived community pressure (CP) is a function of the cumulative load of beliefs held by their managers regarding the perceived weak or strong signals coming from the community that their firm should develop clean technologies (Σcp_b).

$$\text{H}_6\text{: } CP = CP \left(\sum_{b=1}^{15} cp_b \right)$$

Where:

CP is the item that assesses the perceived community pressure
cp_b is the *bth* belief regarding community pressures.

PERCEIVED REGULATORY PRESSURE

In the literature on environmental policy it is widely recognised that the major driver of environmental protection in industry is the enforcement of environmental regulations (e.g., Vig and Kraft, 1990; Tietember, 1992; Levèque *et al.*,1996; Garrod, and Chadwick, 1996; Howes 1996; Langerak *et al.*, 1998; Clayton *et al.*, 1999). The application of regulations has taken the form of direct command-and-control,[15] economic instruments,[16] and voluntary programmes (Barde, 1994; OECD, 1993). These schemes have been generally associated with standards limiting the amount of residuals or hazardous wastes released to the environment through end-of-pipe technologies or waste management practices.[17]

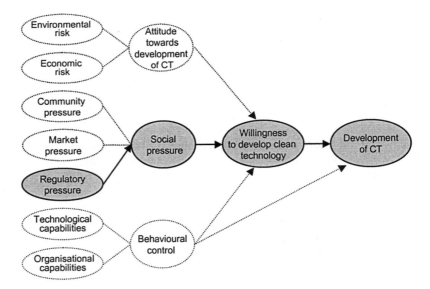

Figure 4.6   Understanding and predicting the firm's willingness to innovate Behavioural domain: Perceived regulatory pressure

There is a vast literature that focuses on the effects of environmental regulations on the behaviour of the firm. From the literature review four groups can be differentiated. The first group focuses on the degree of success of the different types of regulatory instruments. These studies build upon experiences in the implementation process and outcomes of specific regulations. They intend to give prescriptions on how to design and implement environmental policies (e.g., Opschoor and Vos, 1991; OECD, 1991a; OECD; 1991b; Tietenberg, 1992; OECD, 1993; Panayotou, 1993; Barde, 1994; Folmer *et al.*, 1995; OECD; 1995; Lotspeich, 1998).

A second group intends to assess the effects of regulations on the aggregate productivity of a country. Productivity is measured in terms of expenditure in pollution control and its association with variations on GNP (e.g., Gallop and Roberts, 1983; Hazilla and Kopp, 1990; Jorgenson and Wilcoxen, 1990; Barbera and McConnell, 1994; Xu, 2000). The overall conclusion is that environmental regulation does not reduce to any great extent the productivity of the countries or industrial sectors studied. At the micro level some of these studies explore the effects of regulations on competitiveness and financial performance of firms (e.g., Georghiou *et al.*, 1986 Stewart, 1994; Jaffe *et al.*, 1995; Hart and Auhja, 1996; Porter and van der Linde, 1995a, 1995b; Loayza, 1996; Hitchens *et al.*, 1998; Heyes and Heyes, 1999; Slater and Angel, 2000).

The evidence supporting arguments for or against the effects of regulation has been found to be ambiguous or weak. In general, it appears that the effect of environmental regulations on the firm's competitiveness is likely to be minimal (Barbera and McConnell, 1990; Chua, 1999; Xu, 1999). Environmental regulation can itself become a key competitive factor, creating new markets and new opportunities for some firms while negatively affecting others (e.g., OECD, 1985; Howes *et al.*, 1996).

The third group explores the effect of regulations on the type of responses and technologies adopted, and their relationship with the firm's environmental performance and compliance costs (e.g., Irwin and Hooper, 1992; Schmidheiny, 1992; Ashford, 1993; Jaffe and Palmer, 1997; Rondinelli and Vastag, 1996; Lober, 1996; Hass, 1996; Gouldson, and Murphy, 1998; Gray and Shadbegian 1998). These, and the other works mentioned above in general refer to the adoption of technologies either to control pollution or to improvements in housekeeping, not to modifications in process and product designs to eliminate or reduce pollution at source.

The fourth group arises from the advent and gain in currency of the concepts of pollution prevention and clean production. This group implicitly recognises the limits of pollution control technologies and their associated regulations. Technological change is considered to be critical to achieving long-term and cost-effective solutions for the environmental problems generated by the industry (e.g., Fisher and Schot, 1993; Kemp, 1994; Shrivastava, and Hart, 1995; Linnanen *et al.*, 1995; OECD, 1995; den Hond, 1996; Fullerton and Wu, 1998; Norberg-Bohm, 1999; Clayton *et al.*, 1999; PCSD, 1999). As innovations in products and processes generally improve not only features of product and process performance, but also economic efficiency, innovation aiming to reduce pollution at source is assumed to render the same benefits for the firm (e.g., Porter *et al.*, 1995a; Howes *et al.*, 1997; Langerak *et al.*, 1998; Norberg-Bohm, 1999).

Within this group it is argued that regulation under the traditional policy approach has not been successful in promoting pollution prevention at source (Rothwell, 1992; Inwing and Hooper, 1992; OTA, 1992; Jaffe and Palmer, 1997; Kemp, 1998; Sanchez and McKinley, 1998; Granderson, 1999). This has been recognised recently at the government level. It is accepted that the way in which environmental regulations are designed and enforced currently limits the development of clean technologies (CSIS, 1997; ELI, 1998; PCSD, 1999). Emission and discharge rate standards provide no incentive to go beyond the required standard reduction and, as such, they fail to develop a culture of continuous environmental improvement necessary to sustain R&D and investment in innovation. In addition, emission and discharge standards are one-dimensional,[18] and while they require a high level of control for one particular pollutant, they may provide few incentives for overall cleaner production.

PCSD (1999, p. 112) and CSIS (1997, p. 7) indicate that a fundamental reform of the regulatory system is needed in order to remove the many barriers to innovation. Such reform it is suggested should depart, where possible, from technology-based rate standards that focus on end-of-pipe results towards overall plant or regional performance standards that focus on preventing pollution. CSIS (1997) argues that this change will have the effect of removing the need for the review of compliance technology by regulators, which is at the root of many barriers to innovation in the traditional environmental regulatory system.

The above literature offers many insights into and perspectives on the effects of regulations on the behaviour of the firm. According to Kemp (1998) and Chua (1999) although much discussed, there is very little known about the effects of regulations on the firm's technological innovation process and its interactions in the policy game. The relationship between regulation and innovative activities to prevent the generation of pollution is an under-researched topic. From the above review of the literature on the effects of regulation on the performance of the firm we can conclude that it does not help in the exploration of the possible social affective perceptions of firms' managers.

There are few studies that consider the relation of social norms and environmental perceptions of managers (e.g., Gladwin, 1993; Everett *et al.*, 1993; Andrews, 1998), and no studies were found that helped to explain in more detail how the firms or their managers internalised their perceived social norm or socially desirable behaviours. The social norm, understood as a behaviour regarded as desirable to society, can be considered to be embodied in institutions like government regulatory agencies, industrial standards like ISO14000, international trade environmental norms and international treaties for environmental protection. Following the definition given in Chapter 3 concerning the perceived social pressure these institutions are assumed to be the possible important referents that could be seen to be pushing or demanding the development of clean technologies. That is, the sources of regulatory pressure for the firm. These sources are presented in Table 4.6 below.

Table 4.6 Scale to assess regulatory pressure

	Regulators		**International agreements**
rp1	Environmental agencies	rp7	BECC
rp2	Risk of future regulations	rp8	NAFTA
rp3	Regulators' enforcement capability	rp9	Motivation to comply with international agreements
rp4	Motivation to comply with regulators		
	International Standards Organization		
rp5	ISO influence capability		
rp6	Motivation to comply with ISO		

Item sample:

rp$_7$. The new international agreements such as the Border Environmental Cooperation Commission (BECC) will push us to develop clean products and clean production process.

unlikely	1	2	3	4	5	6	7 likely
	extremely	quite	slightly	uncertain	slightly	quite	extremely

The beliefs presented in Table 4.6 constitute the set of beliefs that may contribute to the perceptions held by managers regarding the pressure from diverse normative agencies and treaties to develop clean technologies. Supported by the framework provided above it is proposed that the firms' perceived regulatory pressure is proportional to the connotative accumulated load generated by beliefs regarding the perceived weak or strong obligation to comply with their important normative referents to develop clean technologies. Based on the above discussion and with the aim of testing the link between the normative referents and the overall perceived regulatory pressure the following hypothesis is proposed:

H₇: The firms' perceived regulatory pressure (RP) is a function of the connotative accumulated load generated by beliefs regarding the weak or strong obligation to comply with the perceived norms dictated by their important referents to develop or not to develop clean technologies (Σrp_b).

$$H_7: \quad RP = RP \left(\sum_{b=1}^{9} rp_b \right)$$

Where:

MP is the item that assess the perceived regulatory pressure

rp_b is the bth belief about the normative importance of social referents to develop clean technologies.

Summary

The possible sources of *normative* predisposition among firm managers regarding the development of clean technologies were discussed above. It was proposed that this predisposition stemmed from the importance given to critical referents in the marketplace, the community and regulatory institutions. Hypotheses H_5, H_6 and H_7 relate to the relationship of dependence of the overall perceived social pressure on the specific normative beliefs proposed here. The premise of these hypotheses is that, if such a relationship is empirically confirmed and if hypotheses H_1 and H_2, proposed in Chapter 3, are also accepted, then a chain of causality from *normative* beliefs to willingness would be established. This would enable an assessment of the importance of these three social forces to drive behavioural and technical change in those firms under study in the specific context of the Mexican Northern Border Region.

PERCEIVED CONTROL OVER THE DEVELOPMENT OF CLEAN TECHNOLOGIES

In Chapter 2 the macro determinants of the environmental behaviour of the firm – i.e., technological trajectories and the stages of evolution of the industry – were discussed. The conclusion in Chapter 2, was that clean technology development depends on the creation of a new knowledge base. It was stated that clean technologies refer to a set of new technological paradigms involving a new set of needs to fulfil, new scientific principles to apply, and new material technologies to produce all kinds of consumable goods and services. This section explores the instrumental component proposed to determine the firms' willingness to innovate. The discussion intends to layout the theoretical foundations to assess the perceived ease or difficulty to develop clean technologies. For this, it is necessary to define the capabilities that are essential to undertake the creation of a new knowledge base that may enable the firms to develop clean technologies.

Since the focus of this section is on the capabilities that firms need to function in an environmentally friendly way the literature of the business and the environment was consulted. A number of authors within this literature have attempted to reconcile economic activities with environmental protection. Most of them propose ideal models of clean products (or sustainable firm) for which they provide very general check lists of the features of products and corporations. A wide variety of topics regarding organisations and organisational behaviour are discussed but this literature only goes as far as concluding that the main challenge is to find technological solutions that are in balance with economic optimisation (e.g., Gladwin, 1993; Shrivastava and Hart, 1995; van Someren, 1995; Skidmore, 1995; Linnanen *et al.*, 1995; Chattery, 1995; Steger, 1996; Graedel, 1997; den Hond, 1996). However, it does not provide any insight into which capabilities are necessary to develop clean technologies.

Broadening the perspective to the resource view of the firm without an immediate link to the environment, there is an extensive body of literature about the capabilities that are enabling mechanisms for change and innovation within firms. (e.g., Teece *et al.*, 1990; Hamel and Prahalad, 1994; Huber, 1996; Teece and Pisano, 1994; Leonard-Barton, 1995; Grant; 1996; Panda and Ramanathan, 1996; etc.). Unfortunately, and in agreement with Panda (1996) and Collins (1994), the field is full of ill-definitions and generalisations with no empirical content. There still is no operative normative work that lays the foundation for a generic firm to lead change. The elements needed to enable change are mentioned (Tidd *et al.*, 1997) but no propositions to operationalise them are put forward. The general justification for this is that since there is a large variety of firms, the number of capabilities is enormous and therefore it is not possible to list them all (Collins, 1994).

Furthermore, Penrose's (1959) seminal work introduced the broad classification of capabilities into R&D, design, manufacturing, operation, marketing. This classification implies that the resource view of the firm is directed towards enhancing and reproducing the competitiveness of the firm. Therefore this approach remains within the actual technological regime. As argued in Chapter 2, the development of clean technologies depends on the creation and integration of a new knowledge base progressing from, but not remaining within, the current technological regime. As a result, this literature does not offer the appropriate set of capabilities, nor the categories of capabilities, that might enable the development of clean technologies.

The notion of the creation of a new knowledge base is the central element on the work of Nonaka (1994) and also Roome (1994). Although Nonaka provides a theory that explains the creation and deployment of new knowledge within organisations, he does so only at a generic level. Nonaka's framework helps the understanding of the dynamics of knowledge creation, but does not provide the specific capabilities or categories of capabilities that enable the development of clean technologies.

Building on Nonaka, Roome (1994) proposes that the creation of a clean production paradigm requires a reshaping of the organisational relationships as well as employment of new environmental techniques to inform R&D practice and its integration in the procurement and productive activities of the firm. Roome proposes a model to integrate a set of capabilities that may already exist within an industrial organisation (see Figure 4.7). The scheme outlines six categories of capabilities that are necessary for the creation of a new knowledge base.

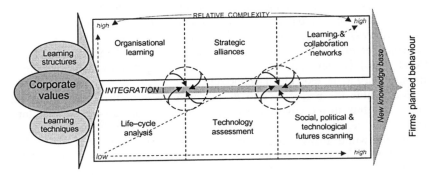

Figure 4.7   Technological regime shift: Core capabilities definition
Figure based on: Roome (1994) and Leonard-Barton (1995)

The *first set of capabilities* (top row of Figure 4.7) refers to the ability to learn quickly and reshape organisational structures and routines that enable change (Senge, 1990; Teece *et al.*, 1997). According to Roome (1994) they can be seen as the existing learning structures within an organisation. Within this set, the first element refers to organisational learning, regarding the capability to organise environmental screening of products via analysis of their life cycle and integrate them into the firm's technologies and activities. The next two capabilities refer to the ability to outsource knowledge, to the ability to form strategic alliances with suppliers, customers or competitors. The last refers to the capability to organise networks of learning and collaboration with universities and public R&D institutions and consulting firms, and to develop relations with other industrial sectors and regulatory institutions and agencies. It is expected that firms are currently practising most elements of the model, with the exception of product life cycle analysis.

The *second set of capabilities* (bottom row of Figure 4.7) refers to technological capabilities, which can be seen as learning techniques: the first element of the set represents the key to starting the process of change. This is in agreement with several authors who have proposed a product life cycle analysis technique (LCA) as the starting point to evaluate, screen and set priorities, in order to environmentally re-engineer or create new products and processes (e.g. SETAC, 1993; Keoleian, 1993; van den Berg *et al.*, 1995; Linnanen *et al.*, 1995; Böhm and Walz, 1996; Steger, 1996; Curran, 1996).[19] The second, refers to the assessment of the environmental implications of the technological path pursued by the firm. The third, refers to the scanning of social, political and technological futures.

Although Roome proposed six categories of capabilities the capabilities involved in technology assessment and futures scanning are not considered here. In the case of technology assessment, it has been argued elsewhere that the scope of this is so broad that traditionally it has been carried out outside the firm by government organisations (e.g., Smits *et al.*, 1995; den Hond and Groenewgen, 1996; Zidaman and Cevidalli, 1987; Tschirky, 1994; Dale and Loveridge, 1996). This type of assessment, although socially desirable, cannot be expected to be conducted by the firm. In the case of strategic planning, the perception of the firm's social context and futures scanning were implicitly considered in the sections of perceived economic risk (pp. 72–74) and perceived social pressure (pp. 75–86). In the following sections the relevant literature on those categories of capabilities considered will be discussed.

TECHNOLOGICAL CAPABILITIES

In Chapter 2 the main features of a new technological regime that might enable environmental conservation were discussed. In the previous section four capabilities were proposed to be a core that must be mastered by the firm in order to be able to develop clean technologies. The proposed model to operate the creation of a new knowledge base implies the use of life cycle analysis (LCA) techniques as a tool in the search for technological solutions (see Figure 4.8).

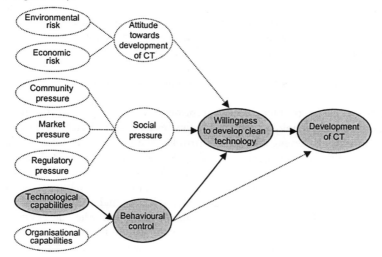

*Figure 4.8   Understanding and predicting the firm's willingness to innovate
Behavioural domain: Perceived technological capabilities*

According to Society of Environmental Toxicology and Chemistry (SETAC, 1993), LCA is a technique used to evaluate the environmental burdens associated with an economic activity by: (1) identifying and quantifying energy and materials used and wastes released; (2) assessing their impact on the environment; and (3) identifying and evaluating opportunities to effect environmental improvements. Such assessments include the entire life cycle of the product (or economic activity). This encompasses the extraction and processing of raw materials; manufacturing, transportation and distribution; use; re-use; maintenance; recycling; and final disposal. LCA must be used routinely at the earliest stages of R&D on products and process to avoid undesirable environmental impacts (SETAC, 1993, p. 2).

The LCA technique represents the appropriate tool and the logical steps to be followed by any firm wanting to develop an environmentally oriented business strategy. Although LCA has the potential to help in the development of clean technologies, its implementation presents several problems. First, LCA links the whole supply chain in terms of causality of externalities and pollution. Consequently, it reduces the accountability of any specific firm in the search for solutions. Second, the weighting of environmental impacts of specific activities is given by the ecological risk perception of 'experts'. As was discussed above, p. 61, the perception of risk is culturally and value determined. The experts' risk perception in combination with the time and costs demands of a LCA, may lead to non-universal weighting and bias according to the interest of who performs or pays for the LCA (Udo de Haes, 1993). Third, as it is costly, small companies are unlikely to be able to afford to specialise in LCA. Fourth, the environmental and economic benefits of investing in LCA may not be immediately apparent. In order to compare the benefits it is necessary to make the LCA complete to see the extent of improvements along the whole cycle. And last, time-to-market pressures to shorten the product development cycle can also impede the use of LCA. That is, the firm faces the risk of being left out of the market due to an obsolete out-of-date product. The extensive time generally required to conduct an LCA may interfere with the regular product development cycle (Keoleian, 1993).

Despite these problems, LCA represents a step forward towards the development of techniques that enable the development of clean technologies. Thus, in order to assess whether the firm has the basic capabilities needed to perform a life-cycle analysis, according to the definition of LCA given by SETAC, four stages are proposed. The first stage could be seen as the foundation for the development of clean technologies.[20] This refers to the creation of an inventory of the critical environmental interventions of the whole production process and product use; and the assessment of environmental impacts that may occur at each stage in the production process. Following van den Berg *et al.* (1995) this stage would require: a process flow chart with an overview of the most relevant processes involved in the LCA striving for a 100% coverage of the production process (*tcpp1*); the quantification of materials and energy used to produce a good (*tcpp3*); the identification of those critical materials and releases of pollutants inherent to, or related to, the production process (*tcpp4*), and their follow up along the whole supply chain (*tcpp5*); the assessment of environmental impacts for those critical spots of the production process (*tcpp 6*), and their follow up along the whole supply chain (*tcpp7, tcpp9*); calculation of the overall mass and energy flows (*tcpp8*); identification of critical suppliers (*tcpp12*); assignment of priorities to action (*tcpp10*); analysis of interrelations and links with suppliers and customers (*tcpp13*); the tracking of environmental impacts of products beyond the firm gates (*tcpp16*); time and resources availability for data collection (*tcpp11*) (SETAC, 1993; Wenzel *et al.*, 1997).[21]

The second stage of development towards a clean product and process relates to the capability of the firm to cooperate with, and influence suppliers and customers towards the implementation of a clean environment culture. The activities that the implementation of a dynamic of cooperation and influence may require are: the procurement of safety data sheets from suppliers of inputs and components (*tcpp2*); allocation of environmental impacts and pollution prevention responsibilities to suppliers (*tcpp14*) and customers (*tcpp15*); creating and enforcing a 'clean production' culture at the firm level via the delegation of authority to the environmental management department (*tcpp37*), generation of awareness (*tcpp39*), training in new skills (*tcpp40*), conciliating demands from other functional areas of the firm (*tcpp41*), and the integration of environmental and growth policies (*tcpp42*).

The third stage focuses on the technological opportunities and availability of the appropriate substitutes of raw materials, inputs and components, and its overall feasibility due to nature of the service that the product provides (*tcpp43*). This entails procurement of 'clean inputs', components (*tcpp17, tcpp25*), machinery and equipment (*tcpp18*); recyclability of inputs, components and containers (*tcpp28, tcpp30, tcpp36*), waste elimination in manufacturing via the re-design of product, process and packing (*tcpp31, tcpp32, tcpp33, tcpp34*).

The fourth stage refers to the actual improvement of those environmentally critical parts of product and production process. Although, the feasibility of clean technologies ultimately depends on both the availability of new technological options for the substitution of noxious inputs and the firm's capability to re-think and re-design product and process. It is the last, the fourth, dimension that is most critical as it refers to the actual realisation improvements through the integration of the knowledge generated in the three previous stages. This integration would require at least the mastering of the following capabilities: concept development (*tcpp21*), R&D (*tcpp22*), design (*tcpp23, tcpp24*), environmental management procedures (*tcpp29*). Table 4.7 summarises the set of beliefs proposed above.

Table 4.7   Scale to assess technological capabilities in product and process environmental improvement

	LCA
tcpp 1	Manufacturing process flow charts
tcpp 3	Mass and energy flows (process)
tcpp 4	Sources of critical environmental interventions
tcpp 5	Supply chain management
tcpp 6	Environmental impact assessment for activities, inputs and components
tcpp 7	Up-stream and down impact assessment follow up
tcpp 8	Mass and energy flows (products)
tcpp 9	Estimate of environmental impacts
tcpp 10	Inventory priorities
tcpp 11	Resources and time availability for data collection
tcpp 12	Critical suppliers identification
tcpp 13	Links with suppliers and consumers
tcpp 16	Environmental impacts tracking
	Cooperation and influence
tcpp 2	Inputs and components safety data sheets collection
tcpp 14	Assigning responsibilities to suppliers
tcpp 15	Assigning responsibilities to consumers
tcpp 37	Authority delegation to environmental department
tcpp 38	Culture enforcement capability
tcpp 39	Culture creation capability
tcpp 40	Training capability
tcpp 41	Conciliation of functional areas demands
tcpp 42	Integration of environmental and growth policies
	Technological opportunities
tcpp 7	Procurement of clean inputs and components
tcpp 18	Procurement of clean machinery and equipment
tcpp 25	Unsafe raw materials and inputs (products)
tcpp 28	Recyclability of raw materials, inputs and components
tcpp 30	Recyclable material and components containers
tcpp 31	Waste elimination via re-design (product)
tcpp 32	Waste elimination via re-design (process)
tcpp 33	Packing method substitution (process)
tcpp 34	Packing substitution (product)
tcpp 36	Re-design for product recyclability
tcpp 43	Product nature
	Improvement
tcpp 21	Concept product development capability
tcpp 22	R&D capability
tcpp 23	Design capability
tcpp 24	Re-design work team assemble
tcpp 26	Certified clean raw materials and inputs procurement
tcpp 27	Unsafe components
tcpp 35	Redisign for easy recyclability of products and maintenance materials
tcpp 29	Environmental management procedures

Item sample:

tcpp41 Integrating a clean production policy with other policies of our organisation is:

difficult	1	2	3	4	5	6	7	easy
	extremely	quite	slightly	uncertain	slightly	quite	extremely	

The four stages described above comprise the set of activities that may generate the managers' beliefs about the technological capabilities of their firm to develop clean technologies. Applying the framework and definitions provided above it is proposed that the firms' perceived technological capability to improve the environmental features of their product and process (*TCPP*) is proportional to the connotative belief load accumulated ($\Sigma tcpp_b$) regarding the perceived ease or difficulty of performing the individual activities needed to carry out LCA practices and the respective product and process improvement. Based on the above discussion the following hypotheses are proposed in order to link the perceived ease or difficulty of the activities required to perform a life-cycle analysis and product and process improvement to the overall perceived technological capability.[22]

H₈: The perceived technological capability (TCPP) is a function of the accumulated connotative beliefs load regarding the perceived ease or difficulty on those activities needed to perform an LCA and the product and process improvement ($\Sigma tcpp_b$).

$$H_8: \quad TCPP = TCPP \left(\sum_{b=1}^{38} tcpp_b \right)$$

Where:

TCPP	is the item that assesses the perceived technological capability
$tcpp_b$	is the *b*th belief of perceived control upon the practice of LCA and product and process improvements.

ORGANISATIONAL LEARNING

For a firm to develop or adopt clean technologies it needs to acquire a new set of knowledge and skills. This process of generating new knowledge in the literature of innovation has been described through the use of the metaphor 'organisational learning' (see Figure 4.9 below). The current literature on strategic management agrees that *organisational learning* is an imperative. This imperative stems from the rapid changes in science and technology and in regulatory and market structures. The basic premise is that large or small firms that do not learn how to respond to changes in their market context will not survive (e.g. Senge, 1990; Dodgson, 1995; Leonard-Barton; 1995, Huber, 1996; Grant, 1996; Tidd *et al.*, 1997). According to Tsang (1997) the learning literature can be broadly classified into two streams.

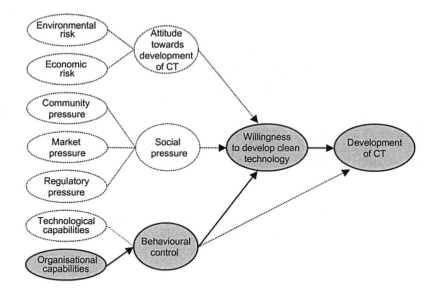

Figure 4.9   Understanding and predicting the firm's willingness to innovate
           Behavioural   domain: Perceived   organisational   learning
           capabilities

The first stream includes authors that aspire to prescribe how an organisation should learn. The main objective of their research is to improve organisational performance by providing analytical tools to practitioners. The prescriptions provided results from the extensive consulting experience of the authors and case study and action research. Tsang argues that there is a tendency to generalise the prescriptions to all types of organisations, because the learning process is considered to imply behavioural change and organisational performance improvement (e.g., Senge, 1990; Peters, 1992).

In the second stream of literature are those authors that attempt to understand how firms learn. Tsang suggests that the main objective is to build theory through rigorous research methods and systematic data collection. The learning process is assumed to provide the potential for a behavioural change with either positive or negative outcomes in the overall organisational performance. They are careful to keep the reader aware of the factors limiting the generalisation of the research results (e.g., Leonard-Barton, 1995; Nonaka, 1994, Nonaka *et al.*, 1996; Argyris and Schön, 1996).

Organisational learning has been defined by many authors (e.g., Hedberg, 1981; March, 1989; Fiol and Lyes, 1985; Huber, 1991; Dodgson, 1995; Miller, 1996). According to Miller (1996), organisational learning refers to the acquisition of new knowledge by actors who are able and willing to apply that knowledge in making decisions or influencing others in the organisation.

This definition is used to assess learning capabilities because it synthesises previous definitions and is in agreement with the frameworks proposed by the theory of planned behaviour and the R&D model proposed by Roome (1994). In contrast to other definitions of learning, Miller (1996) explicitly includes the notion of action, a fact that is suitable for the measurement of behavioural control.

As the focus of this section is to measure the degree of control over action, those works that fall within the descriptive and volitional classification will be used (i.e., Nonaka, 1994, 1996; Leonard-Barton, 1995; and Tidd *et al.*, 1997). Although these works do not present in detail how firms actually learn, they observe specific actions and resources present in those organisations that succeed in innovative activities. The aim of this section is to construct a scale on which to assess the degree of control over the action of organisational learning. This implies volitional control over learning, and hence the scale will be based on those works that fall within the descriptive and volitional classification.

Nonaka (1994) proposes that organisational knowledge is created through a continuous interaction between tacit and explicit knowledge. He presents a cycle of information and knowledge management in order to embed knowledge in the structures of the organisation. He proposes a spiral of knowledge by which the diffusion of knowledge flows in a circular causality; from individual to individual in a process of socialisation; from individual to documentation in a process of externalisation; from documentation to documentation in a combinatory way; and from documentation to individual in a process of internalisation of information.

Although this theory helps us to understand the dynamics of learning as a social phenomenon it does not provide more tangible steps to conduct such a process. In this sense the work of Leonard-Barton complements Nonaka's theory by providing in a more specific way some of the elements needed for organisational learning to occur. Leonard-Barton proposes four core learning capabilities to be mastered: problem solving, implementing and integrating, experimenting, and outsourcing. Only the first two of the core capabilities are considered in this section; outsourcing will be discussed in the section discussing strategic alliances (p. 98), and experimenting is not included as it was considered to be an outcome once the first three other capabilities are present in the firm.

Shared problem-solving capability refers to the availability and deployment of critical knowledge on environment-related disciplines across different cognitive and functional barriers. Three sources of individual differences in problem solving according to Leonard-Barton are: (1) *specialisation* on the deep understanding of a specific field of science or technology. In the present study the crucial knowledge we refer to is knowledge for developing clean technologies (*ol6, ol8*). (2) The term *cognitive styles* refers to the preferred form in which individuals make sense of reality. Team working in any task implies the conciliation of different cognitive styles (*ol4*). (3) *Preferences in tools and methodologies* refers to how specialists cling to one way of developing their tasks once they have mastered them. Such mastering, once seen as their core competencies, are potential core rigidities when the time to learn and change comes (*ol5*) (Leonard-Barton, 1992). In addition, two more capabilities that could be indispensable are proposed by Tidd *et al.*, (1997) regarding the continuous development of human resources. This refers to the importance and value that is given to the acquisition of new knowledge (*ol11*), and the presence of individuals prone to take initiative and responsibilities for knowledge creation and experimentation (*ol12*).

The *integrating capability* refers to the mastering of mechanisms and the availability of resources to manage specialisation, cognitive diversity and methodological preferences. Four capabilities have been proposed as fundamental to the integration of knowledge into the products and processes. The first refers to the availability of a diversity of disciplines related to solving the problem (*ol1*). The second concerns the availability of people who speak two or more professional languages, which enables them to apply knowledge across situations and disciplinary skills (*ol2*). The third implies the presence of mechanisms that encourage depersonalisation of conflicting professional perspectives (*ol3*). The last capability involves effective communication among cross-functional teams and projects (*ol15*) (Leonard-Barton, 1995, Ch.3).

Implementation involves behavioural change; that is, once resources are available and goals are set, influencing people's behavioural change is the challenge. Such a challenge demands individuals with power and influence at the organisational level to promote change (*ol7*). It also requires the minimisation of opposition (*ol9*), and the involvement of individuals to learn new techniques (*ol13*, *ol14*) in a culture of continuous improvement (*ol10*, *ol16*).

Following the definition of organisational learning provided above, the aim of the scale is to capture and measure the perceptions of managers about the ease or difficulty of influencing behavioural change towards specific actions and the availability of specific human resources. These actions and resources have been observed in organisations that succeed in the innovative activity and, thus from the features of an innovative organisation. The premise of the scale is that those managers that perceive it as being easy for their firms to possess high organisational learning capabilities on shared problem solving, integration and implementation of knowledge in concept products, designs, prototypes, and synthesise these into new products and process will be more willing to innovate in clean technologies. The list of beliefs used in the scale to assess the firm's learning capabilities is summarised in Table 4.8.

Table 4.8   Scale to assess organisational learning capabilities

Shared problem solving		**Integrating knowledge**	
ol4	Cognitive styles preferences	ol1	Shared problem solving
ol5	Preferences in tools and methodologies	ol2	Specialisation
ol6	Key individuals (critical knowledge)	ol3	Specialisation
ol8	Key individuals (gate keepers)	ac15	Extensive communication
ol11	Continuous training and development of human resources (knowledge value)		**Implementing**
		ol7	Key individuals (power and influence)
ol12	Continuous training and development of human resources (initiative and responsibility)	ol9	Core rigidities (human rigidities)
		ol10	Core rigidities (culture implementation)
		ol13	Involvement of people (technical change)
		ol14	Involvement of people (organisational change)
		ol16	Continuous improvement involvement
Item sample:			

ol9. For our company minimising employees resistance to learn new techniques and change work practices is:

difficult	1	2	3	4	5	6	7	easy
	extremely	quite	slightly	uncertain	slightly	quite	extremely	

The aspects described above comprise the set of capabilities that may generate the managers' perceptions about the organisational learning capability to generate and integrate new knowledge towards the development of clean technologies. Following the framework and definitions provided above it can be said that the managers' perceived capability to promote organisational learning is proportional to the connotative accumulated belief load of the capabilities needed to organise environmental screening of products via LCA and integrate them into the firm's technologies and activities. Based on the above discussion the following hypothesis is proposed:

H₉: The perceived organisational learning capability (*OL*) is a function of the connotative accumulated load of beliefs regarding the perceived ease or difficulty on those activities and the availability of human resources that a learning organisation requires (Σol_b).

$$H_9: OL = OL\left(\sum_{b=1}^{16} ol_b\right)$$

Where:

OL is the item that assesses the perceived capability on
         organisational learning
ol_b is the bth belief of the perceived control upon organisational
         learning.

STRATEGIC ALLIANCES AND NETWORKS OF COLLABORATION

The third and fourth core capabilities proposed by Roome (1994) refer to the firms' ability to evaluate and outsource the possible emerging clean technologies through engagement in strategic alliances with other firms along the supply chain and in broader external networks of collaboration to track new knowledge and the evolution of the environmental agenda at a societal level (see Figure 4.10). In order to lay the theoretical foundation from which to assess the degree of control over alliances of collaboration to innovate, this section explores two questions: 'What are strategic alliances?' and 'What are the required steps in forming a strategic alliance?'

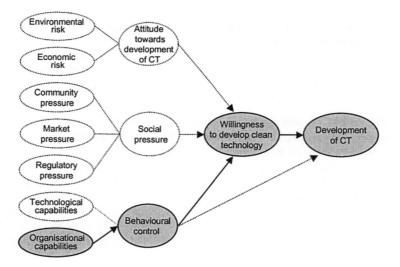

Figure 4.10 Understanding and predicting the firm's willingness to innovate Behavioural domain: Perceived alliances and networks of collaboration capabilities

Porter (1993, p. 25) defined strategic alliances as informal business relationships characterised by tight operational linkages. Such operations tend to be characterised by mutual vested interest in each other's future; strategic orientation; close contact between upper and middle management; reciprocal relationships that share strengths, information, and mutual advantages; and co-ordinated management styles organised around collaboration, not hierarchical power.

According to Contractor and Lorange (1988b), strategic alliances can vary from complete mergers to simple co-operative agreements. For example, some types of alliances may be made for technical training, start-up assistance agreements, patent and know-how licensing, exploration and research partnerships, development and co-production, etc. These types of cooperative agreements are differentiated according to the method of ensuring compensations and appropriability of the benefits of the cooperation, and the level of inter-organisational dependence. In general alliances are formed to obtain more benefits with less efforts and risks (Murray and Murray, 1989).

Some benefits are related to risk reduction; economies of scale; co-opting or blocking competition; overcoming regulations; and vertical quasi-integration (Contractor and Lorange, 1988b). Of particular interest to this work are the benefits that accrue from alliances of cooperation to innovation activities. It is generally accepted that risk is something inherent in innovation (Dosi, 1982). Some of the advantages that encourage firms to cooperate are the possible complementarities in technologies, patents, and know-how to reduce risks in technological developments.

In order to understand the possible perceptions of managers when deciding whether to engage or not in alliances to develop clean technologies, it is nece-

Figure 4.11 Alliances making process
Based on: Porter (1993)

ssary to understand the architecture of any alliance. According to Porter, the steps in the development of an alliance can be broadly described as follows (see Figure 4.11). The origin of an alliance is the parent firm's strategy or goal, which in the case of this study, is the strategy regarding the outsourcing of clean technologies. Such a strategy calls for appropriate partners and this implies an adequate understanding of both partners' profile to ensure good a match. Negotiations can proceed with some assurance that the potential alliance may be realised.

Once negotiations have proceeded a statement of procedures must be produced to outline the principles of the venture including the strategic fit, the posible operational interfaces and the goals and objectives. Next, an operational plan should be jointly created to ensure that the alliance fits properly. By delineating the operational plans before any legal agreements are signed, the firms' teamwork fit can be tested at an operational level. Only once this test is passed by determining the respective functions within the alliance should the organisational, legal agreement and accounting aspects clearly take form and structure (Porter, 1993, Ch. 4).

The process outlined above gives an idea of the inherent challenges of performing any strategic alliance. In order to capture how managers may assess the ease or difficulty of such an endeavour, four aspects are proposed to be measured: access to strategic synergies; availability of support and commitment from top management; the possibility to achieve influence via cooperation; and outsourcing opportunities. The first and second aspects are based on what is proposed by Porter as the essential building blocks of an alliance architecture. These blocks are: the critical driving forces that call for an alliance, strategic fit, great chemistry, operational integration, growth opportunity, win/win deal, and commitment and support.[23] These building blocks are located within the first four stages of the development process of alliances. A summary of the aspects that characterise these building block of and alliance that were included in the scale to assess the perceived opportunities and capabilities to perform strategic alliances and networks of collaboration to outsource knowledge and know-how are shown in Table 4.9 (next page).

The first building block to consider for assessment regards what is generally agreed that making a strategic alliance produces, that is, *strategic synergies* (Coombs *et al.*, 1996). Although they have many potential benefits, alliances present several challenges. The main challenge is identifying the right partners in terms of strategy fit, chemistry and operational match. Without such a match, any alliance is doomed to fail (Porter, 1993, Ch. 4). The strategic fit refers to the strengths and complementarities in innovative capacity and technical know-how. Both partners should have more strength when combined than they would have independently (*al1*).

The chemistry fit concerns the trust, honesty, win/win commitment, good reputation, predictability under pressure and creativity in the face of adversity that the prospective partnering firms may need to have (*al2*). The operational fit refers to the reference framework upon which the prospective partners operate their respective business (e.g. strategic time orientation (long–short term), information and communication methods (formal–informal), management styles (hierarchical–collaborative), labour relations (harmonious–conflictive), technology (familiar–unfamiliar) and business government relations (adversarial–harmonious)) (*al3*) (Porter, 1993, Ch. 6).

Table 4.9   Scale to assess strategic alliances and networks of collaboration capabilities

	Strategic synergy		**Outsourcing opportunities**
al1	Strategic fit	al8	Life cycle analysis expertise
al2	Chemistry fit	al12	Clean product technologies
al3	Operational fit	al13	Clean process technologies
	Support and commitment		**Networks of collaboration**
al4	Win/win negotiation	nwk1	With universities
al5	Values pro-environment	nwk2	With EPA
al6	Support from CEO and shareholders	nwk3	With SEMARNAP
al7	Previous experience on alliances	nwk4	With ISO
	Cooperation-Influence	nwk5	With suppliers
al9	With suppliers (inputs and components)	nwk6	With consulting firms
al10	With suppliers (machinery and equipment)	nwk7	With other firms in the same industrial sector
al11	With customers		

Item sample:

al1   For our firm finding partners for strategic alliances that ensure good strategic fit (with regard to strengths and complementarities in innovative capacity and technical know-how) for the development of a cleaner technology-product portfolio is:

difficult   1   2   3   4   5   6   7   easy
        extremely quite slightly uncertain slightly quite extremely

The second aspect to assess concerns the *support and commitment* that the alliance can receive from the CEO and shareholders (*al6*). Such support it is proposed arises from their perceptions of the opportunities of having win/win negotiations (*al4*), the presence of pro-environmental values (*al5*) and successful experiences with previous alliances (*al7*). The third aspect refers to the possibility of the parent firm *cooperating with and influencing* behavioural change in customers (*al11*) and suppliers regarding the development of cleaner substitutes of inputs, components (*al9*), and equipment and machinery (*al10*). The fourth aspect arises from one of the major assumptions of studies of cooperation-innovation regarding the benefits of strategic alliances (e.g. Tidd *et al.*, 1997; Teece *et al.*, 1990; Contractor and Lorange, 1988). This is that cooperation between firms can provide leverage for precious off-the-shelf technological and know-how resources and opportunities; specifically life cycle analysis expertise and know-how (*al8*); and cleaner product (*al12*) and process technologies (*al13*).

For networks of collaboration within a broader context to follow up sources of new knowledge and the evolving environmental agenda several institutions were considered. Environmental regulatory agencies (*nwk2*, *nwk3*) and standardisation agencies (*nwk4*), institutions such as universities and public R&D (*nwk1*), consultancy firms with clean technology expertise (*nwk6*), other firms in the same sector to transfer technology and expertise (*nwk7*), suppliers of raw materials and other inputs for product integration (*nwk5*).

The aspects described above comprise the set of capabilities and opportunities that may contribute to the perceptions of managers about the alliances capability of their firms to develop clean technologies. It is proposed that the managers' perceived control over strategic alliances is proportional to the connotative accumulated belief load of the perceived ease or difficulty in fulfilling the essential aspects needed to perform strategic alliances to develop clean technologies. In intending to test the link between specific beliefs regarding the overall perceived alliances capability to develop clean technologies the following hypothesis is proposed.

H_{10}:   The strategic alliances perceived capability (*AL*) is a function of the accumulated connotative beliefs load regarding the control upon the individual aspects that performing strategic alliances requires (Σal_b).

$$H_{10}: \quad AL \ = AL \ \left(\sum_{b=1}^{13} al_b \right)$$

Where:

AL is the item that assesses the perceived capability on strategic alliances

al_b is the *b*th belief of the perceived control upon opportunities and essential aspects to perform strategic alliances.

Similarly, it is proposed that the perceived control over the outsourcing of knowledge through networks of collaboration is proportional to the connotative accumulated belief load. This load is generated by the perceived ease or difficulty to engage in external networks of collaboration as a means to track new knowledge that enables clean technology development.

H_{11}:   The perceived control over networks of collaboration (*NWK*) is a function of the accumulated connotative beliefs load regarding the control upon the perceived ease or difficulty to engage in networks of collaboration to outsource new knowledge to develop clean technologies (Σnwk_b).

$$H_{11}: NWK = NWK \left(\sum_{b=1}^{7} nwk_b \right)$$

Where:

NWK   is the direct measure of the perceived networks of collaboration capability

nwk_b is the bth belief of the perceived control upon the performance of networks of collaboration.

Summary

The sources of an *instrumental* predisposition towards the development of clean technologies have been discussed above. This predisposition it was proposed, stems from the perceived ease or difficulty to master four core capabilities to generate and integrate a new knowledge base into products and production processes. Hypotheses H_8, H_9, H_{10}, and H_{11} refer to relationship between the perceived overall technological (*TCPP*) and organisational capability (*OL*, *AL*, and *NWK*) and the perceived instrumental control over the individual activities needed to perform the changes that improve the environmental features of product and production processes. The premise of H_8, H_9, H_{10}, and H_{11} is that, if there is a relationship of dependence between the perceived capability and specific beliefs used in the construction of the scale, then it may be possible to design environmental policies with a better focus in specific areas of diffusion of innovations. Therefore, indirectly, it may be possible to influence perceived control and willingness to innovate in clean technologies.

SYSTEM OF HYPOTHESES

This section summarises the set of arguments presented along the discussion of this chapter by presenting them as a system of hypotheses. Figure 4.12 (next page), displays the whole model as a system that intends to link beliefs to the willingness to innovate. In addition, the following system of hypotheses aims to test the theoretical framework developed in Chapters 3 and 4. The confirmation of the proposed definitional system will enable us to respond to the questions that motivated this study: whether or not it is possible to reconcile the interest of the firm with the social interest regarding environmental protection. If it is not possible, why not? If it is possible, under what conditions?

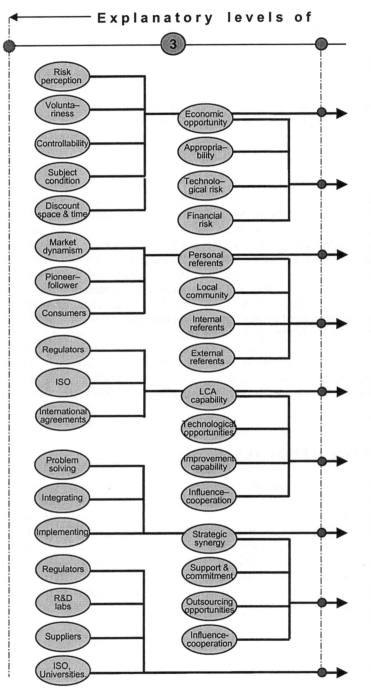

Figure 4.12   Hypotheses of dependence between willingness to innovate in clean technologies and attitude, social pressure, control over innovation; and the behavioural domains indexes

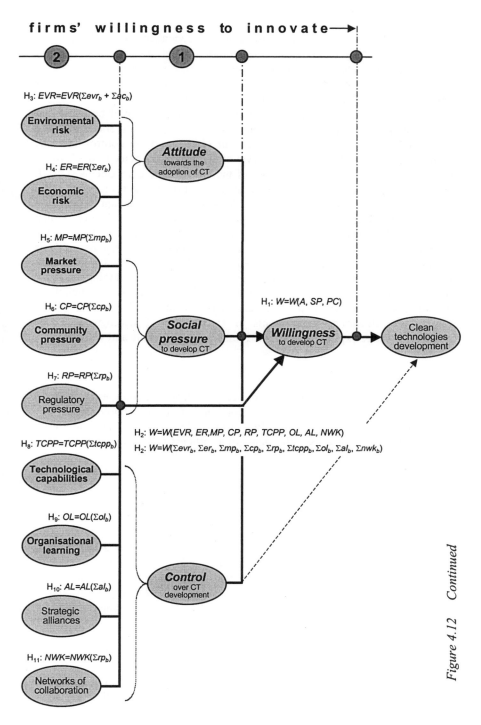

firms' willingness to innovate⟶

2   1

H_3: $EVR=EVR(\Sigma evr_b + \Sigma ac_b)$

Environmental risk

H_4: $ER=ER(\Sigma er_b)$

Economic risk

H_5: $MP=MP(\Sigma mp_b)$

Market pressure

H_6: $CP=CP(\Sigma cp_b)$

Community pressure

H_7: $RP=RP(\Sigma rp_b)$

Regulatory pressure

H_8: $TCPP=TCPP(\Sigma tcpp_b)$

Technological capabilities

H_9: $OL=OL(\Sigma ol_b)$

Organisational learning

H_{10}: $AL=AL(\Sigma al_b)$

Strategic alliances

H_{11}: $NWK=NWK(\Sigma rp_b)$

Networks of collaboration

Attitude towards the adoption of CT

Social pressure to develop CT

Control over CT development

H_1: $W=W(A, SP, PC)$

Willingness to develop CT

Clean technologies development

H_2: $W=W(EVR, ER, MP, CP, RP, TCPP, OL, AL, NWK)$
H_2: $W=W(\Sigma evr_b, \Sigma er_b, \Sigma mp_b, \Sigma cp_b, \Sigma rp_b, \Sigma tcpp_b, \Sigma ol_b, \Sigma al_b, \Sigma nwk_b)$

Figure 4.12   Continued

105

The set of hypotheses tests the relationships of dependence of willingness to innovate in clean technologies with attitude, social pressure, behavioural control; and the behavioural domain indexes. The presentation of the system of hypotheses is divided into three parts with regard to the levels of explanation of willingness to engage in innovative activities.

In Chapter 3 it was proposed that firms' willingness could be explained primarily in terms of attitudes towards the behaviour (A), their social pressure to perform (or not perform) the behaviour (PSP), and the control over the innovation process (PC). A second level of analysis takes place at the level of the behavioural domains within each of the above three components (i.e., A, PSP and PC). Finally, at a third level, the perception within each behavioural domain could be explained by the set of salient beliefs or relevant information held by the firms' managers. Similarly, as proposed in Chapter 3 that presented the mean features of the TPB, here the aim of the system hypotheses is to test whether within the environmental policy realm, it is possible to link salient beliefs to perceptions at the domain level and, in turn, link these perceptions to the willingness to develop clean technologies. If the links are proved to exist, a chain of causality that connects salient beliefs to willingness to innovate and ultimately to behaviour would be established. Figure 4.12 illustrates these levels of explanation of willingness and is intended to make explicit the expected links between beliefs and willingness.

Explanatory level one

H$_1$:   The firms' willingness (W) to develop in clean technologies depends on the attitude towards the development of clean technologies (A), the social pressure to develop clean technologies (PSP) and the perceived control over the innovation process (PC) as perceived by their managers.

$$H_1: W = W(A, PSP, PC)$$

Explanatory level two

H$_2$:   The firms' willingness (W) to develop clean technologies depends on the perceptions of the: environmental risk (EVR), economic risk (ER), community pressure (CP), market pressure (MP), regulatory pressure (RP), technological capabilities $(TCPP)$, organisational learning capabilities (OL), and capabilities on outsourcing strategic alliances (AL) and networks of collaboration (NWK).

$$H_2: W = W(EVR, ER, CP, MP, RP, TCPP, OL, AL, NWK)$$

H$_{2a}$: Proportionality exists between the scores in each domain scale and its respective domain index. This implies that the willingness to innovate can also be explained (and predicted) by the accumulated connotative load of the domain scales.

H_{2a}: $W = W(\Sigma evr, \Sigma er, \Sigma cp, \Sigma mp, \Sigma rp, \Sigma tcpp, \Sigma ol, \Sigma al, \Sigma nwk)$

Explanatory level three

H₃: The managers' environmental risk attitude (*EVR*) is a function of the accumulated connotative load of beliefs that arise from environmental risk perception (Σevr_b) and environmental risk acceptance (Σac_b).

$$H_3: \quad EVR = EVR \left(\sum_{b=1}^{13} evr_b + \sum_{b=1}^{19} ac_b \right)$$

H₄: The managers' economic risk attitude towards clean technologies (*ER*) is a function of the connotative accumulated load of beliefs regarding the good or bad economic consequences for the firm that may arise from developing clean technologies (Σer_b).

$$H_4: \quad ER = ER \left(\sum_{b=1}^{21} er_b \right)$$

H₅: The firm's perceived market pressure (*MP*) is a function of the cumulative load of beliefs held by their managers regarding the weak or strong signals coming from the market place to develop clean technologies (Σmp_b).

$$H_5: \quad MP = MP \left(\sum_{b=1}^{12} mp_b \right)$$

H₆: The manager's perceived community pressure (*CP*) is a function of the cumulative load of beliefs held by their managers regarding the perceived weak or strong signals coming from the community that their firm should develop clean technologies (Σcp_b).

$$H_6: \quad CP = CP \left(\sum_{b=1}^{15} cp_b \right)$$

H₇: The firms' perceived regulatory pressure (*RP*) is a function of the connotative accumulated load generated by beliefs regarding the weak or strong obligation to comply with the perceived norms dictated by their important referents to develop or not to develop clean technologies (Σrp_b).

$$\text{H}_7\text{:}\quad RP = RP\left(\sum_{b=1}^{9} rp_b\right)$$

H₈: The perceived technological capability (*TCPP*) is a function of the accumulated connotative beliefs load regarding the perceived ease or difficulty of those activities needed to perform an LCA and the product and process improvement ($\Sigma tcpp_b$).

$$\text{H}_8\text{:}\quad TCPP = TCPP\left(\sum_{b=1}^{38} tcpp_b\right)$$

H₉: The perceived organisational learning capability (*OL*) is a function of the connotative accumulated belief load of beliefs regarding the perceived ease or difficulty on those activities and human resources that a learning organisation requires (Σol_b).

$$\text{H}_9\text{:}\quad OL = OL\left(\sum_{b=1}^{16} ol_b\right)$$

H₁₀: The strategic alliances perceived capability (*AL*) is a function of the accumulated connotative beliefs load regarding the control upon the individual aspects that performing strategic alliances requires (Σal_b).

$$\text{H}_{10}\text{:}\quad AL = AL\left(\sum_{b=1}^{13} al_b\right)$$

H₁₁: The networks of collaboration perceived capability (*NWK*) is a function of the accumulated connotative beliefs load regarding the control upon the perceived ease or difficulty to engage in networks of collaboration to outsource new knowledge to develop clean technologies (Σnwk_b).

$$\text{H}_{11}\text{:}\quad NWK = NWK\left(\sum_{b=1}^{7} nwk_b\right)$$

SUMMARY

This chapter has explored the content of each of the behavioural domains proposed in Chapter 3. It has shown that the theory of planned behaviour provides a definitional system for the systematic exploration of the possible micro determinants of the development of clean technologies in manufacturing firms. The exploration aimed to gain a better understanding of what could condition firms' managers' perceptions of environmental and economic risk, the social norm arising from the market, community and regulations, and the perceived organisational and technological capabilities. In aiming to link the perceptions or beliefs in each domain to willingness to innovate several hypotheses were proposed.

At a first level of explanation, hypothesis H_1 proposed that the firms' willingness to innovate is dependent on the attitudes, social pressure and perceived control over innovation as perceived by their managers. Hypotheses H_2 and H_{2a} proposed that the firms' willingness to innovate is a function of the overall perceptions on the different behavioural domains. These hypotheses (i.e., H_1, H_2, and H_{2a}) if accepted will partially validate the theoretical framework presented in this chapter. Such validation of the model proposed will enable the simulation of scenarios of policy intervention. Hypotheses H_3, to H_{11} bring into focus the relationship between the behavioural domain scales with their respective direct measures. In the following chapter the method and research strategy to test this system of hypotheses will be presented.

NOTES

1. 'Behavioural domain scales' refer to scores obtained with the addition of several items to obtain a composed single score.
2. 'Direct measures' refers to single items (or questions) that intend to capture the overall connotative load held by the respondent regarding a specific behavioural domain (e.g., the perceived technological capabilities). See the wording of the items (direct measures) in Appendix E.
3. Cars, planes, trains, etc.
4. Some authors see this approach as a challenge to the psychological approach (e.g., Royal Society, 1992).
5. According to Douglas and Wildavsky (1982) this depends on the ideology and values held by the individual or social group.
6. These parenthesis and the acronyms inside are used to identify the number of beliefs within a specific domain. This way of identifying beliefs will be used in the rest of the book. This nomenclature was also used in the questionnaire (see Appendix E) and the matrix of data.
7. This term is not in a standard English dictionary. Vlek and Stalen (1984) used it to denote the willingness of people to voluntarily expose themselves to any given hazard. It will be used here in the same sense.
8. The notion of connotation and its relation to attitude generation was discussed in Chapter 3. The wording of these items and those proposed in the following sections of this chapter is presented in Appendix E.
9. To review the wording of items in this table and in the following, see Appendix E.

10. The addition of items to form a scale to assess a specific behavioural attribute is discussed in Chapter 5.
11. The domain index of risk perception was estimated as: $EVR=EVR_2*(EVR_1/7)$. See the wording of the direct measures of the behavioural domain perceptions in Appendix E, Section V.
12. This represents a partial justification for not using the Ajzen model in a multiplicative fashion of beliefs and outcome probabilities.
13. This word, although not included in a standard dictionary (e.g., *The Compact Edition of the Oxford English Dictionary*) is widely used in the literature of technological innovation to denote 'the capacity to appropriate the benefits' derived from an innovative activity, and will be used here.
14. The perceived influence of suppliers will be considered, p. 91, and, p. 101.
15. Refers to 'measures aimed at directly influencing the environmental performance of polluters by regulating processes or products used, by prohibiting or limiting the discharge of certain pollutants, and/or restricting activities to certain times, areas, etc., through setting standards, zoning, and so on' (OECD, 1991b, Ch. 15).
16. These instruments include charges and taxes, emission charges, user charges, product charges or taxes, administrative charges or fees, subsidies, deposit-refund schemes, marketable permit arrangements, financial enforcement incentives or financial assistance (OECD, 1993).
17. A compendium of these technologies and waste management practices can be found in World Bank (2000).
18. Pollutants are targeted individually and considered to affect a single medium (i.e., water, air or soil) (ELI, 1998).
19. LCA is considered here as one among several methods that could be used to map and screen the spots where the technological portfolio of specific firm has critical relationships with the environment in relation to its supply chain. Other methods include EMS, environmental auditing, etc.
20. Or any other similar method to make an analysis of the critical stages of production and consumption of manufactured goods.
21. The algorithm proposed by van der Berg (1995) provides a set of detailed activities needed to perform an LCA. Here only the headings of clusters of activities are taken into account to assess the perception of managers. Those activities that were considered obviously feasible were not included in the questionnaire.
22. Similarly, as commented on the discussions on the previous domains, the beliefs listed in Table 4.7 have a level of generality that can be applied to several industrial sectors. It can be expected that the generated connotative load will vary from sector to sector and from firm to firm depending on capabilities and the complexity of product.
23. The assessment of the two following building blocks is obviated within this domain: *strategic drivers* are implicitly assessed in the domains of social pressure and economic risk; and *growth opportunity* is assessed in the domain of economic risk.

5. Research method

Chapter 5 presents the research strategy used to answer the research questions; modifications made to the Ajzen model; the connection of the theoretical approach with the research design and unit of analysis; a justification for the selected case study; the criteria for data analysis. It also includes a description of how the research was conducted; how the data were collected; and the criteria for the sample selection.

THE RESEARCH STRATEGY

In any research endeavour the theories that underpin the responses and the research strategy and methods of validation arise from the questions that it aims to respond to. The questions that originated this work were: (1) Is it possible to reconcile the individual interest with the social interest regarding environmental protection?; (2) If so, under what conditions?, and (3) If not, why not? These questions contained a number of hidden questions both at a theoretical and methodological level. Some of the questions that needed a response before an attempt was made to answer the main questions of this work where: *What* are the factors that determine the development of clean technologies on manufacturing firms? *How* can we account for and organise those determinants? *How* can we rate and rank them? *How* can the degree of conflict between the interest of the firm and the protection of the environment be measured? *How* can the research strategy approach be validated?

To answer the research questions, the research strategy required a methodology strongly grounded in theory. In a broad sense, the research strategy adopted can be divided in two stages. The first refers to the proposition of the theory of planned behaviour as theoretical framework that can be seen as a meta-theory to integrate several bodies of theory. Chapters 3 and 4 show that this framework provided a method to search systematically for those bodies of theory that might offer insights into the factors that explain behaviour in specific situations. It also provided guidance to search for those belief systems that might determine the planned behaviour of the firm. The second stage is composed of the fieldwork period used to collect the data, and the statistical validation process of the proposed framework to assess the willingness of the firm to develop clean technologies is presented in the Appendix C.

MODIFICATIONS TO THE AJZEN MODEL

The theory of planned behaviour (TPB) was presented in Chapter 3 in its original form (Ajzen, 1988). In this work several modifications were made to suit the needs of the study. First, the expectancy value model to create the scales of attitude (i.e., $A \propto \Sigma\ b_i e_i$), perceived social norms (i.e., $SN \propto \Sigma b_i m_i$) and perceived behavioural control (e.g., $PBC \propto \Sigma c_i p_j$) was not followed as originally proposed by Ajzen (1991) (see Chapter 3). The reasoning for this is as follows. Ajzen himself has commented that the application and appropriateness of the expectancy value model – for example, multiplying an outcome by its perceived likelihood of occurrence – is still the subject of an unresolved debate (Ajzen, 1991). In addition, according to Shapira (1994) managers are rather insensitive to estimated outcome probabilities: instead, they are better able to assess detailed descriptions of particular events, such as outcome scenarios.

Based on the above, it was found more appropriate to estimate the indexes of attitude, perceived social norms and perceived behavioural control as accumulated semantic loads.[1] The cognitive and evaluative components proposed by Ajzen (1991) were included in almost all items that constitute the scales included in the model developed in Chapter 4. This was done by combining the wording and differential semantic of a single item – the notions of outcomes and the evaluation of its likelihood of occurrence (see Appendix E section v). Using two separate items to assess one belief – as proposed by Ajzen – would have doubled the number of items in the questionnaire making its application impractical. Successful applications of the TPB assessing outcomes and likelihood in a single item can be found in Metselaar (1997).

The second modification to the implementation of the TPB concerns the motivation to comply with important referents (part of the perceived social pressure). This was not generally included for each item as suggested by Ajzen. Instead was included only in those domains of the perceived social pressure where it was considered appropriate. This decision was based on Ajzen's report concerning the contribution of this concept in explaining intention and behaviour. Generally its contribution to explain variance has been limited or negative (Ajzen, 1991). In addition, considering the context for which the questionnaire was developed (i.e., the firm) for some of the items it was not considered suitable to assess. For example, with questions like 'This firm does what the environmental authorities prescribe us to do' (agree–disagree); 'Our firm follows the behaviour of our competitors' (agree–disagree); and 'Our firm always does what our customers prefer' (agree–disagree); it was believed that the questionnaire would lose face value. This is due to the rhetoric tone of the questions.

Third, an extra level of explanation of intention and behaviour was added (see Figure 5.1). The standard application of Ajzen model does not include items assessing the overall perception of the behavioural domains that underlie attitudes, social norms and perceived behavioural control in a single item. The idea to include these items has the goal of capturing in a single item the accumulated connotative load that the scale in a particular domain contains. The addition of this level of explanation enabled the integration of a more detailed model that allowed for the integration of different theoretical bodies into a single model. The appropriateness of this integration – thus the addition of this new level of explanation – has been proved by several statistical tests (see Appendix A), their usefulness in showing the current and future rational expectancies of managers in a summarized form (see Chapter 6, Figure 6.12) and in the simulation of policy scenarios (see Chapter 7). In sum, in this work the TPB was seen as a methodology that could be modified according to the needs of the study, instead of letting the study to be moulded according to the possible rigidities of the model.

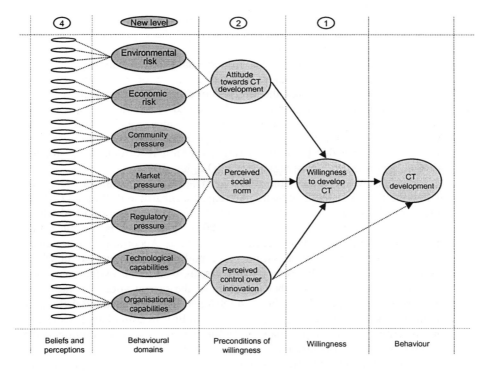

Figure 5.1   Levels of explanation of willingness to innovate in clean technologies

RESEARCH DESIGN

This section discusses the relation of the theoretical approach with the research design and the unit of analysis. Chapter 3 stated that this book makes a simile between the 'perception' the firm as an entity with the perception of its manager. In principle, these are two different units of analysis; firms do not perceive anything – the people who lead or represent the firm do. The adequacy of using a metaphor like 'the willingness of the firm to engage in innovative activities' and of assessing this concept based on the perceptions and beliefs of senior managers perceptions arises from the following.

First, the research questions and the theoretical and methodological approach via the use of self-report questionnaires point to the individual as the unit of analysis. This far no studies survey-based were found that have applied questionnaires to a group of people within an organisation in order to infer the weight or average value of item scores or that have used similar procedures to capture the collective vision of the organisation's strategy within a sample of organisations.

Second, in the literature of organisational studies it is widely argued that senior mangers or CEOs ought to have a vision of the future of their companies. That is, to choose the direction of a firm, its manager must have a clear mental image of the firm's present state and of a realistic and attractive future for their organisation (e.g., Benis and Nanus, 1985; Aguilar, 1988; Mintzberg, 1994). Furthermore, empirical evidence shows that the managers themselves believe that both articulating a vision and formulating a strategy are their key roles within an organisation (Quigley, 1993).

Third, elsewhere it has frequently been argued that strategic decisions within the firm are socially constructed (e.g., Eisenhardt and Zbraracki, 1992; Payne *et al.*, 1992; Ocasio, 1995; Frank *et al.*, 1988; Beach and Mitchell, 1990; Hickson *et al.*, 1986; Shapira, 1994). That is, it is accepted that managers do not always take decisions in solitude. According to Burgelman (1983, 1991), complex organisations have both a planned process in which there is a critical role for senior managers, as well as an evolutionary and iterative process in which other members of the organisation can influence strategy. In this respect, Rotemberg and Saloner (2000) pointed out that at any point in time, senior managers have responsibility for articulating a strategy that is believed to be appropriate given the firm's strategic position and the context it faces. Accordingly, in this construction process, the firms' managers can be considered to be positioned best to express the preferences of their firms. This strategic position enables them to be the hub of information, communication, control and decision-making. Because of this, managers are assumed to be best-informed concerning internal influences and politics, capabilities, resource endowments and the external context in which the organisation operates.

In sum, if we conceptualise the *firm* as an institution that embodies the world views and will of entrepreneurs or businessmen, this vision is embodied in the position of managers and decision makers. They are the trustees of the strategic vision of the firm, that is to say the firm's planned behaviour. Therefore, the unit of analysis to assess the possibility of influencing the resistance or willingness to innovate in firms and at the aggregate level for the industry under study, is the managers of the firms in the sample, as they can provide a vision of what is the planned behaviour of their firm and the context that conditions their strategy. Although the assessment of the managers' perceptions in this book is considered a proxy to infer the planned behaviour of the firm, it is important to emphasise that here we are not interested in the behaviour of the managers but in the behaviour of the firm based on the perceptions of its managers. All the items presented in Appendix E refer to, or ask about, attributes or features related to 'the firm', not the managers.[2] When talking about behaviour or behavioural change, therefore, we refer to the firm.

THE SELECTION OF THE CASE STUDY AND SAMPLE

The research is conducted taking as a case study the determinants of innovative behaviour in clean technologies in the In-Bond industry in the northern region of Mexico, for two reasons. First, as was stated in the introduction to this study, the In-Bond industry is an *ad hoc* sample of those firms with high mobility, seeking the optimal deregulated regions, in search of the perfect flexibility in labour, fiscal and environmental regulations (Icasa, 1993, Sklair, 2000b). These are the common features that many corporations seek when they operate on a global level. It is assumed that by focusing on firms that seek these conditions the results of this study could be useful to other countries or regions with similar contexts. The second reason relates to the knowledge and experience of the author about the region and the industry under study. This experience extends over nine years in activities related to engineering and economics in different areas of manufacturing and in research and development of wastewater treatment systems for industrial applications. This gives access to a network of contacts in industry, regulatory agencies, commissions and academia that facilitated the development of this research.

To test the hypotheses, data were collected through the face-to-face administration of a self-report questionnaire to managers of an inventory of firms generated from listings of the In-Bond Association and The Northern Border College. The selection of companies was limited to those located in the cities of Tijuana, Baja California and Ciudad Juárez, Chihuahua. These Mexican cities were selected because they have the greatest concentration of In-Bond firms on the US–Mexican border. As commented in Chapter 2, the In-Bond industry is very heterogeneous. In order to achieve a higher representativeness, the criteria of industrial sector selection focused on the relative degree of complexity of products and production processes and its relation to the length of its supply chain.

Three sectors were selected: (1) electrical and electronics is assumed here to be the industry with the highest degree of product and production process complexity and the longest supply chain; (2) metal-mechanics was considered to be moderate; and (3) plastics the lowest complexity and shortest supply chain. These sectors were considered to be representative of the complexity of inter-firm trade along the supply chain of those sectors that make up the In-Bond industry. It was believed that the selection of these sectors might provide a sample with a gradient varying from high to low relative difficulty to develop clean technologies (see Figure 5.2). This would give an index that would include other industrial sectors that fall within such a continuum.

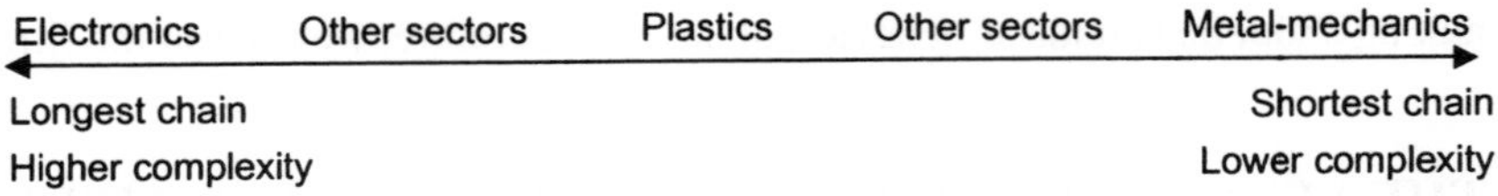

Electronics	Other sectors	Plastics	Other sectors	Metal-mechanics

Longest chain   Shortest chain
Higher complexity   Lower complexity

Figure 5.2   Gradient of supply chain length and inputs composition complexity

DATA COLLECTION PROCEDURE

The application of the questionnaire was done in three stages. The first stage was a test of the particular procedure followed in this book to construct the questionnaire. Ajzen suggests that beliefs should be elicited from a small group of respondents to build up the questionnaire. Afterwards, the questionnaire can be applied to a larger sample of respondents. Instead, in this book the questionnaire was constructed using insights from several bodies of literature. Because of the fact that this book followed a different approach to generate the questionnaire, the first stage of data collection had the goal of comparing the insights offered by the theoretical framework presented in Chapters 3 and 4, and those that could be obtained following the method proposed by Fishbein and Ajzen (1980) to explore the beliefs that might determine the behaviour of interest. An additional goal of this stage was to identify beliefs not found in the literature review and to identify possible bias introduced in the theoretical research. In order to elicit beliefs in accordance with Ajzen's method, salient beliefs were elicited by asking questions regarding the advantages or disadvantages that developing clean technologies could imply; what type of demands from important referents were perceived by the managers; and what type of capabilities and resources their firm would need to develop clean technologies (see Appendix G).

This stage included open-ended interviews with 15 managers known to the author. As commented in Chapter 2, the In-Bond industry has a 'dirty' image due to its past environmental behaviour. Thus, interviewing known managers at this stage was thought to be necessary because of the criticisms that the industry under study had had in the past. It was believed that the exploration of sensitive issues like environmental behaviours would be facilitated in this way. In addition, the elicitation of the managers' beliefs was carried out under strict confidentiality. Although some sensitive information regarding the firms' environmental behaviour was obtained, this was not useful for policy design for the promotion of clean technology development. In addition, the elicited beliefs were mainly those of 'common sense' views of lay people. Such salient beliefs coincided with the beliefs considered *a priori* to be assessed as 'direct measures' within each domain (see Section V in Appendix E).

Although at this stage it was not possible to be statistically conclusive, nor measure the determinants of willingness of the firm to engage in the development of clean technologies, in general, comments about the perception of moderate to low environmental risk perception, high economic risk, the lack of social pressure and minimal capabilities to re-orient technological change coincided with the analysis presented in Chapter 6 were elicited, but no additional information about the underpinnings of such perceptions was obtained.

The theoretical exploration of the behavioural domains and possible beliefs that might determine the behaviour of interest in this study proved to be more fruitful than using solely the method proposed by Fishbein and Ajzen (1980). At this stage, no further statistical analysis was possible due to the small number of respondents and because no quantitative data had been collected. Using the results of this exploratory stage to contrast both approaches, the application of the questionnaire developed *a priori* turned out to be more appropriate.

The second stage was carried out using a larger number of interviewees including the control group interviewed in the first stage. The chief executive officers or highest rank executives in 49 manufacturing firms were contacted by a telephone call that was followed up by personalised letters. The contact was made in batches of ten and only after the batch was completed was the next batch started upon. Each respondent was introduced to the concept of clean technologies as a contrast to pollution control. First, the cycle of pollutants related to end-of-pipe technologies was explained to contrast it with the idea of pollution prevention (see Chapter 2). Second, the notions of product life-cycle analysis and the links between suppliers and customers along the supply chain were discussed using the depiction in Figure 5.3 below.

This presentation aimed to introduce the idea of value cycles and value recovery presented in Chapter 2 to the managers that were interviewed. This had the goal of creating awareness of the firm's implicit dependence on the supply chain and the challenges that this might pose for the development of clean technologies. This stage generated a total of 64 usable questionnaires.

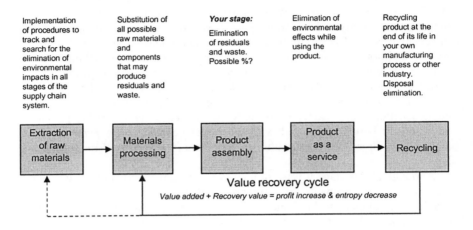

| Implementation of procedures to track and search for the elimination of environmental impacts in all stages of the supply chain system. | Substitution of all possible raw materials and components that may produce residuals and waste. | *Your stage:* Elimination of residuals and waste. Possible %? | Elimination of environmental effects while using the product. | Recycling product at the end of its life in your own manufacturing process or other industry. Disposal elimination. |

Figure 5.3 Product life-cycle chain management
Note: Figure 5.3 is a simplified version of Figure 2.3 presented in Chapter 2

The third stage included contracting and training an interviewer. This stage aimed at testing the reliability of the questionnaire when not applied by the author.[3] Personalised letters were faxed to the chief executive officers or highest ranking executives of 90 manufacturing firms. The letters were faxed in batches of ten and, as in the previous stage, only after a batch was completed was another batch started. This stage had a lower rate of success and yielded 32 usable questionnaires. In total, 97 interviews were included in the analysis and the testing of the system of hypotheses proposed in Chapter 4.

The overall response rate of 61% can be considered very good for this type of research in the particular industry and region selected. As commented before, during the last decade, the In-Bond industry has been highly criticised for its environmental behaviour. As a consequence, the willingness to participate in environmental studies is limited. The relative success of this study is explained by the approach adopted. No questions were included regarding their current environmental behaviour. In addition, the idea that their participation could help to design schemes of collaboration between environmental authorities, research institutions and firms was strongly emphasised. This opened the doors of some firms that traditionally had not been willing to participate in previous studies concerning environmental issues.

STRUCTURE AND CONTENT OF QUESTIONNAIRE

The development of the structure and content of the questionnaire used to assess the determinants of the willingness to innovate in clean technologies was based on two theories. The first, the theory of planned behaviour, guided the theoretical construction of Chapters 3 and 4 upon which the content of the questionnaire is based. The second, the facet theory, helped to develop the structure of the questionnaire based on the principle of contiguity (Shye *et al.*, 1994; Borg, 1994; Borg and Shye, 1995). It proposes that the more similar the items in their conceptual definition, the more related they will be empirically. This principle offers a link between conceptual and empirical structures. It predicts that variables that are similar in their semantic structure will also be related empirically (see Figure 5.4 below). By using this principle, it was possible to predict that the relationship between any given items v and x composed by the generic words $a_1a_2a_3b_4b_5$ and $a_1a_2b_3b_4b_5$ respectively, will be higher than the relationship between the items t and z composed by the generic words $a_1a_2a_3a_4a_5$ and $b_1b_2b_3b_4b_5$. Figure 5.4 shows the expected correlation among a set of items in which their semantic similarity varies from high to low.

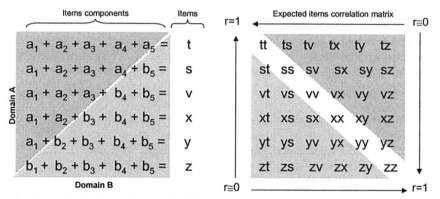

Rule for wording: The bigger the semantic similitude between two items the higher their correlation in the structure of the matrix of correlations can be expected.

Figure 5.4 Co-linearity management for the construction of items
Based on: Borg (1995) and Shye *et al.* (1994).

The above principle helped in the design of a structured questionnaire on the premise that the theoretical constructs that comprise the questionnaire should be linked semantically to the main variable that they intended to predict. The structure of the questionnaire has the following sequence (see Appendix E). First, it asked for general data about the firm and the respondent (Section I). Second, it asked about the characteristics of the firm in terms of the framework of the stage of evolution of industry proposed by Utterback (1994) (Section II). Third, it presented direct measures of intention and willingness, attitude, perceived social pressure and perceived control (Sections III and IV). Fourth, it introduced direct measures of economic and environmental risk perception, the perceived social pressure arising from the market, community and regulatory agencies, and the perceived technological capabilities (Section V). Finally nine scales intending to measure the beliefs in each of the behavioural domains are presented (Section VI). Each of the items presented in the questionnaire links semantically to the next explanatory level. That is, items at the belief level are linked semantically to the questions at the domain level. Items at the domain level link semantically to attitude, social pressure or perceived behavioural control. Lastly, items of attitude, social pressure or perceived behavioural control are linked semantically to willingness.

RATING BY USING DIFFERENTIAL SEMANTICS

The basic operation measuring the constructs presented in Chapter 4 is based upon the assignment of numbers to concepts in a differential semantic scale. These types of scales were devised as a mean to assess the connotative meaning of a concept for any given group of subjects. This connotative meaning comprehends all of its suggestive or implicit significance by association with other concepts. The differential semantic is constructed by making a statement regarding the concept to be ranked coupled with a seven-point scale linking to opposed adjective pairs (Carlsmith *et al.*, 1976).[4] For example:

> In general, the social pressure (e.g., from the community, the marketplace, government agencies and public institutions, etc.) perceived by this company to develop clean products and adopt clean production processes is:

low	1	2	3	4	5	6	7	high
	extremely	quite	slightly	uncertain	slightly	quite	extremely	

In the item above, the concept to be assessed is the perceived social pressure and the differential semantic varies from extremely low to extremely high in an interval (1, 7). According to Carlsmith *et al.*, (1976) the connotative meaning of most concepts can be accounted for by three underlying dimensions: evaluation, potency and activity. It is along these ranges that the differential semantics used in this work were designed (see Sections I to V in Appendix E, for more examples of the application of the differential semantic).

THE NUMBER OF ITEMS INCLUDED IN THE QUESTIONNAIRE

Regarding the number of items that make up the questionnaire, in this study it is accepted that people's capacity for information processing in decision problems is limited. It is taken for granted that no manager could take into account at any given moment all the beliefs included in the questionnaire. This is in agreement with the TPB framework. Ajzen (1991) argues that most people take decisions in specific situations based on a range of seven to fifteen beliefs. As is implicitly stated in the system of hypotheses proposed in Chapter 4, it is expected that willingness and ultimately behaviour in firms will be affected by few beliefs. Specifically, these perceptions refer to the nine direct measures that intend to capture the connotative load in each domain, that is, nine beliefs (see Appendix E, Section V).

SALIENT LIMITATIONS OF THE APPROACH

The limitations of the study are related to its implications for policy recommendations; these limitations arise from three aspects. The first arises from the implicit assumption that negotiation is possible. That is, that for the sake of a *common interest,* parties in conflict are pushed to negotiate and reach conciliation towards a common goal. This implies that the members of society in the long term will be able to learn to understand, respect and collaborate with each other towards the preservation of our environment.

The second is related to the isolation of the firms analysed from the whole context of the politics of the environment. The political process of environmental regulation involves firms, regulatory agencies, NGOs, other economic sectors, and other government agencies. Often the goals of environmental regulatory agencies are in contradiction to other government agencies that normally hold more power to pursue their goals. In addition, countries or regions interact with each other.

The interaction among regions takes the form of transnational competition to deploy regulatory paradigms that promote the expansion of environmental technologies (PCSD, 1999, Ch. 1), although in the literature of environmental policy it is recognised that the actors that directly determine the approaches and solutions to environmental problems are the regulators and firms (Levèque, 1996). The variables relevant to this work are related only to the determinants of decision making in three industrial sectors, the rest are ignored.

The third limitation arises from the methodological approach adopted. This is related to the inferences that can be reasonably made about relations among constructs when all the variables are assessed with self-reports. In the case of a self-report questionnaire, the scores are people's connotative ratings associated with the variables of interest. The application of the TPB framework assumes that people behave having first motivations and cognition, then having goals or intentions and then afterwards a behaviour. For predictive purposes, this assumption has the problem that intentions can change over time; the longer the time interval, the greater the likelihood that unforeseen events will produce changes in intentions. It follows that accuracy of prediction will usually be an inverse function of the time interval between the measurement of intention and observation of behaviour. There may be another source of error if the respondent has little information about the behaviour, when requirements or available resources have changed, or when new and unfamiliar elements have entered into the situation.

Finally, a major objection in studies based on self-reports is related to the cross-sectional design where all data are collected at one point in time. Even though the causality of the variables included in the Ajzen model is widely empirically proven, it has never been used to analyse firms' behaviour. In this case, a longitudinal design would allow for more reliable conclusions about causal relationships, which are difficult in cross-sectional designs, regardless of the measurement method used (Spector, 1994). The statistical analysis carried out in the Appendix C tests the reliability and degree of association between these variables. In the following chapter, Chapter 6, a description of the specific determinants of the innovative behaviour will be presented.

NOTES

1. For example, $A = A(EVR, ER)$ was in turn $EVR=EVR(\Sigma evr_b)$ and $ER=ER(\Sigma er_b)$. The sum indicates that the connotative meaning of items accumulates to give shape to the environmental and economic risk perception. In turn this forms an attitude. The form of the function is not considered to be a simple sum; its mathematical form is to be determined empirically. This last point, here, is considered beyond the scope of this study.
2. The exceptions to this rule are six items in the behavioural domain of environmental risk perception.
3. A presentation and discussion of the differences found on the scales reliability for the stages 2 and 3 of the survey is given in Appendix A.
4. The decision to use a five, seven or nine bipolar scale appears to be arbitrary in the literature of psychometric research. The only criterion is given by the degree of discrimination desired among respondents.

6. Mapping the drivers of the firm's willingness to innovate in clean technologies

In this chapter, the descriptive statistics are presented in order to characterise the sample of firms under study. It provides the first insights into the macro conditions – as described in Chapter 2 – and into the managers' beliefs systems that determine the willingness of the firm to engage in innovative activities towards clean production. The following sections present first the descriptive statistics that characterise the firms in the sample, and second the distribution of responses in each behavioural domain. The description of the distribution of responses starts with the scores of the willingness to innovate, then proceeds to the perceptions in the domains of attitude, perceived social pressure and perceived control. Subsequently, a scenario of the firms' current and long-term environmental planned behaviour is used to respond to two of the main questions of this work.

STAGE OF INDUSTRIAL EVOLUTION OF THE IN-BOND INDUSTRY

This section characterises the In-Bond industry according to the framework that refers to the stage of evolution of products and processes discussed in Chapter 2. This characterisation aims at providing an image of the point of departure to move towards a clean production system for those firms in the sample. Following the framework proposed by Utterback (1994), those manufacturing firms operating on the transitional or rigid stages of the co-evolution cycle of product and process would find it more difficult to move to a new technological regime.

The analysis of the data collected confirms the main traits, discussed in Chapter 2, that characterise this industry as operating with foreign capital, with its production oriented towards exports to the US market. Their capital was found to mainly originate from the USA (88.7%), the remaining 11.3% was reported to be from Europe and Asia. Almost all of the firms (96.9%) export more than 75% of their production, and 94.9% reported exporting their product to the US market (see Appendix D, Figures D2, D3, D4). The sample was composed mainly of medium (56.7%) and small sized firms

(30.9%), with only 12.4% of large firms (see Appendix D, Figure D15). About half of the firms (48.5%) were from the electronics sector, 36.1% from the plastics sector and 15.5% from the metal-mechanics sector (Figure D1). As discussed in Chapter 5 it was expected that more firms with a high willingness to develop clean technology would be found in the metal mechanics sector, as they present the simpler product and production processes and the shortest supply chain. No significant relationship was found between the industrial sector with the willingness to develop clean technologies (W) or with the perceived control upon the innovation process (PC).

Regarding the firms' *main sources of product and process innovations,* 47% reported being dependent mainly on their suppliers of components and materials, 29% on the transfer or licensing of new technologies and 23% on their own R&D laboratories (Appendix D, Figures D5, D6). Concerning their *product maturity*, 43% indicated their products to be mostly undifferentiated and standardised, 31% reported having at least one product design that is stable enough to have significant production volume, and 25% perceived them as diverse in designs and often customised (Figure D7). Similarly, with respect to *process maturity,* 53% reported their process to be efficient, capital intensive, and rigid; 31% indicated their process becoming more rigid, with changes occurring in major stages of the production line; and 15% found their process flexible and inefficient, where major changes could with reasonable ease be accommodated (Appendix D, Figure D8).

Concerning *R&D activities,* 59% indicated these to be focused on incremental changes in product technology with emphasis on improving process technology, 37% reported a focus primarily on specific product or process features, and 4% reported to have an undefined focus due to a high degree of technical uncertainty (Figure D9). The *type of machinery and equipment* mainly described by 47% was special purpose, mostly automatic with labour focused on tending and monitoring equipment; 35% depicted having some islands of automation, and 18% characterised it as mainly composed of general purpose equipment, requiring skilled labour (Figure D10). The *cost of technical change* was considered to be high by 75% of the respondents, while 22.5% believed it to be moderate and 2% perceived it to be low (Figure D11).

With respect to the *number of competitors,* 41% of the respondents indicated that a few companies dominated the market, 34% reported that the number of competitors was declining and 24% reported having few competitors but that these were growing in number (Figure D12). The *competition strategy* was reported to be based on price and quality by the majority of respondents (63%), 25% indicated competition based on product differentiation, and 11% on product performance (Figure D13). The last feature of interest regarded the firms' *organisational control.* Those firms with more informal and entrepreneurial organisational relationships are reported in the literature of innovation to be more innovative. Just under 60%

of the firms reported being in the rigid stage, that is, their labour relationships were described as based on structures, hierarchies and procedures; 21% reported operating in team project structures and 19% indicated their organisation as being informal and entrepreneurial (Figure D14).

In sum, the data collected regarding the stage of evolution of the industry shows a frequency of responses that would locate those firms in the sample operating predominately within the 'rigid' stage of evolution of product and process. By analysing the set of figures presented in Appendix D, it can be said that, approximately 55% of the firms presented some of the traits of the 'rigid' stage of evolution of industry, 29% reported having features of the 'transition' stage, and 16% of the 'fluid' stage. Based on the characteristics of this industry discussed in Chapter 2, it was expected that a larger number of firms would be found to operate within the rigid stage. However, although many managers indicated their firms as having primarily features of the rigid stage, they still reported some features of the transitional and fluid stages.

Despite this lack of discrimination among respondents, it can be clearly seen that the majority of the firms in the sample present features in their product and production processes suggesting that they will find it difficult – due to the nature of their evolution stage – to make radical changes in product and process towards clean technologies. Although it was expected to find significant relationships between the attributes that define the 'fluid', 'transition' and 'rigid' stages of evolving products and processes with the willingness of the firm to develop clean technologies, apart from the attribute 'size' of the firm, no significant relationships were found between any of the attributes and willingness.

Most aspects of the stage of evolution of the firms' technological profile have no significant relationship with the willingness to innovate. This may be explained by the fact that the categories used to assess the stage of evolution refer to structural features that may condition the pace of technical change. These features constitute a state in time that results from a particular technology strategy of the firm and therefore these features cannot be expected to explain the strategy of the firm. The attributes that may condition the technology strategy regarding clean technology development are discussed in the following sections.

Stage Industrial Evolution: Sectoral Differences

This section looks at the relation of the stage of industrial evolution industry with the willingness of the firm to engage on innovative activities in clean technologies. As commented in Chapter 2, the In-Bond industry is very heterogeneous. In order to achieve a highly representative sample of firms, the criteria for the selection of the industrial sector focused on the relative degree of complexity of inputs, products and production processes and its relation to the length of the supply chain. Three sectors were included in the survey: (1) the electrical and electronics sector is assumed here to be the industry with the highest degree of product and production process complexity and with the longest supply chain; (2) plastics was considered to be of moderate complexity; and (3) metal-mechanics the sector of lowest complexity and the shortest supply chain. The selection of these three sectors was considered to provide the extremes of a gradient varying from high to low relative difficulty to develop clean technologies (see Figure 5.2). In addition, following the framework proposed by Utterback (1994), it was expected that those manufacturing firms operating in the transitional or rigid stages of the co-evolution cycle of product and process would find it more difficult to move to a new and cleaner technological regime.

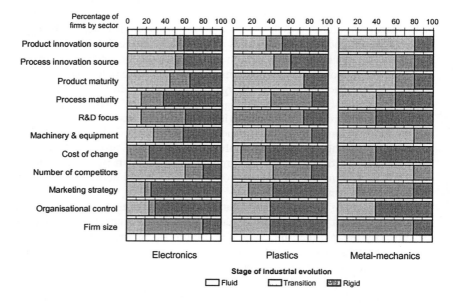

Figure 6.1 Stage of industrial evolution by sector

Figure 6.1 shows the frequency of responses per stage on the features that define the stage of industrial evolution of a specific industrial sector. At first glance, the most flexible industrial sector – although not by much – appears to be composed of firms grouped in the metal-mechanics sector. The source of innovations in product and processes is predominantly their own R&D capacity and they have moderate to high flexibility in their machinery and equipment. They are less dependent on suppliers of materials and components than firms grouped in the plastics and electronics sectors. In addition, metal-mechanics firms face a larger number of competitors and operate with relatively less rigid structures of organisational control. These aspects contrast with the relatively high rigidity concerning the focus of their innovation activities, since metal-mechanic firms reported they focused predominantly on incremental innovation. Some firms in the electronics sector reported that their innovative activities include radical changes in their designs. The three sectors seem to share the feature of large costs of radical technical change.

In general, the data summarised in Figure 6.1 support the notion that firms with a long supply chain will be likely to be more rigid, thus perhaps finding it more difficult to engage in radical innovation towards clean production. In relation to this point – as discussed in Chapter 5 – it was expected that firms in the fluid stage of evolution of industry would be more willing and find it easier to develop clean technologies. An example of this stage was the metal-mechanics sector included in this study, with its relatively simple materials composition, product and production processes and a short supply chain. Contrary to expectations the results displayed in Figure 6.2 do not support this assumption.

Figure 6.2 shows an inter-sectoral comparison of the sample mean on the different behavioural domains and willingness. On average, the three sectors surveyed reported they were unwilling to innovate in clean production. The figure shows remarkably similar patterns with regard to the managers' perception of the internal and external contexts of their firms. The similarity of perceived environmental and economic risks, perceived market, community and regulatory pressures and the perceived technological and organisational capabilities to carry out innovation does not reflect the stages of industrial evolution of the sample of firms.

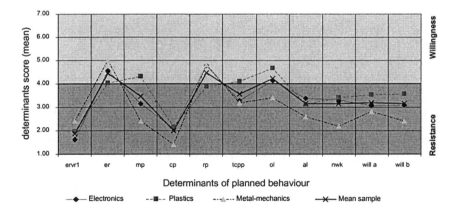

Figure 6.2   Inter-sector comparison of firms' environmental planned behaviour

Contrary to what could be expected, this comparison by sector suggests that, on average, the firms in the sample face similar realities concerning clean technology development. Despite the minimal disparities in the scores achieved for the different behavioural domains and on the willingness to innovate, it can be argued that the most flexible sector is the least willing to engage in innovation towards clean production and also reported the lowest organisational and technological capabilities, thus finding it more difficult to change. Similarly, contrary to the initial assumption, firms grouped in the electronics sector are less willing to innovate than those grouped in the plastics sector.

The apparent disparities between the stages of industrial evolution of the sectors in the sample and the behaviour of the variables of willingness, perceived economic and environmental risks, perceived market, community and market pressures and technological and organisational capabilities can be explained by the lack of significant relationships between the attributes that define the 'fluid', 'transition' and 'rigid' stages with the willingness and the other variables shown in Figure 6.2. Apart from the attribute 'size of the firm', no significant relationships were found between any of the attributes of the stage of evolution of the firms' technological profile described above and the willingness of the firm to innovate in cleaner production. This may be explained by the fact that the categories used to assess the stage of evolution refer to structural features that may condition the pace of technical change. It can be argued that these features constitute a state in time that results from a particular technology strategy and therefore they cannot explain what motivates the strategy of the firm. The attributes that might condition the technology strategy regarding clean technology development are discussed in the following sections.

WILLINGNESS TO INNOVATE IN CLEAN TECHNOLOGIES

For the description of the frequencies and rating of responses in the different behavioural domains summary stacked percentile bar plots are used (Figure 6.3). The scale on the left side of the figure represents the percentile of response frequency per rank in the interval 1 to 7, ranging from low to high. The stacked bars on the extreme right plot the results for the direct measures of perception in each domain. The white diamond denotes the mean value achieved in the sample. The frequency of response in each rank is colour coded with the darkest indicating the strongest sources of resistance to innovate. The lightest tone suggests optimal conditions for the development of clean technologies. Due to the large number of beliefs considered in the questionnaire, the purpose of the figures is to present the distribution and the trend of the responses in a particular domain in a single picture, albeit relevant results are highlighted. The mechanics of reporting the findings for each domain are exemplified in the following section.

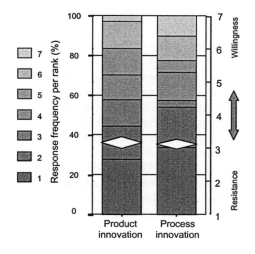

Figure 6.3   Willingness to develop clean technologies

Figure 6.3 shows the firms' willingness to innovate towards clean products and production processes. For this and all subsequent domains, the scores attained and the frequency of responses will be presented as follows. The differential semantic scale used in each question in the questionnaire has two opposing extreme adjectives (e.g., easy–difficult, likely–unlikely, high–low, agree–disagree, etc.). The score in the differential has seven points (i.e., (1, 7)). It can be argued that although the negative extreme has a connotation related to the non-optimum preconditions that induce behavioural change, the positive extreme can be considered as the optimum only if the responses are located at the higher scores (i.e., extremely high (7) or very high (6)). In this sense, Figure 6.3 shows that almost 60% of the sample reported no intention to develop clean technologies, while 27% reported that they are willing to develop clean technologies. The average willingness in the sample was found to be negative (–1) for both product and production process (see white diamonds in Figure 6.3).

With regard to the willingness of their firm to innovate, 13% of respondents reported being uncertain.[1] The above result indicates that up to 80% of the firms in the sample could be said to be unwilling to innovate. In the following sections the preconditions that determine this resistance to develop clean technologies will be presented. In order to simplify the presentation and comparison of the percentages for optimal and non-optimal responses, no mention is made of the percentage of managers that reported being uncertain.

ATTITUDINAL PERCEPTIONS

Environmental Risk Perception

Figure 6.4 presents the plot for environmental risk perception. As predicted in Chapter 4, there is an inverse relationship between the perception and the acceptance of risk. Low scores in perception correspond to high scores in the acceptance of the generation of hazards by the technology currently in use. On the one hand, the results show that the frequency of response per rank, and the average score of managers' perceptions of risk generated by the firms in the sample, is extremely low (*1EVR*, see white diamond in the extreme right). On the other hand, the concentration of responses for risk acceptance shows that all the conditions that predispose someone to accept the generation of hazards are present in most of those managers that participated in the study (see Figure 4.2).

The plot representing the scale developed by Slovic *et al.*, (1984) indicates that on average 80% of the respondents considered the environmental risk generated by the firms' operations to be within the 'safe' zone as described in Chapter 4. The remaining 20% considered the generated hazards to be moderate, that is, outside but close to the 'safe' zone. The generated risk is considered to be highly controllable, not representing a risk to future generations and not affecting the managers themselves; and the economic benefits and environmental costs are considered to be evenly distributed among the population. The risk is also believed to have no global implications or fatal consequences, exposure is believed to be voluntary and known to those exposed to it and with delayed effects for human and environmental health. Furthermore, the generated hazards were considered to be 'old' and known to science.

The above perceptions could be conditioned or reinforced by the managers' acceptance of risk. Chapter 4 argued that the acceptance of risk is mainly contingent on the voluntariness to exposure, controllability of effects, and its perceived rate of discount in time and space. The creation of hazards in general was considered to be somehow involuntary. Three-quarters (vs. 25%) of the managers reported that their firms operated with – or close to – state-of-the-art technology in their industry (*ac1*) while 77% (vs. 23%) considered residuals inherent to all manufacturing activities (*ac2*). This could be considered to be a lack of clean technological options to prevent the generation of residuals. In contrast, almost 85% (vs. 15%) believed they had a high degree of influence and freedom to choose for or against the creation of hazards (*ac3, ac5*) with the current technological options. In addition, 78% (vs. 22%) of the respondents considered that the benefits generated by their firms' operations outweighed any possible impacts on the environment (*ac4*).

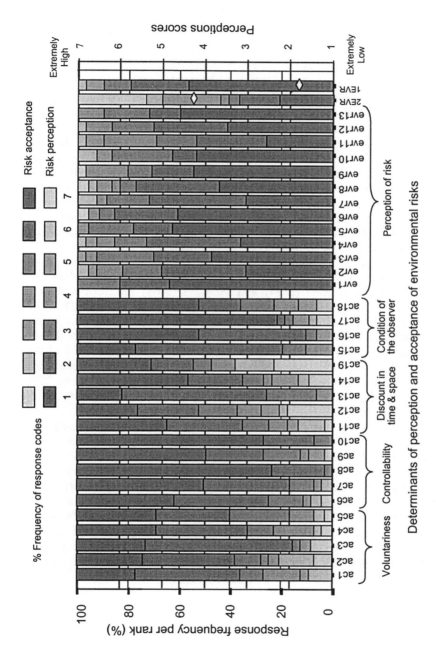

Figure 6.4 Environmental risk perception

The *controllability* of residuals and pollution effects was reported to be high. The majority (92% vs. 8%) of the managers considered that their firms had the appropriate skills, equipment and written procedures to avoid environmental accidents (*ac6*). Likewise, 94% (vs. 6%) considered the probability of accidents to be low (*ac7*), 100% believed pollution effects to be reversible (*ac8*) and 88% (vs. 12%) thought that, in the case of an accident the pollution was extremely likely to be controlled by rescue operations (*ac9*). The whole sample (100%) considered the effects on the environment and human health of recognised pollutants to be controllable (*ac10*).

The *discount in time* of economic benefits and environmental costs were found to have an inverse relationship. Three-quarters (75% vs. 18%) of the respondents considered that the success of the firm lay in profits being obtained in the shortest possible time (*ac11*), and agreed that there were no immediate environmental consequences from the operation of their firms. Environmental effects were considered to be cumulative over the long term by 44% (vs. 29%) of the managers (*ac12*). The *discount in space,* that is, the social distance of the economic benefits, was found to be close to the managers and its effects were perceived as socially distant from them. Almost three-quarters (74% vs. 26%) reported to be well-informed about how the firm's profits were used (*ac14*) and 90% (vs. 10%) indicated that they considered that they benefited greatly from the firm's operations (*ac15*). The majority (85% vs. 15%) did not think they were being affected (*ac17*) and 88% (vs. 12%) believed they were unlikely to be affected in the future (*ac18*) as a result of environmental accidents or pollution. In addition, 50% of the respondents reported that the benefits that their business operations generated for themselves outweighed the possible impacts on the environment, 25% reported moderate disagreement with this idea and the remaining 25% disagreed strongly (*ac19*).

In summary, the lack of clean technological options, the managers' participation and influence in the firms' decision-making process, the personal benefits obtained, the illusion of high controllability of effects, and the characteristics of the discount in time and space of economic benefits and undesirable effects in conjunction with the perception of the operations of the firm as 'safe', produced a very small risk accumulated connotative load in the whole sample (see the extreme right of Figure 6.4).[2] More than 85% of the managers in the sample considered that their firm operated in an environmentally safe manner and more than 90% indicated a high degree of acceptance of the possible hazards generated by the operations of their firms.

Economic Risk Perception

Based on the importance that the literature on innovation studies gives to economic risk and uncertainty, and the very many technological challenges that the development of clean technologies pose, it was expected that a generalised perception of high economic risk would be found. The findings present a somewhat more heterogeneous scenario. Figure 6.5 displays the response frequencies per rank for the beliefs of possible economic risk faced when planning the development of clean technologies. As in the figure of environmental risk perception, the lightest tone represents the optimal and the darkest the poorest conditions for the development of clean technologies.

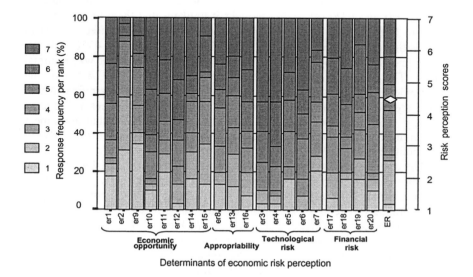

Determinants of economic risk perception

Figure 6.5 Economic risk perception

Concerning the *economic opportunities* arising from the development of clean technologies, the failure to launch a clean product for a new market niche did not represent an economic opportunity for 75% (vs. 25% with the opposite perception) of the firms (*er1*). This belief is linked with the fact that 70% (vs. 25%) of managers considered a clean product to be 'ahead of its time' (*er10*); 65% expected minimal customer willingness to pay more for a cleaner product (*er12*); and 55% (vs. 38%) reported that, with regard to the development of clean technologies, their company preferred to be a follower rather than a pioneer (*er11*). Although most managers preferred the role of follower, 55% (vs. 25%) recognised the advantages of pioneering in terms of the expected benefits arising from the novelty of products and distribution effects (*er9*); similarly, 58% (vs. 30%) acknowledged the opportunity to sustain growth for those firms that ventured into the development of clean technologies (*er15, er14*). Most managers (76% vs. 16%) foresaw great benefit in avoiding environmental regulation risks.

The perceived possibilities to *appropriate the benefits* of developing novel clean products and processes were considered to be minimal by 48% (vs.

32%) of the respondents (*er8*), coupled with 60% (vs. 32%) who believed that if they cooperated by means of strategic alliances (*er16*) and the 40% (vs. 42%) believed that to subcontract the outsourcing of knowledge in LCA practices (*er13*) would result in the loss of their technology secrecy.

The *technological risk* was perceived to be substantial by most managers: 75% (vs. 9%) believed the amount of R&D required was likely to be great (*er3*), 78% (vs. 9%) considered the cost associated with this R&D would be great (*er4*) and 62% (vs. 22%) thought it unlikely that their firm would be able to bear it (*er5*), 65% (vs. 17%) reported that the duration of a clean innovation project is likely to be prolonged (*er6*), and 43% (vs. 47%) held the view that the likelihood of achieving a clean product concept was minimal (*er7*). The *financial risk* was seen to be great by 50% (vs. 41%) of the respondents, and 55% (vs. 38%) believed it unlikely that their firm would have the necessary financial, human and intellectual resources to develop 'timely' clean technologies (*er19*), 54% (vs. 19%) considered that investment in environmental innovative activities would affect the firm's overall competitiveness (*er20*).

The above frequency of responses distribution is captured by the direct measure index of economic risk perception. The average firm perceived the economic risk to be negative ($m = -1$). Although the development of clean technologies was reported to be of relevance to protecting the environment for 56% (vs. 38%) of the respondents (*2EVR*, Figure 6.4, p. 131), 60% (vs. 35%) believed that it would have adverse consequences for the wellbeing of their firm (*ER*). In agreement with the review of the literature on decision making under risk discussed in Chapter 4, it is clear that individuals prefer to take risks when the potential outcomes are likely to be beneficial financially. This indicates a negative predisposition or attitude towards the development of clean technology in the average firm. The relative heterogeneity of the scores in respect to the perceived environmental risk can be attributed to the differences between the three sectors surveyed (i.e., plastics, metal-mechanics and electronics), and as it is shown in Appendix A, to the moderating negative relationship of economic risk with the perception of technological and organisational capabilities.

Summary

The distribution of responses within the domain of environmental risk perception indicated a predominant very low risk perception with a very high acceptance on the part of managers of the possible hazards generated by the firms' operations. For economic risk, the perceptions were more heterogeneous. On average, the managers reported the risk to be negatively moderate. The combination of a very low environmental risk and moderate economic risk suggest a negative predisposition or attitude towards the development of clean technologies.

THE PERCEIVED SOCIAL PRESSURE

Perceived Market Pressure

The scenario presented in Figure 6.6 shows that, on average, the firms in the sample perceived market pressure to develop clean technologies to be very low (see white diamond on *MP* stacked bar). Up to 60% of the managers reported pressure as low, 20% perceived moderate pressure and 20% reported not to be troubled by any market pressures. As proposed in Chapter 4 the sources of market pressures are classified into four sub-scales. These were the perceived pressures from the competitive environment, customers, and, as a consequence of their perception of the above, the necessity of being a pioneer or a follower of clean technologies development.

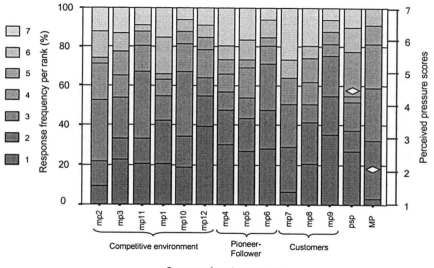

Figure 6.6   Perceived market pressure

More than half (53% vs. 28%) of the managers believed that their *competitors* were not considering the development of clean technologies and 55% (vs. 35%) considered it unlikely that their competitors would be pushing them to develop clean products and adopt clean production processes. These beliefs are coupled with the perception of 68% (vs. 20%) of the managers who did not consider a clean product a good marketing option in the face of intense competition and limited market opportunities.

The pressure from customers was perceived to be low by 52% (vs. 39%) of the managers (*mp8*), because 50% (vs. 35%) of them believed that their customers did not think that they should develop clean technologies (*mp7*). Coupled with these beliefs, and contradicting the general wisdom in the literature on environmental policy and the greening of industry, the motivation to comply with customer expectations was very low. Up to 75% (vs. 20%) of managers reported that their firms, generally speaking, do not do what their customers think they should do regarding environmental issues (*mp9*).

Moreover, 67% (vs. 19%) considered it unlikely that the rate of change in their industry regarding customers' and competitors' behaviour, as well as technological conditions of the industry, would lead them to develop clean technologies in order to pre-empt rival entries (*mp10*). This belief is reinforced by the 55% (vs. 37%) that perceived a moderate technological pace within the sector would not push them to innovate in clean technology. In addition, 64% (vs. 22%) believed the heterogeneity of their markets to be low. According to Zahra (1996), those firms facing heterogeneous markets innovate more often.

With regard to being a *pioneer or a follower* in technological innovation, 58% (vs. 35%) of the respondents reported to be followers in product technology (*mp4*) and 56% (vs. 30%) in process technologies (*mp5*). As a consequence, 72% (vs. 20%) indicated a preference to quickly adopt advances in technology in their industry and that adopting clean technologies would not be an exception (*mp6*). In sum, the reported perceived market pressure regarding the perceived market signals from the competitive environment, and the consumers appears, for the average firm, to be predominantly very low.

Perceived Community Pressure

The perceived community pressure to develop clean technologies arising from the managers' personal important referents, the firms' internal and external referents and the local community for the average firm was found to be quite low (mean = −1.7; see the white diamond on *CP* stacked bar in Figure 6.7). Up to 87% of the managers indicated a perception of low community pressure, 5% reported slight pressure and 8% perceived no pressure. As explained in Chapter 3, the subjective norm or social norm refers to the beliefs held by people about what they think that their important referents think about them in terms of developing, or not developing, clean technologies. In this domain the managers' personal moral norm was included. This refers to whether they personally think that their firm should or should not innovate in cleaner products and processes. In this regard, up to 80% (vs. 18%) of respondents indicated disagreement with the notion that their company should develop clean technologies (*cp1*). In addition, 68% (vs. 25%) reported that they did not perceive any social norm from their personal important referents motivating them to promote the development of clean technologies in their firm (*cp2*).

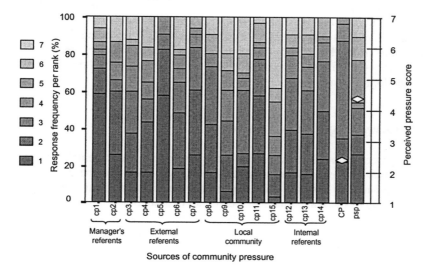

Figure 6.7   Perceived community pressure

Concerning the perceived pressure from the firm's *external referents*: 60% (vs. 27%) indicated that they had no pressure from important outsiders (*cp3*), and 57% (vs. 37%) did not expect pressure from them in the next five years (*cp4*); 90% of the managers disagree with the environmental experts who advocate that it is time for industry to develop clean technologies (*cp5*). Up to 64% (vs. 28%) of managers recorded that their environmental consultants were not suggesting innovative behaviour in clean technologies (*cp6*), and 85% (vs. 10%) disagreed with the idea of following recommendations from environmental consultants in such a direction (*cp7*).

Moreover, 68% (vs. 20%) of managers believed that the *internal referents* of the company, such as the staff, who think it is important for the success of the business are not thinking that their firm should innovate in clean technology (*cp12*), 63% (vs. 25%) believed that it is unlikely that their staff would be promoting or pushing for CT (*cp13*). In addition, the influence of internal staff appeared to be limited as 78% (vs. 16%) of the respondents reported disregarding the suggestions of their staff in relation to environmental issues (*cp14*).

Finally, the *local community* seemed to have the potential for influencing firm behaviour since 73% (vs. 20%) of the respondents responded that the local community was expecting their firm to develop cleaner options (*cp8*). Although 60% (vs. 34%) believed that currently the local community was not a serious lobby (*cp10*), 78% (vs. 16%) expected them to be pushing for the development of clean technology within five years (*cp11*). In this regard, 40% (vs. 45%) of the managers reported the motivation to comply with the community demand (*cp9*), and 27% (vs. 62%) of the respondents admitted feeling little pressure from NGOs (*cp15*). In sum, the accumulated connotative load captured in the direct measure (*CP*) regarding the perceived demand from the important community referents indicates that, on the average, the firms' perceived community pressure to develop clean technologies is very low.

Perceived Regulatory Pressure

The perceived regulatory pressure arising from environmental regulators, ISO14000 and environmental international agreement for the average firm was shown to be low (see white diamond in the *RP* stacked bar in Figure 6.8). Only 18% of the respondents perceived an extremely low pressure, while on the opposite side the same percentage indicated extremely high regulatory pressure, 18% reported quite low pressure, 37% slight pressure, 6% between slight and quite high pressure and 15% reported to perceive no regulatory pressure.

The expected pressure from *international agreements*, like the US–Mexican Border Environmental Cooperation Commission (BECC) and NAFTA, on average, was limited. Up to 60% (vs. 16%) of respondents thought that it is unlikely that BECC will be pushing them to develop clean products and adopt clean production processes within the next five years (*rp7*). Likewise, 70% (vs. 22%) believed that it is unlikely that NAFTA will push them to innovate in clean technologies (*rp8*). In addition, the motivation to comply with the prescriptions of environmental policies from these international agreements was found to be low for 73% (vs. 16%) of the respondents (*rp9*). The perceived pressure to innovate in clean technologies arising from the importance given in the market to the *standard ISO14000* was reported low for 64% of respondents (vs.19%) (*rp6*) and 58% (vs. 14%) believed it unlikely that the preference for such standardisation (ISO) would be pushing their firm to innovate in clean technologies within the next five years (*rp5*).

The *environmental agencies* were perceived as not thinking about the development of cleaner technological options by 50% (vs. 40%) of respondents (*rp1*). In addition, 72% (vs. 23%) believe that the authorities will not be pushing for clean technology within the next five years (*rp2*) and 60% (vs. 33%) thought that the environmental authorities did not have the enforcement capabilities to push for the development of clean technologies (*rp3*). Regarding the motivation to comply with environmental policies within the sample, 40% disagreed and 10% slightly disagreed, and 50% of the respondents disagreed strongly with the idea of following regulatory prescriptions (*rp4*).

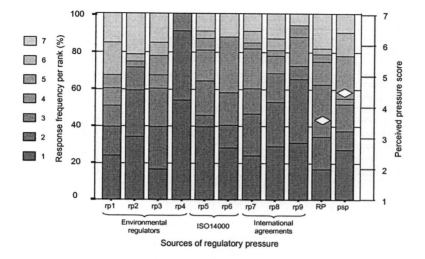

Figure 6.8   Perceived regulatory pressure

Summary

The findings regarding the firms' perceived overall demand arising from the market, the community and the regulatory institutions for them to develop clean technologies is rather limited. That is, the important possible social referents that could generate the motivation to comply with social desirable goals are perceived, on average, as not providing well-defined signals or incentives for the development of clean technologies.

PERCEIVED CONTROL UPON THE INNOVATION PROCESS

Technological Capabilities

Figure 6.9 (next page) presents the scores for the perception of technological capabilities in product and process environmental improvement (*TCPP*). The figure shows the perceived ease or difficulty of performing improvements in those critical environmental attributes on product and production process. The perceived ease to perform such activities is assumed to be associated with (or arise from) strong technological (or organisational) capabilities.

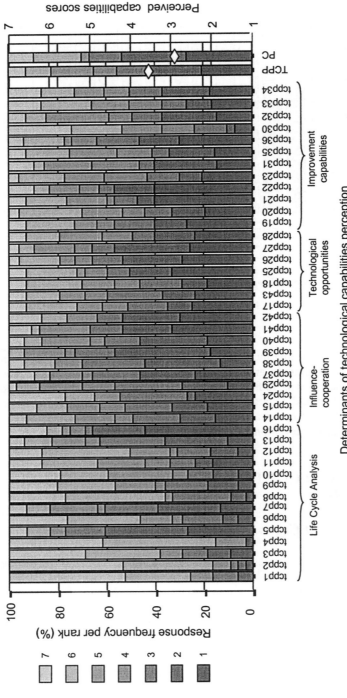

Figure 6.9 Perceived technological capabilities

140

The figure is divided into four types of technological capabilities: life cycle analysis, technological opportunities, influence and cooperation, and improvement capabilities. Although on average the perception of technological capabilities is quite low for 55% of the firms, 45% of them indicated high capabilities (see white diamond in the *TCPP* stacked bar). From the theory discussed regarding the dominance of pollution control technological paradigms and trajectories and the need for a new knowledge base as a prerequisite to develop clean technologies in Chapters 2 and 4, a generalised scenario of extremely low technological capabilities and technological opportunities was expected. The managers interviewed were introduced to the notion of linkage of their firms with the whole supply chain in the practice of a product Life Cycle Analysis, and the almost 'non-existence' of clean technological options. Despite this, Figure 6.9 indicates an optimistic scenario of perceptions for many of the managers in the sample.

Technological Capability in Product Life Cycle Analysis

As described in Chapter 4, the initial stage of an environmentally oriented business strategy includes the creation of an inventory of the firm's possible environmental critical interventions. This inventory involves the gathering of basic data, the assessment of environmental impacts and action priority setting. With regard to this stage Figure 6.9 on its left side displays a perceived ease that suggests high capabilities in gathering the basic data. The first four activities involve only activities within the boundaries of the manufacturing facilities. Most firms (84% vs. 16%) found it easy to construct a detailed manufacturing flow chart with an overview of their manufacturing process and its possible environmental critical interventions (*tcpp1*). Up to 92% (vs. 8%) found it easy to obtain environmental effects specifications for raw materials and inputs (*tcpp2*). The gathering of information about mass and energy flows was reported to be easy for 70% (vs. 30%) of the respondents (*tcpp3*).

Derived from the assessment of the above, 96% (vs. 4%) reported the compiling of a list that identifies all the possible sources of environmental critical interventions to be easy (*tcpp4*). In contrast, linking these critical spots to the relevant suppliers along the supply chain was seen as difficult by 88% (vs. 12%) of the managers in the sample (*tcpp5*). At this point, the challenge of developing clean technologies becomes more difficult, as discussed in Chapter 2, as it implies the cooperation of a broader number of firms along the supply chain.

Regarding environmental impact assessment, 65% (vs. 28%) of the managers found it easy to assess the impacts on the local environment for all their activities, inputs and components in their operations (*tcpp6*), while 60% (vs. 37%) found it difficult to perform such an assessment for the whole life cycle of their product (*tcpp7*). In addition, 60% (vs. 37%) of the respondents thought it difficult to estimate the amounts of the inputs (in terms of mass and energy) used in the manufacturing operations (*tcpp8*).

Setting priorities for action regarding the more relevant environmental aspects was seen as easy by 66% (vs. 26%) of the managers (*tcpp10*). The identification of suppliers of critical inputs and components was reported to be easy for 68% (vs. 28%) (*tcpp12*). However, 70% (vs. 25%) reported it to be difficult to track the environmental impacts from the use of their products beyond the gates of the firm (*tcpp16*). Half of the managers (vs. 34%) indicated that to have the necessary time and resources to perform a life cycle analysis up to the stage of the collection of data that would enable them to define priorities (*tcpp11*).

Capability to Cooperate and/or Influence

From Figure 6.9 it can be seen that the capability to co-operate with, and influence, suppliers and customers and internal staff was reported to be lowest in the domain of technological capabilities. The assignment and negotiation of environmental impacts and prevention responsibilities were reported to be difficult for 49% (vs. 44%) of the managers (*tcpp14*), while to do the same with customers was seen as difficult for 53% (vs. 37%) of the sample (*tcpp15*). More than half (54% vs. 35%) reported it difficult to establish teams to redesign product and process that include environmental considerations (*tcpp24*), 57% (vs. 30%) found difficult the implementation of efficient materials management for waste reduction and prevention of residuals in the plant (*tcpp29*), and the appointment of a responsible person with the corporate authority to control an environmental management system was seen as difficult by 64% (vs. 30%) (*tcpp37*).

Moreover, 70% (vs. 30%) perceived the communication of the firms' commitment to protect the environment and to ensure measures were implemented and maintained at all hierarchical levels (*tcpp38*) to be difficult. Up to 73% (vs. 23%) of the respondents perceived the organising of sessions to create awareness of environmental quality policy (*tcpp39*) to be difficult. Implementation of an environmental culture was reported as difficult by 60% (vs. 33%) of the sample (*tcpp40*). The reconciliation of environmental necessities and demands with the demands and objectives of other functional areas of the firm was perceived as difficult by 67% (vs. 33%) of the respondents   (*tcpp41*). In addition, integrating an environmental policy towards clean technologies with the other policies of the firm was seen as difficult by 63% (vs. 37%) of the managers (*tcpp42*).

Technological Opportunities

The technological opportunities to find off-the-shelf substitutes for inputs and components for products and process were also found to be one of the most difficult tasks when considering clean product and production process concepts. Regarding product technology, 53% (vs. 38%) of the managers reported difficulty in procuring inputs and components that ensured the elimination of noxious residuals and high recyclability of waste (*tcpp17*). In addition, 62% (vs. 28%) indicated that due to the nature of their product, substitution of inputs and components that ensured prevention of residuals and high recyclability was difficult (*tcpp43*).

Concerning the technological options for process substitution, the procurement of machinery and equipment that ensured the elimination of noxious residuals was seen as difficult by 46% (vs. 45%) of respondents (*tcpp18*). The possibility of completely eliminating the use of raw materials and inputs that are not environmentally safe was considered minimal by 60% (vs. 30%) of the managers (*tcpp25*). The procurement of raw materials and components produced with clean technologies was thought difficult by 67% (vs. 25%) of the sample (*tcpp26, tcpp27*), and the procurement of raw materials and inputs that ensured high recyclability of their products at the end of their life was reported as difficult by 50% (vs. 38%) of the sample (*tcpp28*).

Improvement Capability

The above three capabilities are assumed to provide the basis for the improvement of products and processes. It can be expected that if firms have life cycle analysis capabilities, capabilities to move their human external and internal resources and there are technological opportunities, the possibility of developing clean technologies is open. The capabilities to improve the firm technology were divided in product and process improvements.

Regarding product technology, 55% (vs. 40%) of the managers reported the development of a product concept that included the notion of the recycling of its components at the end of its life in the firm's manufacturing process to be difficult (*tcpp21*). The R&D capability to assess the feasibility of such a new product concept was perceived as low by 64% (vs. 29%) of the managers (*tcpp22*). Almost half (47% vs. 33%) perceived difficult the elimination of waste via the redesign of their product (*tcpp31*). The redesign of the product to be easily maintained with materials and spare parts being fully recyclable was thought to be difficult by 55% (vs. 43%) of the sample (*tcpp35*). Similarly, 65% (vs. 26%) perceived the redesign of their product to become fully recyclable at the end of its life to be difficult (*tcpp36*).

Focusing on process technology improvements, the use of materials in bulk or in recyclable containers was considered to be easy by 63% (vs. 25%)

of the managers (*tcpp30*). Achieving the elimination of waste via the redesign of their production process was seen as difficult by 50% (vs. 42%) of the respondents (*tcpp32*); 50% (vs. 38%) perceived the design of packing methods that ensured the elimination of waste and residuals during the packing process to be easy (*tcpp33*) but, equally, ensuring packing functionality while being recyclable was considered difficult by 50% (vs. 40%) of the sample (*tcpp34*).

In sum, although there is a high degree of heterogeneity in the set of scores and capabilities in the sample, the set of activities described above, generated in the average firm an accumulated connotative load of moderately low capabilities to perform improvements to the critical spots of their product and process technological portfolio (see the white diamond in the stacked bar 'TCPP' in Figure 6.9).

Organisational Learning Capabilities

Figure 6.10 shows that on average the managers in the sample reported moderate capabilities to learn and acquire knowledge to develop clean technologies (see *OL* stacked bar). About 20% of managers reported high learning capabilities, 44% considered they had moderate capabilities, 22% responded having low capabilities and 20% indicated they were uncertain. As discussed in Chapter 4, three groups of learning capabilities were considered to be relevant for the development of clean technologies: problem solving, knowledge integration and implementation of change.

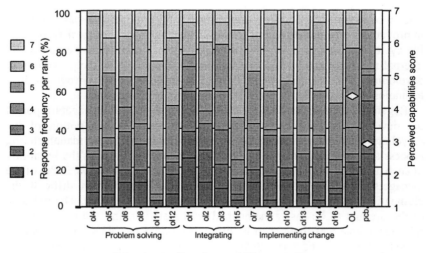

Figure 6.10 Perceived organisational capabilities

With regard to the *capability to solve problems by sharing knowledge*, 70% (vs. 26%) of managers perceived the assembly of problem-solving teams made up of different personality types with a diversity of professional backgrounds to be easy (*ol4*). Likewise, 65% (vs. 28%) perceived no difficulty in overcoming the differences in different perspectives with regard to how to solve the problem in such teams (*ol5*); 50% (vs. 38%) of the respondents indicated that their firms had individuals with the necessary breadth of knowledge to develop clean products (*ol6*). Around 68% (vs. 32%) of managers responded that their staff included several people who regularly collected information regarding clean technologies and passed it on to the people best able to make use of it (*ol8*). In addition, 94% (vs. 4%) of the respondents believed that most people within their firms valued the acquisition of new skills and abilities (*ol11*), and 76% (vs. 22%) indicated it to be easy for their firm to enable people to take more responsibility and demonstrate more initiative (*ol12*).

Concerning the *integration of knowledge* into products and process modifications, the integration of a diversity of professionals to focus on solving the problem of generating a new product concept design that included the notions of reuse/recycling of material and components into the manufacturing process of their firm was perceived as being easy by 28% (vs. 59%) of the managers (*ol1*). About half (52% vs. 42%) reported to have staff who could merge industrial and environmental design skills (*ol2*). Coupled with this latter result, 41% (vs. 39%) considered easy the implementation of mechanisms to translate across different disciplinary languages that encourage depersonalisation and conflicting perspectives among their staff (*ol3*). Moreover, 77% (vs. 15%) of the managers considered achieving effective communication among their staff and across functional teams and projects to be easy (*ol15*).

With respect to the *capability to implement* technological or organisational changes, 58% (vs. 29%) of respondents believed that their firm had individuals with the power to influence the organisation. Although they did not have detailed technical knowledge, they believed in the positive potential of innovating in clean technology (*ol7*). The minimisation of employees' individual opposition to learning new techniques and changing work practices and methods for any new task-technology was thought to be easy for 61% (vs. 38%) of the managers (*ol9*). Gaining people's positive participation in the process of technical and organisational change was thought to be easy by 63% (vs. 27%) of respondents (*ol13, ol14*). Likewise, the promotion of a broad participation in organisation-wide continuous improvement activities towards the development of clean products and clean production processes was believed easy for 77% (vs. 18%) of participants in the sample (*ol16*). As a consequence, 63% (vs. 37%) of respondents believed it would be easy for their firms to implement a clean production culture that eliminated pollution (*ol10*).

In sum, the above description of the perceived organisational learning capabilities on solving technical problems by sharing knowledge, knowledge integration and implementation of improvements portrays a sample of firms in which apparently the majority have those capabilities observed in firms that have succeeded in innovative activities.

Strategic Alliances and Networks of Collaboration Capabilities

The perceived ease or difficulty to outsource skills and knowledge to develop clean technologies through strategic alliances and networks of collaboration is shown in Figure 6.11. The scenario presented indicates that the average firm in the sample perceives low capabilities and possibilities to outsource knowledge and expertise in clean technologies (see *AL* and *NWK* stacked bars).

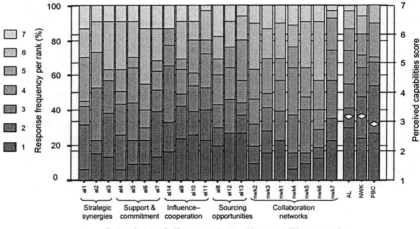

Figure 6.11   Perceived strategic alliance and networks of collaboration capabilities

Concerning alliances, 16% of the managers reported high alliances capabilities, 24% moderate capabilities, 42% low capabilities and 18% reported being uncertain in their response. Regarding networks, 14% of the managers reported high networking capabilities, 31% perceived moderate capabilities and, 48% perceived low capabilities.   Five sub-scales were proposed to assess the perceived alliance and networks of collaboration capabilities to develop clean technologies: strategic synergies; support and commitment; cooperation and influence; outsourcing opportunities; and networks of collaboration.

Regarding *strategic synergies*, the ease or difficulty of finding the right partners to make alliances with, 42 % (vs. 55%) of the managers thought is was difficult to find partners that ensured a good strategic fit with regard to strengths and complementarities in innovative capacity and technical know-how for the development of a cleaner technology-product portfolio (*al1*). Finding partners that ensured a good chemistry fit with regard to trust, honesty, win/win commitment, good reputation, predictability under pressure and creativity facing adversity was thought difficult by 52% (vs. 48%) of the respondents (*al2*). Similarly, 57% (vs. 43%) of the sample thought it difficult to achieve a good operational fit between partners concerning strategic time orientation, information and communication methods, management styles, labour relations, etc. (*al3*).

With regard to *support and commitment* to innovate, 43% (vs. 50%) of the managers believed it would be difficult to reach a point that maximised gains for both partners in a win/win fashion when negotiating strategic alliances (*al4*). Likewise, 43% (vs. 38%) of the respondents perceived it to be a difficult task to find partners that shared the same environmental values (*al5*). Only 30% (vs. 60%) believed it unlikely that the forging of strategic alliances for the development of cleaner technologies would have the support and commitment of the CEO and shareholders (*al6*). Above half (51% vs. 38%) recalled unsuccessful experiences in trying to form strategic alliances in order to innovate. They expected that forming alliances to develop clean products and processes would be similarly unsuccessful (*al7*).

The possibility of influencing or cooperating with suppliers to outsource inputs, components, raw materials and services to develop cleaner substitutes for the actual environmentally sensitive critical parts of their product portfolio with cleaner options was perceived to be low by 50% (vs. 19%) of the respondents (*al9*). Similarly, influencing suppliers of process technologies to find cleaner options was seen as difficult by 53% (vs. 40%) of the sample (*al10*). In addition, 52% (vs. 30%) of managers believed it would be difficult to pass on to customers the costs of the development of clean products (*al11*).

Outsourcing the capability to undertake life cycle analysis for their product portfolio was thought difficult by 43% (vs. 40%) of managers (*al8*). The outsourcing of better product technologies, such as clean designs for inputs, materials and components from the technological marketplace, was believed to be difficult by 46% (vs. 36%) of respondents (*al12*). Likewise, 44% (vs. 43%) of the sample believed the outsourcing of new clean manufacturing process technologies to be difficult (*al13*).

Concerning the perceived capabilities to collaborate with broader network sources of information and knowledge such as regulators, universities, international agreements, etc., 44% (vs. 38%) of the respondents found establishing networks of collaboration with universities to out source know-how and learn how to develop clean technologies to be easy (*nwk1*). Although all the firms visited operate on the Mexican side of the US–Mexican border, 53% (vs. 42%) of the firms considered it would be easy to collaborate with the USEPA's Clean Technologies Program (*nwk2*). Similarly, 50% (vs. 41%) of the sample perceived it as being easy to collaborate with the Mexican environmental authorities (SEMARNAP's) (*nwk3*). Only 37% (vs. 36%) of the managers indicated the ease of collaborating with the International Standards Organization (*nwk4*), 54% (vs. 40%) believed it would be easy to collaborate with suppliers of raw materials and other inputs for product integration (*nwk5*), 60% (vs. 30%) perceived it as easy to collaborate with consulting firms that specialise in clean technologies expertise (*nwk6*), and 27% (vs. 56%) of the managers considered the collaboration to transfer technology and expertise with firms in the same sector easy (*nwk7*).

In sum, the individual perceived capabilities regarding strategic synergies, the possible influence or cooperation with suppliers, the operation of a network to outsource know-how, and the perceived support and commitment of CEOs and shareholders to carry out these activities generated a connotative load on the average firm of low capability in strategic alliances directed towards the development of clean technologies.

Summary

In general, the perceived control over the innovation process was reported to be low across the sample (see white diamonds in Figures 6.9, 6.10 and 6.11). As expected from the heterogeneity of the firms surveyed, the description of the individual activities and capabilities described above have shown a heterogeneous scenario. The connotative loads generated by the set of capabilities in each domain and captured on average scores achieved on the four core capabilities proposed by Roome (1994) are consistent with the average overall perceived control over the development of clean technologies (*PC*) (compare the average scores of *PC* and the four behavioural domains of the capabilities to innovate: *TCPP, OL, AL,* and *NWK*).

THE FIRMS' ENVIRONMENTAL PLANNED BEHAVIOUR

This chapter has presented the distribution of responses in the different behavioural domains. The figures in general presented the trend of the percentages between the optimal and worst conditions that may precondition the development of clean technologies for the firms in the sample. In order to summarise the descriptive statistics presented above, Figure 6.12 shows the optimal conditions in each behavioural domain that may induce the development of clean technologies. It also shows the average scores achieved on the direct measures of the behavioural domain perceptions and willingness, currently and for the long term. These scores were proposed in Chapter 3 and 4 to capture the accumulated beliefs load in their respective domains. The strategic planning of the firm, as already mentioned in Chapter 3, can be considered as the firm's planned behaviour. This planning is generally agreed to be based on the rational expectations of CEOs and top managers. In this sense, Figure 6.12 presents the managers' current, and future rational expectations that may determine the firm's planned behaviour regarding the development of clean technologies.

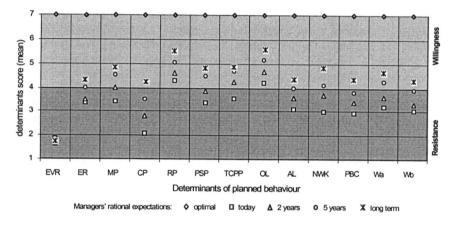

Figure 6.12 Firms' environmental planned behaviour

The willingness to innovate both in product (W_a) and production process (W_b) for the average firm is non-existent for the next five years and minimal in the long term. The scores for the attitudinal domains are extremely low for environmental risk (*1EVR*) and moderate for economic risk (*ER*). It is interesting to note that in the eyes of the managers no changes are expected in the environmental effects of their firms' operations on the environment in the long term. Economic risk and uncertainty that normally are considered to be of paramount importance in innovative projects show only moderate scores. The scores for the domains of social pressure (*PSP*) indicate that the managers do not perceive these at the moment, nor do they expect significant market pressures (*MP*) in the long term. The local community (*CP*) is not expected to impose environmental demands and the regulatory pressures (*RP*) are expected to be moderate only in the long term. Finally, the perceived technological capabilities (*TCPP*) are low at the moment and are expected to improve only marginally in the long term. Regarding organisational capabilities, it is expected that there will be some changes from low to moderate organisational learning capabilities (*OL*), strategic alliances (*AL*) and networks of collaboration capabilities (*NWK*) are foreseen to remain low in the long term.

The above scenario throws some light on the main questions of this work. In the introduction of this book, it was argued that at the core of most environmental problems lies a conflict between the interests of the firm in the short-term with long-term societal interests. The degree of conflict between the interests of the firm with the societal goal of environmental protection can be equated with their degree of willingness to innovate. Those firms with high willingness to develop clean technologies (or already developing) have in practice no conflict with the societal goal of environmental protection. If we consider that in order to reconcile both interests it is a necessary condition that the firm has an optimal willingness to change (i.e., to innovate towards the development of cleaner technological options). The scenario presented in Figure 6.12 indicates that, on average, this optimal willingness does not exist.

If we believe that the framework proposed in Chapters 3 and 4 is valid, we can infer that if willingness is not optimal, it will not be possible to reconcile or balance the interest of the firm with the societal interest regarding environmental protection in the long term if those conditions presented in Figure 6.12 continue. But how *reliable* and *valid* are these scores to make such inference? In addition, do these assumed determinants of the willingness of the firm to develop clean technologies really explain what they are supposed to explain? The question of the empirical validation of the theory arises not only from the test of the proposed system of hypotheses but also from need for advancement in the literature researching the determinants of the 'greening' of industry. Gladwin (1993) and Fuchs and Mazmanian (1998) have argued that one of the main challenges and research agenda for the next decade is to provide comprehensive models with theoretical and methodological rigour to *assess* the determinants that explain the firm's environmental innovative behaviour and also its relative weights.

This assessment implies measurement. The problem of measurement of the variables of interest in this work has been addressed in the Appendix. In a broad sense the Appendix deals with the consistency between the structure and content of the theoretical model and structure of the empirical data. The test of this correspondence enabled the test of the system of hypotheses proposed in Chapter 4. That is, the empirical validation of the proposed theoretical framework for environmental and technology policy analysis. The following paragraphs summarise the results of the validation process.

The *reliability* of the questionnaire used to measure managers' perceptions and the *validity* of theoretical underpinnings that shaped its structure and contents were tested in the Appendix. With regard to the question of reliability, two tests were carried out: item-total correlation and Cronbach's alpha. The results of these tests were highly satisfactory with regard to the stability of measurement (see Appendix A, pp. 201–5). It can be asserted that the questionnaires have produced reliable estimates (measurements) of the overall managers' perceptions in this study and could also produce stable estimates for future applications in other contexts.

With respect to the measurement of the variables of interest, two types of validity were considered: content and construct validity. Regarding content validity, the resulting linear combination of the behavioural domains performed by the principal component analysis explained a large proportion of the variance in the sample. In addition, the clustering of the empirical components extracted (i.e., C1, C2, and C3 for both data sets. See Table A.5, p. 207) in the principal component analysis very closely fits the theoretical structure and contents as hypothesised. This indicates that the proposed nine behavioural domains and their contents represent most parts of the aspects that the model intends to capture, i.e., attitude, social norm and perceived control. Based on these findings, it is concluded that the proposed contents and the structure of the model are valid (see Appendix A, pp. 207–9). Concerning construct validity, several multiple regression analyses were run to test the system of hypotheses proposing a chain of causality by linking beliefs to willingness to innovate. This system of hypotheses was not rejected, consequently the hypothesis of the links of causality can be accepted (see Appendix A, pp. 209–15).

In sum, the results of the tests support the reliability and validity of the measurements operations, including the quantitative character of the constructs assessed. In the light of this evidence it can be said, therefore, that the developed model appropriately measures and predicts a given firm's willingness to innovate towards the development of clean technologies as perceived by its managers. Accepting this, the scenario presented in Chapter 6 (see Figure 6.12, p. 149) represents the planned behaviour of the sample of firms in the longer term. That is, the scenario presented above can be considered valid.

Furthermore, the highly significant results from testing the hypotheses H_2 and H_{2a} confirmed the propositions of proportionality between scales of cumulative belief loads and domain indexes presented in Chapter 3 (e.g., $EVR \propto \Sigma evr_b$, $MP \propto \Sigma mp_b$, $TCPP \propto \Sigma tcpp_b$, etc.). This proportionality implies that the indexes of perception in each domain capture the accumulated connotative load of the beliefs that compose the scale. This confirmed one of the main propositions of the theory of planned behaviour, that is, few salient beliefs determine willingness and ultimately behaviour in specific situations. Here, based upon the regression analysis, it can be argued that the salient beliefs that determine the willingness of the firm to engage in innovative activities directed to protect the environment are the direct measures of perception for each domain (i.e., *EVR, ER, CP, MP, RP, TCPP, OL, AL, NWK*). In the next chapter, these measures are used to assess the importance of each behavioural domain in determining willingness of the firm to innovate. In addition, several scenarios are explored showing upon what terms the firms in the sample may be optimally willing to innovate and some policy implications to foster environmental innovative behaviour are discussed.

NOTES

1. The percentage of response frequency in this rank is obviated in the following sections.
2. This connotative load of beliefs is captured and measured by the item *IEVR*. See Appendix E, Section IV.

7. Strategy follows structure: environmental and technology policy pathways

In Chapters 3 and 4 it was shown that the theoretical insights provided by the literature of the greening of industry could be systematised and further explored within the definitional system provided by the Theory of Planned Behaviour. The TPB framework enabled the integration of several bodies of theory. In the Appendix it is shown that 85% of the variance in the firms' willingness to innovate in clean technologies can be explained in terms of their attitude (A), perceived social pressure (PSP) and the perceived control upon the development of clean technologies (PC) (see Table A.6, p. 215). In addition, through a principal component analysis, it was shown that the empirical data fits the theoretical structure of the determinants of the behaviour under study (see Table A.5, p. 207). Although these findings are theoretically relevant, for policy analysis it is more useful to operate at the second and third levels of explanation of the willingness to innovate (see Figure 4.12, pp. 104–5).

In the following sections, the analysis focuses on the behavioural domains that determine attitudes, perceived social pressure and perceived control. The goal is to identify which domains explain the willingness to innovate, and, more specifically, which perceptions that are currently most relevant and likely to influence behavioural change in firms. This chapter can be seen as an example of how the developed model could be operated to analyse the determinants of willingness to change (i.e., willingness to innovate) and the derivation of policies that may induce behavioural change. The policy suggestions are based on the structural relationships between the salient beliefs and the willingness to develop clean technologies.

In order to operate the model for policy analysis, the following steps were followed. First, a stepwise multivariate analysis was used to assess the weight of the direct measures of perception in each behavioural domain (i.e., EVR, ER, MP, CP, RP, TC, OL, AL, and NWK). In addition, the direct measures in each domain were regressed against the beliefs that corresponded to the domain in order to assess the weight of individual beliefs. Second, the estimated equation at the domain level is used in a simulation process to seek the optimal policy scenario for influencing the firms' willingness to engage in clean technology development. Third, the moderating role of core capabilities for perceived economic risk and its relation with the self-interest of the firm (profit-seeking behaviour) is explored. Finally, based on a selected optimal policy scenario, policy implications are discussed in terms of (a) the limitations that the In-Bond industry scheme presents for policy design and (b) the specific activities that may be needed to maximise willingness and ultimately innovative behaviour in clean technologies for those firms in the sample.

POLICY PATHWAYS

This section seeks to depict the current paths from beliefs to willingness and establish the degree of influence that different behavioural domains exert on willingness to innovate in clean technologies. Figures 7.1a, and 7.1b, pp. 156–9, show respectively the current and the long-term rational expectations of the managers within each behavioural domain and their degree of influence on the firms' willingness to innovate.[1] Regarding the current expectations (i.e., *EVR*, *ER*, *MP*, etc., Figure 7.1a), the regression analysis showed an index of determination of $R^2=0.88$ (see Appendix C1, p. 225, and Appendix C4, p. 228). The results indicate that perceived control (i.e., the perceived ease or difficulty to develop clean technologies) over the development of clean technologies accounted for 46.49% of the explained variance.[2] Within this component, technological capabilities in product and process environmental improvement (*TCPP*) accounted for 39.79% of the variance and capabilities in organisational learning (*OL*) explain 6.61% of the variance on willingness. The domains of strategic alliances (*AL*) and networks of collaboration (*NWK*) showed minimal explanatory significance (see Appendix C2, p. 226).

Within the domain of technological capabilities (*TCPP*), the beliefs were classified into four groups (i.e., scales) according to the arrangement presented in Table 4.7. This grouping resulted in an index of determination of $R^2=0.863$. The scale of product life cycle analysis capabilities explained 2% of the variance, the scale of technological opportunities for the substitution of inputs, materials and components accounted for 22.3% of the variance of the perceived capability, the capability to improve products and process explained 59% and the capability to cooperate with or influence suppliers and customers towards the development of clean inputs explained 3% of the variance in the perceived technological capabilities.

Two beliefs were salient in explaining the variance of the perceived technological capabilities. Within improvement capabilities, the capability to develop clean product concepts (*tcpp21*) accounted for 55.3% of the variance, while within the grouping of technological opportunities the perception that the very nature of the product limits availability of substitutes for product inputs that ensure the elimination of noxious residuals (*tcpp43*) accounted for 17.8% (see Appendix C10).

Within the domain of organisational learning capabilities (*OL*) the tools for implementing changes were the most important. Here the involvement of the firm's personnel in continuous improvement (ol_{16}) explained 58.9% of the variance, and in problem solving the availability of individuals who regularly collect information regarding clean technologies and pass it on to the relevant people who are best able to use it accounted for 12.53% of the variance in the perceived capability on organisational learning (ol_8) (see Appendix C11).

The second most important component to explain willingness was attitude towards the development of clean technologies (*A*). The underlying concept of attitude is an evaluation of possible outcomes arising from the development of clean technologies. As discussed in Chapter 3, environmental and economic risk were considered. Economic risk (*ER*) accounted for 21.38% of the variance on willingness, while environmental risk perception (*EVR*) explained only 6.04% (see Appendix C2).

Within economic risk perception, the financial risk arising from pioneering new clean products due to the possible loss of invested capital in R&D (er_{19}) explained 62.37% of the variance in perceived risk. The reduction of overall competitiveness due to an increase in overheads and R&D costs (er_{20}) explained 11.21%. The possible economic opportunities captured in four items explained only 13.8% (er_1, er_{10}, er_{12}, and er_{15}). These results indicate that the perceived economic outcomes arising from the development of clean product and processes in the eyes of the managers have a negative connotation (see Appendix C6).

In the domain of perceived environmental risk, the managers' perceptions were found to be more diverse. That is, the variance in risk perception is explained more evenly by a higher number of beliefs in contrast with the other domains. Here the grouping of beliefs using the Slovic scale (evr_2, evr_3, evr_5, evr_4, evr_6, and evr_9) explained 35.6% of the perceived safety of the firms' operations. The managers' perceptions of being personally affected by pollution in the past or future accounted for 26.4% (ac_{17}, ac_{18}), and the perceived controllability of the generated hazards explains 17.4% (evr_1, ac_8, ac_{10}) of the variance on the perceived environmental risk and the relevance of developing clean technologies (see Appendix C5).

The least important component to influence the willingness to innovate was found to be the perceived social pressure (*PSP*). Together, the three domains proposed under social pressure explained only 14.67% of the variance in the willingness to innovate. The pressures arising from the market (*MP*) explained 5.75%, the perceived community pressure (*CP*) accounted for 8.22%, and the perceived regulatory pressure accounted for less that one percentile of the willingness to innovate in clean technology (see Appendix C2). As discussed in Chapter 4, the literature that explores the issues of technical change and environmental policies regarded social pressure and especially regulatory pressure as the main driver for undertaking innovative behaviour.

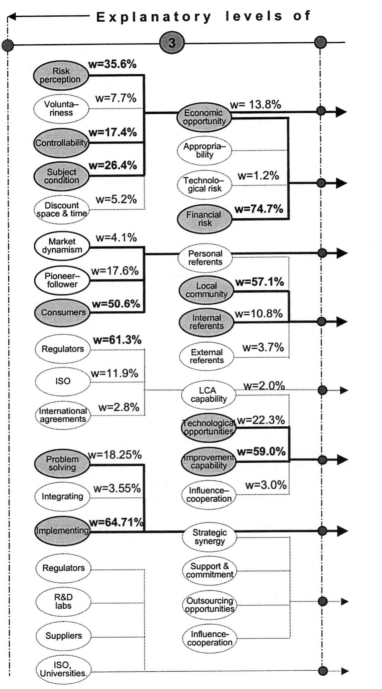

Explanatory levels of

③

Risk perception — w=35.6%

Volunta–riness — w=7.7%

Controllability — **w=17.4%**

Subject condition — **w=26.4%**

Discount space & time — w=5.2%

Economic opportunity — w= 13.8%

Appropria–bility

Technolo–gical risk — w=1.2%

Financial risk — **w=74.7%**

Market dynamism — w=4.1%

Pioneer–follower — w=17.6%

Consumers — **w=50.6%**

Personal referents

Local community — **w=57.1%**

Internal referents — w=10.8%

External referents — w=3.7%

Regulators — **w=61.3%**

ISO — w=11.9%

International agreements — w=2.8%

LCA capability — w=2.0%

Technological opportunities — w=22.3%

Problem solving — w=18.25%

Integrating — w=3.55%

Implementing — **w=64.71%**

Improvement capability — **w=59.0%**

Influence–cooperation — w=3.0%

Strategic synergy

Regulators

R&D labs

Suppliers

ISO, Universities

Support & commitment

Outsourcing opportunities

Influence-cooperation

Figure 7.1a   Behavioural domains explanatory weight (at the moment of the survey)

156

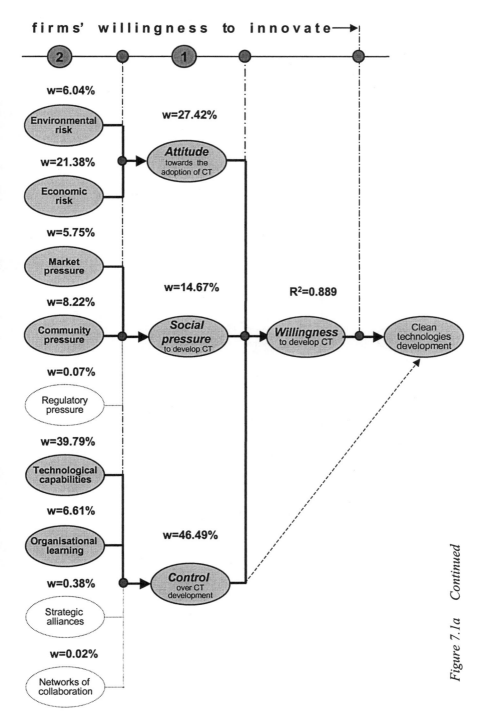

firms' willingness to innovate→

② ● **①** ● ●

w=6.04%

Environmental risk

w=27.42%

w=21.38%

Attitude towards the adoption of CT

Economic risk

w=5.75%

Market pressure

w=8.22%

w=14.67%

$R^2=0.889$

Community pressure

Social pressure to develop CT

Willingness to develop CT

Clean technologies development

w=0.07%

Regulatory pressure

w=39.79%

Technological capabilities

w=6.61%

Organisational learning

w=46.49%

w=0.38%

Control over CT development

Strategic alliances

w=0.02%

Networks of collaboration

Figure 7.1a   Continued

157

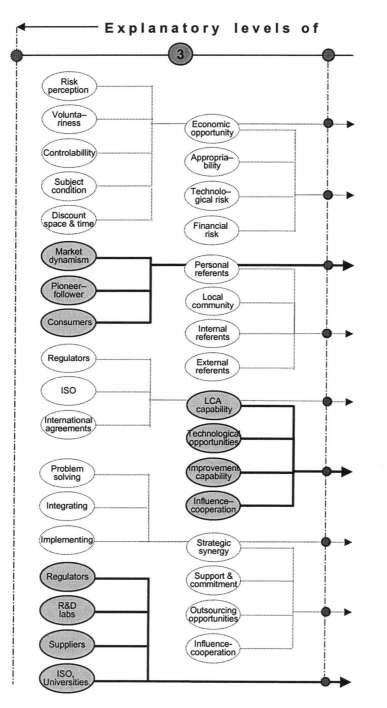

Explanatory levels of

Risk perception

Volunta–riness

Controlabillity

Subject condition

Discount space & time

Market dynamism

Pioneer–follower

Consumers

Regulators

ISO

International agreements

Problem solving

Integrating

Implementing

Regulators

R&D labs

Suppliers

ISO, Universities

Economic opportunity

Appropria–bility

Technolo–gical risk

Financial risk

Personal referents

Local community

Internal referents

External referents

LCA capability

Technological opportunities

Improvement capability

Influence–cooperation

Strategic synergy

Support & commitment

Outsourcing opportunities

Influence-cooperation

Figure 7.1b   Behavioural domains explanatory weight (in the long term)

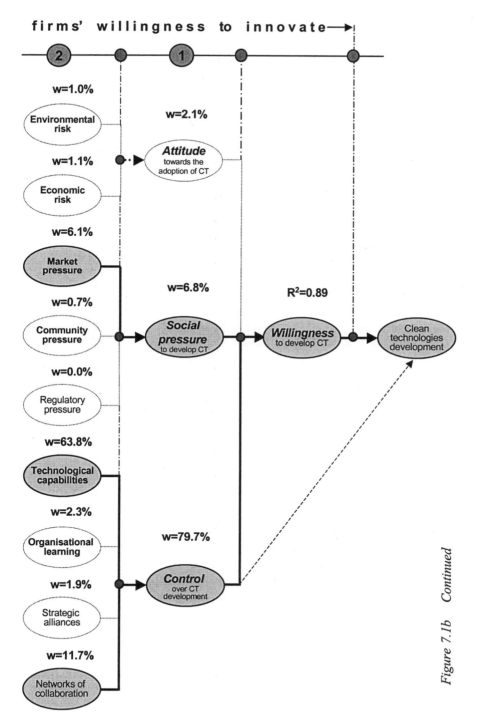

firms' willingness to innovate →

② ①

w=1.0%
Environmental risk

w=2.1%

w=1.1%
Attitude towards the adoption of CT

w=6.1%
Market pressure

w=0.7%
Community pressure

w=6.8%
Social pressure to develop CT

R^2=0.89

Willingness to develop CT

Clean technologies development

w=0.0%
Regulatory pressure

w=63.8%
Technological capabilities

w=2.3%
Organisational learning

w=79.7%
Control over CT development

w=1.9%
Strategic alliances

w=11.7%
Networks of collaboration

Figure 7.1b   Continued

159

The above findings contradict the general wisdom in the field regarding the relative weight of regulatory pressure to influence the environmental behaviour of the firm. This is perhaps due to following reasons. The first concerns the definition used to measure innovative behaviour. In general, the improvements or innovations mentioned in the literature refer to marginal changes either in production process, product design, inputs change or improvements in internal management and practices (e.g., Clayton *et al.*, 1999; Kemp, 1997; CEC, 1996a). In contrast, this book refers to innovation in clean technologies as a reorientation of the business strategy that includes radical preventive measures to eliminate residuals and waste, including radical re-engineering in products and production processes, aiming for the closed-loop and zero emissions factory.

Second, most studies were carried out in industrialised countries where some incipient and discrete samples of '*cleaner technologies*' exist (i.e., Clayton *et al.*, 1999; CEC, 1996a; OECD, 1998). Third, although there is awareness of the local environmental problems in those communities where the firms in the sample are located, in general, they have other more pressing (i.e., social security, income, health, transport, etc.) needs than environmental quality (Ganster and Sanchez, 1996; CEC, 1996a). Fourth, the production of those firms in the sample is oriented to US market preferences (see Appendix D, Figure D4). It is well known that the average consumer in the USA is not much concerned with where and how their consumables are produced (PCSD, 1999).

Last, as discussed in Chapter 2, the capability and focus of Mexican environmental regulation is still oriented to command-and-control BAT-standard based and cleaning operations. The notion of pollution prevention exists only at the highest level of policy analysis documents, but not at the legislative and executive federal levels. These factors can partially explain why the current social pressure for more radical changes could be expected to be minimal.

In summary, two behavioural domains accounted for most of the variance on willingness (61.17%). The perceived economic risk accounted for 21.38% and the perceived technological capabilities explained 39.79% of the variance in the sample. The domains of the perceived market and community pressures jointly accounted for 13.97% and the perceived organisational learning capabilities explained 6.61% of the variance. In each domain, with the exception of the perceived environmental risk, two beliefs accounted for a major part of the variance within the behavioural domain (see Appendixes C5 to C13).[3] Furthermore, at the domain level, nine items (i.e., nine beliefs) accounted for 88.9% of the variance (see Appendix C2). Therefore, the argument of Ajzen (1991) that a few beliefs could explain most human behaviours has been confirmed for this study.[4]

The same analysis was carried out regarding the expected changes in the conditions of the different behavioural domains in the long term (see Figure 7.1b). Here it is interesting to note that the perceived technological capabilities and the perceived capabilities in networks of collaboration account for more than 75% of the variance in willingness to innovate in clean technologies (see Appendix C4). In addition, domains that were important in explaining the current willingness to innovate, like economic risk perception and community and market pressure, are expected to play a minimal role in motivating behavioural change.

In concluding this section, it is important to locate the firms' perceived control in relation to theorised macro-determinants of technical change. The beliefs found to be the most important in explaining the technological capabilities confirm the discussion in Chapter 2 about the significance of technological paradigms and technological trajectories in shaping opportunities to change designs in products and production processes. Following Pavitt's taxonomy of the sectoral patterns of innovation, this taxonomy indicates that manufacturing firms are dependent on other industrial sectors of the economic system including, science-based, materials, and specialised engineering firms (Pavitt, 1984).

POLICY SIMULATION

Although the previous section pointed to the determinants that are currently the most important, this does not necessarily imply that the policy effort should focus on those domains. It is necessary to explore what could happen if the current conditions changed. In this section changes in the preconditions of the firm's willingness to innovate are simulated. In the Appendix B, it is shown that the scores of the domain scales are proportional to those of the direct measures of the perception in each behavioural domain. This allows us to use either score in a simulation exercise. The domain indexes (i.e., nine items with scores 1 to 7) were chosen as their scores simplify the simulation process. In addition, the low standard error of the estimate of willingness indicates a satisfactory level of accuracy of the prediction (see SEE in Table C2a, p. 226). This enables a meaningful prediction of several situations in which the firm may change its predisposition to innovate in clean technologies.

Figure 7.2 below presents several scenarios seeking to optimise willingness by varying the scores on the nine domains that explain behaviour (i.e. *EVR, ER, MP, CP, RP, TC, OL, AL*, and *NWK*). At the top of the figure, the current scenario (AVS) corresponds to the average scores achieved for the firms in sample. The 26 scenarios considered below AVS are sorted by the degree of influence that the optimal scores on specific behavioural domains have on the willingness to innovate. Here, as in the figures presented in Chapter 6, darkest and lightest tones indicate worst and optimal conditions respectively. The tones in between represent scores within the interval (worst (1), optimal (7)) for the behavioural domains and scores within (2, 14) for willingness to innovate.

Environmental and technology policy pre-conditions

	Worst							Optimal
Behavioural domains	1	2	3	4	5	6	7	
Willingness to innovate	2	4	6	8	10	12	14	

Perception scenarios	Environmental risk	Economic risk	Market pressure	Community pressure	Regulatory pressure	Technological capabilities	Organisational learning	Alliances capabilities	Networks capabilities	Estimated willingness
S	EVR	ER	MP	CP	RP	TCPP	OL	AL	NWK	We
AVS	1.86	4.36	3.18	2.35	4.10	3.72	4.21	3.08	2.99	5.44
S1	1.86	4.36	3.18	2.35	7.00	3.72	4.21	3.08	2.99	3.08
S2	1.86	4.36	3.18	2.35	4.10	3.72	4.21	3.08	7.00	5.77
S3	1.86	4.36	7.00	7.00	7.00	3.72	4.21	3.08	2.99	6.03
S4	1.86	4.36	3.18	2.35	4.10	3.72	4.21	7.00	2.99	6.19
S5	1.86	7.00	3.18	2.35	4.10	3.72	4.21	3.08	2.99	6.40
S6	1.86	4.36	3.18	7.00	4.10	3.72	4.21	3.08	2.99	6.81
S7	1.86	7.00	7.00	7.00	7.00	3.72	4.21	3.08	2.99	6.99
S8	1.86	4.36	7.00	2.35	4.10	3.72	4.21	3.08	2.99	7.03
S9	1.86	4.36	3.18	2.35	4.10	3.72	7.00	3.08	2.99	7.32
S10	7.00	4.36	3.18	2.35	4.10	3.72	4.21	3.08	2.99	7.50
S11	1.86	4.36	7.00	7.00	4.10	3.72	4.21	3.08	2.99	8.40
S12	7.00	7.00	3.18	2.35	4.10	3.72	4.21	3.08	2.99	8.46
S13	1.86	4.36	3.18	2.35	4.10	7.00	4.21	3.08	2.99	8.79
S14	7.00	7.00	7.00	7.00	7.00	3.72	4.21	3.08	2.99	9.05
S15	7.00	7.00	3.18	2.35	7.00	7.00	4.21	3.08	2.99	9.44
S16	1.86	4.36	3.18	7.00	1.00	3.72	4.21	3.08	2.99	9.56
S17	1.86	4.36	7.00	7.00	1.00	3.72	4.21	3.08	2.99	10.92
S18	1.86	4.36	3.18	2.35	1.00	7.00	4.21	3.08	2.99	11.32
S19	1.86	4.36	3.18	2.35	4.10	7.00	7.00	7.00	7.00	11.75
S20	1.86	7.00	3.18	2.35	1.00	7.00	4.21	3.08	2.99	12.28
S21	1.86	4.36	7.00	7.00	7.00	7.00	7.00	7.00	7.00	12.35
S22	1.86	4.36	7.00	2.35	1.00	7.00	4.21	3.08	2.99	12.91
S23	7.00	4.36	3.18	2.35	1.00	7.00	4.21	3.08	2.99	13.38
S24	7.00	4.36	3.18	2.35	1.00	7.00	4.21	3.08	7.00	13.71
S25	7.00	7.00	3.18	2.35	1.00	7.00	4.21	3.08	2.99	14.33
S26	7.00	7.00	3.18	2.35	4.10	7.00	7.00	7.00	7.00	14.77

Worst policy scenarios → Optimal policy scenarios (left axis)

Resistance to change → Willingness to innovate (right axis)

AVS= Average score; N=97
Estimated equation used for the scenarios simulation:
$W\infty -3.023+0.4EVR+0.363ER+0.416MP+0.294CP-0.815RP+1.022LCA+0.672OL+0.192AL+0.083NWK$
Scenarios 23, 24 and 25 indicate the optimal technological and environmental policy focus that may induce innovative behaviour in clean products and process, for the sample of firms in the study.

Figure 7.2 Scenarios for the determinants of the firm's willingness to innovate in clean technologies

The simulation proceeds by substituting current average scores with maximum scores for targeted behavioural domains leaving the other correlates unchanged. The turning point from resistance to willingness to innovate in clean products occurs when scores above 7 – along the continuum 'resistance–willingness to innovate' (see Figure 7.2) – have been achieved. The scenario simulation presentation starts with changes in managers' attitudes towards clean technologies development derived from changes in economic and environmental risk perception. Next, changes in perceived social pressure are considered. Then, increases in technological and organisational capabilities are presented. Finally, the optimal policy scenarios that maximise the willingness to develop clean technologies are discussed.

Attitudinal Changes

In the introduction and in Chapter 2 it was pointed out that the literature of environmental policy puts attitude in a central position. The underlying assumption is that radical changes in environmental attitudes of the firms' CEOs and managers implies a reorientation of business strategy or at least its environmental planned behaviour. Three scenarios were considered to contrast this general belief with the empirical evidence. Figure 7.3 shows that extremely favourable changes in environmental (see scenario *S10*) and economic risk perceptions (see *S5*) were considered independently and aggregated (*S12*).[5]

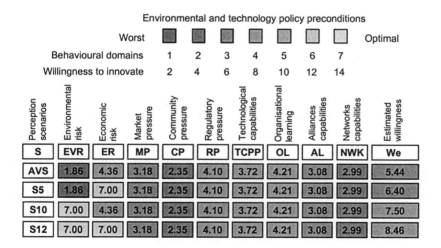

S	EVR	ER	MP	CP	RP	TCPP	OL	AL	NWK	We
AVS	1.86	4.36	3.18	2.35	4.10	3.72	4.21	3.08	2.99	5.44
S5	1.86	7.00	3.18	2.35	4.10	3.72	4.21	3.08	2.99	6.40
S10	7.00	4.36	3.18	2.35	4.10	3.72	4.21	3.08	2.99	7.50
S12	7.00	7.00	3.18	2.35	4.10	3.72	4.21	3.08	2.99	8.46

Figure 7.3 Effects of attitudinal changes on willingness to innovate in clean technologies

From scenario S10 it can be said that, if there is change from the current very low environmental risk perception (average score = 1.86) to an extremely high one (assuming an average score of 7 in the sample), it can be expected to have a greater effect on willingness ($S10 \Rightarrow We = 7.5$) than a situation where the business opportunities are high and economic risk is extremely low (see scenario $S5$). In such a scenario, the change in willingness is lower ($We = 6.4$) than that generated by changes in the environmental risk perception. It was not expected that an optimal economic opportunity with low financial risk would have only minimal influence on the willingness to innovate. This is due to the high and significant inverse correlation between economic risk perception and willingness (see Figure 6.3) and also due to the 21.38% contribution of economic risk in explaining the current willingness to innovate (see Figure 7.1a). In scenario $S12$, the combination of changes in both attitudinal correlates (i.e., EVR and ER) influences willingness up to a score of $We = 8.46$ on a scale of 14 points. Such a change falls just within the boundary of minimal willingness (note the line of demarcation between willingness and resistance to change in Figure 7.2).

The above results contrast with the general wisdom within the environmental policy literature. Scenarios $S4$, $S10$ and $S12$ imply that, by itself, a radical change towards a positive attitudinal disposition to protect the environment arising either from the managers' perception of high environmental risks or from low economic risk with good business opportunities or a combination of both perceptions, is likely to have a minimal influence on managers to promote innovation and behavioural change in their firms. Although the predisposition to innovate in clean technologies increases, it succeeds only in turning a moderate resistance into a minimal willingness.

Changes in the Perceived Social Pressure

As suggested Chapter 1, for more than 30 years environmental authorities have been enforcing regulations that faced strong resistance to compliance by firms. It is interesting to note that the worst policy scenario ($S1$) occurs when there is an increase in the perceived regulatory pressure only by the firm and this is not coupled with changes in any of the other behavioural domains, such as, a positive attitudinal change in risk perception or an increase in technological capabilities. In this scenario ($S1$), the willingness to innovate drops from its current value for the average firm ($W = 5.44$) to $We = 3.08$.

In a scenario where the average firm perceives extremely high pressures to innovate in clean products only from the market ($S8$), willingness has a score of $We = 7.03$ while a perception of extremely high pressure from the community ($S6$) has a lesser effect of $We = 6.01$. In scenario ($S3$) the aggregated effect of the three sources of social pressure ($We = 6.03$) is lower than in scenario ($S11$) when considering only the effect of market and the community and leaving the regulatory pressure with its average value (*We* = 8.03). Considering only market pressures with no regulatory pressure (*S16*), willingness moves up to *We* = 9.56. The negative impact of regulatory pressure on willingness to innovate is more evident in scenario (*S17*) when considering the aggregated effect of the three sources of social pressure, but assuming that the regulatory pressure is perceived as extremely low by the firm. In this scenario willingness moves up to *W* = 10.92.

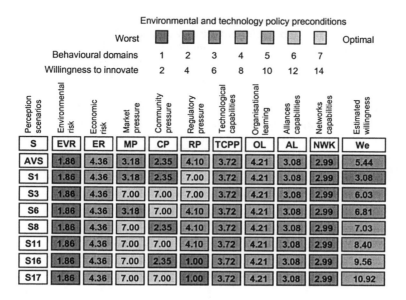

Figure 7.4   Effects of social pressures changes on willingness to innovate in clean technologies

As in the case of attitude, this simulation did not generate the expected results. It was assumed that by maximising regulatory pressure willingness to innovate would increase. This was expected because, as discussed in Chapter 4, environmental regulation has been seen as one of the main drivers of technological innovation in environmental technologies. The negative influence of regulatory pressure can be interpreted as the natural response of any firm to an ill-designed policy that aims to force change, not taking into consideration the lack of clean technological options. As discussed in the section on economic risk perception (Chapter 4), the uncertainties regarding technical feasibility, R&D time and costs, and time to market would present particular difficulties to the promotion of innovation in clean technology. This is especially the case as it is widely accepted that clean technologies are at their very early stage of development (e.g., PCSD, 1999; Clayton *et al.*, 1999; AIST, 1993; CEC, 1999).

Changes in the Perceived Control over Technological Change

Perceived control over the innovation process was expected to be the most important determinant of willingness and ultimately the predictor of behaviour for two reasons. First, Chapter 3 argued that in the case of any given firm having optimal attitudinal and normative predispositions to innovate, it was its volitional control that would ultimately determine the performance of any given behaviour. That is, firms with low control over their technical change after evaluating the possible environmental and economic outcomes and social pressures would not be able to innovate in clean technologies even if they were willing to do it. The second reason to believe that this is the case for many firms in the sample arises from the discussion presented in Chapter 2, regarding virtual non-existence of clean technology and the need to generate a new knowledge base to develop them. This is confirmed by the level of variance explained by the two beliefs concerning the capability to develop clean product concepts and the technological opportunities to substitute the current materials and components by clean options, and by scenarios *S14*, *S21* and *S24* where technological and organisational capabilities are assumed to be optimal (see Figure 7.5).

Environmental and technology policy preconditions

	Worst							Optimal
Behavioural domains	1	2	3	4	5	6	7	
Willingness to innovate	2	4	6	8	10	12	14	

Perception scenarios	Environmental risk	Economic risk	Market pressure	Community pressure	Regulatory pressure	Technological capabilities	Organisational learning	Alliances capabilities	Networks capabilities	Estimated willingness
S	EVR	ER	MP	CP	RP	TCPP	OL	AL	NWK	We
AVS	1.86	4.36	3.18	2.35	4.10	3.72	4.21	3.08	2.99	5.44
S2	1.86	4.36	3.18	2.35	4.10	3.72	4.21	3.08	7.00	5.77
S4	1.86	4.36	3.18	2.35	4.10	3.72	4.21	7.00	2.99	6.19
S9	1.86	4.36	3.18	2.35	4.10	3.72	7.00	3.08	2.99	7.32
S13	1.86	4.36	3.18	2.35	4.10	7.00	4.21	3.08	2.99	8.79
S14	7.00	7.00	7.00	7.00	7.00	3.72	4.21	3.08	2.99	9.05
S19	1.86	4.36	3.18	2.35	4.10	7.00	7.00	7.00	7.00	11.75
S21	1.86	4.36	7.00	7.00	7.00	7.00	7.00	7.00	7.00	12.35
S26	7.00	7.00	3.18	2.35	4.10	7.00	7.00	7.00	7.00	14.77

Figure 7.5 Effects of perceived control changes on the willingness to innovate in clean technologies

In the case that the average firm has an extremely positive attitude and a perception of high social pressure while having only average capabilities (see scenario *S14*), its willingness to innovate could be expected to be minimal (*We* = 9.05). In contrast, there is a significant difference when the perceived behavioural control is increased to its optimal value. On the one hand, while maintaining the current average attitude and perceiving high social pressure (*S21*), the average firm's willingness increases to *We* = 12.35. On the other hand, in scenario *S24*, if the firm has an extremely positive attitude with the current average perceived social pressure accompanied by high control upon the innovation process, willingness could be expected change to *We* = 14.77, the highest score scenario of all presented.

The stronger influence of technological capabilities on product and process environmental improvement (*TCPP*) is confirmed when its value is maximised and the other domains of behavioural control are fixed at their current average scores. The expected influence of *TCPP* on willingness (*S13* $\Rightarrow$ *We* = 8.79) is comparatively higher than all of the other domains when taken independently. The effect of optimal organisational learning capabilities (*S9*) moves willingness from its average value (*W* = 5.44) to *We* = 7.32, optimal strategic alliances capabilities shift willingness to We = 6.19 and optimal capabilities in networks of collaboration (*S2*) marginally moves willingness from 5.44 to 5.77. The aggregated influence of an extremely high technological and organisational control on willingness (*S19* $\Rightarrow$ *We* = 11.75) is higher compararared to the aggregated influences of a extremely positive attitude to develop clean technologies and an extremely high perceived social pressure (*S14* $\Rightarrow$ We = 9.05).

Optimal policy scenarios: strategy follows structure

In Chapter 1 it was argued that current environmental policy practice tends to select its policy instruments without knowing the preconditions upon which firms take decisions. Here it is suggested that policy efforts could be better allocated and have more chance of success if the structural determinants of the behaviour to regulate are explicitly taken into account. The environmental policy strategy discussed in the following arises from the paths indicated by the weight of the different behavioural domains explored in previous chapters. This simulation allows a more realistic scenario to be generated.

Scenarios *S23*, *S24*, and *S25* are proposed to be optimal as they yield the highest scores in the willingness to innovate in clean technologies with minimal policy efforts. These scenarios do not take into consideration behavioural domains in which governmental intervention is unlikely to occur. Some room for government policy intervention is assumed to exist in the domains of environmental and economic risk perceptions, environmental regulations, technological capabilities and networks of collaboration. The domains not optimised are used with their average score in the sample. These scenarios are depicted in Figure 7.6 below.

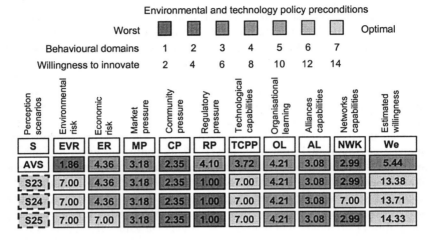

Figure 7.6 Optimal policy scenarios

Scenario *S23* shows that if there is an extremely high environmental risk perception (*EVR*) coupled with high technological capabilities (*TCPP*) and minimal regulatory pressure (*RP*) on the average firm, the willingness to innovate shifts up to We = 13.38. This is a better scenario than *S20* (*We* = 12.28), in which the firm perceives optimal economic and business opportunities, high technological capabilities and minimal regulatory pressure. By adding optimal conditions in networks of collaboration (*NWK*) to scenario *S23*, scenario *S24* is generated.

In this new scenario (*S26*), there is only a marginal change in willingness from *We* = 13.38 in *S23* to *We* = 13.71. This contrasts with a considerable change in willingness when removing networking capabilities and adding optimal economic conditions to develop clean technologies in scenario *S25*. In this scenario, the expected willingness goes up to *We* = 14.33, which is the highest score of the three scenarios considered. These are the conditions upon which the firms under study would be optimally willing to venture on innovative activities towards the development of clean product concepts and the adoption of clean production processes.

Scenario *S23* shows unexpected results because of the comparatively weak correlation between environmental risk perception (*EVR*) and willingness (see Appendix F, Tables F1 and F2) and the low proportion of variance in willingness that *EVR* explains (6.04%, see Figure 7.1a). Likewise, in the case of scenarios *S20* and *S24*, it was expected that the perceived economic risk would play a more important role in the determination of willingness to innovate. This expectation was based on three aspects. First, a highly significant negative correlation between economic risk and willingness (see Appendix F, Tables F1 and F2) and to the high proportion of the variance of willingness explained by the beliefs aggregated under the domain of economic risk perception that had been established in previous steps of the analysis (21.38%, see Figure 7.1a). The second aspect was the long standing focus of environmental regulations trying to regulate the self-interest of firms. Third, innovation theories indicate that the economic opportunities provided by innovations are supposed to organise and foster entrepreneurial innovative activities.

The simulation results (see scenarios *S19, S21, S26* in Figure 7.2) suggest that, even in the case of large business opportunities, the final determinant of willingness and, ultimately, innovative behaviour in clean technologies is highly dependent on technological and organisational capabilities. Before suggesting some policy implications and recommendations derived from scenario *S23*, a brief discussion is developed regarding the self-interest of the firm and economic risk.

THE MODERATING ROLE OF CORE CAPABILITIES UPON THE SELF-INTEREST OF THE FIRM

In the introduction to this book it was argued that the assumption of the current policy making paradigm is that the self-interest of the firm explains its current environmental behaviour. Based on this assumption, policies have been designed to change the firm's behaviour directly without knowing what the determinants of such behaviour are. Here, the self-interest of the firm was assessed by measuring the perceived economic risk considering potential gains and losses. The simulated policies indicate that although economic risk showed a significant and negative correlation with the willingness to innovate (see Appendix F, Table F1) and although it currently explains 21.38% of the variance in willingness (see Figure 7.1a), at the moment its score for the average firm is only moderate (see Figure 6.12).

Economic risk is apparently even less important in determining firms' behaviour when there are high environmental risk perception and optimal technological and organisational capabilities, even when the perception of risk is high (see scenarios *S25* and *S24* in Figure 7.2). These findings can be misleading as they suggest that, provided the appropriate technological opportunities exist, the self-interest of the firm (*the profit-seeking behaviour*) is not in contradiction with the broader social interest of environmental health. The following findings indicate that the self-interest of the firm has to be placed in context.

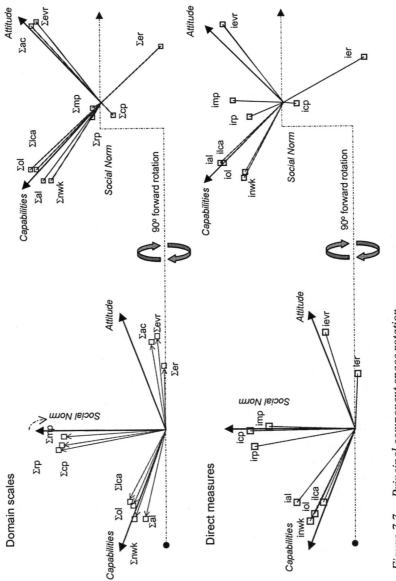

Figure 7.7   Principal component space rotation

170

Figure 7.7 shows the principal components plots for the 'domain scales' and the 'direct measures' presented in the Appendix (see Figure A.1, p. 209). The nine behavioural correlates that determine innovative behaviour in clean technologies cluster in three components (i.e., attitude, perceived social pressure and perceived behavioural control). The left side of the figure repeats the plots shown in Figure A.1, p. 209, while the right side presents a 90° forward rotation of the plot. This rotation reveals graphically what is indicated by a negative load of perceived economic risk in the behavioural control component (C1) shown in Table A.5, p. 207, a relationship of *independence* between the data vectors of environmental and economic risk perceptions.[6]

Figure 7.7 also shows an *opposition* between the activities needed to develop clean technologies and economic risk perception. It can be argued that perceived economic risk is inversely proportional to the perceived control over those abilities needed to develop clean technologies. That is, the higher the capabilities, the lower the degree of uncertainty associated with the innovation process. This opposition is also indicated by the significant negative bi-variate correlation between economic risk (ER) and perceived technological capabilities (TC), organisational learning (OL), strategic alliances (AL) and network of collaboration (NWK) (see Appendix F).

From the evidence presented above, regarding the variance explained by specific beliefs, and the negative correlation presented in Tables F1 and F2 (Appendix F), it can be inferred that the perceived economic risk (either low or high) for the average firm may arise from, or at least is indirectly influenced by, the lack of technological capabilities for product and process improvement (see Appendix C10, Table C10a). Such a moderating role of technological capabilities does not imply that the other capabilities are not important and should be neglected for policy analysis. The analysis of variance indicates the weight of those beliefs (or rational expectations) that are most salient *at the time* of the survey.

It is important to highlight again the inverse relationship of perceived economic risk (ER) with *all the domains that integrate the capabilities* to develop a clean product, (i.e., $TCPP$, OL, AL, and NWK). This implies that any of the other capabilities potentially can become salient depending on which barriers to the development of clean technologies are removed. It can be expected that once technological capabilities and technological opportunities[7] become available in the market, capabilities in organisational learning (OL) or strategic alliances (AL) have the potential to became crucial.

For example, for organisational learning, the stepwise regression (see Appendix C11, Table C11a) indicates that the expected organisational resistance towards the implementation of a culture of continuous improvement – in production processes – is the most important element in explaining the current perceived organisational learning capabilities (beliefs ol_7, ol_{13}, ol_{14}, and ol_{16} explain 63.34% of the perceived learning capabilities). The same analysis is applicable to strategic alliances and networks of collaboration capabilities. That is, the four capability domains are sources of uncertainty, therefore they are potentially sources of economic risk.

In the light of this finding it may be necessary to consider a complementary perspective to what has long been seen as a contradiction between the economic interest of the firm's activities and its inherent environmental effects. As discussed in Chapters 1 and 3, the perceived economic risk represents the interest of the firm and the perceived environmental risk is associated intrinsically with the social interest. The factor analysis indicates no explicit opposition between both 'perceived' interests (or both factors) such as that between economic risk and the capabilities, but cognitive independence. That is, in the perception of the managers there is no contradiction but independence between their firm's activities and its environmental effects, as neither perceptions are cognitively associated.

Three sources support this idea. First, the orthogonal relationship between *EVR* and *ER* shown by the above factor analysis. Second, the null correlation between environmental and economic risks perceptions (see Appendix F, Tables F1 and F2). Last, the scenario simulation indicates that when the managers are assumed to be aware – that is when they cognitively associate – the possible environmental effects of their firms' operations, they are expected to perceive that their firm will be more willing to innovate in clean technologies.

In sum, in addition to the financial risk, the regime of appropriability of the benefits generated by the innovative activities and the economic opportunities arising from new market niches, the self-interest of the firm can be expected to be mediated by the inverse relationship between economic risk and the degree of behavioural control over activities such as product life cycle analysis, product concept designs, the learning capabilities, etc. Once the appropriate capabilities are available, the importance of economic risk reduces as the uncertainty of failing in the innovation endeavour decreases due to a higher behavioural control. This last finding will be further explored below.

ENVIRONMENTAL POLICY STRATEGY FOLLOWS STRUCTURE

The discussion up to this point has focused on developing a conceptual framework to explore, differentiate and assess the set of structural relationships among determinants and their influence on the *environmental planned behaviour* of the firm. This had the aim of looking inside the firm and identifying the specific conditions that constitute the sources of resistance to innovate in clean technologies. The question arises about how such relationships can be influenced by policy? In the literature of social psychology, there is a general agreement that the path to a successful programme of behavioural change for a specific target group includes a number of steps. First, it is necessary to expose people to new information. Then, to create awareness of the socially desirable behaviour. Next, intentions, willingness or goals must be generated. Finally, the conditions for the new behaviour to be fixed or performed must be facilitated (Kuhl and Beckmann, 1985).

The structure of the developed policy analysis model is fully in agreement with this strategic path for a program of induced behavioural change. This path points to the three factors outlined by the TPB model and analysed in this work. The first activity in a behavioural change programme regarding the provision of new information refers to attitude, the cognitive component of the model. The second activity refers to the generation of subjective norms in people, the affective component (i.e., social norm). The last activity concerns the logistics required by the firms to carry out the behaviour, that is the instrumental or capabilities component to actually be able to carry out the development of clean technologies. The simulation of policy scenarios above enabled the identification of those conditions in which the firms in sample would be optimally willing to develop clean technologies. Figure 7.8 shows those domains that were the most relevant in scenario *S23* (compare Figure 7.8 with Figures 1.1, 1.2, and 3.4).

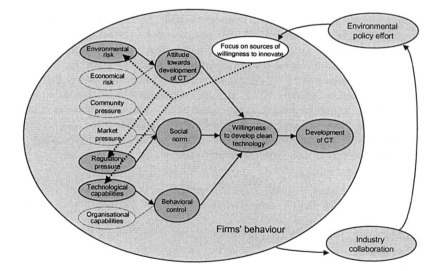

Figure 7.8   *Focus of the policy effort to promote a virtuous cycle of willingness to develop clean technologies*

In the scenario shown in Figure 7.8, by assuming high environmental risk perception and high technological capabilities with minimal regulatory pressure, willingness was optimised. As commented on above, although it does not reach the maximum expected willingness, this scenario optimises the policy effort. This is because it focuses the effort on those areas of policy intervention where the government has some degree of influence. The path for a policy programme that may induce a virtuous circle of collaboration between industry and regulatory agencies towards the development of clean technologies for those firms in the sample would be the following.

First, it would be necessary to provide the decision makers within the firm with the appropriate information about environmental risk to influence their environmental risk perception. This should have the aim of increasing the awareness of environmental hazards generated by the firm's operations. Second, the social desirability of innovative behaviour should be diffused by the environmental institution and authorities in collaboration with industry. Last, appropriate policies to facilitate the creation and implementation of a new knowledge base for the development of clean technology need to be in place. In the following sections, some policy suggestions for what may need to be done to address these aspects are put forward.

The proposed path is assumed to work for the following reason. Currently the willingness to innovate in clean technologies is mainly explained by the lack of technological capabilities and their associated economic risk, while the perceived environmental risk is very low. If it is possible to bridge the cognitive dissociation between economic and environmental risk, the managers will be very aware of the environmental effects of industrial activities. At the same time, if the required technological capability ($TCPP$) is available to start a deliberate innovative process it can be expected that the perceived economic risk (ER) will be reduced (this assertion arises from the negative correlation between $TCPP$ and ER, see Appendix F, Tables F1 and F2). From this, it can be inferred that, if the firms' managers perceive a real environmental problem and they perceive that they have the appropriate capabilities with minimal economic risk, they would be more willing to promote innovation in their firms in order to protect the environment.

Shifting the Managers' Environmental Risk Perception

The policy suggestions for an attitudinal change arising from a modification to the managers' environmental risk perception refer to those risk communication activities undertaken by the Mexican environmental authorities and institutions. The following format for an initiative is taken from the literature of risk communication, in particular from the works of Fischhoff (1994), Bostrom *et al.* (1994), and Atman *et al.* (1994). According to Atman *et al.* (1994), the guiding principle for any risk communication is that the message should cover the basic facts that are relevant to the recipient's decisions. Thus, the first step is to create a *mental risk model* of the managers and compare this with an expert's model for the same risk problem. The communication content should be based upon the gaps between the expert's model and managers' model. In the following subsection, the first part of such an expert's model is discussed. This refers to the environmental risk perception beliefs system of the managers that participated in the survey.

As discussed in Chapter 4, and tested in the Appendix, the conditions upon which the operations of the firms under study are considered environmentally safe are those where the generated hazards are meant to be controllable; not dreaded; not catastrophic; the benefits and social costs are equally distributed; of low risk for future generations; voluntary for those exposed; observable and not affecting the observer; of delayed effects; old and familiar; and known to science. Likewise, the acceptance of the generation of environmental hazards was considered mainly contingent upon the managers' voluntariness of exposure, the perceived controllability of 'environmental accidents', the discount of the economic benefits and environmental costs in time and social space and finally the condition of the observer (see Chapter 4, p. 65).

According to what was described in Chapter 6, more than 85% of the managers considered the generated hazards very low, while 90% considered them very acceptable (see Figures 6.4 and 6.5). Also due to the positive correlation of environmental risk perception scale (Σevr) and the negative relationship of the acceptance of the creation of hazards (Σac) with willingness to innovate (W) (see Tables F1 and F2 in Annex F), it can be argued that the managers considered the development of clean technologies to be irrelevant. That is, in terms of attitudinal predisposition to innovate, they did not evaluate the expected environmental improvements derived from the development of clean technologies as significant or good enough. In addition, if we consider the inverse relationship of economic risk (ER and Σer) and the willingness to innovate (Tables F1 and F2 in Annex F), it can be asserted that the managers have a negative attitude towards clean technology development despite its implicit social desirability.

The distribution of the frequencies of response for each belief presented in Figure 6.4 gave a picture of the perceptions in the sample. This figure indicates that in general the managers have a very low environmental risk perception and high acceptance of the generated hazards at the time of the survey. Furthermore, the managers' rational expectations (displayed in Figure 6.12) indicate that they do not expect any changes that may modify such a perception in the long term. Within this distribution of responses the beliefs that explain 92.3% of the variance in perceived risk are shown in Table C5a.[8] The perception of the firms' operations as environmentally safe accounted for 35.6% of the variance. The aspects of the perceived risk that contributed to this factor are the controllability of hazards (*evr1*), the scale of the impact perceived as not global (*evr2*), not catastrophic (*evr5*) and not representing risk for future generations (*evr6*). In addition, the generated hazards for the managers appear to have no fatal consequences (*evr3*), and the benefits and costs of the generated risks are thought to be evenly distributed (*evr4*).

The discount in time and space in conjunction with the perceived better-off condition of the manager that assesses the risk explained 31.16% of the variance in the sample. Within this aspect, the managers' lack of personal experience in environmental accidents (*ac17*) and the minimal perceived likelihood of being personally affected by pollution in the future (*ac18*) accounted for 26.4% of the variance on risk perception, the latter belief accounting for 24.4%. In addition, the distance of the managers' home locations from the firm facilities (*ac13*) and the delay of pollution effects (*ac12*) explained 2% of the variance respectively.

Chapter 6, described that 90% of the managers reported to benefit highly from the firm's operations. According to Vlek (1984), the discount in time and space refers to the distribution of consequences of firms' operations in a socio-geographical time-space. This refers to when and who reaps the benefits and who bears the undesirable consequences of industrial activities. To the extent that the benefits of the firm's operations are enjoyed 'here' while the undesirable costs are borne 'elsewhere', the emotional involvement of the managers (or shareholders) gradually decreases with increased socio-geographical distance. This refers to the location of the source of hazards and how likely they think it is that such hazards will affect people other than the managers themselves or their families.

The controllability of the possible consequences of hazards explained 17.4% of the variance. Perceived control depends on the knowledge and imaginability about possible consequences of hazardous releases and the measures to control them. In this regard, the managers' perceived controllability is composed of the beliefs that the generated hazards are controllable (*evr1*, *ac8*), and that in the case of accidents the likely effects of pollution could be contained by rescue operations (*ac10*).

The voluntariness *of exposure* accounted for a weight of 7.7% of the variance. Three beliefs composed the voluntariness. The technical options available can be considered as minimal since 75% of managers considered their technology to be the state-of-the-art in their industry (*ac2*). The managers perceived high influence in technological profile of the firm (*ac3*) and in the supply chain (*ac5*). These beliefs indicate that to the extent that the managers perceive themselves as co-authors of the firm's behaviour, they present higher voluntariness to accept the creation of hazards.

In summary, the most important aspects that explain the current environmental risk perception of managers are the scale of Slovic (1987) in assessing whether a technological activity is perceived as risky or safe; the position of the managers in the distribution of the benefits and undesirable effects of their industrial activities; and the perceived controllability of hazards. In the following section, the relationships among these aspects of risk are further explored in a correlation analysis of the managers' environmental risk perception beliefs system.

Managers' Environmental Risk Perception Beliefs System

Table 7.1 shows the managers' environmental risk perception correlation analysis. The table shows the set of relationships among the beliefs that explain the perception of environmental risk. The correlation analysis was carried out following the classification of beliefs in sub-scales as presented in the Tables 4.2, p. 67, and 4.3, p. 73. The scores obtained in each sub-scale were then correlated to assess if there were any significant relationships. The results from the correlation analysis indicate that if, there are low scores in the scale *sr* and high scores in the scales *cs* and *ctr*, then low scores in *EVR* can be expected. That is, a general low environmental risk perception (EVR) corresponds with the perception of the firm's operations as being environmentally safe, the generated hazards being highly controllable and the managers being better off in the distribution of economic benefits and environmental costs and consequences. Conversely, high risk perception corresponds ith low controllability, environmentally risky manufacturing operations and the managers being worse off.

Table 7.1   Correlation among the semantic loading of the different aspects of risk

	Aspects of risk			
EVR	Environmental risk perception index (domain)			
sr	The firms' operations are environmentally safe			
vol	Voluntariness of exposure			
ctr	Controllability of hazards' consequences			
dts	Discount in time and space			
cs	Condition of the subject			

	EVR	sr	vol	ctr	dts
sr	.351**	1.000			
vol	.014	−.306**	1.000		
ctr	−.321**	−.415**	.064	1.000	
dts	.060	−.081	.248*	−.002	1.000
cs	−.539**	−.422**	.057	.395**	.017

** Correlation is significant at the 0.01 level (2-tailed), N=97
 * Correlation is significant at the 0.05 level (2-tailed)

In addition, the results show a significant and negative correlation between the scale assessing the perception of the firm operations as 'safe or risky' (*sr*) and voluntariness (*vol*), controllability (*ctr*) and the condition of the subject (*cs*). For example, the relationship between the scale '*sr*' and the scale '*cs*' could be read as follows: if the hazards or pollution generated in the manufacturing operations are perceived as highly controllable, with no global impact, very unlikely to have fatal consequences, not catastrophic, and with very low risk for future generations, it is likely up to the level of a probability of .001 that by association the beliefs referring to the condition of the subject (*cs*) will be such that the managers perceive themselves better off because of their minimal experience with the effects of pollution, that they do not expect to be affected by pollution in the long term, they believe that they have a good knowledge of the current and possible environmental effects of the firm's operations and they value the economic benefits more than the inherent environmental effects.

Similarly, it is likely that perceived safety of the firms' operations is associated with beliefs of high controllability of hazards and pollution, such as the perceived availability of skills and safety procedures, minimal likelihood of environmental accidents combined with high possibility of rescue operations and reversibility of pollution effects. A similar analysis can be made with the other scales (i.e., *dts*, *vol*). As correlation is a two-way function, the relevance of this associations is revealed when the scores are considered in the opposite direction. High values on risk perception correspond with low scores on the controllability of pollution, low voluntariness of exposure and the perception of being worse off in the distribution of the benefits and costs. This can be expected to minimise the acceptance of the generation of hazards. In turn, linked by association with this perception, a higher overall environmental risk perception can be predicted and, as a consequence, a higher willingness to innovate in clean technologies.

The relationships described above suggest that changes in one of the correlates can have indirect effects in the others. For example, changes to a worse-off personal condition in the managers' perception would be accompanied by changes to a low controllability, low voluntariness of exposure and perception of the firms' operations as environmentally risky. The change in a single belief (*ac18*), referring to the condition of the subject (*cs*), that is, the managers perceived likelihood of being affected by pollution in the future could be expected to affect a high proportion of the variance in risk perception (i.e., 24.6%, see Table C5a).

Environmental Risk Communication Policy Design

From the variance and correlation analyses, it can be inferred that the policy effort should focus on the modification of those beliefs referring to the scales of 'risky or safe' operations, the condition of the subject and the perceived controllability of possible hazards. The correlation described above as the managers' environmental risk perception belief system corresponds to the logic and relationships among correlates presented in the theoretical section of environmental risk (Chapter 4). Assuming that the socio-psychological theories of attitudinal change are correct, it can be expected to influence the general predisposition to believe in the relevance of the development of clean technologies. This could become possible by a focus on the communication policy effort to provide the managers with new information as shown in Figure 7.9.

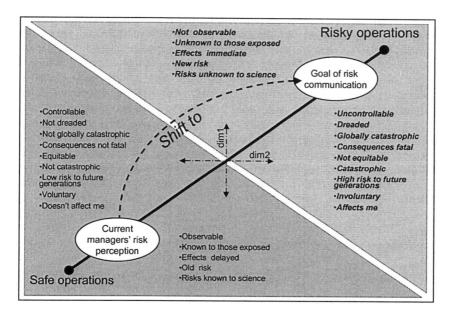

Figure 7.9 Risk perception policy

That is, according to the above analyses of correlation and variance it is possible to modify the managers' perception regarding their firms' operations as environmentally *safe* (*sr*) to environmentally *risky* through the modification of the beliefs that compose the Slovic scale or by changing the loading of the condition of the subject (*cs*) and controllability (*ctr*). Similar policies on environmental risk communication could be designed to raise awareness of the implications of environmental risk perception through the modification of the beliefs that motivate the acceptance of the generation of hazards. The type of information contained in the communication initiative will depend upon the type of sector or firms to be addressed, as different firms in different sectors use different technologies and generate different risks and therefore face different decision loads.

Although based upon the above belief system structure, the content of risk communication is expected to vary from sector to sector or firm to firm. A communication policy component common to all industrial activities would be to generate decision makers' mindfulness of the environmental implications of two aspects related with the transformation of matter and energy. The first regards the intrinsic generation of solid and, in many cases, hazardous wastes in the industrial production systems and its relation with the cycle of pollutants in the environment. That is, as described in Chapter 2, once the pollutants are generated, they can be expected in the long term to travel through water, soil or air, thus polluting the environment. The second aspect refers to the intrinsic generation of residuals in any work or matter transformation. This implies that at the end of the product life cycle, the product has to be ready to be reabsorbed by the economic system instead of being the environment perceived as the natural sink of waste.

In sum, this section has intended to show that it may be possible to generate a fundamentally different environmental risk perception for those managers in the sample. This could be achieved through the appropriate campaign focusing on the managers' notions of controllability, their condition as observers but also subjects to environmental hazards, and the perception of their technological activities as entailing some degree of risk. The expected outcome of such a campaign would be to bridge the managers' cognitive disassociation between firm operations and their inherent environmental effects.

Limitations for Technological Policy Design

Given the importance of the presence of clean technological capability in explaining the willingness to innovate, it is necessary to propose a policy to build up such capability. The previous section made suggestions for environmental policy design (i.e., risk communication) that, from their very conception, can be foreseen to be difficult to implement in a programme that includes the whole In-Bond industry. The design of policies to build up clean technology capability even is more problematic for the following reasons.

First, in Chapter 4 it was argued that four types of capabilities are required to generate a new knowledge base that might enable the development of clean technologies. Within the domain of technological capabilities, the perceived capabilities were classified into product life cycle analysis, technological opportunities, cooperation and influence, and improvement capabilities. The beliefs accounting for the capabilities in the product life cycle analysis explained 2% of the variance; the capability to cooperate or influence suppliers and customers towards the development of clean inputs 3%; the scale of technological opportunities for the substitution of inputs, materials and components 22.3%; and the capability to improve products and process accounted for 59% of the variance in perceived technological capabilities.

From the analysis of Table C10a (see Appendix C10) it can be said that two beliefs were salient. The capability for concepts development to improve the environmental qualities of the product (*tcpp21*) accounted for 55.3% of the variance, while the technological opportunities for substitutes of the current inputs and product components that ensure the elimination of noxious residuals and high recyclability (*tcpp43*) accounted for 17.8%. These two perceptions account for 73.1% of the perceived technological capabilities. Here it is interesting to notice that the belief *tcpp43* refers to the limitations and difficulties that arise from the very nature of the product.

It is not difficult to infer a relationship between both capabilities if we look at the procedures of product concept development (see Table C10d in Appendix C10). Generally, once a concept is generated, the next step is to assess its feasibility by finding the appropriate materials and machinery that will enable its manufacture. So the perceived challenge for the firms in the sample to develop clean products and processes does not arise from the difficulty of product life cycle analysis practices nor the capability to buy-in suppliers to collaborate, but from the very nature of the product itself. This refers to the service it provides and the particular combination of qualities that constitute this service. This implies that it might be possible to generate a clean product concept but it can be very difficult or impossible to develop it. This suggests the necessity for those firms that reported low capabilities (i.e., minimal possibilities to change) to search for new technological paradigms for product concept development as discussed in Chapter 2.

A second limitation for policy design, closely linked to the above, is the stage of technological evolution of the In-Bond industry (discussed in Chapter 2). All firms in the sample are in the so-called *rigid stage of evolution of industry* in a continuum of flexibility–rigidity to change technologically (see Appendix D, Charts D5 to D11). As their activities are focused mainly on standardised mass production, the sources of products and process innovations are principally suppliers and they focus their R&D efforts primarily on marginal changes in process efficiency and cost reduction. It could be expected that the firms in the sample would find it extremely difficult to shift into a new technological paradigm. This due not only to the focus of their own innovative activities but also because of their dependence on their suppliers of inputs, components, machinery and equipment for technical changes.

Third, as discussed in Chapter 2, the environmental institutions and regulatory agencies in charge of environmental management along the US–Mexican border are finding it difficult to cope with current environmental problems. Most activities, with minimal institutional and technological capabilities, are related to control and remediation of pollution. Very little attention is given to policies that promote pollution prevention and there is no awareness of the importance and implications of the dynamics of technical change for environmental policy design.

Last, further limitations for policy design directed at promoting innovation are imposed by the nature of the industrial organisation of the In-Bond industry. Common features in all the firms visited were foreign investments, high geographic mobility, high rates of openings and closures, and exemption from taxes upon revenues as their operations in Mexico are considered to be cost centres. The question of how to promote and facilitate technical change that will benefit the firms while aiming at protecting the environment presents additional challenges. Any investment by the Mexican government to promote these changes will only increase the level of subsidies in terms of low wages and tax exemptions that these firms already enjoy.[9] In addition, the fact that these firms are cost centres constrains the level of decision making at the local level regarding radical technical changes. That is, ultimately the overall technology strategy is linked to marketing and the growth of the firm is defined at its headquarters beyond the national boundaries of the manufacturing plant.

To sum up, the results from the analysis of variance carried out in this chapter, the two main beliefs that explain the perceived technological capabilities, and the important role of the latter in explaining the firm's willingness to innovate in clean technologies confirm what was discussed in Chapter 2. That is, that there is a need to create a new knowledge base that enables the development of new product and process concepts such as clean technologies. The current limitations imposed by the lack of technological capabilities and opportunities that might enable the development of clean products and process; the stage of technological evolution and the nature of the industrial organisation of the In-Bond industry, and the lack of attention and technological and organisational capabilities to promote clean technology development by the regulatory agencies and institutions along the US–Mexican border, leave the technological component of the proposed environmental policy still wide open and unfocused. The policy suggestions in the following section are a consequence of the analysis of variance of those beliefs classified under technological capabilities; and they are suggested with recognition of the limitations presented above.

Suggestion of Policy to Enable Clean Technology Capabilities Building

This section suggests there should be creation of a minimal institutional infrastructure and mechanisms that may enable the accumulation of clean technology capabilities in the Mexican Northern Region. Therefore, the following policy suggestions consider the above results from the statistical analysis and the regional reality by focusing on the 'soft' component of the process of innovations' diffusion. Here the diffusion refers to the process by which an *innovation* (i.e., the clean technology concept) is *communicated* through certain channels over *time* among the members of a *social system* (Rogers, 1995). Therefore, the considered activities focus on the promotion of a better understanding of what clean technologies are, their possible economic benefits to the firms and the management methods employed to move forward. In this sense, five activities are recommended to link to a sixth level of responses within the firm.

First, the creation and implementation of clean technology capabilities to protect the environment can be expected to be a lengthy process that will necessarily involve the participation of wide and heterogeneous sectors of society, such as legislators, firms, government, academia, the community and financial institutions. As this work has focused on the industrial sector, the immediate links are regulators and the sources of basic and applied research. To promote the participation of several sectors, it is necessary to create a binational agency (US–Mexican) or task group especially designed to merge the efforts of environmental agencies, academia and industrial chambers into a body that enables the generation of synergies. This recommendation arises from the necessity to buy in champions at the highest level of the corporate boards in industry, as this group has been absent in all environmental initiatives along the US–Mexican border. Forums and examples for the creation of such agency already exist with the creation of BECC and the CEC.

Second, as discussed in Chapter 2, the development of clean technologies for pollution prevention is gaining currency as an important part of environmental policy. This seems to be the appropriate approach as it represent lower costs for achieving real environmental protection in the long term, and it increases the overall economic efficiency at the firm level. In addition, it has been recognised lately that it can become a new multiplier of economic growth in those countries that endorse and promote this paradigm. This is particularly apparent in the latest documents for technology policy and the environment in the USA, Canada, and Japan (e.g. PCSD, 1999, US-White House, 1998; CEC, 1996a; AIST, 1993). Although this *vision* is mentioned in documents at government policy level for promoting cleaner technologies, many of the interviews carried out with the firms' managers revealed that the concept and the benefits of clean technologies – in terms of economic efficiency – are poorly understood. Therefore, it is necessary to create a common vision with common goals through consensus mechanisms among regulators and industry while promoting information exchange. Among these mechanisms, is the organisation of regular conferences and workshops to deploy information about the latest environmental management systems and the long-term benefits for the firms, the community and for the environment on both sides of the border.

Third, it is interesting to note different approaches to the same problem. While in Japan and Canada there are close links between industry, government and academia, in the USA and Mexico the linear model of technological 'push' is still present in the documentation intending to promote technical change towards sustainability. This assertion arises from analysis of the policy initiatives of these countries (US-White House, 1998; EPA, 1998; AIST, 1993; MPW, Canada, 1999). This model has already proved to be inefficient to promote technical change, because very frequently the products of basic research in universities and research centres do not reach the industrial and commercial stage.

There are some initiatives in process already that intend to address the problem of pollution prevention in the NAFTA region (CEC, 1999). Unfortunately, these activities have not included the representatives of the In-Bond industry in the region. It can be expected that any environmental initiative seen by this industry to stem from 'outside' will be viewed with distrust by industry. This is the result of a history of conflictive relationships between industry and environmental agencies. Therefore, it is necessary to promote the applied research projects linking academic institutions and environmental agencies to industry in specific problems of pollution prevention assistance.

Fourth, already much potential exists in academic and R&D infrastructure along the border that has not yet been linked to applied research.[10] These collaborations could generate immediate benefits for the firms that participate and spin-off for the community and other industries in the region. Assistance can be carried out at different levels of cleaner response, depending on the stage of evolution of the product and process of specific firms. This arises from the recognition that it cannot be expected that firms that historically have been known as 'dirty' begin the complete redesign of their products and process, especially when the core problem in their perceived capabilities lies in the very nature of their products. In this regard, the agreements between industry, academia and environmental agencies should explicitly differentiate and aim to provide assistance at the following six levels of possible responses for cleaner behaviour on the part of the firm:

- Improvement of operating techniques, working routines and upgraded housekeeping;
- Implementation of internal recycling mechanisms to reintroduce waste materials into their own production system;
- Implementation of external recycling to recover and sell waste materials onto another party;
- Introduction of incremental improvements in the process technology aimed at reducing waste and residuals in the short term and eliminating them in the long term;
- Development of new product or service concepts;
- Involvement in a wider process of product chain management, where environmentally oriented change takes place across the inter- and intra-firm trade and supply chain for those companies that are large enough to influence suppliers and intermediate or final customers (Clayton *et al.*, 1999).

Fifth, few of the interviewed managers were aware of the concept of clean technology. The knowledge and tools for the undertaking of an innovation programme are lacking. The region lacks professionals or firms that provide services in EMS implementation and innovation management. This training is absent from the education programmes of the regional professional education system. Therefore it is necessary to link regulation activities to the Ministry of Education to promote the creation of an infrastructure to train the required human resources in order to provide services and assistance in firms' future pollution prevention programmes.

Sixth, as was shown in this chapter the managers' economic risk perception arises not so much from the lack of economic opportunities but is indirectly due to the lack of technological and organisational capabilities. One of the ways to persuade managers of the benefits of the development of clean technologies is through the presentation of evidence projects and through the creation of demonstration projects. For this activity, it is necessary to search for successful cases of implementations of radical or incremental innovations either in products or processes, and deploy such information where appropriate.

Last, local reinforcements and social norms have been proven to be important motivations for individual behaviour (Ajzen, 1988, 1991; Cross and Guyer, 1980). Therefore it is necessary to make an effort to institutionalise local reinforcements and social recognition to the efforts of those firms (or managers) that show significant environmental improvements. Mechanisms for, and experiences of, how to create awareness and social desirability of a specific activity are abundant. These are prizes, titles, honorary positions, special mentions, etc. The features common to them all is the need of distinction and the generation of high social recognition and status. The creation of social desirability could be expected to arise from the creation of short-term local reinforcements to give signals of immediate benefits that fix the new behaviour into constant improvement.

In sum due to the limitations imposed by the nature of the firms in the sample, the lack of technological opportunities and the lack of attention to pollution prevention by environmental authorities the need arises to create a basic infrastructure of institutions. The task of these institutions would be the promotion of the concept of clean technology and the deployment of knowledge and innovation management tools towards this technological development. Such an institutional infrastructure in conjunction with activities on environmental risk communication can be expected to trigger a virtuous circle of willingness towards continuous improvement in the environmental performance of the firm.

Summary

This chapter described the relative influence of the different behavioural domains upon the current and long-term degree of willingness of the firms in the sample; it has simulated scenarios to find the optimal conditions under which the firms would be optimally willing to innovate; and it has discussed the critical role of the capabilities to perform innovation to moderate the perceived economic risk. These analyses were carried out taking a socio-psychological perspective from which it was possible to find better ways of promoting improvements on the environmental performance of the firm other than through direct regulation. The underlying assumption was that in order to improve this performance, it is a primary condition to reduce the level of conflict between the firm's self-interest and the social interest that embodies environmental protection. This conflict is presumed to be minimal when the firm is optimally willing to reorient its long-term business strategy to be environmentally responsible. The main findings in the analysis carried out were:

- Currently two behavioural domains explain the major part of the variance in the willingness of the firm to innovate: (a) the technological capabilities derived mainly from the perceived capacity to develop clean product concepts due to the vary nature of the product; and (b) the perceived economic risk derived from the possible loss of capital associated with the uncertainty that an innovation process entails.
- The perceived economic risk depends not only on the lack of economic opportunities and capital risk, but is also strongly moderated by the firm's degree of control over the innovation process. The higher the capabilities, the lower the perceived economic risk.
- The simulation process revealed several points: first, the negative impact of environmental regulation upon the willingness to develop clean technology. Second, optimal attitudes (i.e., very high environmental risk and optimal economic opportunities) and very high overall social pressure to develop clean technology are not sufficient to foster the innovative behaviour of the average firm. Third, optimal policy scenarios arise only in the presence of high technological capabilities. Finally, a scenario that relates high environmental risk and high technological capabilities with minimal direct environmental regulation was considered to optimise the policy effort while maximising the willingness to innovate.
- The policy suggestions for the above scenario are related to two types of activity on the part of the government. The first relates to the bridging of the cognitive independence between the firms' operations and their environmental consequences. It is suggested that this be addressed via the undertaking of risk communication activities aimed at increasing awareness of the firms' managers regarding the creation of environmental hazards generated by the operations of their firms for the host communities. The second type of activity refers to the creation of a minimal institutional infrastructure directed at promoting the diffusion of the concept of clean technologies and innovation management tools. This was suggested due to the limitations of the type of industrial organisation and the stage of technological evolution that characterise the In-Bond industry, together with the scant attention that environmental regulators

in Mexico give to pollution prevention which make it difficult to specify a clear and specific technology policy.

In the light of these conclusions, at this point it is opportune to reflect on the main question of this book (Is it possible to reconcile the interest of the firm with the broader social interest regarding environmental protection?) and the concept of 'social traps' put forward in Chapter 1. This challenge faced by policy makers and firms presents all the features of a social trap as defined in the taxonomy proposed by Cross and Guyer (1980). These are: (1) *Time delay*: the benefits of industrial technology are expected to be obtained in the short term. If the technology implies negative impacts, very frequently these are perceived only in the long term after a cumulative process. (2) *Ignorance*: linked to the previous point, the negative aspects of a technology are unknown at the time of its development or early diffusion and use. (3) *Slider reinforcer*: there is a potential regress when tackling the negative effects of a specific technology with a new technological fix with unknown secondary effects in the long term. (4) *Externalities*: the benefits obtained by the producer and user of a specific technology do not match the pay-offs incurred by others.

Firms benefit from technology in their economic activities. On a broader scale, society as a whole has benefited for several generations with consumable products and services enabled by advances in science and technology. Whatever the benefits, these have been obtained by applying specific scientific and technological paradigms to industrial activities that have evolved over decades into the current techno-economic regime. These structural determinants have oriented people, organisations or whole societies in a direction or a set of relationships that have proved to be difficult or impossible to get out of. This is because individual advantage or perceived needs in the short term prevent innovative behaviour that might, in the long term, be of great benefit to the group or society as a whole. It is also due to a lack of agency and power to carry out the required changes. Thus, paraphrasing Cross and Guyer (1980), this situation is one characterised by multiple but conflicting rewards or local reinforcements.

The local reinforcements of the current behaviour of the firm can be equated with the determinants explored under the concept of behavioural domains in this thesis. The local reinforcement (i.e., the perceptions in each behavioural domain) can be seen as the signals that guide the behaviour of the firms and equate the sources of the conflict with the social interest. The suggested initiatives in risk communication and clean technology capability building are conceptualised taking into consideration the minimisation of these sources of conflict. This approach to environmental policy analysis represents a radical shift from the current practice of policy design in which the behaviour of the firm is explained merely in terms of self-interest. To overcome this reality, the policy approach suggested for the specific region of northern Mexico that would be carried out partly in collaboration with the firm would enable the regional environmental authorities to approach the conflict in a more constructive fashion.

NOTES

1. The weight of each domain results from an 'enter' multivariate analysis performed on the data set of the direct measures of the perception on the different behavioural domains. The estimation of the weight of each domain was assessed by accounting for the amount of variance that was explained in the sample after each domain was introduced in the regression analysis.
2. It was proposed in Chapter 3 that the assumption underlying the measurement of the perceived capabilities was that those firms with lower capabilities would perceive more difficulty in the developing clean products and processes and vice versa. This assumption is confirmed in Appendix F (Table F3). There is a positive correlation between capabilities and the perceived control upon the innovation process.
3. Check the proportions of the variance explained for the two first beliefs in the Model summary Tables in Appendix C.
4. This argument was presented in Chapter 3.
5. This figure repeats elements from Figure 7.2 to highlight outcomes of the simulation referring only to attitude changes. The same procedure is followed for social pressure and perceived behavioural control.
6. In vector analysis, orthogonal vectors are considered to be linearly independent (Marsden and Tromba, 1996). That is, if we consider that a principal components analysis plot represents a set of Euclidean distances that create a space with the minimal possible dimension by a linear combination of the variables included in the analysis (e.g., the variables being the vectors Σevr, Σer, Σmp, Σcp, Σrp, $\Sigma tcpp$, Σol, Σal, Σnwk), what we have in the plot represents a set of vectors clustering along three orthogonal dimensions (i.e., attitude, social pressure and perceived control).
7. New raw materials, components, and in general inputs highly recyclable and biodegradable.
8. Those beliefs that accounted for most of the variance in the sample were considered the more influential in the perception and acceptance of environmental risk. For a methodological note and the verification of the contribution of each belief to explain the environmental risk perception see Table C5a (Appendix C5), and Figure 7.1a.
9. For example, the net capital transfer to foreign firms in 1998 due to wage differentials amounted to 14 billion dollars. This calculation was done considering differentials only on minimal wages of 1:5.25 dollars per hour per one million direct jobs generated in 1998 by this industry (*Source*: INEGI, 1999).
10. There are already seven state universities with many campuses, twelve federal technological institutes plus several prestigious private universities along the border.

8. Conclusions

SUMMARY OF FINDINGS

At the outset of this book it was stated that the primary goal of the firm is the optimisation of profits for their shareholders. Experience has shown that this goal is in contradiction with broader societal goals, one of which is environmental protection. In this respect, ideally, environmental policies are conceptualised as a means of making these opposing interests compatible. The challenge is to design ways of achieving socially desirable goals while allowing people to pursue their individual self-interests. The first research question of this study was whether or not it is possible to reconcile the interest of the firm with the social interest regarding environmental protection. The analysis of the data in Chapter 6 indicated that the firms in the sample, currently and in the long term, are not willing to develop clean technologies. This suggests that it is not possible to reconcile these interests, either at the moment or in the long run, if the current social and technological conditions that determine the firms' willingness to change continue.

The second research question concerned finding an explanation as to why the firms in the sample are not willing to undertake a business strategy that includes radical preventive measures to eliminate residuals and waste, such as changing product designs and manufacturing processes that aim at the ideal recycling and zero emissions factory. Following the framework developed here, the willingness in the firm to develop clean technologies could be sparked by three factors (separately or in combination). The first factor, attitude, refers to the managers' positive predisposition arising from the positive evaluation of the development of clean technologies in terms of (a) presenting good economic opportunities with low capital risk; and/or (b) the perception of CT development as a permanent solution to environmental pollution resulting from the firms managers' high environmental risks awareness. The second factor, perceived social pressures, concerns the internalisation of social norms that encourage the development of clean technologies arising from the market, the community or the regulatory agencies. The third factor, the perceived control over the behaviour, regards the perceived technological and organisational capabilities to innovate.

From the analysis of the data in Chapters 6 and 7, we can conclude that the average firm is not willing to develop clean technologies because of the perceived low technological and organisational capabilities and the lack of economic opportunities owing to the lack of demand and willingness to pay for clean products on the part of the customers. As a consequence, this generates a negative perceived economic risk. In addition, the perceived social pressure arising from the market, the community and the regulatory and normative institutions are minimal. Environmental governmental agencies, traditionally seen as the main drivers of environmental protection, have little influence and can be expected to have a negative impact on the willingness to innovate in clean technologies if these are enforced by law. As discussed in Chapters 2 and 7, the main factor that accounts for the minimal perceived regulatory pressure is that regulatory agencies in Mexico are still oriented to command-and-control BAT-standard based enforcement of regulation, without explicit consideration of the development of clean technologies. The proportion of the contribution of each determinant to willingness is presented in Figure 8.1.

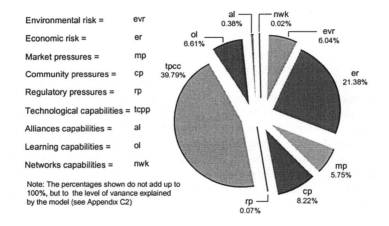

Figure 8.1   Relative weight of the determinants of the firms' willingness to develop clean technologies

The third research question addressed the conditions upon which the firm would be willing to re-orient its main goal to include radical preventive measures that avoid the generation of residuals. According to the results of the simulation exercise, the firms in the sample would be optimally willing to innovate in two scenarios. These scenarios have two common features. The first feature implies the mastering of the proposed technological capabilities and the availability of technological opportunities to substitute inputs, materials and components in order to develop clean product and process concepts. The second common feature concerns the minimal regulatory pressure as conceptualised today, that is, the enforcement of norms and standards. This regulation may need to take the form of collaboration on specific policies to find solutions as proposed in Chapter 7.

The difference between the two scenarios is that one requires optimal economic opportunities derived from the opening of new market niches. This is assumed to imply minimal capital risk as the firms ideally would encompass the appropriate technological capabilities to carry out the innovation process. As discussed in Chapter 7, the negative risks arise mainly from the lack of technological and organisational capabilities to innovate. The other scenario requires that the firms' managers perceive the residuals and waste generated by their firm as non-controllable, and non-voluntary for those exposed to them, and that these managers perceive themselves very likely to be personally affected in the future by pollution. In this sense, a new form of regulation could take the form of risk communication activities and the promotion and facilitation of technological capabilities.

THE SCIENTIFIC VALUE AND PRACTICAL USE OF THE DEVELOPED MODEL

The above findings arise from the operation of a behavioural theory, adapted to the environmental policy realm. The developed model enabled us to explain, measure and predict firms' willingness to innovate in clean technologies as well as its determinants. The framework provided a set of definitions to search systematically and construct a broader definitional system that enabled the test of hypotheses regarding dependence upon specific factors as well as their importance in influencing willingness and ultimately behavioural change.

The introduction of this book mentioned that, over the last decade, the literature on the 'greening' of industry has provided important insights about the firm's environmentally responsible behaviour. Two common features of these studies are that they emphasise isolated determinants of cleaner behaviour of the firm while neglecting the effect of others, and lack hypotheses and methodological rigour to test the importance of those factors in explaining behaviour. This work differentiates itself from those studies in that it has provided a theoretical framework with a systematic approach that allowed the derivation and testing of hypotheses and to differentiate those factors that determine the decision of the firm to engage in the development of clean technologies.

It also differentiates itself from previous works on environmental policy analysis that are based mainly on theories of distribution and power, assuming that the environmental behaviour of firms is explained only by the notion of self-interest or rent-seeking behaviour. This philosophy underlying policy making in the last 30 years has produced strong conflictive positions between firms and regulators. On the contrary, this work is in agreement with approaches in the constructive conflict analysis focused on gaining a better understanding of the sources of the conflict. This study set out to search and distinguish between the values, cognitions, fears and goals of the firm, seeking for those conditions that may enable the design of better policies based on the notion of collaboration instead of conflict. This new approach to environmental policy is summarised and depicted in Figure 8.2. In addition, this work contributes to the field of innovation studies by providing an example of how behavioural models can be applied within the field to better understand the propensity of the firm to engage in innovative activities.

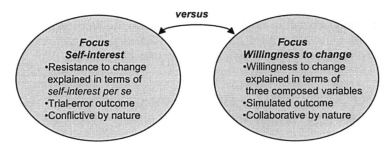

Figure 8.2   Comparison of environmental policy approaches

An additional contribution of the research strategy adopted in this study to the area of environmental policy analysis is that it evolves from a positive to a normative approach by proceeding from the explanation to the prediction of the willingness of firms. It is positive insofar as it first explores and describes the possible determinants of the dependent variable. Only after testing the association between dependent and independent variables through empirical validation did it attempt to use the developed framework at a normative level. In this sense, it can be seen as more robust than previous studies in the field, as it bases its policy suggestions on sound theoretical and empirical grounds. As a consequence, this work further advances the methods used in previous works of environmental policy analysis. The practical uses of the developed model arise from the diagnosis of the different degrees of predisposition to innovate in clean technologies. It is possible to differentiate between firms and industrial sectors. As a consequence, it is possible to allocate the policy effort to those areas of policy intervention that result in being more relevant to the achievement of socially desirable goals.

IMPLICATIONS FOR POLICY DESIGN

The main ·policy implication of this study concerns the approach to environmental policy analysis. This work proposes an instrument for environmental policy analysis that allows us to gain a better understanding and to assess the possible sources of conflict between firms and regulators when promoting clean technology development. As described in Chapter 2, the Northern Border Region of Mexico has experienced very rapid industrial growth due to the relocation of foreign firms, the In-Bond industry. This industry has traditionally had a 'dirty' image regarding its environmental behaviour. Recently, with the advent of NAFTA, there has been an upsurge of debates in the governments of the USA and of Mexico regarding the promotion of sustainability on the US–Mexican border. At present, the two main institutions promoting sustainability involve only marginally the main source of environmental problems in the region, that is, industry.

As shown in Chapter 7, this work can help to increase the understanding of the nature of the challenges that the promotion of clean technology development may entail. It is assumed that the policy-making process can be better handled if the stakeholders (i.e. industry and regulators), have a better understanding of what is being negotiated; what is and what is not possible to do. This study shows that very little can be expected from the firms under study in terms of contributing to the sustainability of the region. Their social context in Northern Mexico, the way they perceive the effects of their operation on the environment and their capabilities to change and the benefits they perceive do not encourage significant changes in their behaviour.

In order to change the above conditions to those that promote behavioural change in firms, it is necessary to provide the decision makers within the firm with the appropriate information about environmental risk in order to influence their environmental awareness, and their perception of the relevance of clean technology development. This should have the aim of increasing the awareness of environmental hazards generated by the firms' operations. Second, the social desirability of innovative behaviour should be disseminated by environmental institutions and authorities in collaboration with industry. Finally, the appropriate policies to facilitate the creation and implementation of a new knowledge base aimed at the development of clean technology need to be in place.

Following the results of the policy simulation in Chapter 7, one way of promoting changes in firms' behaviour would require the undertaking of risk communication activities to reduce the gaps between a risk expert model and the environmental risk belief system of managers. A positive attitude towards clean technologies is assumed to be founded upon modified perceptions of the pollution generated by the firm as non-controllable, and non-voluntary for those exposed and of the perception that the managers themselves are likely to be affected in the future by pollution. In turn, this positive attitude can be expected to optimise the willingness to innovate.

For the building of technological capability the creation of a binational agency or task group appointed to coordinate the efforts of environmental agencies, academia and industrial organisations into a body that would enable the generation of synergies was suggested. These efforts should aim to create mechanisms to arrive at a common vision with common goals among regulators and industry while promoting information exchange; they should aim at promoting joint ventures of applied research projects linking academic institutions and environmental agencies to industry in dealing with specific problems of pollution prevention assistance.

In this regard, the joint ventures between industry, academia and environmental agencies should explicitly aim to provide assistance at different levels of possible responses to implement cleaner behaviour on the part of the firm. This would require the linking of regulation activities to the Ministry of Education in order to promote the creation of an infrastructure to train the human resources that would be required to provide services and assistance to the firms future' pollution prevention programmes. Finally, it would be necessary to make an effort to institutionalise positive local reinforcement and social recognition of the efforts of those firms (or managers) that show significant environmental improvements.

Another way of using the results might be for the policy makers just to be knowledgeable of these determinants, how they interact with each other and to use this knowledge in the process of any policy negotiations. In these respects, the policy makers need to be aware that the clean technology development is by no means under the firms' volitional control. This is indicated by the salient beliefs within the domain of perceived behavioural control. The two beliefs accounting for most of the variance in perceived technological capabilities point to a systematic dependence on technical changes along the whole supply chain. This fact will limit the control of an individual firm. This determinant can be seen as a primary cause of the perceived lack of control.

Once this barrier is removed, it is very likely that other organisational factors, like organisational learning or outsourcing knowledge through strategic alliances or networks of collaboration, gain more relevance. Due to the negative correlation between economic risk with the perceived control over the innovation process and with the willingness to innovate, it can be expected that the above activities reduce the perceived risk owing to higher technological control and, as a consequence, the firm can be expected to be more willing to innovate. The relative importance of these factors is depicted in Figure 8.1.

An additional policy implication concerns the role of the environmental agencies. From the negative impact that the perceived regulatory pressure has on willingness, it can be said that its current role and *modus operandi* must change if these agencies intend to promote clean production. They would need to reorient their capabilities from the enforcement of standards to the facilitation and promotion of technical change. This suggests that regulatory agencies need to increase their capability in operating environmental management systems and above all, in understanding the dynamics of technical change in manufacturing firms. This may enable them to better promote technical change in the firms that they intend to regulate.

The above policy suggestions could be criticised from the point of view that it was not necessary to develop such an elaborate model to propose them. In principle, this is wrong in that the goal of policy analysis is to gain a better understanding of the possible ways of acting and of the possible responses to specific determined policies. The above suggestions are intended to address one aspect of environmental policy implementation that has not previously been taken into account. That is, the perceived environmental risks; and the specific considerations involved in the acceptance of hazards and pollution generation. Prior to the present study, the policy instruments mentioned in the literature of environmental policy had not included initiatives such as risk communication, targeting the managers in firms. In addition, the literature around the 'greening' of industry and environmental policy analysis previously had not assessed the availability of technological capabilities needed to develop clean technologies.

How to implement a programme of risk communication and actually create and deploy a new knowledge base to develop clean technologies is beyond the scope of this work. Once the behaviour has been explained, the question of actually influencing behavioural change remains open. The suggested initiatives in risk communication and clean technology capability building are conceptualised as taking into consideration the minimisation of the sources of conflict between the interest of the firm and the interest of society regarding environmental protection. It is assumed that the activities carried out in collaboration with the firm will enable an approach towards resolving conflicts between the interests of the firm and societal interest regarding environmental protection in a more constructive fashion.

GENERALISATIONS

Regarding possible generalisations, these arise from the proposed method of policy analysis in two ways. First, owing to the construction of the model based on relevant bodies of literature rather than on elicited beliefs as originally suggested by Ajzen, the model can be regarded as generalisable and applicable in other national contexts and industries. The literature is not location-specific but this would have been the case if the model had been compiled using more conservative belief elicitation methods. The In-Bond industry presents a specific context in which the model has been tested. Second, the proposed framework essentially consists of a system of hypotheses linking a number of attributes (i.e., beliefs held by managers about their firms' internal and external context) to the willingness of the firm to develop clean technologies. As discussed in the Appendix, the empirical verification and the consistency of the findings, in terms of statistical *reliability* and *validity* of the theoretical model developed, are satisfactory.

The values of the parameters that test the *reliability* of the items used in the questionnaire were, in general, above the standard recommended by the norms of psychometric tests. As to its *validity,* the structure of the empirical data was confirmed to correspond with the proposed theoretical model. Items assessing environmental and economic risk perception cluster to form a cognitive dimension (attitude). Items assessing community, market and regulatory pressures cluster to form a normative dimension (social norm). Items assessing technological and organisational capabilities cluster to form an instrumental dimension (behavioural control). In addition, several multiple regression analyses tested the explanatory and predictive power of the model. The coefficient of determination of willingness was found to be satisfactory. Similar results were obtained in the multiple regression analyses for the different domains. Based on these findings, it can be said that the model developed measures and predicts appropriately firms' planned behaviour regarding the development of clean technologies as perceived by their managers.

Therefore, it can be asserted that the model developed here can be used to assess and predict the same behaviour in different contexts. The application of the model in other contexts might result in other behavioural domains being more important in explaining the willingness to develop clean technologies. In settings where environmental awareness is above the basic struggle for subsistence or minimal consumption, the social norm (i.e., market and community pressures) can be expected to play a more important role in influencing the willingness in firms. This can be expected to imply a higher demand for clean products, which would mean that firms would perceive economic opportunities and therefore would have a higher willingness to change. The challenge remaining for the firm would be to acquire the appropriate technological and organisational capabilities.

FINAL REMARKS

Two final remarks: first, traditional economic models of the firm and the consumer behaviours are constructed upon psychological assumptions either stemming from the behaviourist school of the 1920s to 1960s (stimulus and reaction) or, as recently, they are constructed upon purely cognitive approaches (bounded rationality). The introduction of new theories from social psychology developed in the 1980s and early 1990s related to the psychology of action can give new insights into the economic behaviour of social agents. These new theories shed new light by linking cognitive, motivational, normative and instrumental factors into the explanation of the dissonance between cognition, motivations, intentions, goals, plans and actions. A very promising new branch of research can be considered to be open with the introduction of the notion of psychological economics applied to policy analysis, as this work implies.

Second, concerning the main question in this study: is it possible to reconcile the interest of the firm with the broader social interest regarding the environment? In sum, although the case study focused on a few firms in three industrial sectors in Northern Mexico, its theoretical underpinnings might be generalised in terms of method for environmental and technology policy analysis for those manufacturing firms that operate globally. If this is accepted, then this work suggests that policy makers, and society as a whole, have two big challenges. On the one hand, there is the need to change the local reinforcements of the self-interest that predispose and form environmental risk perceptions and, as a consequence, determine environmental attitudes. On the other hand, it is necessary to make a shift in the current dominant technological paradigms and trajectories. This is indicated by the two beliefs that explain the perception of technological capabilities. In turn, this technological shift is perceived as risky, conditioning economic risk perception, that is, the self-interest of the firm.

This implies that, in principle, the firm will not pursue a path of behavioural change that goes at least against its main goal (i.e., profit making), and that at most may threaten its own survival in the market. This represents a massive social trap in which local reinforcements do not allow firms (i.e., managers, decision makers) to see beyond their short-term plans, as a radical change in their intrinsic logic of operation may go against its own survival. At this point, it is appropriate to mention that in some instances what is relevant for the individual or the group may also be crucial for the collective. This was expressed by Charles Darwin in his proposal of the 'law' of the survival of species and paraphrased by Theodore Sturgeon:

> Implicit in this law was humanity. With it, the base of survival emerged, a magnificent ethic: *the highest command is in terms of the species, the next is survival of group. The lowest of three is survival of self.* All good and all evil, all morals, all progress, depend on this order of basic commands. *To survive for the self at the price of the group is to jeopardise species. For a group to survive at the price of the species is manifest suicide.* Here is the essence of good and of greed, and the wellspring of justice for all of mankind. (Sturgeon, 1950, p. 183, emphases added).

Appendix A: Validation of theory structure and its contents

RELIABILITY AND VALIDITY OF MEASUREMENT

In Chapters 3 and 4 the structure and content of a decision-making model to assess a beliefs system were proposed. The purpose of this model was to explain and predict the willingness (or propensity) of the firm to innovate in clean technologies. Concerning environmental and technology policy analysis, the model is intended to assess the determinants' relative importance in explaining and influencing the environmental innovative behaviour of the firm. This assessment implies the measurement of the behavioural correlates involved. In this sense, this appendix deals with the validation of the structure and contents of the proposed model.

The validation of measurements of abstract constructs in psychometric research has been under debate for long time (Kline, 1998; Michell, 1997). According to Korzybsky, a 'measurement represents nothing else but a search for *empirical structure* by means of extensional, ordered, symmetrical and asymmetrical relations. Thus, when we say that a given length measures five feet, we have reached this conclusion by selecting a unit called 'foot', an *arbitrary and unspeakable* affair, then laying it end to end five times in a definite *extensional order* and so have established the asymmetrical, and, in each case, five times as many as the arbitrary selected unit' (1994, p. 259, original emphases). Similarly, Michell (1997, p. 358) defines scientific measurement 'as the estimation or discovery of some magnitude of a quantitative attribute to a unit of the same attribute'. In contrast, in psychometric research – building upon the work of Stevens – measurement has been traditionally defined as 'the assignment of numerals to objects or events according to rules' (Stevens 1946, p. 667).[1]

The difference between the definitions of measurement used in the natural sciences and in psychometrics arises from two facts. First, measurement in psychometrics tests – in contrast to measurements developed in the natural sciences – does not have units of measurement (Kline, 1998, p. 47). An example of this fact is the arbitrariness of the number of items that compose the scales proposed here to assess the managers' perceptions. These scales represent a typical example of what happens in the field of psychometrics. Second, doubt arises about validity when considering the measurement of beliefs and perceptions. According to Michell (1997, pp. 368–72), the *ad hoc* definition of measurement used in psychometric research was intended to solve a long-standing conceptual problem that entails the assignment of numbers to psychological attributes in the search for quantification.

Measurement assumes that the variables assessed are quantitative in nature. Michell (1990, p. 19) argues that Stevens' definition mistakes measurement for numerical coding (labelling, tagging), and that the notion that psychological traits are quantitative cannot be established *a priori*, it has to be empirically demonstrated (*ibid.*, p. vii). That is, for a construct to be quantitative it must be proven to possess *order and additive structure* in order to claim that any measurement has been achieved. The failure to confirm that the construct is quantitative leaves the proposed measurement procedures to be 'considered at best as a speculation and, at worst, a pretence at science' (Michell, 1997, p. 359). Michell (1997, pp. 360–61) points out that this fact has been largely neglected in the whole field of psychometrics research that is constructed upon the definition of measurement proposed by Stevens.

This explains why within psychometric research there is an ongoing debate about the methods used for the measurement of abstract constructs. Despite this debate, it is widely accepted that measurements of this type are considered good or scientific if the instrument used to measure has the following characteristics: it is based at least on interval scales; it can discriminate among respondents; and it is reliable and valid (Kline, 1998, p. 29; Loewenthal, 1996).[2]

The first two features can be easily demonstrated. Regarding the first, in this work, the designed questionnaire uses interval scales ranging from 1 to 7. This ensures that the scales can be linearly transformed into common scales, thus allowing comparison of scores (Kline, 1986). Concerning the second, the smallest scale ranges from 2 to 14, and the largest ranges from 38 to 266, this indicates a potential large range of variance. This fact ensures that the developed scales can discriminate among the respondents (Kline, 1986).

The third and fourth features of good tests are not so straightforward to establish. Before intending to make any inferences derived from the perceptions of managers regarding the planned behaviour of their firms, therefore, it is necessary to test whether the proposed constructs to assess these perceptions are reliable and valid. In the following sections, these two terms will be briefly explained along the testing process.[3] It will also be shown that the methods used here to validate the effectuated measurement operations are in agreement with the definitions given by Korzybsky and Michell. That is, it will show the quantitative nature of the construct assessed. Therefore, here we have avoided any problems that have been identified with Stevens' definition.

RELIABILITY STATISTICS

The Meaning of Reliability of Measurement in Psychometric Research

An unreliable measure is of limited value. If different questions or items in the questionnaire give inconsistent results, then nothing is being assessed. Therefore the reliability of a questionnaire refers to the extent to which the outcome of a test remains unaffected by variations in the conditions and procedures of testing (Loewenthal, 1996). Thus, in psychometrics, the reliability of a test (or scale) refers to its consistence, internally and over time.[4] According to Kline (1998, p. 30), in psychometrics, if any given scale intends to measure a particular variable then it is obvious that each item in the scale should also measure attributes of that variable. If each item in the scale measures attributes of the same variable, then the test can be expected to be internally consistent. This ensures that the test is as unvaried (or one-dimensional) as possible measuring only one variable. Table A.1 shows items for the assessment of economic risk perception. Here, managers were asked to respond to a number of test items regarding the possible outcomes derived from innovative activities towards the development of clean technologies.

Table A.1   Example of one-dimensional items

Item	Diff. Semantic
er1 For our firm failing to launch a clean product for a new market niche may imply a great opportunity loss:	(unlikely–likely)
er2 The benefit this firm can gain from the development of clean technologies in order to avoid the uncertainty of change in environmental regulations is likely to be:	(great–minimal)
er3 The amount of R&D required to create an ideal clean product and develop a clean production process is likely to be:	(minimal–great)
er4 The cost associated with this level of R&D is likely to be:	(minimal–great)
er6 The duration of a clean product innovation project is likely to last:	(short–long time)
er7 The certainty that a venture developing a clean product concept can be accomplished is:	(great–minimal)

The total score obtained is one-dimensional insofar as all the items in the scale are designed to generate a connotation of possible outcomes in terms of good or bad consequences for the firm. This gives an overall estimate of economic risk perception. The procedure is expected to work in the same way to provide estimates of the connotative load of the perceived social pressures and the perceived capabilities to carry out the development of cleaner products and processes.

The desirability of scales with minimal internal variance derives from the definition of measurement. A common feature in the three definitions of measurement given above is the requisite of additivity of the unit of measurement. This implies that the unit of measurement needs to be stable, not to vary, in order to ensure that its addition will produce the same results over time. In this sense, the addition of scores assigned to items intends to equate the notion of ratio additivity common to most measures in the natural sciences. This emulation makes it desirable that each item that composes a scale refers only to particular attributes of the construct being assessed. In addition, this emulation also makes it desirable that interval scales in which all points are equal are used, as this allows the transformation of scores to common scales and the comparison between scores (Kline, 1986).

The most accepted test of reliability is the Cronbach alpha (α). The alpha index is considered the appropriate measure when several items are summed to make a composite score or summated scale. This index is based on the mean correlation of each item in the scale with every other item. It provides a measure of reliability that can be obtained from one administration of a questionnaire (Morgan and Griego, 1998). The higher the correlation among items the greater the alpha. Alpha can vary from 0 to 1. What are the criteria of acceptability for reliability coefficients? According to Cronbach (1994) and Kline (1986), scales with reliability values ranging from 0.60 to 0.80 are acceptable, while aiming to produce scales close to or above 0.80. The British Psychological Society Steering Committee on Test Standards (1992) suggest that 0.70 might be acceptable.

Results of the Reliability Tests

A summary of the Cronbach reliability test (α) of all scales and subscales is presented in the Tables A.2, A.3 and A.4. Items with item–scale correlation below 0.20 were excluded from further analysis. The average cohesiveness (i.e., item–scale correlation) for all the items included in the questionnaire was found to be very satisfactory; only five items were excluded from further analysis. Table A.2 below shows the results of the reliability test for the scales of the attitudinal domains.

High reliability was found for the scales of environmental risk perception (α=0.80); low reliability for the scale of the acceptance of environmental risk (α=0.39) for the total sample (97 managers); and high reliability for acceptance (α=0.82) in the control group sample. High reliability was also found for the scale of economic risk perception (α=0.85). The average internal cohesiveness (i.e., μ = item–scale correlation) for the three scales of attitude towards clean technologies was found highly satisfactory. For items of environmental risk the average item–scale correlation was (μ= 0.4262) with a standard variance[5] of σ^2 = 0.1246; for items of risk acceptance for the control group (μ= 0.6480, σ^2 = 0.2693) and for the total sample (μ= 0.1321, σ^2 = 0.2110). For items of economic risk perception the average item–scale correlation was μ= 0.4649 with a standard deviation of σ^2 = 0.1330.

Table A.2 *Cronbach's alpha reliability for the scales to assess the managers' attitude towards the development of clean technologies*

Scales of the attitude domains	(α) Scale reliability	(α) Subscales reliability	No. of items
Environmental risk perception (EVR)	0.8024		13
Acceptance of environmental risk (AC) (sample 97)	0.3902		
Voluntariness of exposure		-0.3058	5
Controllability of hazards		0.4157	5
Discount in time and space of effects and benefits		-0.0232	5
Condition of the subject		0.6444	4
Acceptance of environmental risk (AC) (control group)	0.8248		
Voluntariness of exposure		0.7359	4
Controllability of hazards		0.8772	4
Discount in time and space of effects and benefits		0.6580	4
Condition of the subject		0.5217	3
Economic risk perception (ER)	0.8555		
Economic opportunity		0.7379	8
Appropriability of benefits		0.0620	3
Technological risk and uncertainty		0.6082	6
Financial risk		0.8435	4

Table A.3 presents the results of the reliability analysis for the scales of the domains of perceived social pressure. High reliabilities were found for the three scales proposed to assess the social norm. Market pressures had a reliability of α=0.89; community pressures α=0.88 and regulatory pressure α=0.87. The average internal cohesiveness (μ) (item–scale correlation) for the three scales of social pressure was found to be highly satisfactory. For items of market pressure the average item–scale correlation was (μ=0.6031) with a standard variance of σ^2 = 0.1229; for items of community pressure μ=0.5615, and σ^2 = 0.1689; and for the items of regulatory pressure

μ=0.6212, and σ^2 = 0.1431 Here it is interesting to notice the difference between the index of reliability (α) on scales of risk acceptance for the control group (15 managers) and the whole sample. This may be explained by the fact that some questions in that section of the questionnaire involved the disclosure of the respondents' societal values. Such disclosure could be affected by the degree of familiarity that the managers in the control and non-control groups had with the interviewer. Those more acquainted with the interviewer are assumed to have responded more openly to this section of the questionnaire. No significant differences were found on any of the other scales of the questionnaire for either group.

Table A.3 *Cronbach's alpha reliability for the scales to assess the managers' perceived social pressure to develop clean technologies*

Scales of the perceived social pressure domains	(α) Scale reliability	(α) Subscales reliability	No. of items
Market pressure (MP)	0.8901		
Market dynamism		0.8918	6
Pioneer–follower		0.8802	3
Consumers		0.6287	3
Community pressure (CP)	0.8838		
Manager's moral norm		0.7616	2
Firm's important external referents		0.6668	5
Local community		0.7881	5
Firm's important internal referents		0.6888	3
Regulatory pressure (RP)	0.8777		
Regulators		0.7423	4
International Standards Organisation		0.7575	2
International agreements		0.7834	3

Table A.4 below presents the results of the reliability analysis for the scales proposed to measure the perceived behavioural control over the development of clean technologies. High reliabilities were encountered for the four scales proposed to assess the perceived technological and organisational capabilities to develop clean technologies. The technological capabilities for product and process improvements scale show a reliability of α=0.95; organisational learning capabilities of α=0.93; strategic alliances to outsource technologies and knowledge scale had α=0.94; and networks of collaboration with α=0.86.

The average internal cohesiveness (item–scale correlation) for the four scales of perceived behavioural control was found to be highly satisfactory. For items of technological capabilities the average item–scale correlation was

(μ= 0.5841) with a standard variance of (σ^2 = 0.1213); for items of organisational learning (μ= 0.6805, σ^2 = 0.0926); for items of strategic alliances (μ= 0.7319, σ^2 = 0.0820); and for networks of collaboration items (μ= 0.6346, σ^2 = 0.1883).

Table A.4   Cronbach's alpha reliability for the scales to assess the managers' perceived control over the development of clean technologies

Scales of the perceived behavioural control domains	(α) Scale reliability	(α) Subscales reliability	No. items
Technological capabilities (TC)	0.9590		
Life cycle analysis capability		0.9241	13
Cooperation and influence capability		0.8677	9
Technological opportunities		0.8663	11
Improvements feasibility		0.9315	11
Organisational learning (OL)	0.9381		
Shared problem-solving capability		0.7876	6
Integrative knowledge capability		0.7410	4
Implementation capability		0.7110	6
Strategic alliances (AL)	0.9476		
Strategic synergy		0.8757	3
Support and commitment		0.9036	4
Cooperation-influence		0.8810	3
Outsourcing opportunities		0.9086	4
Networks of collaboration (NWK)	0.8633		7

Summary

In general all the scales proposed to measure the different behavioural domains showed high indexes of reliability, that is, high internal consistence. The Cronbach alpha was on average above 0.85, a value taken as good in psychometric research. This index indicates that the attributes (or items) included in each of the scales contribute towards the measurement of the perceptions within their respective behavioural domain. That is, any given item within any given scale asks or refers only to those attributes of the behavioural domain that the given scale intends to assess. The addition of items assessing different attributes to produce an estimate of the perceptions of managers in a specific behavioural domain, therefore, can be considered justified according to the methods used in psychometric research. As a consequence, the nine scales can be expected to produce reliable estimates (measurements) of the overall perceptions of manager in this study and also to produce stable estimates in future applications of the same test.

As a final remark, it is interesting to note that the scales to do with disclosure of societal values or response to the connotation of social norms and responsibility (i.e., environmental risk acceptance, community pressure, regulatory pressure) showed relatively lower reliabilities than those scales that did not imply direct social responsibility (i.e., technological capabilities, organisational learning, strategic alliances, economic risk, and market pressures). This may be explained by the level to which the managers themselves or the way their firms operate felt questioned about their social responsibility regarding environmental protection. This is suggested by the high reliability attained with the scores obtained from the control group of managers. The relation of environmental risk perception and the willingness of the firm to develop clean technologies were discussed in Chapter 7.

VALIDITY STATISTICS

Meaning of Validity of Measurement in Psychometric Research

In psychometric research it is agreed that a test is *valid* if it measures what it claims to measure (Kline, 1986; Ghiselli *et al.*, 1981; Anastasi, 1988; Oppenheim, 1992). Again, as with the notion of reliability, here the difference of validity between measurements in natural sciences and those of psychology is evident. According to Kline (1998, p. 49), psychometric scales differ from those in the natural science 'even in measures of the simplest kind, such as length and weight, in that these unquestionably measure what they measure and can be shown to be accurate because they agree with other purported measures of those variables'. Most of these measures have concrete presence in the real world. On the contrary, psychological constructs refer to 'intangible or non-concrete characteristics or qualities in which individuals differ' (Ghiselli *et al.*, 1981, p. 280).[6] This implies that the validity of any given measurement has to be demonstrated. In this sense, according to Ghiselli *et al.* (1981, p. 266), 'validity refers to the appropriateness of inferences from test scores or other form of assessment'. That is, 'given a set of specific questions we want a psychological measure to help answer, how useful or appropriate (that is, valid) are the answers (that is, the information) provided by the test scores?' (Ghiselli *et al.*, 1981, p. 266).

In psychometric research, there are various types of validity of measurements. There is agreement on five types of validity: face, concurrent, predictive, content and construct validity (Kline, 1998). Here it is of interest to establish the last two types of validity: content and construct. These types of validity are of interest in this work because they intrinsically demonstrate or falsify the quantitative nature of the constructs of interest. In addition, in establishing these types of validity it can be said that the theory supporting the production of the tests (constructs) can be considered as empirically confirmed (Loewenthal, 1996; Kline, 1986; Ghiselli *et al.*, 1981).

Content Validity

According to Ghiselli *et al.*, the '*content validity* of set of measurement operations[7] refers to the degree to which those operations measure the characteristics we wish to measure, as *judged* from the appropriateness of the *content* of those operations' (1981, p. 274, original emphasis). Such a judgement refers to the consideration of two aspects: the extent to which each scale of the test pertains to the variable of interest as it is defined, and the extent to which the entire set of scales represent all aspects that the designated model intends to capture (Ghiselli *et al.*, 1981). In this respect, a confirmatory principal components analysis was performed on two sets of data.[8] The first data set was comprised of the scores on the behavioural domain scales (e.g., Σevr_b, Σmp_b, $\Sigma tcpp_b$, etc.) and the second was composed of the scores on the direct measures of the behavioural domains overall perception (e.g., *EVR*, *MP*, *TCPP*, etc.).

Three outcomes were expected from this analysis. The first outcome of the test, although not related to content validity, concerned the confirmation of the proportionality between the domain scales scores and the scores of the direct measures of perceptions for all the domains, one of the implicit propositions of the theory of the planned behaviour. For example: the scores achieved in the scale of economic risk should be proportional to the scores achieved in its direct measure (i.e., $ER \propto \Sigma er_b$, $MP \propto \Sigma mp_b$, $OL \propto \Sigma ol_b$, etc.).[9] To confirm such proportionality, the results of the principal components analysis in both data sets should produce similar structural clustering and should show a set of similar loading within each factor for both domain scales and direct measures.

The second outcome regards the confirmation that the proposed scales measure what they are supposed to measure (i.e., attitudes; social pressure; and behavioural control). That is, if the content of the proposed model consists of nine scales – two for attitude, three for the perceived social pressure and four the perceived control over the development of clean technologies – then the clustering of the scales resulting from their inter-correlation should be consistent with the nature of the factors in the construct definition (Ghiselli *et al.*, 1981). This would establish that the empirical structure of the data fits or corresponds to the proposed theoretical structure and contents of the main determinants of the environmental planned behaviour of the firm regarding the development of clean technologies as hypothesised in Chapter 3.

The third outcome concerns how well the entire set of scales represents all aspects that the model is intended to capture. This refers to the amount of variance on the sample explained by the linear combination of the proposed behavioural domains. The higher the explained variance, the more comprehensive the model. If both tests produce desirable results, this will show that the measurements carried with proposed scales have content validity.

Results of the Content Validity Tests

The results of the principal component analysis are summarised in Table A.5 (next page).[10] In the analysis of the first data set, the number of factors to be extracted was set to three following the model structure proposed in Chapter 3. This extraction resulted in three orthogonal factors with eigenvalues[11] of 3.95, 2.97, and 1.8, explaining 82.58% of the total variance in the sample.

The first component (C_1) explaining 38.43% of the total variance, consists of the perceived capabilities to innovate towards the development of clean products and production processes ($\Sigma tcpp_b$, Σol_b, Σal_b, Σnwk_b); and the perceived economic risk (Σer_b) inherent to the performance of those activities required to develop clean technologies. The second component (C_2) explains 25.54% of the variance in the sample, and includes market pressure (Σmp_b), community pressure (Σcp_b), and regulatory pressure (Σrp_b), the elements of perceived social pressure. Finally, the third factor attitude (C_3), explains 18.69% and is composed of the environmental risk perceptions (Σevr_b) and acceptance of environmental hazards (Σac_b) (see Figure A.1 below).

The analysis of the second data set (the direct measures) produced very similar results. Similarly, as with the first data set, the number of factors to be extracted was set to three. Three orthogonal factors with eigenvalues of 3.88, 2.22, and 1.05, explaining a total of 79.64% of the variance in the sample were confirmed. The first component (C_1) explaining 43.12% is composed of the perceptions of the firm's capabilities to innovate (*TCPP, OL, AL, NWK*) and the economic risk (*ER*). The second component (C_2) explaining 24.7% of the variance of the sample, is composed of *MP*, *CP*, and *RP* the direct measures of the perceived social pressure. Finally, the third component (C_3) that explains 11.77% corresponds to the index of perception of environmental risk (*EVR*).

From these results it can be said that the three expected outcomes were confirmed. With respect to the first expected outcome, the comparison of the clustering for both data sets presented in Table A.5 show that the loading values on the two sets of data are very similar. This fact is also indicated on the graphic representation of the loads of the different domains on their respective components (see Figure A.1). This evidence indicates that the scores achieved on the direct measures are proportional to those scores achieved on the domain scales.

Table A.5   Principal component analysis for the domain scales and the direct measures of domain perceptions. Rotated components matrix

Behavioural Domains	Domains Abbrevia-tions	Components		
		C3: attitude	C2: social pressure	C1: behavioural control
Scales (set 1)				
Environmental risk perception	Σevr_b	0.926		
Acceptance of envir. risks	Σac_b	0.953		
Economic risk	Σer_b	0.220		−0.729
Market pressures	Σmp_b		0.838	
Community pressures	Σcp_b		0.927	
Regulatory pressures	Σrp_b		0.915	
Technological capabilities	$\Sigma tcpp_b$			0.890
Learning capabilities	Σol_b			0.928
Strategic alliances capabilities	Σal_b			0.875
Networks of collaboration	Σnwk_b			
Direct measures (set 2)				
Environmental risk perception	*EVR*	0.923		
Economic risk	*ER*	0.311		−0.826
Market pressures	*MP*		0.817	
Community pressures	*CP*		0.921	
Regulatory pressures	*RP*		0.809	
Technological capabilities	*TCPP*			0.888
Learning capabilities	*AL*			0.818
Strategic alliances capabilities	*OL*			0.729
Networks of collaboration	*NWK*			0.835

The second outcome regards the first judgement of content validity. The results presented above indicate that the empirical components extracted (i.e., C_1, C_2, and C_3 for both data sets) in the principal component analysis fit very closely with the theoretical structure and contents as hypothesised in Chapters 3 and 4. The scales measure what they are supposed to measure. With the exception of economic risk perception (with loading of −.729 and −.826 cluster on behavioural control (C_1)), all the other scales cluster on those domains to which they are supposed to belong. For the clustering of the perceived economic risk, this domain loads in the attitudinal (C_3) and the control (C_1) components. The loading in the attitudinal factor was relatively low compared to its load on behavioural control.

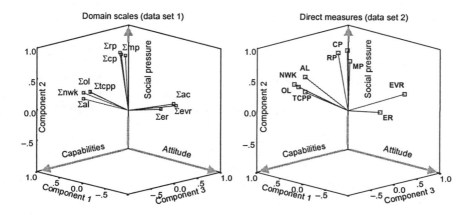

Figura A.1 Principal components analysis

This indicates a strong relationship between the attitude towards the development of clean technologies and the perceived control over the innovation process. The interpretation of this fact in relation to the degree of willingness of the firm to develop clean technologies is discussed in Chapter 7. Finally, the third outcome considered refers to the second judgement of content validity. The results show that the linear combination of the behavioural domains performed by the principal components analysis in both data sets explains a large proportion of variance in the sample. This indicates that the proposed nine behavioural domains and their contents represent most parts of the aspects that the model intends to capture – i.e., attitude, perceived social pressure and perceived behavioural control. In sum, the results from the principal components analyses have shown that the hypothesised structure and its contents correspond to the structure of the empirical data. That is, in other words, the proposed *contents* of the model are valid.

Construct Validity

Construct validity refers to a process pertinent to any theory. This process takes place whenever the primary objective is to develop a measure of a characteristic of an individual (or people), and we want to know how well the rating (or ranking) operations, measure this characteristic. In this sense according to Ghiselli *et al.* (1981) construct validation is a deductive process, and 'construct validity is established to the extent that specific hypotheses deduced from a theory are substantiated in empirical studies' (Ghiselli *et al.*, 1981, p. 283).[12] In agreement with the above definition, the model developed in Chapters 3 and 4 essentially consists of a system of hypotheses linking beliefs to willingness to perform a specific behaviour, in which each hypothesis requires empirical verification.

In that system, it was hypothesised that the beliefs proposed in each of the behavioural domain scales explain the overall perception in their respective domain. In turn, it was proposed that those perceptions at the domain level explain the willingness to innovate. Finally, it was also proposed that the direct measures of attitude, perceived social pressure, and the perceived control over the innovation process could also explain the willingness to develop clean technologies (see Chapter 4). By testing these links, the construct validity of the measurements presented in Chapter 6 will be established or refuted. In this sense, establishing the validity of construct implies the validation of the underpinning theory that supports the development of the instrument used to measure the constructs.

The procedure to test the hypothesised links between the beliefs held by managers and the firms' willingness to innovate towards the development of clean technologies will be the following: first, a regression will carried out with the 'direct measures' of attitude toward the development of clean technologies (A), perceived social pressure (PSP) and the perceived control over the innovation process (PC).[13] The set of scores in these three direct measures should explain a major part of the variance on the scores achieved on the willingness (W) of firms to develop clean technologies as perceived by their managers. Then, regressions will be performed upon the data set of the behavioural domain scales (Σevr, Σer, Σcp, Σmp, Σrp, $\Sigma tcpp$, Σol, Σal, Σnwk) and the data set of the behavioural domain direct measures (EVR, ER, CP, MP, RP, $TCPP$, OL, AL, NWK). The set of nine scales and the set of nine direct measures separately should also explain a major part of the variance on the scores achieved on the willingness to develop clean products and to adopt clean production processes. Last, regressions were carried out upon the data sets of belief scores in the different behavioural domains.

Similarly, as with the above, the beliefs proposed to explain the overall perceptions in their respective domains should explain a major part of the variance on the scores achieved in their respective direct measures. The complete reports for all the performed regressions are presented in Appendix C.

Results of the Construct Validity Tests

Explanatory Level One

In order to avoid excessive repetition, the meaning of the results presented in Table A.6 will be explained only for hypotheses H_1 and H_2 in reference to what these hypotheses intend establish. As discussed in Chapter 3, the work of Ajzen has established that people's behaviour can be expressed or formulated in the following form:

$$B \sim I \propto w_0 + w_1 A + w_2 SN + w_3 PBC \qquad (3.4)$$

Hypothesis H_1 intends to test whether the main proposition of the TPB can be applied to describe the firms' willingness to innovate towards the development of clean technologies. For this purpose, the proposition presented in equation four was expressed in the following form:

H₁: The firms' willingness (W) to develop clean technologies can be explained in terms of the attitude towards the development of clean technologies (A), the perceived social pressure to develop clean technologies (PSP) and the perceived control over the innovation process (PC) as perceived by their managers.

$$H_1: W = W(A, PSP, PC) \qquad (3.5)$$

The mathematical expression of H_1 (eq. 3.5) can also be expressed in a similar fashion as presented in equation (3.4):

$$B \sim W \propto w_0 + w_1 A + w_2 PSP + w_3 PC \qquad (A.1)$$

Where:

B	is the behaviour of interest;	
W	is the willingness to engage in innovative activities	
$\propto$	indicates proportionality between the levels of willingness and the values achieved in the explanatory variables; [14]	
w_n	are influence weighting parameters empirically determined; and	
$\sim$	suggests that willingness is expected to predict behaviour provided that the criterion stated in Chapter 3, p. 40, is met.	

The formal expression given in equation A.1 facilitates the test of the hypothesis H_1. In the postulate of H_1, strictly, we face two hypotheses: a null ($H_{1,0}$) and an alternative ($H_{1,1}$). The null hypothesis asserts that W is not associated with A, PSP, and PC. To accept this hypothesis, the degree of influence of the independent variables (weighted by w_n) upon the dependent variable must be zero.[15] On the contrary, the alternative hypothesis states that

W is associated with A, PSP, and PC. In this case, the influence (w_n) must be different from zero.

That is: $H_{1,0}$: $w_0 = w_1 = w_2 = w_3 = 0$ (null hypothesis)

$H_{1,1}$: $w_0 \neq w_1 \neq w_2 \neq w_3 \neq 0$ (alternative hypothesis)

The test of H_1 (i.e., $H_{1,0}$ and $H_{1,1}$) concerns the confirmation or rejection that there is a linear relationship of dependence between the dependent (W) and the independent variables (A, PSP, PBC). The existence of such a relationship can be accepted if, and only if, $H_{1,0}$ is rejected. In this regard, the results of the regression presented in Table C1c (see Appendix C1, p. 226) indicate that the individual influence of the independent variables upon the dependent variable weighted by the coefficients w_0, w_1, w_2, and w_3 is different from zero. The level of significance of this difference according to the 't' statistic show a probability level of $(p<0.002)$ for all the coefficients.[16] In the light of these results, therefore, the hypothesis null $(H_{1,0})$ is rejected and the alternative $(H_{1,1})$ accepted.

From these results it is possible to infer that H_1 can be accepted. That is, the willingness of the firm to develop clean technologies is dependent on – or can be explained by – the attitude towards clean technology development, the perceived social pressure and the perceived control upon the innovation process. The values of the coefficient of determination $(R^2 = 0.85)$; the standard error of the estimate $(SE = 1.36)$; the F test $(F = 191.65)$; and the significance of the probability levels that the estimated coefficients are different form zero $(Sig. = 0.000)$ indicates that the goodness of fit of the data set to the proposed model (i.e., equation A.1) that sets out the relationship between the variables of interest is satisfactory.

Explanatory level two

The test of hypothesis H_1 represents the standard application of the TPB followed in those studies referred to in Chapter 3. The proposition of the hypotheses H_2 and H_{2b} are a deviation from this standard. Although the test of H_1 is relevant to establish the validity of the adaptation of the TPB to assess willingness to innovate, with respect to policy analysis, it is more appropriate to carry out the analysis at the domain level, if our intention is, at a latter stage, to simulate scenarios. For this reason, the direct measures of the overall perceptions at the domain level $(EVR, ER, CP, MP, RP, TCPP, OL, AL,$ and $NWK)$ were included in the adaptation presented in Chapter 3. In a similar, way as with hypothesis H_1, hypothesis H_2 is presented assuming a linear relationship of dependence between these direct measures and the willingness of the firm to develop clean technologies (W). Here H_2 is repeated:

H_2: The firms' willingness (W) to develop clean technologies depends on the perceptions of: environmental risk (EVR), economic risk (ER), community pressure (CP), market pressure (MP), regulatory pressure (RP), technological capabilities ($TCPP$), organisational learning capabilities (OL), capabilities on outsourcing strategic alliances (AL) and networks of collaboration (NWK).

$$H_2: W = W(EVR, ER, CP, MP, RP, TCPP, OL, AL, NWK) \qquad (3.6)$$

In a similar fashion, as with H_1, H_2 is expressed as:

$$W = w_0 + w_1 EVR + w_2 ER + w_3 MP + w_4 CP + w_5 RP + w_6 TC + w_7 OL + w_8 AL + w_9 NWK$$

$$(A.2)$$

Where:

$H_{2,0}$: $w_0 = w_1 = w_2 = w_3 = w_4 = w_5 = w_6 = w_7 = w_8 = w_9 = 0$; and
$H_{2,1}$: $w_0 \neq w_1 \neq w_2 \neq w_3 \neq w_4 \neq w_5 \neq w_6 \neq w_7 \neq w_8 \neq w_9 \neq 0$;

are the null and the alternative hypotheses.

The results of the regression analysis presented in Table C2c (see Appendix C2, p. 226) indicate that the individual influence of the independent variables upon the dependent variable weighted by the coefficients w_0, w_1, w_2, w_3, w_4, w_5, w_6, w_7, w_8, and w_9 is not zero. Upon the evidence of these results, the hypothesis null ($H_{2,0}$) is rejected and the alternative ($H_{2,1}$) accepted. In turn, it is possible to infer that H_2 can be accepted. In addition, the values of the coefficient of determination ($R^2 = 0.88$); the standard error of the estimate (SE = 1.25); the F test (F = 77.43); and the probability level of significance of (Sig. = 0.000) indicate that the fit of the data set to the proposed model (i.e., equation A.2) that sets out the relationship between the variables of interest is satisfactory. That is, the willingness of the firm to develop clean technologies is dependent on, or can be explained by, the environmental (EVR) and economic risk (ER) perceptions; the perceived social norms arising from the community (CP), the market (MP), and regulatory institutions (RP); and the perceived technological ($TCPP$), learning (OL), strategic alliances (AL) and networks of collaboration (NWK) capabilities to develop clean technologies.

As predicted in Chapter 3 some behavioural domains were found to be better predictors than others. The capabilities to outsource new knowledge (i.e., strategic alliances and networks of collaboration) proved to be bad predictors. The probability level significance (p) of the coefficients of AL and NWK (i.e., w_8, and w_9, respectively) is relatively low compared with the rest of the coefficients (see Appendix C2, Table C2c). This was an expected finding, since the TPB stipulates that goals, intentions, or willingness of people can be predominantly under the influence of either attitude, subjective norms, or the perceived behavioural control.

This stipulation can be made extensive to the level of the behavioural domains. The willingness was expected to be influenced in an unsymmetrical fashion by the different behavioural domains. For the firms in the sample of this study the domains of strategic alliances and networks of collaboration resulted in being poor predictors. Following the TPB framework, it can be expected that different predictors would arise with other samples of firms in other contexts at a different point in time. These differences would imply the perception of different outcomes evaluation (i.e., generating different attitudes); different degrees of social pressures; and different organisational and technological capabilities (i.e., therefore generating different perceived control over the innovation process).

With respect to H_{2a}, the results of the regression analysis indicate that the connotative load of the scales on the different behavioural domains can also explain the willingness to innovate, although with a smaller coefficient of determination (see Appendixes C2 and C3). The comparison of the factor loading of the explanatory variables in both data sets indicates that the scores of the domain scales and the direct measures of the overall perception on the behavioural domains are proportional. Similar results on the principal components analysis point to the same fact. These proportionality of these scores validates the use of the scores of the direct measures of the behavioural domains overall perceptions for the simulation of policy scenarios.

Explanatory level three

In the previous section, the link between the perceptions at the behavioural domain level to the willingness to innovate was tested. As said before, explanatory level three refers to the explanation of willingness through the connection of the beliefs, classified in the different behavioural domains, to their respective behavioural domains' direct measures. The test of hypotheses H_3 through H_{11} proceeded in a similar fashion as the testing of hypotheses H_1, H_2, and H_{2a}. In order to evade repetition, a summary of the main parameters to consider when gauging how good are the predictors and the fit of the model resulting from the multiple regression is presented in Table A.6 below. At this point of the analysis it is sufficient to say that the results of the regressions presented in the Appendix C (C3 to C13) confirmed the propositions of hypotheses H_3 through H_{11} presented in Chapter 4 regarding the link between beliefs and willingness and the moderating role of the perceptions arising from different domains.

Table A.6 *Summary of multivariate analyses of variance at three levels of explanation of the firms' willingness to develop clean technologies*

Hypotheses		R^2	SE	F	Sig.
		\multicolumn{4}{c}{ANOVA Results}		
Explanatory level one					
C1 H_1: W = W(A, PSP, PBC)		0.85	1.36	191.6	0.000
Explanatory level two					
C2 H_2: W = W(EVR, ER, CP, MP, RP, TC, OL, AL, NWK)		0.88	1.35	65.84	0.000
C3 H_{2a}: W = W(Σevr, Σer, Σcp, Σmp, Σrp, Σtcpp, Σol, Σal, Σnwk)		0.73	1.83	31.19	0.000
Explanatory level three					
C5 H_3: EVR	$= w_0 + w_b\Sigma evr_b + w_b\Sigma ac_b$	0.92	0.29	72.85	0.000
C6 H_4: ER	$= w_0 + w_b\Sigma er_b$	0.89	0.60	105.63	0.000
C7 H_5: MP	$= w_0 + w_b\Sigma mp_b$	0.72	1.14	84.48	0.000
C8 H_6: CP	$= w_0 + w_b\Sigma cp_b$	0.71	0.81	49.41	0.000
C9 H_7: RP	$= w_0 + w_b\Sigma rp_b$	0.76	0.99	51.64	0.000
C10 H_8: TCPP	$= w_0 + w_b\Sigma tcpp_b$	0.86	0.72	107.5	0.000
C11 H_9: OL	$= w_0 + w_b\Sigma ol_b$	0.85	0.70	55.76	0.000
C12 H_{10}: AL	$= w_0 + w_b\Sigma al_b$	0.69	1.02	37.65	0.000
C13 H_{11}: NWK	$= w_0 + w_b\Sigma nwk_b$	0.64	1.14	35.70	0.000

Summary

In general, the tests carried out in this appendix confirmed the validity of the measurement operations. Regarding *content* validity, the analysis confirmed the correspondence between the theoretical structure of the model and the empirical data. In addition, the developed model captures a major part of the variance that it is intended to explain. With respect to *construct* validity, the proposed system of hypotheses linking beliefs to willingness to innovate was accepted. Based on this fact, therefore, it can be asserted that the hypothesised structure and contents of the proposed model are valid.

THE QUANTITATIVE NATURE OF THE MANAGERS' PERCEPTIONS

The results of the tests carried out in this appendix support the validity of the measurements. This assertion brings us back to the definition of measurement and the establishment of the quantitative character of the variables involved in this study. It was argued above that when dealing with measurement operations of abstract constructs, the quantitative nature of these constructs has to be demonstrated before claiming that any measurement has been done. The two features that define quantity were said to be order and additive structure. That is, 'to show that a variable is quantitative is to show it has a definite kind of structure: its values stand in ordinal and additive relations to one another' (Michell, 1990, p. vii). This does not imply finding empirical analogues of numerical addition but finding empirical evidence in favour of underlying additive structure (*ibid.*). These features have been demonstrated to coexist (Michell, 1997). That is, where there is additive structure there is order, and *vice versa* (Michell, 1990).

The quantitative character of the constructs operated here will become apparent when explaining the underlying basic algebraic operations of factor analysis and regression analysis. If we remember the definition of measurement given above 'a measurement represents nothing else but a search for *empirical structure* by means of extensional, ordered, symmetrical and asymmetrical relations' (Korzybsky, 1994). Michell (1990) in agreement with Korzybsky, stipulates that the process of measurement implies empirical relationships between quantities. The test of the correspondence between the theoretical and the empirical structure of the contents carried out here is intended to resemble what is the main objective of any scientific measurement, that is, the search for *empirical structure*.

The test of correspondence is made through methods of multidimensional scaling based on *ordered* monotonic relationships.[17] The additive structure of the relationships of the constructs is demonstrated by their contribution to the formation of three-dimensional space in which the two basic operations are: (1) all the components[18] of the data set taken as pairs (i, j) until (k, l) are ordered in a rank (in this book, the rank varies between the correlation interval values $(-1, 1)$) and (2) the calculus of the Euclidean inter-point distance d_{ij} for any given pair of correlation (i, j) to a common origin such that $d_{ij} < d_{kl}$. These two basic operations present in all multidimensional scaling methods (including principal component analysis) show that the constructs assessed in this book possess order and additive structure.[19] Further evidence of the quantitative character of the constructs assessed here is provided by the significant asymmetric relationship between the criterion 'willingness' and its determinants (i.e., *EVR, ER, CP, MP, RP, TCPP, OL*) established by the estimation of the coefficients of proportionality in the multiple regression analyses carried out above. The notion of additive structure is more evident here than in the methods of multidimensional scaling.

Ajzen's model proposes that the constructs included in the model contribute to explain people's predisposition to behave in specific situations and contexts. In its simpler form the model is presented as a linear equation (a sum of variables – each one with an estimated different effect on the dependent variable). Here it is not suggested – for any future applications of the model for policy analysis – that the same assumption should be made. Thus, in this study the assumption of a linear relationship was not assumed a priori. In this book it was preferred to leave the possible type of relationship between dependent and independent variable as an implicit function. This is explicitly stated in hypothesis H_1 and H_2; where W is an implicit function of *A*, *PS* and *PC* (i.e., $W = W(A, PS, PC)$; and also $W = W(EVR, ER, RP, CP, MP, TCPP, OL, AL, NWK)$. The form or character of the function between variables should be accepted for the purposes of measurement of the phenomena only after the estimated function is found to be appropriate via parametric or non-parametric methods.

As it is obvious in Chapter 7, the analysis and interpretation of the resulting empirical function for policy design does not necessarily imply a sum of factors needed to generate the conditions that might induce behavioural change in those firms under study. Furthermore, the implementation of the different aspects that compose the policy suggested in Chapter 7 should not be seen as a simple and mechanistic sum of policy activities that will produce the expected outcome. Concerning the additivity of the model here it is appropriate to paraphrase Michell (1990, p. 53). The interpretation of the additive relation of $A+PSP+PC = W$ does not mean that *A* added to *PSP* and *PC* is the same as W. Rather $W = A+PSP+PC$ is a relation between *A*, *PSP*, *PC* and W. It is the relation of W as being entirely composed by discrete parts of *A*, *PSP*, and *PC*.

NOTES

1. Very similar definitions are given by Ghiselli *et al.* (1981); Kline (1986); Anastasi (1988); Oppenheim (1992); and Cramer (1998). For example, according to Ghiselli *et al.* (1981, p. 478), measurement can be defined as 'a quantitative description of individuals or objects on variables (constructs) involving the use of numbers or values that can be manipulated to give further information about the variables. Measurement deals with the assignment of numbers according to specific rules'.
2. For a detailed discussion of these concepts see: Anastasi (1988); Ghiselli *et al.* (1981); Kline (1986, 1998).
3. To follow the tests presented in this chapter, the reader will need to be familiar with the standard statistical tools to test the reliability and validity of conjoint measurements of theoretical constructs. These include factor, correlation, multivariate and reliability analyses.
4. Establishing reliability over time involves the application of the questionnaire several times to a control group. Because of this, only the first type of reliability was considered.

This is due to limited time and willingness of the managers to participate in such test re-testing. In addition, according to Loewenthal (1996) one test is sufficient to test the reliability of a battery of items, and to (Bryman, 1992, p. 57) 'high internal consistency is a more exacting requirement than test re-test over time'.

5. σ^2 is an index of dispersion around the mean (μ). The smaller the σ^2, the more unvaried is the measure.

6.   In the case of this work, the constructs refer to characteristics or qualities in which those firms in the sample differ.

7.   'Measurement operations' can be also called items, scales, or tests.

8.   For a short explanation of the nature of this analysis, see Appendix B.

9.   The direct measures scores range from 1 to 7 and the scales range depends on the number of items that compose a specific scale.

10. The complete results of the factor analysis are presented in Appendix B.

11. '*Eigenvalues*: indicate the size of the factors. These are calculated by squaring and adding the loading on each factor. The larger the eigenvalue the bigger the factor in the sense that it accounts for more variance. Each variable has an eigenvalue of 1. Thus a factor must, at least, have an eigenvalue greater than 1 if it is to be of any importance' (Kline, 1998, p. 58).

12. In this work this process can be seen also as establishing *criterion validity*. Such validity is in question when we are interested on verifying how well the scores on the test correspond to, are related to, or predict scores on another variable called a *criterion* (Ghiselli *et al.*, 1981, p. 267).

13. Regression refers to the short name given to the Ordinary Least Squares Multiple Linear Regression (OLS). OLS is the simplest of a family of numerical methods to estimate an equation that best describes or fits a data set regarding the hypothesis of causal relationships between a dependant and several explanatory or independent variables (Allison, 1999, p. 2).

14. The symbol $\propto$ indicates proportionality. This is because the relationships between variables in social sciences – in contrast with the natural sciences – are always inexact. In this sense, $\propto$ indicates the presence of an error in the estimate (Lewis-Beck, 1993, p. 2).

15. These parameters (w_n) indicate the rate of change, degree of influence or effect, slope, etc., between the independent and dependent variables. For an introduction to regression analysis, see Allison (1999) and Lewis-Beck (1993).

16. The standard regression textbook indicates that the smaller the value of p, the stronger the evidence that the coefficient is not zero. A probability of $p<0.002$ indicates a chance of two in one thousand of estimating a coefficient equal to zero (Allison, 1999, pp. 14–6).

17. A monotonic relationship occurs when the transformation of any given variable is one to one. That is, if we have the function $X=f(X)$ the transformation of X will give us a transformation of $f(X)$. There are increasing and decreasing monotonic functions (Chiang, 1984). Factor analysis is based on monotonic functions (see Appendix B).

18. In the case of this book, these 'components' refer to any given correlation between two items (or beliefs).

19. For a complete demonstration of the presence of order and additive structure in multidimensional scaling methods, see Michell (1990, pp. 109–27).

Appendix B: Content validity analysis

FACTOR ANALYSIS
(*Confirmatory principal components analysis*)

Principal components analysis is one method of factor analysis. In turn, factor analysis pertains to a more broad family of multidimensional scaling (MDS) methods. The basic nature of any multidimensional scaling method (e.g. principal components) is the following: We are given, for every two 'objects' (*i* and *j*) in some set of *n*, a datum s_{ij} representing the similarity, substitutability, affinity, association, interaction, correlation, or, general proximity between them. We seek, simply, that the configuration of *n* points in an Euclidean space of smallest possible dimension is such that, to an acceptable degree of approximation, the resulting inter-point distances d_{ij} are *monotonically* related to the given proximity data in the sense that:

$$d_{ij} < d_{kl} \quad \text{whenever} \quad s_{ij} > s_{kl}$$

All these methods share three properties: (1) they are based upon the same assumption: monotonic relation between the inter-point distances and the given data; (2) they use an iterative procedure of adjusting the co-ordinates for points to achieve a closer and closer approximation to the desired monotonic relation, and (3) they yield to spatial representations that are typically indistinguishable, for practical purposes, when applied to the same matrix of data. The basic algorithm for MDS is as follows:

1. Given any set of data all its components taken as pairs from (*i, j*) until (*k, l*) will be rank ordered. In the case of ordered correlation the rank is [−1, 1].
2. The rank will be set taking into account the frequency assigning the same rank to all the pairs (*i, j*) with the same value;
3. Within an Euclidean space a common origin is set up. Based on this origin Euclidean distances d_{ij} are calculated for each pair (*i, j*) such that $d_{ij} < d_{kl}$;
4. The graphic representation of these distances into a minimal Euclidean space is done by scaling them (s_{ij}) having as a restriction the preservation of the rank such that: $d_{ij} < d_{kl}$ whenever $s_{ij} > s_{kl}$ (Coxon and Davis, 1982).

5. Afterwards the transformation is tested to check the goodness of fit. This
    test consists of measuring the degree of monotonicity of the
    transformation by plotting $d_{ij} = f(s_{ij})$. A good fit implies strong
    monotonicity, this test is known as the stress of the monotonic
    transformation (stress $\to 0$) (Shepard, 1972).

These methods are all called non-metrics because they are based on the
ordering of the set of data by their rank. A more in-depth discussion of these
methods can be followed in Shepard *et al.* (1972a) and Coxon and Davis
(1982).

B1: Principal components analysis for the behavioural domain scales.

The principal components confirmatory analysis was set at three dimensions.
The scales assessed intent to capture the connotative meaning generated by
each question and measure accumulated semantic load of the beliefs that
composed the scale

Table B1a   Total variance explained by the model

Component	Initial eigen-values			Extraction sums of squared loading
	Total	% of variance	Cumulative %	Total
1	3.950	39.503	39.503	3.950
2	2.479	24.785	64.288	2.479
3	1.830	18.297	82.585	1.830

Component	% of variance	Cumulative %	Rotation sums of squared loading	% of variance	Cumulative %
			Total		
1	39.503	39.503	3.835	38.348	38.348
2	24.785	64.288	2.555	25.546	63.895
3	18.297	82.585	1.869	18.691	82.585

Table B1b   Component matrix and component rotated matrix

Domains Component matrix		Components 1	2	3
Σevr_b	Environmental risk perception		-.318	.881
Σac_b	Acceptance of environmental risks	.222		.934
Σer_b	Economic risk	-.655		.423
Σmp_b	Market pressures	.358	.799	
Σcp_b	Community pressures		.887	.268
Σrp_b	Regulatory pressures	.348	.823	.234
$\Sigma tcpp_b$	Technological capabilities	.905		
Σol_b	Learning capabilities	.943		
Σal_b	Strategic alliances capabilities	.836	-.244	
Σnwk_b	Networks of collaboration	.892		

Rotated matrix*		Components 1	2	3
Σevr_b	Environmental risk perception			.926
Σac_b	Acceptance of environmental risks			.953
Σer_b	Economic risk	-.729		.220
Σmp_b	Market pressures		.838	-.207
Σcp_b	Community pressures		.927	
Σrp_b	Regulatory pressures		.915	
$\Sigma tcpp_b$	Technological capabilities	.890		
Σol_b	Learning capabilities	.928		
Σal_b	Strategic alliances capabilities	.875		
Σnwk_b	Networks of collaboration	.903		

* Rotation method: Varimax with Kaiser normalisation.
  Rotation converged in 4 iterations.

B2: Principal components analysis for the direct measures of the overall perception in the behavioural domains
Confirmatory analysis set at three dimensions

*Table B2a	Total variance explained by the model*

Component	Initial eigen-values			Extraction sums of squared loading
	Total	% of variance	Cumulative %	Total
1	3.881	43.120	43.120	3.881
2	2.228	24.755	67.876	2.228
3	1.059	11.770	79.646	1.059

Component	% of variance	Cumula-tive %	Rotation sums of squared loading		
			Total	% of variance	Cumulative %
1	43.120	43.120	3.419	37.988	37.988
2	24.755	67.876	2.503	27.808	65.797
3	11.770	79.646	1.246	13.849	79.646

*Table B2b	Component matrix and component rotated matrix*

	Domains	Components		
	Component matrix	1	2	3
EVR	Environmental risk perception		.608	-.745
ER	Economic risk	-.612	.461	.413
CP	Market pressures	.490	.680	.396
MP	Community pressures	.524	.661	
RP	Regulatory pressures	.542	.681	
TCPP	Technological capabilities	.813	-.308	
OL	Learning capabilities	.856		
AL	Strategic alliances capabilities	.836	-.244	
NWK	Networks of collaboration	.892		

Table B2b   Continued

	Component matrix[*]	Components		
		1	2	3
EVR	Environmental risk perception			.923
ER	Economic risk	-.826		.311
CP	Market pressures		.921	
MP	Community pressures		.817	
RP	Regulatory pressures		.809	
TCPP	Technological capabilities	.888		
OL	Learning capabilities	.818		
AL	Strategic alliances capabilities	.875		
NWK	Networks of collaboration	.903		

* Rotation method: Varimax with Kaiser normalisation
  Rotation converged in 5 iterations

Appendix C: Construct validity analysis

The aim of this appendix is to show the level of statistical reliability and power of the theoretical model developed in this book. It shows the links in a chain of causalities between beliefs held by managers and firms' planned innovative behaviour towards clean technologies (see figure A.2). The chain of causalities between beliefs and willingness to innovate is tested in the following way: first by showing that a more general level willingness can be explained in terms of attitudes towards the behaviour (A), the perceived social pressure to behave or not to behave in certain way (PSP) and the perceived control upon the innovation process (PC) (Appendix C1); second, by presenting the regressions of the behavioural domains (i.e., EVR, ER, MP, CP, RP, $TCPP$, OL, AL, and NWK) from which arise the managers A, PSP, and PC and linking those domains to firms' willingness (Appendixes C2, C3 and C4); finally, by regressing beliefs against the behavioural domains that explain willingness (Appendixes C5 to C13). In this way a link between specific beliefs and the firms' planned innovative behaviour in clean technologies is tested and confirmed.

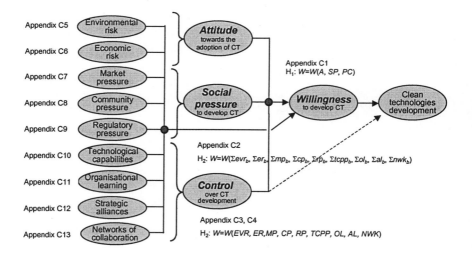

Figure A2. Linking beliefs to willingness to develop clean technologies

C1: Regression of willingness to innovate in CT against attitude (*A*), the perceived social pressure (*PSP*) and perceived control (*PC*)

Table C1a Model summary

Model	R	R^2	Adjusted R^2	SEE*
1	.928	.861	.856	1.362

Predictors: (constant), *PC*, *PSP*, *A*
Dependent variable: *W*
* Note: The interval of the scales to assess willingness ranges from 2 to 14. The SEE should be compared against this value.

Table C1b ANOVA

	Sum of squares	df	Mean Square	F	Sig.
Regression	1067.14	3	355.71	191.65	.000
Residual	172.61	93	1.85		
Total	1239.75	96			

Table C1c Coefficients

CONCEPT	Unstandardised Coefficients		Standardised Coefficients	t	Sig.
	B	SE	Beta		
(Constant)	-.70	.65		-1.07	.284
A	-.18	.05	-.12	-3.11	.002
PSP	.71	.07	.36	9.49	.000
PBC	1.74	.08	.86	21.82	.000

C2:   Regression of willingness to innovate against the behavioural domains indexes

Managers' expectations at the moment of the survey

Table C2a   Model summary

	Domains	R	R^2	Adj. R^2	% E	SEE
EVR	= Environmental risk	.24	.06	.05	6.04	3.50
ER	= Economic risk	.52	.27	.25	21.38	3.09
MP	= Market pressure	.57	.33	.31	5.75	2.98
CP	= Community pressure	.64	.41	.38	8.22	2.81
RP	= Regulatory pressure	.64	.42	.38	0.07	2.80
TCPP	= Technological capabilities	.90	.81	.80	39.79	1.57
OL	= Organisational learning	.94	.88	.87	6.61	1.26
OAL	= Strategic alliances	.94	.88	.87	0.38	1.25
NWK	= Networks of collaboration	.94	.88	.87	0.02	1.25

Dependent variable: W
EVR is a weighted variable [i2evr*(i1evr/7)]

Table C2b   ANOVA

	Sum of squares	df	Mean square	F	Sig.
Regression	1102.17	9	122.46	77.44	.000
Residual	137.57	87	1.58		
Total	1239.75	96			

Table C2c   Coefficients

	Domains	Unstd. coef. B	SE	Std. coef. B	t	Sig.
	Constant	-3.02	.74		-4.08	.000
EVR	Environmental risk	.40	.07	.29	5.31	.000
ER	Economic risk	.36	.10	.20	3.43	.001
MP	Market pressure	.41	.10	.23	3.87	.000
CP	Community pressure	.29	.15	.12	1.92	.058
RP	Regulatory pressure	-.81	.14	-.46	-5.47	.000
TCPP	Technological capabilities	1.02	.10	.64	9.64	.000
OL	Organisational learning	.67	.13	.38	4.85	.000
AL	Strategic alliances	.19	.14	.10	1.29	.199
NWK	Networks of collaboration	.08	.17	.04	.47	.635

Predictors: (constant), EVR, CP, ER, RP, MP, TCCP, OL, AL, NWK
Note: Equation used in the simulation in Chapter 7 is the following.
W= −3.023+0.4EVR+0.363ER+.416MP+0.294CP−
0.815RP+1.022TCPP+0.672OL+0.192AL+0.083NWK

C3: Regression of willingness to innovate in clean technologies against the behavioural domain scales (*i.e.,* Σevr, Σer, Σmp, Σcp, Σrp, $\Sigma tcpp$, Σol, Σal, and Σnwk)

Table C3a   Model summary

Model	R	R^2	Adjusted R^2	SEE
1	.87	.76	.73	1.83

Dependent variable: W

Table C3b   ANOVA

	Sum of squares	df	Mean square	F	Sig.
Regression	946.49	9	105.16	31.20	.000
Residual	293.26	87	3.37		
Total	1239.75	96			

Table C3c   Coefficients

	Domain scales	Unstd. coef. B	SE	Std. coef. B	t	Sig.
	Constant	5.79	2.61		2.21	.029
Σevr	Environmental risk	-.11	.01	-.36	-6.15	.000
Σer	Economic risk	-1.3E-02	.01	-.08	-1.01	.315
Σmp	Market pressure	7.9E-04	.01	.00	.04	.966
Σcp	Community pressure	5.3E-02	.03	.22	1.64	.103
Σrp	Regulatory pressure	-7.5E-02	.04	-.26	-1.63	.105
$\Sigma tcpp$	Technological capabilities	2.3E-02	.00	.40	2.90	.005
Σol	Organisational learning	6.6E-02	.03	.39	1.99	.049
Σal	Strategic alliances	-2.0E-03	.01	-.01	-.11	.908
Σnwk	Networks of collaboration	4.2E-03	.03	.01	.11	.908

Predictors: (constant), SWK, SCP, SEVR, SER, SMP, SRP, STCPP, SL

C4:   Regression of willingness to innovate in clean technologies (W) against the behavioural domains indexes (i.e., *EVR, ER, MP, CP, RP, TCPP, OL, AL,* and *NWK*)

Managers' long-term expectations

Table C4a   Model summary

	Domains	R	R^2	Adj. R^2	%E*	SEE
EVRL	Environmental risk	.00	.00	-.01	1.0	2.79
ERL	Economic risk	.00	.00	-.02	1.1	2.80
MPL	Market pressure	.33	.11	.08	6.1	2.66
CPL	Community pressure	.35	.12	.08	0.7	2.65
RPL	Regulatory pressure	.36	.13	.08	**	2.65
TCPP	Technological capabilities	.86	.74	.72	63.8	1.45
OLL	Organisational learning	.87	.76	.74	2.3	1.39
ALL	Strategic alliances	.88	.78	.76	1.9	1.33
NWK	Networks of collaboration	.94	.89	.88	11.7	.94

Dependent Variable: WL
* Explained variance
** Note: Removed

Table C4b   ANOVA

	Sum of squares	df	Mean square	F	Sig.
Regression	1097.09	7	156.72	97.77	.000
Residual	142.66	89	1.60		
Total	1239.75	96			

Table C4c   Coefficients

Model 9	Domains	Unstd. coef. B	SE	Std. coef. B	t	Sig.
	Constant	2.18	1.2		1.71	.090
EVRL	Environmental risk	.01	.19	-.00	-.06	.952
ERL	Economic risk	.47	.09	.25	5.11	.000
MPL	Market pressure	.53	.12	.41	4.23	.000
CPL	Community pressure	-.38	.07	-.30	-4.86	.000
RPL	Regulatory pressure	-.25	.25	-.15	-1.00	.316
TCPPL	Technological capabilities	.82	.18	.53	4.58	.000
OLL	Organisational learning	-.74	.18	-.25	-4.10	.000
ALL	Strategic alliances	.22	.25	.13	.89	.374
NWKL	Networks of collaboration	.92	.09	.52	9.52	.000

Predictors: (Constant), NWKL, ERL, EVRL, CPL, MPL, OLL, TCPPL, ALL

C5: Environmental risk perception
Stepwise plus forward regression[*]

Table C5a   *Model summary*

	R	R^2	Adj. R^2	%E	SE	Variance explained by each aspect of environmental risk
ac_{18}	.50	.25	.24	24.4	.93	The firms' operations are environmentally safe
evr_2	.62	.38	.37	13.0	.85	$sr = evr_2+evr_3+evr_5+evr_4+evr_6+evr_9$
evr_1	.68	.46	.45	7.6	.79	$= 35.6\%$
ac_8	.72	.53	.51	6.0	.75	
evr_4	.75	.57	.55	4.2	.71	Condition of the subject
evr_5	.78	.62	.59	4.6	.68	$cs = ac_{17}+ac_{18}=$ 26.4%
ac_{13}	.81	.66	.63	3.7	.64	
evr_6	.84	.70	.68	4.6	.60	Controllability of hazards
evr_3	.88	.77	.75	7.5	.53	consequences
ac_2	.90	.81	.79	4.1	.48	$ctr = evr_1+ac_8+ac_{10}=$ 17.4%
ac_{10}	.92	.85	.83	3.8	.43	
ac_3	.93	.87	.85	2.0	.40	Voluntariness of exposure
ac_{12}	.94	.88	.87	1.5	.38	$vol = ac_2+ac_3+ac_5 =$ 7.7%
ac_{17}	.95	.90	.89	2.0	.35	
evr_9	.96	.92	.90	1.7	.32	Discount in time & space benefits and effects
ac_5	.96	.93	.92	1.6	.29	$dts = ac_{12}+ac_{13}=$ 5.2%

Dependent variable: *EVR*
Predictors: (constant), AC18, EVR2, EVR1, AC8, EVR4, EVR5, AC13, EVR6, EVR3, AC2, AC10, AC3, AC12, AC17, EVR9, AC5

Table C5b   *ANOVA*

Model		Sum of squares	df	Mean square	F	Sig.
18	Regression	103.74	16	6.48	72.85	.000
	Residual	7.12	80	8.901E-02		
	Total	110.86	96			

[*] Methodological note: The screening of what beliefs need to be influenced or changed in order to modify the managers' attitudes towards the development of clean technologies was done in two steps. First a stepwise regression was used to screen those beliefs that accounted for most part the variance. Second, the beliefs included in the selected model from the stepwise regression were run again in a forward regression to assess their individual contribution to explain the dependent variable. Those beliefs that accounted for most part of the variance in the sample were considered the more influential in the perception and acceptance of environmental risk. The same procedure was followed in the remaining behavioural domains that will be presented in this section of the Appendix.

Table C5c   Coefficients

Beliefs		Unstd coeff. B	SE	Std. coef. B	t	Sig.
	Constant	1.47	.24		5.92	.000
ac_{18}	Likelihood of being affected by pollution	.47	.03	.71	12.9	.000
evr_2	Hazards have no global impact	.77	.06	.96	12.0	.000
evr_1	Hazards are controllable	−.66	.05	−.47	11.4	.000
ac_8	Controllability by rescue operation	1.73	.12	.82	14.4	.000
evr_4	Risk are evenly distributed	−.08	.05	−.09	−1.6	.104
evr_5	Risk are not catastrophic	.60	.05	.51	10.7	.000
evr_3	Fatal consequences	−.99	.07	−.99	13.4	.000
ac_3	Influence and power in the firm	.26	.03	.39	8.47	.000
ac_{10}	Controllability of pollution effects	−.61	.08	−.34	−7.4	.000
ac_{12}	Discount of pollution effects in time	−.17	.03	−.35	−5.9	.000
ac_{17}	Personal past experience with pollution	.17	.03	.29	5.70	.000
ac_{13}	Managers' home is located	−.65	.06	−.47	−9.9	.000
evr_6	Low risk for future generations	−.52	.05	−.65	-10.4	.000
ac_2	Minimal technological options	−.17	.02	−.31	−7.0	.000
evr_9	Hazards are observable	.17	.03	.23	5.1	.000
ac_5	Firm's influence in the supply chain	−.11	.02	−.16	−4.2	.000

Table C5d   Correlations amongst the semantic loads of the aspects of risk

Aspects of risk

EVR	Environmental risk perception index (domain)
sr	The firms' operations are environmentally safe
vol	Voluntariness of exposure
ctr	Controllability of hazards consequences
dts	Discount in time and space of benefits and effects of the firm operations
cs	Condition of the subject

	EVR	sr	vol	ctr	dts	cs
sr	.351**	1.000				
vol	.014	−.306**	1.000			
ctr	−.321**	−.415**	.064	1.000		
dts	.060	−.081	.248*	−.002	1.000	
cs	−.539**	−.422**	.057	.395**	.017	1.000

** Correlation is significant at the 0.01 level (2-tailed).
* Correlation is significant at the 0.05 level (2-tailed)

C6: Economic risk perception
Stepwise regression

Table C6a   Model summary

Beliefs	R	R^2	Adj R^2	SEE	Variance explained by each aspect of economic risk
er_{19}	.79	.62	.62	1.15	Financial risk =
er_{20}	.86	.74	.73	.96	$er_{18}+er_{19}+er_{20}$ = 74.7%
er_{15}	.89	.80	.79	.85	
er_1	.92	.85	.84	.73	Economic opportunity =
er_{12}	.93	.87	.86	.68	$er_1+er_{10}+er_{12}+er_{15}$ = 13.8%
er_{21}	.94	.88	.88	.65	
er_{18}	.94	.89	.89	.62	Technological risk =
er_{10}	.95	.90	.89	.60	er_{21}= 1.22%

Dependent variable: ER

Table C6b   ANOVA

	Sum of squares	df	Mean square	F	Sig.
Regression	307.765	8	38.47	105.63	.000
Residual	32.050	88	.36		
Total	339.814	96			

Table C6c   Coefficients

Model 8	Beliefs	Unstd. coef. B	S.E.	Std. coef. B	t	Sig.
	(Const.)	.68	.28		2.36	.020
er_{19}	Capital risk	.62	.04	.65	14.43	.000
er_{20}	Competitiveness uncertainty	.25	.04	.26	5.53	.000
er_{15}	Market uncertainty	.38	.04	.39	9.25	.000
er_1	Opportunity loss	-.20	.03	-.23	-6.52	.000
er_{12}	Customer expectancies	-.26	.04	-.26	-5.40	.000
er_{21}	Compound risk	.02	.02	.12	3.60	.001
er_{18}	Resources timing	.15	.05	.17	3.02	.003
er_{10}	Entry timing	.08	.03	-.09	-2.63	.010

Predictors: (constant), ER19, ER20, ER15, ER1, ER12, ER21, ER18, ER10

C7:   **Perceived market pressure**
Stepwise regression

Table C7a   Model summary

Beliefs		R	R^2	Adj. R^2	% E	SEE
mp_9	Motivation to comply with customer expectancies	.71	.51	.50	50.6	1.52
mp_6	Our firm is a fast follower	.83	.68	.68	17.6	1.22
mp_{12}	Market heterogeneity	.85	.73	.72	4.1	1.14

Table C7b   ANOVA

	Sum of squares	df	Mean square	F	Sig.
Regression	330.94	3	110.31	84.48	.000
Residual	121.42	93	1.30		
Total	452.37	96			

Table C7c   Coefficients

Model	Beliefs	Unstd. coef. B	SE	Std. coef. B	t	Sig.
	Constant	2.854E-02	.34		.08	.935
mp_9	Motivation to comply with customer expectancies	.819	.07	.82	11.10	.000
mp_6	Our firm is a fast follower	.555	.06	.57	8.67	.000
mp_{12}	Market heterogeneity	-.398	.10	-.33	-3.86	.000

Predictors: (Constant), MP9, MP6, MP12
Dependent Variable: MP

C8: **Perceived community pressure**
Stepwise regression

Table C8a   Model summary

	Beliefs	R	R^2	Adj. R^2	% E	SEE
cp_{15}	NGOs pressure	.69	.48	.48	48.3	1.10
cp_{10}	Community lobbying current capability	.76	.58	.57	8.8	1.00
cp_3	Outsiders social norm	.78	.62	.60	3.7	.96
cp_{13}	Staff capacity pressure	.82	.68	.67	6.6	.87
cp_{14}	Motivation to comply with staff pressures	.85	.73	.71	4.2	.81

Table C8b   ANOVA

	Sum of squares	df	Mean square	F	Sig.
Regression	307.03	6	51.17	51.69	.000
Residual	89.09	90	.99		
Total	396.12	96			

e Predictors: (constant), CP15, CP10, CP3, CP13, CP14
f Dependent variable: CP

Table C8c   Coefficients

Model 5	Beliefs	Unstd. coef. B	SE	Std. coef. B	t	Sig.
	Constant	-1.49	.41		-3.57	.001
cp_{15}	NGOs pressure	.42	.06	.46	6.98	.000
cp_{10}	Community lobbying current capability	.37	.05	.51	7.35	.000
cp_3	Outsiders social norm	.49	.07	.65	7.02	.000
cp_{13}	Staff capacity pressure	-.52	.08	-.65	-6.08	.000
cp_{14}	Motivation to comply with staff pressures	.29	.07	.29	3.83	.000

C9:   **Perceived regulatory pressure**
Stepwise regression

Table C9a   Model summary

	Beliefs	R	R^2	Adj. R^2	% E	SEE
rp_1	Environmental agencies	.72	.51	.51	51.4	1.41
rp_5	ISO 14000 influence	.79	.62	.61	10.2	1.25
rp_3	Enforcement capability	.83	.69	.68	7.0	1.13
rp_9	Motivation to comply with international agreements	.85	.72	.71	2.8	1.08
rp_2	Regulatory risk	.87	.75	.74	2.9	1.02
rp_6	Motivation to comply with ISO	.88	.77	.76	1.7	.99

Table C9b   ANOVA

Model 6	Sum of squares	df	Mean square	F	Sig.
Regression	307.03	6		51.17	51.69	.000
Residual	89.09	90	.99		
Total	396.12	96			

f Predictors: (constant), RP1, RP5, RP4, RP9, RP2, RP6
g Dependent variable: RP

Table C9c   Coefficients

	Beliefs	Unstd. coef. B	SE	Std. coef. B	t	Sig.
	Constant	-4.52	1.12		-4.01	.000
rp_1	Environmental agencies	.36	.10	.302	3.54	.001
rp_5	ISO 14000 influence	.48	.06	.556	7.91	.000
rp_3	Enforcement capability	-.62	.08	-.615	-7.63	.000
rp_9	Motivation to comply with intern. agreements	.33	.08	.311	3.87	.000
rp_2	Regulatory risk	.82	.21	.267	3.90	.000
rp_6	Motivation to comply with ISO	.18	.06	.187	2.72	.008

C10: Technological capabilities
Stepwise and forward regression

Table C10a   Model summary

	R	R^2	Adj. R^2	% E	SEE	Variance explained by each technological capability
$tcpp_{21}$	.74	.55	.55	55.3	1.30	Product life cycle analysis capability ($tcpp_{13}$) = 2.0%
$tcpp_{43}$	.85	.73	.73	17.8	1.01	Co-operation and influence ($tcpp_2$) = 3.0%
$tcpp_{32}$	.88	.78	.77	4.5	.92	Technological opportunities ($tcpp_{43}+tcpp_{32}$) =22.3%
$tcpp_2$	.90	.81	.80	3.0	.86	Improvement implementation $tcpp_{21}+ tcpp_{24}$ = 59%
$tcpp_{13}$	.91	.83	.82	2.0	.81	
$tcpp_{24}$	.93	.87	.86	3.7	.72	

Table C10b   ANOVA

	Sum of squares	df	Mean square	F	Sig.
Regression	327.07	7	46.72	107.00	.000
Residual	38.86	89	.43		
Total	365.93	96			

Table C10c   Coefficients

Model 6	Beliefs	Unstd coeff. B	SE	Stand. coef. B	t	Sig.
	Constant	-1.41	.08		-16.74	.000
$tcpp_{21}$	Concept product development capability	.08	.02	.09	3.43	.001
$tcpp_{43}$	Product nature	.59	.01	.59	39.53	.000
$tcpp_{32}$	Waste elimination via re-design (process)	-.14	.01	-.13	-10.37	.000
$tcpp_2$	Inputs and components data safe sheets collection	.19	.01	.13	14.05	.000
$tcpp_{13}$	Links with suppliers and consumers	-1.34	.02	-1.21	-50.07	.000
$tcpp_{24}$	Re-design work team assemble	.18	.01	.17	13.15	.000

Dependent Variable: TCPP
Predictors: (Constant), TCPP21, TCPP43, TCPP32, TCPP2, TCPP13, TCPP24

Table C10d   Correlation between willingness (W), perceived control over the innovation process (PC) and the components of technological capabilities

	W	PC	LCAI	LCA II	LCA III	TOP PRC	TO PPRD	IC PRC	IC PRD	CI INT
PC	.69**									
LCAI	.35**	.41**								
LCAII	.49**	.51**	.81**							
LCAIII	.50**	.53**	.69**	.75**						
TOPPRC	.62**	.69**	.45**	.48**	.63**					
TOPPRD	.63**	.73**	.54**	.66**	.61**	.83**				
ICPRC	.42**	.41**	.03	.04	.24	.39**	.41**			
ICPRD	.76**	.76**	.34**	.49**	.53**	.80**	.78**	.57**		
CIINT	.54**	.47**	.35**	.51**	.61**	.45**	.57**	.64**	.60**	
CIEXT	.32**	.50**	.45**	.52**	.74**	.70**	.55**	.14	.57**	.32**

** Correlation is significant at the 0.01 level (2-tailed).
* Correlation is significant at the 0.05 level (2-tailed)

C11: Organisational learning capabilities
Stepwise regression

Table C11a   *Model summary*

	R	R^2	Adj. R^2	% E	SEE	Variance explained by each aspect of learning
ol_{16}	.76	.59	.58	58.9	1.17	
ol_8	.84	.71	.70	12.53	.98	Implementing changes =
ol_{11}	.86	.73	.73	2.36	.94	$ol_7+ol_{13}+ol_{14}+ol_{16}= 63.32\%$
ol_{15}	.87	.75	.74	2.00	.91	
ol_{13}	.88	.77	.76	1.51	.88	Problem solving =
ol_{14}	.89	.80	.78	2.75	.83	$ol_6+ol_8+ol_{11}+ol_{12}= 18.25\%$
ol_6	.90	.82	.80	1.83	.80	
ol_3	.91	.83	.82	1.55	.77	Integrating knowledge =
ol_{12}	.92	.85	.83	1.55	.73	$ol_3+ol_{15}= 3.55\%$
ol_7	.93	.86	.85	1.55	.70	

Table C11b   *ANOVA*

Model 10	Sum of squares	df	Mean square	F	Sig.
Regression	275.40	10	27.54	55.76	.000
Residual	42.47	86	.49		
Total	317.87	96			

Table C11c   *Coefficients*

	Beliefs	Unstd. coeff. B	SE	Std. coef. B	t	Sig.
	Constant	.07	.39		.17	.859
ol_{16}	Involvement of continuous improvement	.77	.11	.66	6.90	.000
ol_8	Key individuals (gate keepers)	.19	.06	.19	3.04	.003
ol_{11}	Knowledge value	-.39	.08	-.25	-4.43	.000
ol_{15}	Extensive communication	.43	.11	.34	3.77	.000
ol_{13}	Involvement (technical change)	.94	.16	.89	5.59	.000
ol_{14}	Involvement (org. change)	-.80	.20	-.71	-3.95	.000
ol_6	Key individuals (critical knowledge)	-.39	.07	-.41	-5.23	.000
ol_3	Specialisation	.22	.06	.20	3.49	.001
ol_{12}	Continuous training	-.32	.07	-.31	-4.15	.000
ol_7	Key individuals (power and influence)	.25	.08	.26	3.13	.002

Dependent variable: OL
Predictors: (Constant), OL16, OL8, OL11, OL15, OL13, OL14, OL6, OL3, OL12, OL7

C12: Strategic alliances capabilities
Enter regression

Table C12a   *Model summary*

	Beliefs	R	R^2	Adj. R^2	% E	SEE
al_{10}	Co-operation and influence with suppliers	.73	.53	.53	53.2	1.26
al_1	Strategic fit	.78	.61	.60	7.7	1.15
al_7	Past experience	.81	.65	.64	3.5	1.10
al_{13}	Sourcing opportunities	.82	.68	.67	2.6	1.06
al_6	Support from CEO and Share holders	.83	.70	.68	1.5	1.03
al_{11}	Influence and Cupertino with customers	.84	.71	.69	1.1	1.02

Table C12b   *ANOVA*

	Sum of squares	df	Mean square	F	Sig.
Regression	235.54	6	39.25	37.65	.000
Residual	93.81	90	1.04		
Total	329.36	96			

TableC12c   *Coefficients*

Model 6	Beliefs	Unstd. coef. B	SE	Std. coef. B	t	Sig.
	Constant	-.31	.36		-.860	.392
al_{10}	Co-operation and influence with suppliers	.39	.09	.43	3.98	.000
al_1	Strategic fit	.24	.09	.21	2.52	.013
al_7	Past experience	-.34	.08	-.36	-3.99	.000
al_{13}	Outsourcing opportunities	.27	.09	.30	3.03	.003
al_6	Support from CEO and Share holders	.17	.08	.18	2.15	.034
al_{11}	Influence and co-operation with customers	.18	.08	.18	2.08	.040

Predictors: (constant), AL10, AL1, AL7, AL13, AL6, AL11
Dependent variable: AL

C13: Networks of collaboration capabilities
Stepwise regression

Table C13a   Model summary

	Beliefs	R	R^2	Adj. R^2	% E	SEE
nwk$_5$	With suppliers	.65	.42	.41	41.8	1.46
nwk$_7$	With firms in the same industrial sector	.74	.54	.53	12.1	1.30
nwk$_3$	With SEMARNAP	.78	.61	.60	6.1	1.21
nwk$_1$	With universities	.79	.63	.62	2.1	1.18
nwk$_2$	With US-EPA	.81	.66	.64	2.3	1.14

Table C13b   ANOVA

	Sum of squares	df	Mean square	F	Sig.
Regression	234.05	5	46.811	35.70	.000
Residual	119.30	91	1.311		
Total	353.36	96			

Table C13c   Coefficients

Model 5	Beliefs	Unstd. coef. B	SE	Std. coef. B	t	Sig.
	Constant	-.94	.35		-2.67	.009
nwk$_5$	With suppliers	.46	.09	.44	5.01	.000
nwk$_7$	With firms in the same industrial sector	.32	.08	.28	4.03	.000
nwk$_3$	With SEMARNAP	.24	.07	.25	3.13	.002
nwk$_1$	With universities	-.44	.12	-.47	-3.66	.000
nwk$_2$	With US-EPA	.41	.15	.39	2.64	.010

Predictors: (constant), NWK5, NWK7, NWK3, NWK1, NWK2
Dependent variable: NWK

Appendix D: Characterisation of the sample of firms

The characterisation of the sample was done putting emphasis on those features that would help to explain the firms' capabilities to change towards a new technological regime. For this reason the sample was characterised mainly by using the framework provided by the stages of evolution of industry proposed by Utterback (1994).

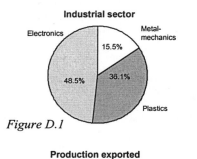

Figure D.1

Figure D.2

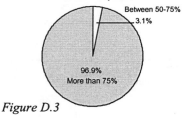

Figure D.3

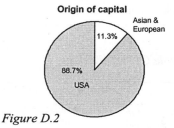

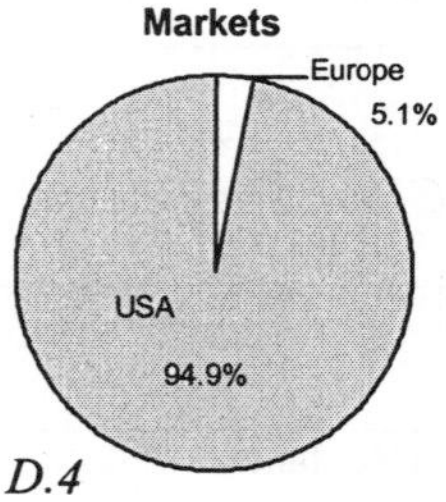

Figure D.4

Stage of evolution of the In-Bond industry

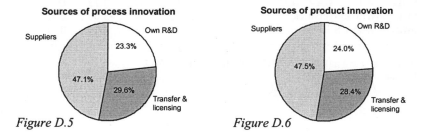

Figure D.5

Figure D.6

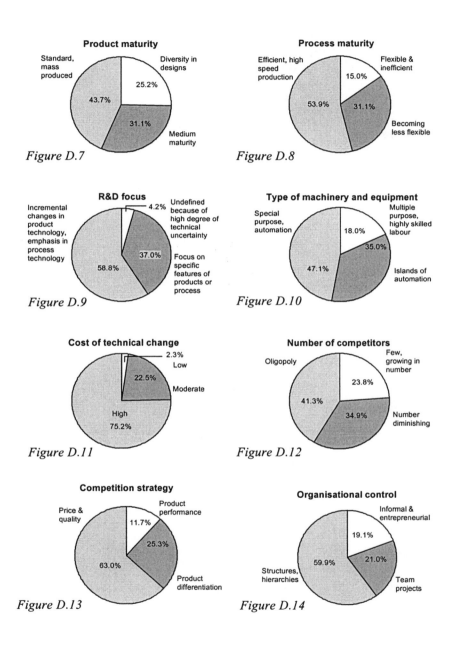

Product maturity

Standard, mass produced

Diversity in designs

25.2%

43.7%

31.1%

Medium maturity

Figure D.7

Process maturity

Efficient, high speed production

Flexible & inefficient

15.0%

53.9%

31.1%

Becoming less flexible

Figure D.8

R&D focus

Incremental changes in product technology, emphasis in process technology

Undefined because of high degree of technical uncertainty

4.2%

37.0%

58.8%

Focus on specific features of products or process

Figure D.9

Type of machinery and equipment

Special purpose, automation

Multiple purpose, highly skilled labour

18.0%

35.0%

47.1%

Islands of automation

Figure D.10

Cost of technical change

2.3% Low

22.5%

Moderate

High 75.2%

Figure D.11

Number of competitors

Oligopoly

Few, growing in number

23.8%

41.3%

34.9%

Number diminishing

Figure D.12

Competition strategy

Price & quality

Product performance

11.7%

25.3%

63.0%

Product differentiation

Figure D.13

Organisational control

Informal & entrepreneurial

19.1%

59.9%

21.0%

Structures, hierarchies

Team projects

Figure D.14

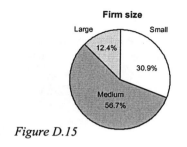

Figure D.15

Appendix E: Questionnaire

Firm   : _____
Respondent   : _____
Position   : _____
Date   : _____

I. General

(a) What is the main activity of this firm?
(b) How many people were employed in the last year?
(c) Amount of net sales in 1997?

More than a billion	5
$ 100 – 1 billion	4
$ 10 – 100 million	3
$ 1 million – 10 million	2
Less than 1 million	1

(d) % of total sales that are export?

More than 50%	5
25 – 50%	4
5 – 25 %	3
Less than 5%	2
Zero (no exports)	1

(f) What are your main export markets (rank the three most important)?

North America	6
Latin America	5
Europe	4
Japan	3
Other Asian countries	2
Other regions	1

II. Stage of evolution of industry

In this section you may tick only one of the three options in each question.

(g)   What do you regard as the main source of *product* innovations in your company?

Our own R&D laboratories and human resources   ☐

We transfer or license major parts of our product   ☐
technology from other firms

We often obtain new inputs and components for our   ☐
product from our suppliers

(h)   What do you regard as the main source of *process* innovations in your company?

Our own R&D laboratories and human resources   ☐

We transfer or license major parts of our process   ☐
technology from other firms

We often obtain new inputs and components for our   ☐
process from our suppliers

(j)   What do you believe is the main feature that could describe the maturity of your product?

Diverse in design, often customised   ☐

At least one product is stable enough to have significant   ☐
production volumes

Undifferentiated standard products   ☐

(k)   What do you believe is the main feature that describes the maturity of your production process?

Flexible and inefficient, major changes can be fairly easily   ☐
accommodated

Becoming more rigid, with changes occurring in major   ☐
stages of the process

Efficient, intensive in capital, not flexible with high costs   ☐
of change

(l)   What are your research and development activities normally focused on?

Unspecified because of high degree of technical   ☐
uncertainty

On specific products or process features   ☐

On incremental changes of product technology; emphasis   ☐
on process technology

(m)   Type of equipment used in your plant can be mainly described as:

General purpose, requiring skilled labour	☐
Some stages of the process are automated	☐
Special purpose, mostly automatic, labour focus on tending and monitoring equipment	☐

(n) The cost of changing production process technologies for your company is likely to be

Low	☐
Moderate	☐
High	☐

(o) The number of competitors in your industry is likely to be:

Few, but growing in numbers with widely fluctuating market share	☐
Declining in number	☐
Few, companies that dominate the market	☐

(p) The major basis for competition for your company is:

Functional product performance	☐
Product variation; fitness for use and differentiation	☐
Price and/or quality	☐

(q) The organisational control in your company is mainly performed via:

Informal and entrepreneurial relations	☐
Through project and task groups	☐
Structures, rules and goals	☐

(r) The size of your company is:

Small	☐
Medium	☐
Large	☐

III. Direct measures of willingness

Our firm has plans to develop cleaner options in our product designs

Our firm has plans to develop cleaner options for our production process

I What is the likelihood that your company would undertake a business strategy that includes radical preventive measures to eliminate residuals and waste, such as changing product designs and manufacturing process that aim for the ideal recycled and zero emissions factory?

At the moment:

unlikely	1	2	3	4	5	6	7	likely
	extremely	quite	slightly	uncertain	slightly	quite	extremely	

Within the next two years:
Within the next five years:
In the long term:

I.   How willing do you believe is your firm to develop clean technologies?

IV. Direct measures of attitude, perceived social pressure and perceived control upon the innovation process.

• Attitude towards the development of clean technology

A. For our firm the development of cleaner products and adoption cleaner processes seems to have:

At the moment:

good consequences	1	2	3	4	5	6	7	bad consequences
	extremely						extremely	

Within the next two years:
Within the next five years:
In the long run:

A.   The development of cleaner products and adoption cleaner processes seems to have for the local and regional environment:

At the moment:
Within the next two years:
Within the next five years:
In the long run:

1	2	3	4	5	6	7	good consequences
no		slightly		quite			extremely

• Perceived social pressure

PSP. In general the social pressure (e.g. from the community, the marketplace, government agencies and public institutions, etc.) perceived by this company to develop clean products and adopt clean production processes is:

At the moment:
Within the next two years:
Within the next five years:

In the long run:

low	1	2	3	4	5	6	7	high
	extremely	quite	slightly	uncertain	slightly	quite	extremely	

- Perceived control over the innovation process

PC1. For our company the development and implementation of clean technologies is:

difficult	1	2	3	4	5	6	7	easy
	extremely	quite	slightly	uncertain	slightly	quite	extremely	

PC2. Our company has the necessary economic and technological and organisational resources to develop clean products and clean production processes.

disagree	1	2	3	4	5	6	7	agree
	extremely	quite	slightly	uncertain	slightly	quite	extremely	

V. Direct measures of the perception on the behavioural domains

- Perceived environmental risk[1]

EVR1. The environmental hazards created by this company are likely to be:

low	1	2	3	4	5	6	7	high
	extremely	quite	slightly	uncertain	slightly	quite	extremely	

EVR2. As a consequence, the development of clean technologies for this firm is:

irrelevant	1	2	3	4	5	6	7	relevant
extremely		quite	slightly	uncertain	slightly	quite		extremely

- Perceived economic risk

ER. For our firm developing cleaner products and adopting cleaner processes seems to imply economic:

benefits	1	2	3	4	5	6	7	losses
great		moderate	small	uncertain	small	moderate		great

- Perceived market pressure

MP. In general, it can be said that the signals (or demand) we are perceiving from the marketplace (i.e., customers, suppliers and competitors) tell us we should develop clean products and adopt clean production processes.

weak	1	2	3	4	5	6	7	strong
	greatly		moderate	small	uncertain	small	moderate		highly

- Perceived community pressure

CP. In general, the demand on this company from the community (i.e. local and regional NGO's, universities & households associations, unions) to develop clean products and adopt clean production processes is:

weak	1	2	3	4	5	6	7	strong
	great	moderate	small	uncertain	small	moderate		great

- Perceived regulatory pressure

RP Several regulatory institutions (i.e. Environmental agencies, ISO 14000, The Commission for Environmental Protection and The Border Environmental Co-operation Commission) are pushing us to develop clean products and adopt clean production processes.

disagree	1	2	3	4	5	6	7	agree
	extremely	quite	slightly	uncertain	slightly	quite	extremely	

- Perceived technological capabilities in product and process improvement

TCPP. Our company has the capability to identify and quantify the energy and materials; assess their impact in the environment; and to identify and evaluate opportunities of modification of inputs, product design and/or manufacturing process. The latter in order to develop clean products and to adopt clean production processes.

disagree	1	2	3	4	5	6	7	agree
	extremely	quite	slightly	uncertain	slightly	quite	extremely	

- Perceived organisational learning capability

OL. I can affirm that our company has the human resources with capabilities to generate the necessary new knowledge and apply it to reshape organisational structures and routines in order to develop clean products and adopt clean production processes.

disagree	1	2	3	4	5	6	7	agree
	extremely	quite	slightly	uncertain	slightly	quite	extremely	

- Perceived strategic alliances capability

AL. Our company finds the formation of strategic alliances to procure or develop substitutes of the environmentally sensitive parts of our technological portfolio:

difficult	1	2	3	4	5	6	7	easy
	extremely	quite	slightly	uncertain	slightly	quite	extremely	

- Perceived networks of collaboration capability

NWK. Establishing networks of collaboration with external sources to acquire know-how to develop clean technologies for our company is:

difficult	1	2	3	4	5	6	7	easy
	extremely	quite	slightly	uncertain	slightly	quite	extremely	

VI. Scales to assess the perception on the behavioural domains

- Scale to assess the perceived environmental risk

The environmental hazards generated by the operations of our company for this region are likely to be:

controllable	1 2 3 4 5 6 7	uncontrollable
don't have global impact	.	have global impact
consequences not fatal	.	fatal consequences
evenly distributed	.	unevenly distributed
not catastrophic	.	catastrophic
low risk to future generations	.	high risk to future generations
voluntary for those exposed	.	involuntary for those exposed
doesn't affect me	.	affects me
observable	.	not observable
known to those exposed	.	unknown to those exposed
delayed effects	.	immediate effects
old risk	.	new risk
risks known to science	1 2 3 4 5 6 7	risks unknown to science

- Scale to assess the acceptance of the generation of environmental risks:

ac1 The way we manufacture our product is state of the art in terms of the environmental technology in our business.[2]

ac2 All forms of manufactured goods generate pollution.

ac3 The degree of influence I wield in my position and perception in the way we operate and produce in this firm is:

ac4 The benefits generated by our business outweigh the possible impacts on the environment.

ac5 My freedom to choose for or against the creation of hazards or risk for the environment as part of a social production system is:

ac6 Good environmental management depends upon (trained) human skills, the existence of adequate written regulations, and the appropriateness of required equipment. In general, the likelihood of environmental impacts caused by the operation of this firm is:

ac7 Accident probabilities are dependent upon opportunities for human error and equipment failures. The chance of an environmental accident due to the operations of this firm are:

ac8 In case of any environmental accident in our firm the likelihood that its effects can be contained by rescue operations is:

ac9 The environmental impacts of the operations of this firm, if any, are likely to be:

ac10 In general, the effects of released pollutants on the environment and human health are controllable.

ac11 It is important for the success and survival of this firm that the expected profits from our operations are obtained at the shortest term possible:

ac12 Undesired consequences of production systems may have immediate or delayed effects. I don't believe there are immediate environmental consequences from the operation of this firm; if any, they remain to be accumulated in the long term.

ac13 My home is located:
  1. ☐ near this production facility
  2. ☐ in other suburb in this city
  3. ☐ in the USA near the border
  4. ☐ in the USA distant from the border
  5. ☐ in other country.

ac14 What is the likelihood of you knowing where the direct benefits from the operation of this plant go:

ac15 My personal benefits from the manufacturing operations of this firm are:

ac16 My knowledge about the possible effects of our operation on the local environment is:

ac17 In the past I have been affected personally by environmental accidents or by pollution:

ac18 The likelihood that I may be affected personally by environmental accidents or by pollution is:

ac19 The benefits our business generates for me outweigh the possible impacts on the environment.

- Scale to assess the perceived economic risk

er1 For our firm failing to launch a clean product for a new market niche may imply a great opportunity loss.

er2 The benefit this firm can gain from the development of clean technologies in order to avoid the uncertainty of change in environmental regulations is likely to be:

er3 The amount of R&D required to create an ideal clean product and develop a clean production process is likely to be:

er4 The cost associated with this level of R&D is likely to be:

er5 The likelihood that this firm can bear the costs is:

er6 The duration of a clean product innovation project is likely to last:

er7 The certainty that a venture developing a clean product concept can be accomplished is:

er8 The opportunities to appropriate the benefits of developing clean products (via patents, licensing, transferring technology, etc) are likely to be:

er9 For our firm the advantages (e.g. novelty of product and distribution effects) of pioneering the launch of clean products are likely to be:

er10 We believe launching a clean product venture would be 'ahead of its time':

er11 In developing clean technologies our company prefers to be a follower rather than a pioneer.

er12 Our customers' willingness to pay for a more expensive yet cleaner product is likely to be:

er13 When doing a life cycle analysis via subcontracting or forming strategic alliances to outsource know-how and/or new materials, the likelihood of losing control over your own technology secrecy is likely to be:

er14 The growth opportunities that arise from forming strategic alliances to develop clean products and clean process are likely to be:

er15 Entering new markets with new products that utilise new technologies have rendered great benefits for some firms. The development of clean technologies provides opportunities to sustain growth for this firm are likely to be:

er16 Strategic alliances create an opportunity for positioning the participating company in a leadership or growth position to sell a new product or service, or to secure access to technology or clean raw materials. Comparatively the risks of losing control of your own technology secrecy and appropriability are likely to be:

er17 The chances of losing trained human resources for the development of clean technologies because of turnover is likely to be:

er18 What is the likelihood that you will have the necessary financial, human, and intellectual resources timely to develop clean technologies?

er19 If your company were to pioneer the development of clean products, what is the chance that you would lose your capital investment?

er21 What is the likelihood that such an investment would affect your fixed costs and overhead, and therefore your overall competitiveness?

er22 What do you see as new areas risks associated with developing clean technologies for your company?

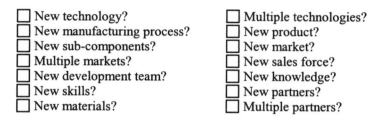

☐ New technology?   ☐ Multiple technologies?
☐ New manufacturing process?   ☐ New product?
☐ New sub-components?   ☐ New market?
☐ Multiple markets?   ☐ New sales force?
☐ New development team?   ☐ New knowledge?
☐ New skills?   ☐ New partners?
☐ New materials?   ☐ Multiple partners?

• Scale to assess the perceived market pressures

mp1 The pace of technological innovation in our sector is very rapid. Soon we will be moving towards the development of clean technologies.

mp2 Our competitors are thinking of developing clean products and adopting clean production processes.

mp3 Competition in the marketplace will push us to develop clean products and adopt clean production processes

mp4 Generally speaking, this company is a pioneer in our industry with regard to advances in technology of *products*. Developing clean *products* is not an exception.

mp5 Generally speaking, this company is a pioneer in our industry with regard to advances in *processes* technology. Developing clean *processes* is not an exception.

mp6 Generally speaking, this company adopts quickly advances in technology of processes and products in our industry; adopting clean technologies is not an exception.

mp7 Our customers think this company should develop clean products and adopt clean production processes.

mp8 Our customers will be pushing us to develop clean products and adopt clean production processes.

mp9 Generally speaking, this company does what our customers think we should do regarding environmental issues.

mp10 The rate of change in our industry, the unpredictability of the behaviour of customers and competitors, and the shifts in the industry's technological conditions will lead us to develop CT in order to pre-empt rival entries.

mp11 The competition in our industry is fierce. This creates an unfavourable business climate, with intense competition and limited market opportunities. Clean products are a good strategy for marketing new products an appealing option.

mp12 The market for our firm is very heterogeneous. We are constantly challenged to maintain a broad line of products to match the diversity of customers' needs. A clean product is a good option to introduce in the market.

- Scale to assess the perceived community pressure

cp1 Personally I think our company should develop clean products and adopt clean production processes.

cp2 Personally, most people that are important to me think our company should develop clean products and adopt clean production processes.

cp3 Most outsiders who are important for the success of this company think we should develop clean products and adopt clean production processes.

cp4 Most outsiders who are important for the success of this company will be pushing us to develop clean products and adopt clean production processes within the next five years.

cp5 Environmental experts from universities and research institutions are convinced that it is time for industry to develop clean technologies. This company agrees with such belief.

cp6 Our environmental consultants think we should develop clean products and adopt clean production processes.

cp7 Generally speaking, this company does what environmental consultants think we should do regarding environmental issues; developing clean technologies is not an exception.

cp8 The local community thinks our company should develop clean products and adopt clean production processes.

cp9 Generally speaking, this company does what the local community thinks our company should do regarding environmental issues.

cp10 The local community (currently) can lobby and pressure us to develop clean products and adopt clean production processes.

cp11 The local community will be pushing us to develop clean products and adopt clean production processes within the next five years.

cp12 Most of the staff who are important for the success of our company think we should develop clean products and adopt clean production processes.

cp13 Most of the staff who are important for the success of our company will be pushing to develop clean products and adopt clean production processes within the next five years.

cp14 Generally speaking, this company does what our key staff think we should do.

cp15 Several non-governmental organisations in the region have appealed to us to develop clean products and adopt clean production processes.

- Scale to assess the perceived regulatory pressure

rp1   Environmental authorities think our company should develop clean products and adopt clean production processes.

rp2   Environmental authorities will be pushing us to develop clean products and adopt clean production processes within the next five years.

rp3   Environmental authorities have the enforcement capabilities to force us to develop clean products and adopt clean production processes.

rp4   Generally speaking this company does what the environmental authorities think our company should do.

rp5   The demand in the market of ISO14000 will push us to develop clean products and adopt clean production processes within the next five years.

rp6   Generally speaking, this company does what the International Standards Organization (ISO) prescribe in order to be certified. Developing clean technologies is not an exception.

rp7   New international agreements such as the Border Environment Cooperation Commission (BECC) will push us to develop clean products and adopt clean production processes within the next five years.

rp8   International agreements such as NAFTA will push us to develop clean products and adopt clean production processes.

rp9   Generally speaking, this company does what international institutions and agreements such as ISO, BECC and NAFTA prescribe about environmental protection.

- Scale to assess the perceived technological capabilities

tcpp1   For our firm making a detailed *manufacturing process flow chart* to have an overview of our manufacturing process, focusing in the most relevant stages, components and raw inputs with environmental critical interventions is:

tcpp2   Ensuring that all our suppliers provide all the specifications and details of our inputs and raw materials and its possible effects when combing with water, air and soil is for our firm:

tcpp3   For our firm gathering information about mass and energy flows for our inputs and residuals (emissions, discharges, solid waste, etc.) is:

tcpp4   For our firm making a list of activities, inputs and components used in our manufacturing process and identifying all the *possible sources* of environmental critical interventions is:

tcpp5   Making the above for the entire life cycle of our product is:

tcpp6   For our firm making a table with the impacts in our local environment for all the activities, inputs and components used in our operations is:

tcpp7   Making the above for the entire life cycle of our product is:

tcpp8   For this firm calculating the amounts of inputs used in manufacture of our products (energy and materials) is:

tcpp9   As part of a LCA estimating the environmental impacts generated by our products and processes through an inventory table is:

tcpp10 Upon the above inventory giving priorities to those relevant environmental aspects (e.g. water acidification, toxicity, ozone layer, etc.) is:

tcpp11 Our firm has the necessary time and resources to gather the necessary data to make a life cycle analysis of our product:

tcpp12 For our firm detecting and associating with our *manufacturing process flow chart* the suppliers of those inputs and components environmentally critical is:

tcpp13 Upon the above chart of associations making a description and analysis of the interrelations and links with our suppliers and consumers is:

tcpp14 Assigning and negotiating environmental impact and prevention responsibilities with our suppliers is:

tcpp15 Assigning and negotiating environmental impact and prevention responsibilities with our consumers is:

tcpp16 For our firm, tracking environmental impacts of the use of our products beyond the limits of our factory is:

tcpp17 Procuring inputs and components that ensure the elimination of noxious residuals and high recyclability for this firm is:

tcpp18 The procurement of machinery and equipment that ensure us the elimination of noxious residuals in our production process is:

tcpp21 Developing concepts of pro-environmental design for our products and manufacturing process that eliminate noxious residuals and waste for our firm is:

tcpp22 The R&D capability to evaluate the feasibility of new product concepts having as guide the notion of prevention of noxious residuals generation in our firm is:

tcpp23 Defining and designing at least the principal subsystems of a clean product for our firm is:

tcpp24 Establishing teams for re-designing environmentally our products and process is:

tcpp25 Eliminating completely the use of raw materials and inputs that aren't environmentally safe for our firm is:

tcpp26   Procuring *raw materials* that are produced via processes and technologies environmentally clean for our firm is:

tcpp27   Procuring *components* that are produced via processes and technologies environmentally clean for our firm is:

tcpp28   Procuring *raw materials and inputs* ensure that high recyclability of our products at the end of their life is:

tcpp29   Implementing an efficient management of materials and inputs that ensure the elimination of residuals in the operation of our plant is:

tcpp30   Using materials available in bulk or in recyclable containers for our firm is:

tcpp31   Achieving the elimination of waste via re-design of our product is:

tcpp32   Achieving the elimination of waste via re-design of our process is:

tcpp33   Designing packing methods that ensure the elimination of waste and residuals during the packing process for our firm is:

tcpp34   Designing packing methods that ensure functionality while being reusable, recyclable and/or biodegradable is for our firm:

tcpp35   Re-designing our product to be easily maintained with materials and spare parts fully recyclable for our firm is:

tcpp36   Re-designing our product to be fully recyclable or biodegradable at the end of its life is:

tcpp37   Appointing a responsible person with enough corporate authority to manage an environmental management system is:

tcpp38   Communicating our commitment to protect the environment and ensure that our policy is clearly understood, implemented and maintained at all hierarchical levels in our firm is:

tcpp39   Organising sessions to create awareness of aspects of environmental quality assurance for our firm is:

tcpp40   Implementing a new environmental culture via the training and education at all level of this firm is:

tcpp41   Reconciling environmental necessities and demands with other demands, necessities and objective of other functional areas in our firm is:

tcpp42   Integrating an environmental policy towards clean production with other policies of our organisation is:

tcpp43   Due to the nature of our product substituting inputs and components that ensure prevention of residuals and high recyclability for our firm is:

• Scale to assess the perceived organisational learning capabilities

ol1   The integration of a diversity of professionals to solve the problem of generating a new product concept design and introducing the notions of reuse/recycling of materials/components into the manufacturing process for our firm is:

ol2 We count on employees that speak two or more professional languages and can see the world from two or more different professional perspectives (e.g. T-shaped skills in industrial and environmental design).

ol3 For our firm the implementation of mechanisms that translate across different disciplinary languages that encourage depersonalisation of conflicting perspectives among our professionals is:

ol4 The assembly of problem-solving teams made up of different personality types is important for ensuring a creative atmosphere for projects undertaken by this firm. For us to put this team together is:

ol5 Overcoming preferences in different perspectives regarding how to solve the same problem within our team projects is:

ol6 Our firm counts on individuals as sources of critical knowledge, or who have the breadth of understanding regarding the technology necessary to develop clean products.

ol7 Our organisation counts on individuals with the power to influence the organisation; they do not need to have detailed technical knowledge but must believe in the potential to positively influence innovation towards clean technologies.

ol8 Our firm has several people who regularly collect information regarding clean technologies and pass it on to the relevant people best able to make use of it.

ol9 For our company minimising employees' individual opposition to learning new techniques and change work practices, and methods for any new task-technology is:

ol10 As a consequence of the above it can be said that for our company implementing a clean production culture that eliminates residuals and waste and pollution is:

ol11 Most people within our firm value the experience of acquiring new skills and abilities; they also feel they are valued as part of the organisation.

ol12 For our firm, enabling people to take more responsibility and demonstrate more initiative is:

ol13 For our firm to achieve that most people participate positively in the process of *technological change* rather than resist it is:

ol14 For our firm achieving an effective communication among our employees, cross-functional teams and projects is:

ol15 For our firm promoting a broad participation in organisation-wide continuous improvement activities towards the development of clean products and clean production process is:

• Scale to assess the perceived strategic alliances

al1 Finding partners for strategic alliances that ensure good *strategic fit* (with regard to strengths and complementarities in innovative capacity and technical know-how) for the development of a cleaner technology-product portfolio is:

al2   Finding partners for strategic alliances that ensure a good *chemistry fit* (with regard to trust, honesty, win/win commitment, good reputation, predictability under pressure and creativity facing adversity) is:

al3   In creating strategic alliances reaching a good *operational fit* for both partners (i.e. strategic time orientation (long–short term), information and communication methods (formal–informal), management styles (hierarchical–collaborative), labour relations (harmonious–conflictive), technology (familiar–unfamiliar) and business government relations (adversarial–harmonious)) is:

al4   In the process of negotiating strategic alliances reaching a point that *maximises gain and value* for both partners in a win/win fashion is:

al5   The task of finding partners for strategic alliances that share the same environmental action values is:

al6   The creation of strategic alliances for the development of cleaner technologies has the support and commitment of our CEO and shareholders of this company.

al7   Our company has successful experiences making strategic alliances in order to innovate. Making alliances to develop clean products and processes would be the same.

al8   For this firm, outsourcing via alliances with suppliers the capability to undertake *Life Cycle Analysis* practices for our products portfolio.

al9   For our firm, influencing our suppliers of *inputs, components, raw materials and services* to develop cleaner substitutes for the actual environmentally sensitive critical parts of our product portfolio with cleaner options is:

al10 For our firm, influencing our suppliers of *production process technologies* to develop substitutes of the actual environmentally sensitive critical parts of our manufacturing technologies portfolio with cleaner options.

al11 For our firm, influencing our customers to participate (absorbing part of the costs of) in the development of clean products is:

al12 Outsourcing better *product technologies* such as clean designs for inputs, materials and components for our products from the technological marketplace is:

al13 Outsourcing new clean *manufacturing process technologies* for inputs, materials and components from the technological marketplace is:

•   Scale to assess the perceived networks of collaboration capabilities

nwk1 For our company, establishing networks of collaboration with universities to outsource know-how to develop clean technologies is:

nwk2   For our company, establishing networks of collaboration with EPA's clean technologies programme to outsource know-how to develop clean technologies is:

nwk3   For our company, establishing networks of collaboration with SEMARNAP's clean technologies programme to outsource know-how to develop clean technologies is:

nwk4   With the International Standards Organisation (regarding ISO 14000)?

nwk5   With suppliers of raw materials and other inputs for product integration?

nwk6   With consulting firms that specialise in clean technologies?

nwk7   With other firms in the same sector to transfer technology and expertise?

NOTES

1. EVR_2 is a factor of weight for the relation of environmental risk perception and the possible outcomes for environment protection arising from the development of clean technologies. The index of risk perception was then estimated as: $EVR = EVR_2 * (EVR_1/7)$.

2. The remaining parts of the questionnaire do not display the differential semantic for each question. The complete questionnaire can be obtained upon request to the author.

Appendix F: Correlation analysis

Table F1   Correlation analysis for the domains scales

Domains	W	Σac	Σevr	Σer	Σmp	Σcp	Σrp	Σtcpp	Σol	Σal
Σac	−.26**									
Σevr	.41**	.50**								
Σer	−.56**	−.05	.09							
Σmp	.15	−.09	.02	.01						
Σcp	.12	−.20	−.14	.15	.70**					
Σrp	.07	−.06	−.17	.00	.67**	.82**				
Σtc	.70**	.01	−.15	−.55**	.21*	.13	.16			
Σol	.59**	.01	−.04	−.54**	.17	.04	.22	.79**		
Σal	.56**	−.10	−.08	−.55**	.07	.06	.15	.69**	.78**	
Σnwk	.55**	−.17	−.07	−.52**	.13	.15*	.30**	.62**	.68**	.75**

** Correlation is significant at the 0.01 level (2–tailed). N=97
* Correlation is significant at the 0.05 level (2–tailed).

Table F2   Correlation analysis for the items direct measures of domain perceptions

Domains	W	EVR	ER	MP	CP	RP	TCPP	OL	AL
EVR	0.32**								
ER	−0.52**	−0.20							
MP	0.50**	0.38**	−0.35**						
CP	0.10	0.13	0.08	0.39**					
RP	0.30**	0.35**	−0.08	0.33**	0.35**				
TC	0.65**	0.09	−0.61**	0.30**	0.12	0.26*			
OL	0.48**	−0.11	−0.41**	0.19	0.12	0.39**	0.55**		
AL	0.70**	0.31	−0.53**	0.30**	0.18	0.51**	0.64**	0.54**	
NWK	0.73**	0.10	−0.45**	0.31**	0.09	0.42**	0.52**	0.60**	0.69**

** Correlation is significant at the 0.01 level (2–tailed). N=97
* Correlation is significant at the 0.05 level (2–tailed).

Table F3   *Correlation between the perceived behavioural*
control and the capabilities to innovate in clean technologies

Domain		PBC	TCPP	OL	AL
Perceived behavioural control	PBC				
Technological capabilities	TCPP	.79**			
Learning capabilities	OL	.55**	.55**		
Strategic alliances	AL	.70**	.64**	.54**	
Collaboration networks	NWK	.70**	.52**	.60**	.69**

Appendix G: Questionnaire application: Phase I

These are the questions for the semi-structured interviews carried out in Phase I of the empirical research to elicit beliefs related to the behaviour under study.

Behavioural beliefs (attitudinal construct)

1. What do you see as the advantages/gains/benefits of your company's engagement in clean technology development?
2. What do you see as the disadvantages/drawbacks of your company's engagement in clean technology development?
3. Is there anything else, either positive or negative, that you associate with clean technology development of your company?

Normative beliefs (normative construct)

1. Are there any people or institutions who you think want/push your company to engage in clean technology development?
2. Are there any people or institutions that you think oppose your company developing clean technology?
3. Does anybody else come to mind when you think about your company developing clean technology?

Control beliefs (instrumental construct)

Respond to these questions in terms of resources, time opportunity and skills.
1. What kind of skills or abilities do you think your company needs to develop clean technology?
2. What does your company need to know to engage in clean technology development?
3. What experience do you think your company needs to engage in clean technology development?

4. What kind of information do you think your company needs to engage clean technology development?
5. What additional resources in terms of time/money do you think your company needs in order to develop clean technology?
6. Are there any people or institutions from which your company needs help to develop clean technologies?
7. Are there any particular circumstances/opportunities you think your company relies on for developing clean technologies?
8. Are there any constraints you think are stopping your company from developing clean technologies?

References

Abelson, R.P. and A. Levi (1985), 'Decision making and decision theory', in G. Lindzy and E. Aronson (eds), *The Handbook of Social Psychology*, 3rd edn, vol. 1, New York: Random House, pp. 231–309.

Abernathy, W.J. and K.B. Clark (1984), 'Innovation: mapping the winds of creative destruction', *Research Policy*, **14** (1), 3–22.

Abernathy, W.J. and J.M. Utterback (1975), 'A dynamic model of product and process innovation', *Omega International Journal of Management Science*, **3** (6).

Aguilar, F.J. (1988), *General Managers in Action*, New York: Oxford University Press.

AIST (1993), *New Sunshine Program*, Agency of Industrial Science and Technology of the Ministry of International Trade and Industry Japan, http://www.aist.go.jp/index_e.html.

Ajzen, I. (1985), 'From intentions to actions: A theory of planned behavior', in J. Kuhl and J. Beckmann (eds), *Action–Control: From Cognition to Behavior*, Heildeberg: Springer, pp. 11–39.

Ajzen, I. (1988), *Attitudes, Personality, and Behavior*, Chicago: Dorsey Press.

Ajzen, I. (1991), 'The theory of planned behavior', *Organizational Behavior and Human Decision Process*, **50**, 179–211.

Ajzen, I. (1996a), 'The social psychology of decision making', in E.T. Higgins and A.R. Kruglansky (eds), *Social Psychology: Handbook of Basic Principles*, New York: Guilford Press, pp. 297–325.

Ajzen, I. (1996b), 'The moderating effects of attitude in decision making', in P.M. Gollwitzer and J.A. Bargh (eds), *The Psychology of Action: Linking Cognition and Motivation to Behavior*, New York: Guilford Press.

Ajzen, I. and D. Krebs (1994), 'Attitude and measurement: implications for survey research', in I. Borg and P. Mohler (eds), *Trends and Perspectives in Empirical Social Research*, New York: Walter de Gruyter, pp. 250–62.

Ajzen, I. and M. Fishbein (1969), 'The prediction of behavioral intentions in choice situation', *Journal of Experimental Social Psychology*, **5**, 400–416.

Ajzen, I. and M. Fishbein (1980), *Understanding Attitudes and Predicting Social Behavior*, Englewood Cliffs, NJ: Prentice Hall.

Ali, A. (1994), 'Pioneering versus incremental innovation: review and research propositions', *Journal of Product Innovation Managament*, 11, 46–61.

Allen, F.W. (1987), 'Towards a holistic appreciation of risk: The challenges for communicators and policy makers', *Science, Technology and Human Values*, **12**, 138–43.

Allison, P.D. (1999), *Multiple Regression: A Primer*, Thousand Oaks, CA: Pine Forge Press.

Alvarez, J. and V.M. Castillo (eds) (1986), *Ecología y Frontera. Ecology and the Borderlands*, Mexico City: UABC.

Anastasi, A. (1988), *Psychological Testing*, New York: Macmillan.

Andrews, C.J. (1998), 'Environmental business strategy: corporate leaders' perceptions', *Society and Natural Resources*, **11**, 531–40.

Argyis, C. and D.A. Schön (1996), *Organizational Learning II: Theory, Method and Practice*, Reading, MA: Addison-Wesley.

Armitage, C.J., M. Conner, J. Loach, D. Willetts (1999), 'Different perceptions of control: Applying an extended theory of planned behavior to legal and illegal drug use', *Basic and Applied Social Psychology*, **21** (4), 301–316.

Arthur D. Little (1996), *'Sustainable Industrial Development: Sharing Responsibilities in a Competitive World'*, The Hague: Conference Paper on Behalf of The Ministry of Housing and Ministry of Economic Affairs.

Ashford, N. (1993), 'Understanding technological responses of industrial firms to environmental problems', in K. Fisher and J. Schot (eds), *Environmental Strategies for industry: International Perspectives on Research Needs and Policy Implications*, Washington, DC: Island Press, pp. 277–307.

Atman, C.J., A. Bostrom, B. Fischhoff and M.G. Morgan (1994), 'Designing risk communication and correcting mental models of hazardous process: Part I', *Risk Analysis*, **14** (5), 779–88.

Baas, L., N. Duffy, B. Ryan, G. Spinardi and R. Williams (1999), 'Petrochemical sector', in A. Clayton, G. Spinardi and R. Williams (eds), *Policies for Cleaner Technology*, London: Earthscan, pp. 53–72.

Baker, G. (1989), 'Costos sociales e ingresos de la industria maquiladora', *Comercio Exterior*, **39** (10), 893–906.

Baker, G. (1990), 'Mi comida con Andrés: Non Traditional Approach to Fiscal Equity and Academic Collaboration in Northern Mexico', in B. Gonzalez-Arechiga and J.C. Ramirez (eds), *Subcontratación y Empresas Trasnacionales: Apertura y Restructuración en la Maquiladora*, Mexico, D.F.: El COLEF-Fundación Friedrich Ebert, pp. 489–554.

Baker, S., D. Ponniah, and S. Smith (1998), 'Techniques for the analysis of risks in major projects', *Journal of the Operational Research Society*, **49** (6), 567–72.

Bamberg, S. (1999), 'Pro-environmental behavior – A question of moral or right incentives?' *Zeitschrift fur Sozialpsycologie*, **30** (1), 57–76.

Bamberg, S. and P. Schmidt (1997), 'Theory driven evaluation of an environmental policy measure: using the theory of planned behavior', *Zeitschrift fur Sozialpsycologie*, **28** (4), 280–97.

Barbera, A.J. and V.D. McConnell (1994), 'The impact of environmental regulations on industry productivity: direct and indirect effects', *Journal of Environmental Economics and Management*, **18** (1), 50–65.

Barde, J.P. (1994), *Economic instruments in environmental policy: Lessons from the OECD experience and their relevance to developing economies*, Technical Papers No. 92, OECD Development Centre, Paris.

Baumol, W.J. (1972), 'On taxation and the control of externalities', *American Economics Review*, June.

Baumol, W.J. and W.E. Oates (1975), *The Theory of Environmental Policy*, Englewood Cliffs, NJ: Prentice Hall.

Baumol, W.J. and W.E. Oates (1993), 'The use of standards and prices for protection of the environment', in A. Markandya, and J. Richardson (eds), *Environmental Economics*, London: Earthscan.

Beach, L.R. and T.R. Mitchell (1990), 'Image theory; a behavioral theory of decision making in organizations', *Research in Organizational Behavior*. **12**, 1–41.

Beck, U. (1995), *Ecological Politics in an Age of Risk*, Cambridge: Polity Press.

Beck, L. and Ajzen, I. (1991), 'Predicting dishonest actions using the theory of planned behavior', *Journal of Research in Personality*, 25, 285–301.

Beladi, H., C.C. Chao and R. Frasca (1999), 'Foreign investment and environmental regulations in LDCs', *Resource and Energy Economics*, **21** (2), 191–99.

Benis, W.G., and Nanus, B. (1985), *Leaders: Strategies for Taking Change*. New York: Harper and Row.

Bernard, C.I. (1938), *The Functions of the Executive*, Cambridge, MA: Harvard University Press.

Berne, E. (1964), *Games People Play*, New York: Grove.

Bhatnagar, S. and M. Cohen (1997), '*The Impact of Environmental Regulation on Innovation*', working paper, Owen Graduate School of Management, Vanderbilt.

Bhoovaraghavan, S., A. Vasudevan and R. Chandran (1996), 'Resolving the process vs. production innovation dilemma: A consumer choice theoretic approach', *Management Science*, **42** (2), 232–46.

Binswanger, H., M. Faber and R. Manstetten (1990), 'The dilemma of modern man and nature: an exploration of the Faustian imperative', *Ecological Economics*, **2**, 197–223.

Boehmer-Christiansen, S. (1995), 'Reflections an the politics linking science, environment and innovation', *Innovations*, **8** (3), 275–87.

Böhm E. and R. Walz (1996), 'Life cycle analysis: a methodology to analyse ecological consequences within a technology assessment study', *International Journal of Technology Assessment, Special Issue in Technology Assessment*, **11** (5–6), 554–65.

Bojórquez, L. A. and E. Ongay (1992), 'International lending and resource development in Mexico: can environmental quality be assured?', *Ecological Economics*, **5**, 197–211.

Boldero, J. (1995), 'The prediction of household recycling of newspapers: The role of attitudes, intentions, and situational factors', *Journal of Applied Social Psychology,* **25** (5), 440–62.

Borg, I. (1994), 'Evolving notions of facet theory', in I. Borg and P. Mohler (eds), *Trends and Perspectives in Empirical Social Research,* New York: Walter de Gruyter, pp. 178–200.

Borg, I. and S. Shye (1995), *Facet Theory: Form and Content,* Thousand Oaks, CA: Sage Publications.

Bostrom, A., C.J. Atman, B. Fischhoff and M.G. Morgan (1994), 'Evaluating risk communications and correcting mental models of hazardous process: Part II', *Risk Analysis*, **14** (5), 789–98.

Boyd, B., G.G. Dess and A. Rasheed (1993), 'Divergence between archival and perceptual measures of the environment: causes and consequenses', *Academy Management Review*, **18**, 204–26.

Boyd, R. and Uri, N.D. (1991), 'The cost of improving the quality of the environment', *Environment and Planning*, **23**, 1163–82.

Brann, P. and Foddy, M. (1988), 'Trust and the consumption of a deteriorating common resource', *Journal of Conflict Resolution*, **31** (4), 615–30.

Braver, S.L. and L.A. Wilson II (1986), 'Choices in social dilemmas: effects of communication within subgroups', *Journal of Conflict Resolution*, **30** (1), 51–62.

Brawn, E. (1995), *Futile progress: Technology's Empty Promise*, London: Earthscan.

Brealey, R.A. and S.C. Myers (1991), *Principles of Corporate Finance*, 4th edn, New York: McGraw Hill.

British Psychological Society Steering Committee on Test Standards (1992), *Psychological Testing: A Guide,* Leicester: British Psychological Society.

Brown, J. (1985), 'An introduction to the uses of the facet theory', in D. Canter (ed.) *Facet Theory*, New York: Springer-Verlag, pp. 16–57.

Bryman, A. (1992), *Research Methods and Organization Studies*, London: Routledge.

Buckley J.P. and M. Casson (1988), 'A theory of cooperation in international business', in F.J. Contractor and P. Lorange (eds), *Cooperative Strategies in International Business*, Lexington, MA: Lexington Books, pp. 31–53.

Burgelman, R. (1983), 'A model of the interaction of strategic behaviour, corporate context, and the context of strategy', *Academy Management Review,* **8**, 61–70.

Burgelman, R. (1991), 'Inter-organizational ecology of strategy making and organizational adaptation: Theory and field research', *Organization Science*, **2**, 239–62.

Canavos, G. C. (1990), *Probabilidad y Estadística: Aplicaciones y Métodos*, Mexico: McGraw Hill.

Canter, D. (1985), 'How to be a facet researcher', in D. Canter (ed.), *Facet Theory*, New York: Springer-Verlag, pp. 265–75.

Canter, L.W., D.I. Nelson and J.W. Everett (1993), 'Public perception of water quality risks; influencing factors and enhancement opportunities', *Journal of Environmental Systems*, **22** (2), 163–87.

Carlsmith, J.M., P.C. Ellsworth, and E. Aroson (1976), *Methods of Research in Social Psychology*, Reading, MA: Addison Wesley.

Carrillo, J. (ed.) (1986), *Reestructuración Industrial: Maquiladoras en la Frontera de México–Estados Unidos*, Mexico City: El Colef–Conaculta.

Casagrande, D.J. and J.H. Morgan (1995), *Support to the Border Environmental Cooperation Commission: Capabilities and Concepts*, Tijuana, B.C.: MITRE.

Casson, M. (1990), *Multinational Corporations*, Harvard Press, Elgar Reference Collection.

CDMA, (1990), *Nuestra Propia Agenda*, New York: Comisión de Desarrollo y Medio Ambiente de America Latina y el Caribe, IBD/UNDP.

CEC (1996a), *Status of Pollution Prevention in North America*, Quebec: Commission for Environmental Cooperation.

CEC (1996b), *Assessing Latin American Markets for North American Environmental Goods and Services*, Report prepared for CEC by: ESSA Technologies Ltd., The GLOBE Foundation of Canada, SIAC de Mexico S.A. de C.V., and CG/LA Infrastructure, Quebec: Commission for Environmental Cooperation.

CEC (1999), *North American Agenda for Action 1999–2001*, Quebec: Commission for Environmental Cooperation.

Chapman, C. and S. Ward (1997), *Project Risk Management: Processes, Techniques and Insights*, Chichester: John Wiley and Sons.

Chattery, D. (1995), 'Achieving leadership in environmental R&D', *R&D Management*, March–April, 37–42.

Cheung, S.F., D.K.S. Chan, and Z.S.Y. Wong (1999), 'Re-examining the theory of planned behavior in understanding wastepaper recycling', *Environment and Behavior*, **31** (5), 587–612.

Chiang, A.C. (1984), *Fundamental Methods of Mathematical Economics*, New York: McGraw-Hill.

Chua, S. (1999), 'Economic growth, liberalization, and the environment: A review of the economic evidence', *Annual Review of Energy and the Environment*, 24, 391–430.

Clark, J. and K. Guy (1998), 'Innovation and competitiveness: A review', *Technology Analysis and Strategic Management*, **10** (3), 363–95.

Clarke, A.F. and N.J. Roome (1995), 'Managing for environmentally sensitive technology: Networks for collaboration and learning', *Technology Analysis and Strategic Management*, **7** (2), 191–215.

Clayton, A., G. Spinardi and R. Williams (1999a), *Policies for Cleaner Technology*, London: Earthscan.

Clayton, A., G. Spinardi and R. Williams (1999b), 'What shapes the implementation of cleaner technology?', in Clayton A., G. Spinardi and R. Williams (eds), *Policies for Cleaner Technology*, London: Earthscan, pp. 218–65.

Coase, R. (1960), 'The problem of social cost', *Journal of Law and Economics,* **3**, 44.

Collins, D.J. (1994), 'Research note: how valuable are organizational capabilities?', *Strategic Management Journal*, **15**, 143–52.

Collins, P.D., J. Hage and F.M. Hull (1988), 'Organizational and technological predictors of change in automacity', *Academy of Management Journal*, September, 512–36.

Colmer, G., M. Dunkley, K. Gray, P. Pugh and A. Williamson (1999), Estimating the cost of new technology products', *International Journal of Technology Management*, **17** (7–8), 840–46.

Conner, M., R. Warren, S. Close, and P. Sparks (1999), 'Alcohol consumption and the theory of planned behavior: An examination of the cognitive mediation of past behavior', *Journal of Applied Psychology*, **29** (8), 1676–704.

Conrad, J. (1995), 'Developments and results of research on environmental management in Germany', *Business Strategy and the Environment*, **4** (2), 51–61.

Contractor, F.J. and P. Lorange (eds) (1988a), *Cooperative strategies in international business,* Lexington, MA: Lexington Books.

Contractor, F.J. and P. Lorange (1988b), 'Why should firms cooperate? The strategy and economics basis for cooperative ventures', in F.J. Contractor and P. Lorange (eds) *Cooperative Strategies in International Business*, Lexington, MA: Lexington Books, pp. 4–30.

Coombs, R. (1988), 'Technological opportunities and industrial organization', in G. Dosi, C. Freeman, R. Nelson, G. Silverberg and L. Soete (eds), *Technical Change and Economic Theory*, London: Pinter Publishers.

Coombs, R., A. Richards, P.P. Saviotti and V. Walsh (1996), *Technological Collaboration: The Dynamics of Cooperation in Industrial Innovation*, Cheltenham, UK and Brookfield, US: Edward Elgar.

Costanza, R. (1987), 'Social traps and environmental policy: why do problems persist when there are technical solutions available?' *Bioscience*, **37** (6), 407–12.

Costanza, R., (ed.) (1991), *Ecological Economics: The Science and Management of Sustainability,* New York: Columbia University Press.

Cote, R. and J. Hall, (forthcoming), 'Industrial Ecology: An Integrated Approach to Environmental Management', *Journal of Cleaner Production*.

Covello, V.T. (1983), 'The perception of technological risks: a literature review', *Technological Forecasting and Social Change*, **23**, 285–97.

Coxon, A.P.M. and P.M. Davis, (1982), *User Guide to Multidimensional Scaling*, London: Heinemann.

Cramer, J. and J. Schot (1993), 'Environmental comakership among firms as a cornerstone in the striving for sustainable development', in K. Fisher and J. Schot (eds), *Environmental Strategies for Industry: International Perspectives on Research Needs and Policy Implications*, Washington, DC: Island Press.

Cronbach, T. (1994), *Essential of Psychological Testing*, London: Hamper and Row.

Cross, J.G. and M.J. Guyer (1980), *Social Traps*, Ann Arbor: University of Michigan Press.

CSIS (1997), *The Environmental Protection System in Transition*, Washington, D.C.: Center for Strategic and International Studies, CSIS Press.

Curran, M.A. (1996), *Environmental Life Cycle Assessment*, New York: McGraw-Hill

Dake, K. (1992), 'Myths of nature: culture and the social construction of risk', *Journal of Social Issues*, **48** (4), 21–37.

Dale, A. and D. Loveridge (1996), 'Technology assessment – where is it going?' *International Journal of Technology Assessment, Special Issue in Technology Assessment*, **11** (5–6), 715–23.

Daly, H. (1990), 'Toward some operational principles of sustainable development', *Ecological Economics*, **2**, 1–6.

Daly, H.E. (1995), 'On Nicholas Georgescu-Roegen's contributions to Economics: an obituary essay', *Ecological Economics*, **13**, 149–54.

Damanpour, F. (1991), 'Organizational innovation: a meta-analysis of the effects of determinants and moderators', *Academy of Management Journal*, **34**, 555–90.

Damanpour, F. (1996), 'Organizational complexity and innovation: Developing and testing multiple contingency models', *Journal of Management Science*, **42** (5), 693–716.

De la O, M.E. and C. Quintero (2000) 'Las industrias maquiladoras en México: Orígenes comunes, futuros distintos', paper presented at the international conference on free trade and the future of the Maquila Industry: Global production and local workers. El Colegio de la Frontera Norte – Comisión Económica para América Latina y el Caribe Naciones Unidas, Tijuana, Mexico.

den Hond, F. (1996), In Search of a Useful Theory of Environmental Strategy: A Case Study on the Recycling of End-of-life Vehicles from the Capabilities Perspective, Amsterdam: M.L. Brookman.

den Hond, F. and P. Groenewegen (1993), 'Solving the automobile shredder waste problem', in K. Fisher and J. Schot (eds), *Environmental Strategies for industry: International Perspectives on Research Needs and Policy Implications*, Washington, DC: Island Press, pp. 343–68.

den Hond, F. and P. Groenewgen (1996), 'Environmental technology foresight: new horizons for technology management', *Technology Analysis and Strategic Management*, **8** (1), 33–46.

Deuthsch, M. (1994), 'Constructive conflict resolution: principles, training, and research', *Journal of Social Issues,* **50** (1), 13–32.

Dewar, R.D., and Dutton, J. (1986), 'The adoption of radical and incremental innovations', *Management Science*, 32 (11), 1422–33.

Dillon, P. and Baram, M.S. (1993), 'Forces shaping the development of product stewardship in the private sector', in K. Fisher and J. Schot (eds), *Environmental Strategies for Industry: International Perspectives on Research Needs and Policy Implications*, Washington, DC: Island Press, pp. 329–42.

Dodgson, M. (1995), 'Organizational learning: A review of some literatures', *Organization Studies*, **14** (3), 375–94.

DOFM (1971), *Ley federal para prevenir y controlar la contaminación ambiental*, Diario Oficial de la Federación Mexicana, 23 March 1971.

DOFM (1983), *Decreto para el fomento de la industria maquiladora de exportación*, Diario Oficial de la Federación Mexicana, August 1983.

DOFM (1993), *Tratado de Libre Comercio de America del Norte: Acuerdos Paralelos*. Diario Oficial de la Federación Mexicana, 8 December 1993.

Dosi, G. (1982), 'Technological paradigms and technological trajectories', *Research Policy*, **11**, 147–62.

Dosi, G. (1988), 'The nature of the innovative process', in G., Dosi C. Freeman, R. Nelson, G. Silverberg, and L. Soete (eds), *Technical Change and Economic Theory*, London: Pinter Publishers, pp. 221–38.

Dosi, G., C. Freeman, R. Nelson, G. Silverberg, and L. Soete (eds) (1988), *Technical Change and Economic Theory*, London: Pinter Publishers.

Dougals, M. (1990), 'Risk as a forensic resource', *Daedalus,* **119** (4), 1–16.

Dougals, M. (1992), *Risk and Blame,* London: Routledge.

Douglas, M. and A. Wildavsky (1982), *Risk and Culture*, Berkeley: University of California Press.

Duffy, N., B. Ryan, L. Baas, F. Boons, O.L. Hansen and G. Spinardi (1999a), 'Pharmaceutical sector', in A. Clayton, G. Spinardi and R. Williams (eds), *Policies for Cleaner Technology*, London: Earthscan, pp. 107–29.

Duffy, N. B. Ryan, L. Baas, F. Boons, I. Thompson and R. Williams (1999b), 'Fine chemicals', in A. Clayton, G. Spinardi and R. Williams (eds), *Policies for Cleaner Technology*, London: Earthscan, pp. 92–106.

Duncan, C. (1998), '*Fundamental Statistics for Social Research*, London: Routledge.

Echeverri-Gent, J. (1992), 'Between autonomy and capture: Embedding government agencies in their societal environment', *Policy Studies Journal*, **20** (3), 342–64.

Edmundson, E.W., W.R. Koch and S. Silverman (1993), 'A facet analysis to content and construct validity', *Educational and Psychological Measurement*, **53**, 351–68.

Edney, J.J. and C. Harper (1978), 'The effects of information in a resource management problem: a social analogue trap', *Human Ecology*, **6**, 386–95.

Edwards, W. (1954), 'The theory of decision making', *Psychological Bulletin*, **51**, 380–417.

Eisenhardt, K.M. and M.J. Zbraracki (1992), 'Strategic decision making', *Strategic Management Journal*, **13**, 17–37.

ELI (1998), *Barriers to Environmental Technology Innovation and Use*, Washington, DC: Environmental Law Institute–EPA.

EPA (1995), *Compendium of EPA Binational and Domestic US/Mexico Activities*, Washington, DC: United States Environmental Protection Agency, EPA 160–B–95–001.

EPA (1996), *US–Mexico Border XXI Program: Framework Document*, Washington, DC: United States Environmental Protection Agency, EPA160–R96–003.

EPA (1998), *Stakeholder Attitudes on the Barriers to Innovative Environmental Technologies*, Washington, DC: United States Environmental Protection Agency, EPA 236–R–98–001.

Everett, M., J.E. Mark and O.R. Toward (1993), 'Greening in the executive suite', in K. Fisher and J. Schot (eds), *Environmental Strategies for Industry: International Perspectives on Research Needs and Policy Implications*, Washington, DC: Island Press, pp. 68–78.

Fagerberg, J. (1996), 'Technology and competitiveness', *Oxford Review of Economic Policy*, **12** (3), 39–51.

Fassnacht, G. (1982), *Theory and Practice of Observing Behavior*, London: Academic Press.

Ferrer, N. (1986), 'El abuso de la gestion ambiental', *Ecología Política*, **6** (3), 23–32.

Fiol, C.M. and M. Lyles (1985), 'Organizational learning', *Academy of Management Review*, **10**, 803–13.

Fischer, G.W., M.G. Morgan, B. Fischhoff, I. Nair, and L.V. Lave (1991), 'What risks are people concerned about?' *Risk Analysis*, **11** (2), 303–14.

Fischhoff, B. (1994), 'Risk perception and communication unplugged: twenty years of process', *Risk Analysis*, **15** (2), 137–45.

Fischhoff, B., P. Slovic, S. Lichtenstien, S. Read and B. Combs (1978), 'How safe is safe enough? A psychometric study of attitudes towards technological risks and benefits', *Policy Sciences*, **9**, 127–52.

Fischhoff, B., S.R. Watson and C. Hope (1984), 'Defining risk', *Policy Sciences,* **17**, 123–39.

Fischhoff, B., A. Bostrom and M.J. Quadrel (1993), 'Risk perception and risk communication', *Annual Review of Public Health*, **14**, 183–203.

Fishbein, M. and I. Ajzen (1975), *Belief, Attitude, Intention, and Behavior: An Introduction to Theory and Research,* Reading, MA: Addison-Wesley.

Fishbein, M. and I. Ajzen (1980), 'Predicting and understanding consumer behavior: Attitude behavior correspondence', in I. Ajzen and M. Fishbein (eds), *Understanding Attitudes and Predicting Social Behavior,* Englewood Cliffs, NJ: Prentice Hall, pp. 149–72.

Fishbein, M., I. Ajzen and R. Hinkle (1980a), 'Predicting and understanding voting in American elections: Effects of external variables', in I. Ajzen and M. Fishbein (eds), *Understanding Attitudes and Predicting Social Behavior,* Englewood Cliffs, NJ: Prentice Hall, pp. 174–216.

Fishbein, M., I. Ajzen and J. McArdle (1980b), 'Changing the behavior of alcoholics: Effects of persuasive communication', in I. Ajzen and M. Fishbein (eds), *Understanding Attitudes and Predicting Social Behavior,* Englewood Cliffs, NJ: Prentice Hall, pp. 218–42.

Fishbein, M., J.J. Jaccard, A.R. Davison, I. Ajzen and B. Loken (1980c), 'Predicting and understanding family planning behaviors: Beliefs, attitudes and intentions', in I. Ajzen and M. Fishbein (eds), *Understanding Attitudes and Predicting Social Behavior,* Englewood Cliffs, NJ: Prentice Hall, pp. 130–47.

Fisher, K. and J. Schot (eds) (1993), *Environmental Strategies for industry: International Perspectives on Research Needs and Policy Implications,* Washington, DC: Island Press.

Fisher, R.J. (1994), 'Generic principles for resolving inter-group conflict', *Journal of Social Issues,* **50** (1), 47–66.

Fleishman, J.A. (1988), 'The effects of decision framing and others' behavior on cooperation in a social dilemma', *Journal of Conflict Resolution,* **32** (1), 162–80.

Florida, R. (1996), 'Lean and green: the move to environmentally conscious manufacturing', *California Management Review,* **39** (1), 80–105.

Foa, U. (1965), 'New developments in facet design and analysis', *Psychological Review,* 72, 262–74.

Folmer, H., H.L. Gabel and J.B. Opschoor (eds) (1995), *Principles of Environmental Economics: A Guide for Students and Decision Makers,* Aldershot: Edward Elgar.

Franco, R.B. (1991), 'Disposición de residuos industriales en la frontera: posibles impactos del Tratado de Libro Comercio', Paper presented for the Plan Integral Ambiental Fronterizo México–Estados Unidos in Cd. Juárez, September 19, 1991.

Frank, H., P. Drenth, P. Koopman and V. Rus (1988), *Decisions in Organizations,* London: Sage Publications.

Fransman, M. (1994), 'Information, knowledge, vision and theories of the firm', *Industrial and Corporate Change,* 3 (3), 713–57.

Freeman III, A. M. (1982), *Air and Water Pollution Control: A Benefit–Cost Assessment,* New York: Wiley and Sons.

Freeman, C. (1971), 'Technology assessment and its social context', *Studium Generale*, **24**, 1038–50.

Freeman, C. (1996), 'The greening of technology and models of innovation', *Technological Forecasting and Social Change*, **53**, 27–39.

Freeman, C. and C. Perez (1988), 'Structural crisis of adjustment, business cycles and investment behavior', in G. Dosi, C. Freeman, R. Nelson, G. Silverberg, and L. Soete (eds), *Technical Change and Economic Theory*, London: Pinter Publishers.

Fuchs, D.A. and D.A. Mazmanian (1998), 'The greening of industry: needs of the field', *Business Strategy and the Environment*, **7**, 193–203.

Fullerton, D. and W. Wu (1998), 'Policies for green design', *Journal of Environmental Economics and Management*, **36**, 131–48.

Gabaldón, A.J. (1994), 'Desarrollo sostenible y reforma del Estado', in Colegio de Mexico, *Primer Foro del Ajusco: Desarrollo sostenible y reforma del Estado en America Latina y el Caribe*. Mexico City: El Colegio de Mexico, pp. 13–64.

Gallop, F. and M.J. Roberts (1983), 'Environmental regulations and productivity growth: the case of fossil-fueled electric power generation', *Journal of Political Economy*, **91**, 654–74.

Ganster, P. and R.A. Sanchez (1998), *Sustainable Development in the San Diego–Tijuana Region*, San Diego, CA.: Center for US–Mexican Studies, UCSD.

Garcia-Guadilla, M.P. and J. Blauert (eds) (1994), *Retos Para el Desarrollo y la Democracia: Movimientos Ambientales en America Latina y Europa*, Caracas: Nueva Sociedad.

Garrod, B. and P. Chadwick (1996), 'Environmental management and business strategy: toward a new strategic paradigm', *Futures*, **28** (1), 37–49.

Gassert, T.H. (1985), *Health Hazards in Electronics: a Handbook*, Hong Kong: Asia Monitor Resource Center.

Geffen, C. and S. Rothenberg (1997), 'Sustainable development across firm boundaries', Paper presented at the GIN Conference, Santa Barbara, CA.

Georgescu-Roegen, N. (1971), *The Entropy Law and the Economic Process*, Cambridge, MA: Harvard University Press.

Georgescu-Roegen, N. (1976), *Energy and Economic Myths: Institutional and Analytical Economic Essays*, New York: Pergamon Press Inc.

Georghiou, L.J., S. Metcalfe, M. Gibbons, T. Ray and J. Evans (1986), *Post-innovation Performance: Technological Development and Competition*, London: Macmillan.

Gereffi, G. and D.I. Wyman (eds) (1992), 'Paths of Industrialization: An Overview', *Manufacturing Miracles: Paths of Industrialization in Latin America and East Asia*, Princeton, NJ: Princeton University Press.

Ghiselli, E.E., J.P. Campbell, and S. Zedeck (1981), *Measurement Theory for Behavioral Sciences*, San Francisco: W.H. Freeman.

Gladwin, T.N. (1993), 'The meaning of greening: A plea for organizational theory', in K. Fisher and J. Schot (eds) (1993), *Environmental Strategies for industry: International Perspectives on Research Needs and Policy Implications*, Washington, DC: Island Press, pp. 37–61.

Godinez, J.A. and A.G. Mercado (1996), 'Fuentes de eficiencia de la y competitividad en la industria maquiladora de exportacion en México', *Frontera Norte,* Tijuana: El Colegio de la Frontera Norte.

Gollwitzer, P.M. and J.A. Bargh (eds) (1996), *The Psychology of Action: Linking Cognition and Motivation to Behavior*, New York: Guilford Press.

Gonzalez-Arechiga, B. and R. Barajas (1988), *Las maquiladoras: ajuste estructural y desarrollo regional*, Working Paper, México City: Fundación Friedrich Ebert.

Gonzales-Arechiga, B. and R. Barajas (eds) (1989), *Las maquiladoras: ajuste estructural y desarrollo regional*, Tijuana, BC: El Colegio de la Frontera Norte and Fundacion Friedrich Ebert.

Gonzalez-Arechiga, B., R. Barajas, N. Fuentes and J.C. Ramirez (1988), *La industria maquiladora mexicana en los sectores electrónico y de autopartes*, Working Paper, México: Fundación Friedrich Ebert.

Gonzalez-Arechiga, B. and J.C. Ramirez (eds) (1990), *Subcontratación y Empresas Trasnacionales. Apertura y Restructuración en la Maquiladora*, Mexico City: El COLEF–Fundación Friedrich Ebert.

Gopalakrishnan, S. and F. Damanpour (1994), 'Patterns of generation and adoption of innovation in organizations: contingency models of innovation attributes', *Journal of Engineering and Technology Management*, **11** (2), 95–116.

Gopalakrishnan, S. and F. Damanpour (1997), 'A review of innovation research in economics, sociology and technology management', *Omega International Journal of Management Science*, **25** (1), 15–28.

Gouldson, A. and J. Murphy (1998) *Regulatory Realities: The Implementation of Industrial Environmental Regulation,* London: Earthscan.

Graedel, T.E. (1997), 'Designing the ideal green product: LCA/SCLA in reverse', *International Journal of Life Cycle Assessment*, **2** (1), 25–31.

Granderson, G. (1999), 'The impact of regulation on technical change', *Southern Economic Journal*, **65** (4), 807–22.

Grant, R. (1996), 'Prospering in dynamically-competitive environments: Organizational capability as knowledge integration', *Organization Science*, **7** (4), 357–87.

Grant, R.M. (1997), 'The knowledge-based view of the firm: implications for management practice', *Long Range Planning,* **30** (3), 450–54.

Gray, W.B. and R.J. Shadbegian (1998), 'Environmental regulation, investment timing, and technological choice', *Journal of Industrial Economics*, **46** (2), 235–56.

Griffin, R.J., S. Dunwoody and K. Neuwirth (1999), 'Proposed model of the relationship of risk information seeking and processing to the development of preventive behaviors', *Environmental Research*, **80** (2), S230–45.

Grin, J. and H. van de Graaf (1996), 'Technology assessment as learning', *Science Technology and Human Values*, **21** (1), 72–99.

Gustavsson, P., P. Hansson and L. Lundberg (1999), 'Technology, resource endowments and international competitiveness', *European Economic Review*, **43**, (8), 1501–30.

Guttman, L. (1954), 'A new approach to factor analysis: the radex', in P.F. Lazarsfeld (ed.) *Mathematical Thinking in the Social Sciences*, Glencoe, IL: Free Press.

Guttman, L. (1959), 'A structural theory for inter-group beliefs and action', *American Sociological Review*, **24**, 318–28.

Guttman, L. (1971), 'Social problem indicators', *Annals of the American Academy of Political and Social Science*, **393**, 40–46.

Guttman, R. and C.W. Greenbaum (1998), 'Facet theory: its development and current status', *European Psychologist*, **3** (1), 13–36.

Hafkamp, W.A. (1994), *Economic-Environmental Modeling in a National–Regional System*, Amsterdam: Elsevier Science Publishers.

Hahn, R.W. (1989), *A Primer on Environmental Policy Design*, New York: Harwood Academic Publishers.

Hahn, R.W. and R.N. Stavins (1991), 'Incentive-based environmental regulation: A new era from an old idea?' *Ecology Law Quarterly*, **18** (1), 1–42.

Hall, J.K. (1999), 'Reducing environmental impacts through the procurement chain, unpublished DPhil. Thesis: University of Sussex.

Hall, S. and N. Roome (1995), 'Strategic choices and sustainable strategies', in P.K. Gronewegen Fischer, E.G. Jenkis and J. Schot (eds) *The greening of industry: Resource guide and bibliography*, Washington, DC: Island Press.

Hamel, G. and C.K. Prahalad (1994), *Competing for the Future*, Cambridge. MA: Harvard Business School Press.

Harland, P., H. Staats and H.A.M. Wilke (1999), 'Explaining proenvironmental intention and behavior by personal norms and the theory of planned behavior', *Journal of Applied Social Psychology*, **29** (12), 2505–28.

Harlow, R.L. (1974), 'Conflict reduction environmental policy', *Journal of Conflict Resolution*, **18** (3), 536–52.

Harman, H.H. (1967), *Modern Factor Analysis*, Chicago: University of Chicago Press.

Harret, G. (1968), 'The tragedy of the commons', *Science*, **162**, 1243–48.

Harrison, D.A., P.P. Mykytyn and C.K. Riemenschneider (1997), 'Executive decisions about adoption of information technology in small business: theory and empirical tests', *Journal Systems Research*, **8** (2), 171–95.

Hart, S. and G. Ahuja (1996), 'Does it pay to be green? An empirical examination of the relationship between emission reduction and firm performance', *Business Strategy and the Environment*, **5**, 30–37.

Hartenian, L.S., P. Bobko and P.K. Berger (1993), 'An empirical validation of bipolar risk perception', *Journal of Applied Social Psychology*, **23** (5), 335–51.

Hartman, C., and E. Stafford (1997), *'Green alliances: forging corporate – environmental group collaborative relationships'*, Paper presented at the GIN Conference, Santa Barbara, CA.

Hass, J.L. (1996), 'Environmental "green" management typologies: an evaluation, operationalization and empirical development', *Business Strategy and the Environment*, **5**, 59–68.

Hazilla, M. and R.J. Kopp (1990), 'Social cost of environmental quality regulations: a general equilibrium analysis', *Journal of Political Economy*, **98** (4), 853–73.

Hedberg, B.L.T. (1981), 'How organizations learn and unlearn', in P.C. Nystrom and W.H. Starbuch (eds), *Handbook of Organizational Design*, London: Oxford University Press, pp. 8–27.

Heider, F. (1944), 'Social perception and phenomenal causality', *Psychological Review*, **51**, 358–74.

Hence, B.J., C. Chess and P.M. Sandman (1988), *Improving Dialogue With Communities: A Risk Communication Manual for Government*, Trenton, NJ: Department of Environmental Protection.

Henriksen, A.D.P. (1995), 'A technology assessment primer for management of technology', *International Journal of Technology Management*, **13** (5–6), 615–38.

Henriquez, I. and P. Sadorsky (1996), 'The determinants of an environmentally responsive firm', *Journal of Environmental Economics and Management*, **30** (3), 381–95.

Heyes, A.G. and C.L. Heyes (1999), 'Corporate lobbying, regulatory conduct and the Porter hypothesis', *Environmental and Resources Economics*, **13** (2), 209–18.

Hickson, D.J., R.J. Butler, D. Cray, G.R. Mallory and D.C. Wilson (1986), *Top Decision: Strategic Decision-making in Organization,* Oxford: Basil Blackwell.

Highhouse, S. and P. Yüce (1996), 'Perspectives, perceptions, and risk-taking behavior, *Organizational Behavior and Human Decision Process*, **65** (2), 159–67.

Hippel, E. and M.J. Tyre (1995), 'How learning by doing is done: problem identification in novel process equipment', *Research Policy*, **24**, 1–12.

Hitchens, D.M.W.N., J.E. Birnie, A. McGowan, U. Triebswetter and A. Cottica (1998), *Environment and Planning A*, **30**, (9), 1585–602.

Holtgrave, D.R. and E.U. Weber (1993), 'Dimensions of risk perception for financial and health risks', *Risk Analysis*, **13** (5), 553–58.

Howes, R., J. Skea, and B. Whelan (1996), *Clean and Competitive? Motivating Environmental Performance in Industry*, London: Earthscan.

Huber, G.P. (1991), 'Organizational learning: the contributing process and the literatures', *Organization Science*, 2, 88–115.

Huber, G.P. (1996), 'Organizational learning: a guide for executives in technology-critical organisations', *International Journal of Technology Management*, **11** (7/8), 821–32.

Hukkinen, J. (1995), 'Corporatism as an impediment to ecological sustenance: the case of Finnish waste management', *Ecological Economics*, **15**, 59–75.

Hull, J.C. (1980), *The Evaluation of Risk in Business Investment,* Oxford: Pergamon Press.

Hymer, S. (1972), *Empresas Multinacionales*, Buenos Aires: Editorial Periferia.

Iarrera, M. and G. Vickery (1997), 'Clean technologies', *OECD Observer*, Paris: OECD, June, pp. 24–7.

Icasa, L.P.A. (1993), 'Marco teorico de la industria maquiladora de exportación', *Comercio Exterior*, **43** (5), 415–29.

INEGI (1995), *Avance de información económica: industria maquiladora de exportación (1985–1995)*', Colección Avances, Aguascalientes: Instituto Nacional de Estadistica Geografia e Informatica (INEGI).

INEGI (1995), *Estadísticas de Medio Ambiente*, Mexico City: Instituto Nacional de Estadistica Geografia e Informatica (INEGI).

INEGI (1998), *Estadísticas de la industria maquiladora de exportación*, Aguascalientes: INEGI, Septiembre 1998.

INEGI (1999) *Estadistica de la industria maquiladora de exportacion*, Aguascalientes: INEGI. Octubre 1999.

IOD (Institute of Directors) (1995), 'Attitudes towards environmental management', *Business Strategy and the Environment*, **4**, 40–41.

Irwin, A. and P.D. Hooper (1992), 'Clean technology, successful innovation and the greening of industry', *Business Strategy and the Environment*, **1** (2), 1–12.

Jaffe, A.B. and K. Palmer (1997), 'Environmental regulation and innovation: A panel data study', *Review of Economics and Statistics*, **79** (4), 610–19.

Jaffe, A.B., S.R. Peterson, P.R. Portney and R. Stavins (1995), 'Environmental regulation and the competitiveness of U.S. manufacturing: What the does the evidence tell us?', *Journal of Economic Literature*, **33** (1), 132–63.

Janis, I.L. (1972), *Victims of Groupthink*, Boston: Houghton Mifflin.

Jonas, K. and J. Doll (1996), 'A critical evaluation of the theory of reasoned action and the theory of planned behavior', Zeitschrift für Sozialpsychologie, **27**(1), 18-31.

Jordan, J.E. (1978), 'Facet theory and the study of behavior', in S. Shye (ed.) *Theory Construction and Data Analysis in the Behavioral Sciences,* San Francisco: Josey-Bass, pp. 26–34.

Jorgenson D.W. and P.J. Wilcoxen (1990), 'Environmental regulation and U.S. economic growth', *Rand Journal of Economics*, **21**, 314–40.

Jungermann, H. and S. Femers (1995), 'Multiple perspectives on risk measures and comparisons', European *Review of Applied Psychology*, **45** (1), 43–8.

Kahneman, D. and A. Tversky (1979), 'Prospect theory: an analysis of decision under risk', *Academy of Management Review,* **11**, 145–63.

Kemp, R. (1993), 'An economic analysis of cleaner technology: Theory and evidence', in K. Fisher and J. Schot (eds), *Environmental Strategies for Industry: International Perspectives on Research Needs and Policy Implications*, Washington, DC: Island Press, pp. 79–113.

Kemp, R. (1994), 'Technology and the transition to environmental sustainability: The problem of technological regime shifts', *Futures*, **26** (10), 1023–46.

Kemp, R. (1996a), *Environmental Policy and Technical Change: A Comparison of the Technological Impact of Policy Instruments*, Maastricht: Datawyse/Universitaire Press Maastricht.

Kemp, R. (1996b), *Technological Impact of Environmental Policies: A Review of Past Experiences and Policy Guide for the Future*, Paper for Conference "Environment: the new business challenge", Turin, 2 December 1995, MERIT/University of Limburg.

Kemp, R. (1998), 'Environmental regualtion and innovation: Key issues and questions for research', position paper for IPTS-DG III project 'Innovation and Regulation', MERIT/Maastricht University.

Kemp, R. and Soete, L. (1992), 'The greening of technological progress: an evolutionary perspective', *Futures*, **24** (5), 437–57.

Kerndrup, S., L. Baas, N. Duffy, O.E. Hansen and B. Ryan (1999a), 'Sugar sector', in Clayton A., G. Spinardi and R. Williams (eds), *Policies for Cleaner Technology*, London: Earthscan, pp. 161–85.

Kerndrup, S., L. Baas, U. Nielsen and J.S. Haas (1999b), 'Electroplating', in Clayton A., G. Spinardi and R. Williams (eds), *Policies for Cleaner Technology*, London: Earthscan, pp. 204–17.

Keoleian, G.A. (1993), 'The application of life cycle assessment to design', *Journal of Cleaner Production*, **1** (3–4), 143–9.

King, A. (1997), 'Cooperative Self-regulation in the Chemical Industry: Impact and Implications, paper presented at the GIN Conference, Santa Barbara, CA.

Kirkwood, C.W. (1985), Risk assessment to support management of a hazardous spill clean up', *IEEE Transaction on Systems Man and Cybernetics*, **15** (5), 601–7.

Kirschman, J.C. (1984), 'Building an adequate risk assessment data-base', *Food Technology*, **38** (10), 103–6.

Klemmensen, B., L. Ball, N. Duffy, B. Hansen, B. Ryan, G. Spinardi and R. Williams (1999), 'Refinery sector', in A. Clayton, G. Spinardi and R. Williams (eds), *Policies for Cleaner Technology*, London: Earthscan, pp.

52–72.

Kline, P. (1986), *A Handbook of Test Construction: Introduction to Psychometric Design,* London: Matheu and Co.

Kline, P. (1998), *The New Psychometrics: Science, Psychology and Measurement,* London: Routledge.

Kline, S.J. and N. Rosenberg (1986), 'An overview of innovation', in R. Landau and N. Rosenberg (eds), *The Positive Sum Strategy,* Washington, DC: National Academy Press.

Koido, A. (2000) 'Territorialized nexus of transnational production chain and its disjunctive with local structure: Development of industrial agglomeration of CTV in US–Mexican border and its limits', paper presented at the international conference on free trade and the future of the Maquila Industry: Global production and local workers. El Colegio de la Frontera Norte – Comisión Económica para América Latina y el Caribe Naciones Unidas, Tijuana, Mexico.

Konar, S. and M.A. Cohen, (1997), 'Why do firms pollute (and reduce) toxic emissions?', Working paper, Owen GSM, Vanderbilt University.

Kondo, T. (1990), 'Some notes on rational behavior, normative behavior, moral behavior and cooperation', *Journal of Conflict Resolution,* **34** (3), 495–530.

Kopinak K., and S.G. García (2000) 'Industrial hazardous waste in Tijuana and its proximity to local populations'. Paper presented at the international conference on free trade and the future of the Maquila Industry: Global production and local workers. El Colegio de la Frontera Norte – Comisión Económica para América Latina y el Caribe Naciones Unidas, Tijuana, Mexico.

Korzybsky, A. (1994), *Science and Sanity: An Introduction to Non-Aristotelian Systems and General Semantics,* 5th edn, Englewood, N.J: Institute of General Semantics.

Kruskal, J.B. and M. Wish (1978), *Multidimensional Scaling,* London: Sage.

Krut, R. (1998), *ISO 14000: A Missed Opportunity for Sustainable Global Industrial Development,* London: Earthscan.

Kuhl, J. (1985), 'Volitional mediators of cognition-behavior consistency: Self-regulatory processes and action versus state orientation', in J. Kuhl and J. Beckmann (eds), *Action–Control: From Cognition to Behavior,* Heidelberg: Springer, pp. 101–28.

Kuhl, J. and J. Beckmann (eds) (1985), *Action–Control: From Cognition to Behavior,* Heidelberg: Springer.

Kunreuther, H. and P. Slovic, (1996), 'Science, values and risk', *Annals of the American Academy of Political and Social Science,* **54** (5), 116–25.

Kuyper, H. and C. Vlek (1984), 'Contrasting risk judgements among interest groups', *Act Psychologica,* **56**, 205–18.

Lam, S.P. (1999), 'Predicting intentions to conserve water from the theory of planned behavior, perceived moral obligation, and perceived water right', *Journal of Applied Social Psychology,* **29** (5), 1058–71.

Lander, E. (1994), 'Opciones civilizatorias, movimientos ambientales y democracia', in M.P. Garcia-Guadilla and J. Blauert, (eds), *Retos Para el Desarrollo y la Democracia: Movimientos Ambientales en America Latina y Europa*, Caracas: Nueva Sociedad, pp. 7–14.

Langerak, F., E. Peelen and M. van der Veen (1998), 'Exploratory results on the antecedents and consequences of green marketing', *Journal of Market Research Society*, **40** (4), 323–35.

Lee, D.R. and R.B. McKenzie (1994), 'Corporate failure as a means to corporate responsibility', *Journal of Business Ethics*, **13**, 969–78.

Lee, K.A. (1993), 'Greed, scale mismatch, and learning', *Ecological Applications*, **3** (4), 560–64.

Leff, E. (1986), *Ecología y Capital*, México City: UNAM.

Leonard-Barton, D. (1992), 'Core capabilities and core rigidities: a paradox in managing new product development', *Strategic Management Journal*, **13**, 111–25.

Leonard-Barton, D. (1995), *Wellspring of Knowledge: Building and Sustaining the Sources of Innovation*, Boston, MA: Harvard School Press.

Levèque, F. (ed.) (1996), *Environmental Policy in Europe: Industry, Competition and the Policy Process*, Cheltenham, UK and Brookfield, US: Edward Elgar.

Levy, S. (1976), 'Use of the mapping sentence for coordinating theory and research: a cross cultural example', *Quality and Quantity*, **10**, 117–25.

Levy, S. (1985), 'Lawful roles of facets in social theories', in D. Canter (ed.) *Facet Theory*, New York: Springer-Verlag, pp. 59–96.

Lewis-Beck, M.S. (ed.) (1978), *Factor Analysis and Related Techniques*, London: Sage Publishers.

Lewis-Beck, M.S. (ed.) (1993), *Regression Analysis*, London: Sage Publications.

Ley general de equilibrio ecológico y la protección al medio ambiente (1989). Mexico City: Porrúa.

Lindblom, C.E. (1959), 'The science of muddling through', *Public Administration Review*, **19**, 79–88.

Linnanen, L., T. Boström, and P. Miettinen (1995), 'Life cycle management integrated approach: towards corporate environmental issues', *Business Strategy and the Environment*, **4**, 117–27.

Lipshitz, R. and O. Strauss (1997), 'Coping with uncertainty: A naturalistic decision-making analysis, *Organizational Behavior and Human Decision Process*, **69** (2), 149–63.

Loayza, I.F. (1996), 'Competitiveness, environmental performance and technical change: The case of the Bolivian mining industry', Unpublished DPhil. thesis, University of Sussex.

Lober, D. (1996), 'Evaluating the environmental performance of corporations', *Journal of Managerial Issues*, **8** (2), 184–205.

Loewenthal, K.M. (1996), *An Introduction to Psychological Tests and Scales*, London: UCL Press.

Logsdom, J.M. (1985), 'Organizational responses to environmental issues: Oil refining companies and air pollution', in L.E. Preston (ed.), *Research in Corporate Social Performance and Policy,* vol. 1, Greenwich, CT: Jai Press.

Lopes, L.L. (1994), 'Psychology and economics: perspectives on risk, cooperation, and the marketplace', *Annual Review of Psychology,* **45**, 197–227.

Lostpeich, R. (1998), 'Comparative environmental policy: market type instruments in industrialized capitalist countries', *Policy Studies Journal,* **26** (1), 85–104.

Lovallo, D. and D. Kahneman (1993), 'Timid choices and bold forecasts – A cognitive perspective on risk taking', *Management Science,* **39** (1), 17–31.

Lynne, G.D., C.F. Casey, A. Hodges and M. Rahmani (1995), 'Conservation technology adoption decisions and the theory of the planned behavior', *Journal of Economic Psychology,* **16** (4), 581–98.

MacCrimmon, K.R. and D.A. Wehring (1986), *Taking Risks: The Management of Uncertainty,* New York: The Free Press.

Maler, K.G. and R.E. Wyzda (1976), *Economic Measurement of Environmental Damage. A Technical Handbook,* Paris: OECD.

Mantel, N. (1985), 'Quantitative approaches for cancer risk assessment', *Risk Analysis,* **5** (1), 5–6.

March J.G. (1989), *Decision and Organizations,* New York: Blackwell.

March J. and Z. Shapira (1992), 'Variable risk preferences and the focus of attention', *Psychological Review,* **99**, 172–83.

Markandya, A. and J. Richardson (eds) (1993), *Environmental Economics,* London: Earthscan.

Marsden, J.E. and A.J. Tromba (1996), *Vector Calculus,* New York: Freeman.

Martin, B. (1995), 'Foresight in science and technology', *Technology Analysis and Strategic Management,* **7** (2), 139–86.

Matten, D. (1995), 'Strategy follows structure: environmental risk management in commercial enterprises', *Business Strategy and Environment,* **4**, 107–16.

Maxwell, J., S. Rothenberg, F. Briscoe and K. Oye (1997), 'A comparison of environmental performance at US and Japanese automobile plants', paper presented at the GIN Conference, Santa Barbara, CA.

McDaniels, T., L.J. Axelrod, and P. Slovic (1995), 'Characterising perception of risk', *Risk Analysis,* **15** (5), 575–88.

McDaniels, T., L.J. Axelrod and P. Slovic (1996), 'Perceived ecological risk of global change: A psychometric comparison of causes and consequences', *Global Environmental Change, Human and Policy Dimensions,* **6** (2), 159–71.

Mendez, M.E. (1995), 'La industria maquiladora en Tijuana: riesgo ambiental y calidad de vida', *Comercio Exterior,* Febrero, 159–63.

Mercado A. (2000) 'Comportamiento de las maquiladoras con respecto al cumplimiento de las normas ambientales'. Paper presented at the international conference on free trade and the future of the Maquila Industry: Global production and local workers. El Colegio de la Frontera Norte – Comisión Económica para América Latina y el Caribe Naciones Unidas, Tijuana, Mexico.

Mesch, G.S. (1996), 'The effect of environmental concerns and governmental incentives on organised action in local areas', *Urban Affairs Review*, **31** (3), 346–66.

Messick, D.M. and C.L. McClelland (1983), 'Social traps and temporal traps', *Personality and Social Psychology Bulletin*, **9** (1), 105–10.

Michell, J. (1990), *An Introduction to the Logic of Psychological Measurement*, Hillsdale, NJ: Lawrence Erlbaum Associates.

Michell, J. (1997), 'Quantitative science and the definition of measurement in psychology', *British Journal of Psychology*, **88**, 355–83.

Miller, D. (1987), 'The structural and environmental correlates of business strategy', *Strategic Management Journal*, 8, 55–76.

Miller, D. (1996), 'A preliminary typology of organizational learning: synthesising the literature', *Journal of Management*, **22** (3), 485–505.

Mintzberg, H. (1994), *The Rise and Fall of Strategic Planning*. New York: The Free Press.

Mirvis, P.H. (1996), 'Historical foundations of organization learning', *Journal of Organizational Change Management*, **9** (1), 13–31.

Montalvo, C.C. (1992), *Costo Ambiental del Crecimiento Industrial: Caso de Estudio de la Maquiladora Electronica en Tijuana, B.C.*, Mexico City: Friedrich-Ebert Foundation.

Montes, J. M. and E. Leff (1986), 'Perspectiva ambiental del desarrollo del conocimiento', in O. Sunkel and N. Gligo (eds), *Estilos de Desarrollo y Medio Ambiente en la América Latina,* Mexico City: Fondo de Cultura Económica, pp. 22–44.

Moreh, J. (1985), 'Utilitarian and the conflict of interests', *Journal of Conflict Resolution*, **29** (1), 137–59.

Morgan, G.A. and O.V. Griego (1998), *Easy Use and Interpretation of SPSS for Windows*, Mahwah, N.J.: Laurence Erlbaum Associates.

Morrison, R. (1997), 'Sustainability and the role of financial institutions', paper presented at the GIN Conference, Santa Barbara, CA.

Mortimore, M. (2000) 'Globalización y el rol de las empresas transnacionales: Como interpretar el fenómeno de la inversión extranjera directa en América Latina y el Caribe', paper presented at the international conference on free trade and the future of the Maquila Industry: Global production and local workers. El Colegio de la Frontera Norte – Comisión Económica para América Latina y el Caribe Naciones Unidas, Tijuana, Mexico

Mowery, D. and N. Rosemberg (1989), *Technology and the Pursuit of Economic Growth*, Cambridge: Cambridge University Press.

MPW, Canada. (1999), *Progress in Pollution Prevention 1997–1998: Annual Report of the Pollution Prevention Coordinating Committee*, Ottawa: Minister of Public Works and Government Services Canada. Copy of this document is available from: <http://www.ec.gc.ca/p2progress>.

Mulvey, J.M., D.P. Rosenbaum and B. Shetty (1997), 'Financial risk management and operations research', *Journal of the Operational Research Society*, **97** (1), 1–16.

Murphy, M.J. (1986), 'Environmental risk assessment of industrial facilities – Techniques, regulatory intitiatives and insurance', *Science of the Total Environment*, **51**, 185–96.

Murray, A.I. and C. Murray (1989), *Joint Ventures and Other Alliances*, Morristown, NJ: Financial Executives Research Foundation.

Nelson, R.R. and S.G. Winter (1977), 'In search for a useful theory of innovation', *Research Policy*, **6**, 36–76.

Nelson, R. R. and S. G. Winter (1982), *An Evolutionary Theory of Economic Change*, Cambridge, MA: Harvard University Press. Belknap Press.

NSF (2000), *New Technologies for the Environment: Program Solicitation*, National Science Foundation: Directorate of Engineering. NSF 00–49. < http://www.nsf.gov/cgi–bin/getpub?nsf0049>.

Nonaka, I. (1994), 'A dynamic theory of knowledge creation', *Organization Science*, **5** (1), 14–37.

Nonaka, I., H. Takeuchi and K. Umemoto (1996), 'A theory of organizational knowledge creation', *Journal of Technology Mangement*, **11** (7–8), 833–45.

Norberg-Bohm, V. (1999), 'Stimulating "green" technological innovation: An analysis of alternative policy mechanisms', *Policy Sciences*, **32** (1), 13–38.

Ocasio, W. (1995), 'The enactment of economic adversity: A reconciliation of theories of failure-induced change and threat-rigidity', *Research in Organizational Behavior*, **17**, 287–331.

OECD (1984), *Environmental and Economics. Issue Papers, Environmental Directorate*, Paris: OECD.

OECD (1985), *Environmental Policy and Technical Change*, Paris, OECD.

OECD (1991a), *State of the Environment*, Paris: OECD.

OECD (1991b), *Environmental Policy: How to Apply Economic Instruments*, Paris: OECD.

OECD (1992), *Government Policy Options to Encourage Cleaner Production and Products in the 90s*, Paris: OECD.

OECD (1993), *Economic Instruments for Environmental Management in Developing Countries*, Paris: OECD.

OECD (1995), *Policies to Promote Technologies for Cleaner Production and Products: Guide for Government Self-assessment*, Paris: OECD.

Ojeda, M. (1995), 'Presentación' in El Colegio de Mexico, *Primer Foro del Ajusco: Desarrollo Sostenible y Reforma del Estado en America Latina y el Caribe*, Mexico City: El Colegio de Mexico – Programa de Naciones Unidas para el Medio Ambiente.

Onishi, Y., A.R. Olsen, M.A. Parkhurst and G. Whelan (1985), 'Computer-based environmental exposure and risk assessment', *Journal of Hazardous Materials*, **10** (2–3), 389–417.

Oppenheim, A.N. (1992), *Questionnaire Design, Interviewing and Attitude Measurement*, London: New Edition.

Opschoor, J.B. and H.B. Vos (1991), *Economics Instruments for Environmental Protection*, Paris: OECD.

Orsatto, R. (1997), 'The political ecology of organizations: a study of the greening of the European automobile industry', paper presented at the GIN Conference, Santa Barbara, CA.

Ortolano, L. (1984), *Environmental Planning and Decision Making*, New York: John Wiley and Sons.

OTA, (1992), *Green Products by Design,* Washington, DC: United States Office of Technology Assessment, OTA–E–541.

Panayotou, T. (1993), 'Economic incentives for environmental management in developing countries', *OECD Documents,* Paris: OECD, pp. 23–9.

Panda, H. and K. Ramanathan (1996), 'Technological capability assessment of a firm in the electricity sector', *Technovation*, **16** (10), 561–88.

Parks, C.D. and A.D. Vu (1994), 'Social dilemma behavior of individuals from highly individualistic and collectivist cultures', *Journal of Conflict Resolution*, **38** (4), 708–18.

Pavitt, K. (1984), 'Sectoral patterns of technical change: towards a taxonomy and a theory', *Research Policy*, **13** (6), 343–73.

Payne, J., J.R. Bettman and E.J. Johnson (1992), 'Behavioral decision research: a constructive processing perspective', *Annual Review of Psychology*, **43**, 87–131.

PCSD (1999), *Towards a Sustainable America: Advancing Prosperity, Opportunity and a Healthy Environment for the 21st Century*, Washington, DC: President's Council on Sustainable Development, US/Government Printing Office.

Pearce, D. W. (1985), *Economía Ambiental*, México: FCE.

Pearce, D. W. and R. K. Turner (1991), *Economics of Natural Resources and the Environment*, New York: Harvester Wheatsheaf.

Penrose, E. (1959), *The Theory of the Growth of the Firm*, London: Basil Blackwell.

Perrera, F. (1986), 'New approaches in risk', *Risk Analysis*, **6**, 195–201.

Perry, D., R.A. Sanchez, W.H. Glaze and M. Mazary (1990), 'Binational Management of Hazardous Waste: The Maquiladora Industry at the US–Mexico Border', *Environmental Management*, **14** (4), 441–50.

Peters, T. (1992). *Liberation Management,* New York: Knopf.

Petts, J., H. Herd and M. O'Heocha, (1998), 'Environmental responsiveness, individuals and organizational learning: SME experience', *Journal of Environmental Planning and Management*, **4** (6), 711–30.

Pigou, A.C. (1924), *The Economics of Welfare*, 2nd edn, London: Macmillan.

Platt, J. (1973), 'Social traps', *American Psychologist*, August, 641–51.

Porter, M. (1985), *Competitive Advantage*, London: Macmillan.

Porter, M.E. and C. van der Linde (1995a), 'Green and competitive: ending the stalemate', *Harvard Business Review*, **70**, 73–93.

Porter, M.E. and C. van der Linde, (1995b), 'Towards a new conception of the environment-competitiveness relationship', *Journal of Economic Perspectives*, **9** (4), 97–118.

Porter, R.L. (1993), *Business Alliances Guide*, New York: John Wiley and Sons.

Prakash, A. (1997), 'A logic of corporate enviromentalism', paper International Studies Association, Toronto.

Quiley, J. V. (1993), *Vision: How Leaders Develop it, Share it, and Sustain it*. New York: McGraw Hill.

Rapoport, A. (1988a), 'Experiments with n-person social traps I: Tragedy of the commons', *Journal of Conflict Resolution*, **32** (3), 473–88.

Rapoport, A. (1988b), 'Experiments with n-person social traps I: Prisoner's dilemma, weak prisoner's dilemma, volunteer's dilemma, and largest number', *Journal of Conflict Resolution*, **33** (3), 457–72.

Rodgers, C. (1998), 'Producer responsibility and the role of industry in managing waste from electrical and electronic equipment', Unpublished D.Phil. thesis: University of Sussex.

Rodriguez, S.B. and D.J. Hickson (1995), 'Success in decision making: different organizations, differing reasons for success', *Journal of Management Studies,* **32** (5), 655–78.

Rogers, E.M. (1995), *Diffusion of Innovations*, New York: Free Press.

Rondinelli, D. and G. Vastag, (1996), International environmental standards and corporate policies', *California Management Review,* **39** (1), 106–22.

Roome, N. (1994), 'Business strategy, R&D management and environmental imperatives', *R&D Management,* **24** (1), 65–82.

Rosenbloom R.S. and C.M. Christensen (1994), 'Technological discontinuities, organizational capabilities, and strategic commitments', *Industrial and Corporate Change*, **3** (3), 655–83.

Rotemberg, J.J., and Saloner G. (2000), 'Visionaries, managers, and strategic direction', RAND *Journal of Economics*, **31** (4), 693–716.

Rothwell, R. (1992), 'Industrial innovation and government environmental regulations: Some Lessons from the past', *Technovation*, **12** (7), 447–58.

Royal Society (1992), *Risk Analysis, Perception and Management*, London: Royal Society.

Sanchez, C.M. and W. McKinley (1998), 'Environmental regulatory influence and product innovation: the contingency effects of organizational characteristics', *Journal of Engineering and Technology Management*, **15** (4), 257–78.

Sanchez, R.A. (1990a), *El Medio Ambiente Como Fuente de Conflicto en la Relación Binacional México–EUA*, Tijuana: El COLEF.

Sanchez, R.A. (1990b), 'Otra manera de ver la maquiladora: riesgos en el medio ambiente y la salud', in B. Gonzalez-Arechiga and J.C. Ramirez (eds), *Subcontratación y Empresas Trasnacionales. Apertura y Restructuración en la Maquiladora*, Mexico City: El COLEF–Fundación Friedrich Ebert, pp. 553–70.

Sanchez, R.A. (1991), 'El Tratado de Libre Comercio en América del norte y el medio ambiente de la frontra norte', *Frontera Norte*, **3** (6), 5–28.

Sarver, V.T., Jr. (1983), 'Ajzen and Fishbein's "Theory of reasoned action"; A critical assessment', *Journal for the Theory of Social Behavior*, **13**, 155–63.

Sax, N.I. (1974), *Industrial Pollution*, New York: Van Nostrand Reinhold.

Sax, N.I. (1977), *Dangerous Properties of Industrial Materials*, New York: Van Nostrand Reinhold.

Schelling, T. (1971), 'The ecology of the micromotives, *Public Interest*, **25**, 61–98.

Schmidheiny, S. (1992), *Changing Course: A Global Perspective on Development and the Environment*, Cambridge, MA: MIT Press.

Schoemaker, P.J.H. (1993a), 'Strategic decisions in organisations: rational and behavioral views', *Journal of Management Studies*, **30** (1), 107–29.

Schoemaker, P.J.H. (1993b), 'Determinants of risk-taking: behavioral and economic views', *Journal of Risk and Uncertainty*, **6**, 49–73.

Schoemberger, E. (1990), 'From fordism to flexible accumulation: technology, competitive strategies and International Location', *Environmental and Planning D: Science and Space*, **6**, 245–62.

Schot, J., R. Hoogma and B. Elzen (1994), 'Strategies for shifting technological systems: The case of the automobile system', *Futures*, **26** (10), 1060–76.

SECOFI (1990), 'Plan nacional de modernización industrial y del comercio exterior', *Comercio Exterior*, February, 164–77.

SEDESOL (1990), *Programa Nacional para la Proteccion del Medio Ambiente 1990–1994*, Mexico City: Secretaria de Desarrollo Social.

SEDUE (1991), *Aspects of the Environmental Situation in Mexico and Related Policies*, México City: Secretaría de Desarrollo Urbano y Ecología.

SEDUE-EPA (1992), *Integrated Environmental Plan for the Mexican–US Border Area, First Stage (1992~1994)*, Washington, DC: Secretaría de Desarrollo Urbano y Ecología and Environmental Protection Agency.

Senge P.M. (1990), *The Fifth Discipline*, London: Century Business.

Senge, P. (1991), 'The learning organization made plain', *Training and Development*, October.

SETAC (1993), *Guidelines for Life cycle Assessment: A Code of Practice*, Brussels: Society of Environmental Toxicology and Chemistry.

Shapira, Z. (1994), *Risk Taking: A Managerial Perspective*, New York: Russell Sage Foundation.

Shrivastava, P. and S. Hart, (1995), 'Creating sustainable corporations', *Business Strategy and the Environment*, **4**, 154–65.

Shye, S. (ed) (1978), *Theory Construction and Data Analysis in the Behavioral Sciences,* San Francisco: Josey-Bass.

Shye, S. (1985a), *Multiple Scaling*, Amsterdam: North Holland.

Shye, S. (1985b), *Multiple Scaling: Theory and Application of Partial Order Scalogram Analysis*, Amsterdam: North Holland.

Shye, S., D. Elizur and M. Hoffman (1994), *Introduction to Facet Theory: Content Design and Intrinsic Data Analysis in Behavioral Research*, Thousand Oaks, CA: Sage Publications.

Simon, H.A. (1945), *Administrative Behavior*, New York: Free Press.

Simon, H.A. (1977), *The New Science of Management Decision*, Englewood Cliffs, N.J: Prentice Hall.

Sitkin, S.B. and A.L. Pablo (1992), 'Reconceptualizing the determinants of risk behavior', *Academy of Management Review*; **17** (1), 9–38.

Sitkin, S.B. and L.R. Weingart (1995), 'Determinants of risky decision-making behavior: A test of the mediating role of risk perceptions and propensity', *Academy of Management Journal*, **38** (6), 1573–92.

Sjöberg, L. (1996), 'A discussion of the limitations of the psychometric and cultural theory approaches to risk perception', *Radiation Protection Dosimetry*, **68** (4), 219–25.

Skea, J. (1995), 'Environmental technology', in H. Folmer, H.L. Gabel and J.B. Opschoor (eds), *Principles of Environmental Economics: A Guide for Students and Decision Makers,* Aldershot: Edward Elgar, pp. 55–78.

Skidmore, D. (1995), 'Managing responsiveness to pressures for change in environmental performance', *Business Strategy and the Environment*, **4**, 95–98.

Sklair, L. (1993), *Assembling for Development*, La Jolla: University of California San Diego, Center for US–Mexican Studies.

Sklair, L. (2000a), 'Global capitalism and sustainable development: exploring the contradictions', in L. E. Herzog (ed.), *Shared Space: Rethinking the U.S.–Mexico Border Environment*, La Jolla, CA.: Center for US–Mexican Studies, University of California San Diego, 17–40.

Sklair, L. (2000b), 'The transnational capitalist class and globalizing corporations: integrating the maquila industry into the global capitalist system', paper presented at the international conference on free trade and the future of the Maquila Industry: Global production and local workers. El Colegio de la Frontera Norte – Comisión Económica para América Latina y el Caribe Naciones Unidas, Tijuana, Mexico.

Sklair, L. (2000c), *The Transnational Capitalist Class*, Oxford: Blackwell.

Slater, J. and I.T. Angel (2000), 'The impact and implications of environmentally linked strategies on competitive advantage: A study of Malaysian companies', *Journal of Business Research*, **47** (1), 75–89.

Slovic, P. (1987), 'Risk perception', *Science*, **236**, April, 280–85.

Slovic, P., B. Fischhoff and S. Lichtenstien (1980), 'Facts and fears: understanding perceived risk', in R.C. Schwing and W.A. Albers (eds) *Societal Risk Assessment: How Safe is Safe Enough?* New York: Plenum Press, pp. 181–216.

Slovic, P., B. Fischhoff and S. Lichtenstein (1984), 'Behavioral decision theory perspectives on risk and safety', *Act Psychologca,* **56**, 183–203.

Smith, M.V. (1984), 'The use of risk assessment in regulatory decision-making', *Food Technology*, **38** (10), 113–18.

Smith, P.G. (1999), 'Managing risk as product development schedules shrink', *Research-Technology Management*, **42** (5), 25–32.

Smits, R., J. Leyten and P. den Hertog (1995), 'Technology assessment and technology policy in Europe: New concepts, new goals, new infrastructures', *Policy Sciences*, **28**, 271–99.

Sockolowska, J. and T. Tyska (1995), 'Perception and acceptance of technological and environmental risks: Why are poor countries less concerned?', *Risk Analysis*, **15** (6), 733–43.

Spector, P.E. (1994), 'Using self-report questionnaires in OB research: a comment on the use of a controversial method', *Journal of Organizational Behavior*, **15**, 385–92.

S.P.S.S. (1998), *SPSS Base 8.0: Applications Guide*, Chicago: SPSS.

Star, C. (1969), 'Social benefits versus technological risk', *Science*, **165**, 1232–38.

Stavins, R.N. and B.W. Whitehead (1992), 'Pollution charges for environmental protection: A policy link between energy and environment', *Annual Review Energy and Environment*, **17**, 187–210.

Steger, U. (1993), 'The greening of the board room: how German companies are dealing with environmental issues', in K. Fisher and J. Schot (eds), *Environmental Strategies for industry: International Perspectives on Research Needs and Policy Implications*, Washington, DC: Island Press, pp. 63–78.

Steger, U. (1996), 'Managerial issues in closing the loop', *Business Strategy and the Environment*, **5**, 252–68.

Stevens, S.S. (1946), 'On the theory of scales of measurement', *Science*, **103**, 667–80.

Stevenson, M.K., J.R. Busemenyer and J.C. Naylor (1990), 'Judgement and decision making theory', in M.D. Dunette and L.M. Hough (eds), *Handbook of Industrial and Organizational Psychology*, 2nd edn, vol. 1, Palo Alto, CA: Consulting Psychologists Press, pp. 283–374.

Stewardson, R. (1993), 'From elephants to mice: The development of EBMUD's program to control small source wastewater discharges', *Ecology Quarterly Law*, **20**, 441–514.

Stewart, R. (1994), 'Environmental regulation and international competitiveness', *Yale Law Journal*, **103**, 2039–22.

Sturgeon, T. (1950), *The Dreaming Jewels,* New York: Dell Publishing.

Taha, H. A. (1989), *Operations Research*, New York: Macmillan Publishing, pp. 27–9.

Taylor, L. (2000), 'The origins of the maquila industry in Mexico. Paper presented at the international conference on free trade and the future of the Maquila Industry: Global production and local workers', El Colegio de la Frontera Norte – Comisión Económica para América Latina y el Caribe Naciones Unidas, Tijuana, Mexico.

Taylor, S. and P.A. Todd (1995), 'Understanding information technology usage: a test of competing models', *Information Systems Research*, **6** (2), 144–76.

Taylor, S. and P.A. Todd (1997), 'Understanding the determinants of consumer composting behavior', *Journal of Applied Social Psychology*, **27** (7), 602–28.

Teece, D.J. and G. Pisano (1994), 'The dynamic capabilities of firms: an introduction', *Industrial and Corporate Change*, **3** (3), 537–56.

Teece, D.J. (1986), 'Profiting from technological innovation: implications for integration, collaboration, licensing and public policy', *Research Policy*, **15**, 285–305.

Teece, J.D., G. Pisano and A. Shuen (1990), *Firm capabilities, resources and the concept of strategy*, Consortium on Competitiveness and Cooperation, working paper No. 90–8. University of California at Berkeley.

Templet, P.H. (1995), 'Grazing the commons: an empirical analysis of externalities, subsidies and sustainability', *Ecological Economics*, **12**, 141–59.

Terry, D.J. (1993), 'Self-efficacy expectancies and the theory of the reasoned action', in. D.J. Terry, C. Gallois and M. McCamish (eds), *The Theory of Reasoned Action: Its Application to AIDS–preventive Behavior*, London: Penguin.

Thaler, R.H. and E.J. Johnson (1990), 'Gambling with the house money and trying to break even: the effects of prior outcomes on risky choice', *Management Science*, **36**, 643–60.

Thompson, I., L Baas, N. Duffy and B. Ryan (1999), 'Dairy Sector', in Clayton A., G. Spinardi and R. Williams (eds), *Policies for Cleaner Technology*, London: Earthscan, pp. 130–45.

Thompson, K.M. (1999), 'Developing univariate distributions from data for risk analysis', *Human and Ecological Risk Asessment*, **5** (4), 755–83.

Tidd, J., J. Bessantand and K. Pavitt (1997), *Managing Innovation: Integrating Technological, Market and Organizational Change*, Chichester: John Wiley and Sons.

Tietenberg, T.H. (1992), *Environmental Policy Innovation,* Aldershot: Edward Elgar.

Tietenberg, T.H. (1994), *Economics and Environmental Policy*, Aldershot: Edward Elgar.

Tirole, J. (1988), *The Theory of Industrial Organization*, Cambridge, MA: MIT Press.

Tsang. E.W.K. (1997), 'Organizational learning and the learning organization: A dichotomy between descriptive and prescriptive research', *Human Relations,* **50** (1), 73–89.

Tschirky, H.P. (1994), 'The role of technology forecasting and assessment in technology management', *R&D Management,* **24** (2), 121–9.

Turner, J.V. and J.L. Hunsucker (1999), 'Effective risk management: a goal based approach', *International Journal of Technology Management,* **17** (4), 438–58.

Udo de Haes, H.A. (1993), 'Applications of life cycle assessment: expectations, drawbacks and perspectives', *Journal of Cleaner Production,* **1** (3–4), 131–7.

Ulrich, T.K. and S.D. Eppinger (1995), *Product Design and Development,* New York: McGraw–Hill.

US–White House (1998), *National Environmental Technology Strategy,* Washington, DC: The White House, Access the document at <http://www.whitehouse.gov/NCST>.

Utterback, J.M. (1994), *Mastering the Dynamics of Innovations,* Boston, MA: Harvard Business School Press.

van de Ven, A.H. (1986), 'Central problems in the management of innovation', *Management Science,* **32** (5), 590–607.

van den Berg, N.W., C.E. Dutilh and G. Huppes (1995), *Beginning LCA: A Guide into Environmental Life Cycle Assessment,* Rotterdam: National Reuse of Waste Research Program (NOH), Netherlands.

van Groenendaal, W.J.H. and J.P.C. Kleijnen (1997), 'On the assessment of economic risk: factorial design versus Monte-Carlo methods', *Reliability Engineering and System Safety,* **57**, 91–102.

van Ryn, M. and A. Vinokur (1992), 'How did it work? An examination of the mechanisms through which a community intervention influenced job-search behavior among an unemployed sample', *American Journal of Community Psychology,* **33**, 793–802.

van Someren, T.C.R. (1995), 'Sustainable development and the firm: Organizational innovations and environmental strategy', *Business Strategy and the Environment,* **4**, 23-33.

van Weenen, J. (1995), 'Towards sustainable product development', *Journal of Cleaner Production,* **3** (1–2), 95–100.

Varian, H.R. (1978), *Microeconomic Analysis,* New York: W.W. Norton.

Vaughan, E. (1993), 'Individual and cultural differences in adaptation to environmental risks', *American Psychologist,* **48**, 673–80.

Velleman, P. and L. Wilkinson (1994), 'Nominal, ordinal, and ratio typologies are misleading', in I. Borg and P. Mohler (eds), *Trends and Perspectives in Empirical Social Research,* New York: Walter de Gruyter, pp. 161–75.

Vig, N.J. and M.E. Kraft (1990), *Environmental Policy in the 1990's,* Washington, DC: Congressional Quarterly Press.

Vlek, C. and Stallen P.J. (1980), 'Rational and personal aspects of risk', *Acta Psychologica*, **45**, 273–300.

Williams, H.E., J. Medhurst and K. Drew (1993), 'Corporate strategies for a sustainable future', in K. Fisher and J. Schot (eds), *Environmental Strategies for Industry: International Perspectives on Research Needs and Policy Implications*, Washington, DC: Island Press, pp. 117–146.

Wandersman, A.H. and W.K. Hallman (1993), 'Are people acting irrationally? Understanding public concerns about environmental threats', *American Psychologist*, **9** (6), 681–6.

Ward, H. (1993), 'Game theory and the politics of the global commons', *Journal of Conflict Resolution*, **37** (2), 203–35.

Watson, S.R. (1981), 'On risks and acceptability', *Journal of the Society of Radiological Protection*, **1** (4), 21–5.

Weber, E.U. and R.A. Milliman (1997), 'Perceived risk attitudes: relating risk perception to risk choice', *Management Science*, **43** (2), 123–44.

Welford, R. (1995), 'Attitudes towards environmental management', *Business Strategy and the Environment*, **4**, 40–1.

Wehn de Montalvo, U.W.C. (2001), *Crossing organisational boundaries: Prerequisites for spatial data sharing in South Africa*, Unpublished DPhil Thesis, Brighton: SPRU – Science and Technology Research, University of Sussex.

Wenzel, H., M. Hauschild and L. Alting (1997), *Environmental assessment of products: Methodology, tools and case studies in product development*, Vol. 1, London: Chapman and Hall.

Wisniewskt, T.K.M. (1983), 'Risk assessment in insurance', *Journal of the Operational Research Society*, **34** (12), A24.

World Bank (2000), *Pollution Prevention and Abatement Handbook, 1998*, Washington, DC: World Bank.

WCED (World Commission on Environment and Development) (1987), *Our Common Future*, Oxford: Oxford University Press.

World Resources Institute (1994), *World Resources, 1994–95: A Guide to Global Environment*, London: Oxford University Press.

Xu, X.P. (1999), 'Do stringent environmental regulations reduce the international competitiveness of environmentally sensitive goods? A global perspective', *World Development*, **27** (7), 1215–226.

Xu, X.P. (2000), 'International trade and environmental policy: how effective is "eco–dumping"?', *Economic Modelling*, **17**, 71–90.

Yúnez-Naude, A. (1994), *Medio Ambiente: Problemas y Soluciones*, Mexico City: El Colegio de Mexico.

Zahra, S.A. (1996), 'Technology strategy and financial performance: examining the moderating role of the firm's competitive environment', *Journal of Business Venturing*, **11**, 189-219.

Zidaman, B. and G. Cevidalli (1987), 'Project evaluation: Externalities must not be disregarded', *R&D Management*, **17** (4), 269–76.

Ziman, J. (1984), *An Introduction to Science Studies: The Philosophical and Social Aspects of Science and Technology,* Cambridge: Cambridge University Press.

Index